THE POOR MAN'S

MORNING PORTION;

BEING

A SELECTION OF A VERSE OF SCRIPTURE,

WITH SHORT OBSERVATIONS,

FOR EVERY DAY IN THE YEAR;

INTENDED FOR THE USE OF THE POOR IN SPIRIT,

"WHO ARE RICH IN FAITH AND HEIRS OF THE KINGDOM."

BY ROBERT HAWKER, D. D.

LATE VICAR OF CHARLES, PLYMOUTH.

Reformed Church Publications
P.O Box 171 Zeeland, Mi 49464

PREFACE.

THE title page of this humble work, sufficiently explains itself. It is designed as a means, in the divine hand, to promote the Redeemer's glory, and his people's happiness. It hath often struck me, that such a method, under the blessing of the Lord, might prove eminently useful. By publishing in this cheap way, some sweet portion of Scripture, for every day in the year, it might come within the reach of all pockets, be within the reach of all hands, and bid fair to be read, when larger books are laid aside and forgotten.

It was, indeed, with the same view, that some few years since I sent forth a *Diary* of this kind. But, in that work, the selection was confined wholly to the *Promises*. Experience hath since shown, that reference may be occasionally had, with great advantage, to other parts of the word of God. In this therefore, I have enlarged the plan. And besides making extracts from the whole Scripture, I have ventured to add, under each passage, such thoughts as passed over my own mind in the perusal, hoping that the Lord might render them profitable to others.

It will be scarcely necessary to go over the same ground, by way of preface, as was then done. But it cannot be too often said, by way of reminding the believer, that the promises of God in Christ, are evidently meant, by the gracious Giver of them, for the daily comfort of his people. And what is said of the *Promises*, may be equally applied to the whole tenor of covenant love, which runs through the Bible. Indeed, if the truly awakened soul did but consider the word of God in this point of view, and make use of it, upon every occasion, as his own circumstances are found to require, it could not fail of opening to his mind a perpetual source of joy and consolation all the day.

For what are the promises, but so many bonds and engagements of a Covenant God in Christ? In them, the Lord hath pledged himself to his people, as they stand related to Christ; and by the fulfilment of them, they prove his faithfulness. So that strictly and properly speaking, God's promises are our Charter: His word our security: His Verily and Amen, the breasts of consolation from whence God's little ones are nourished. And if the Lord's people would seek from the Holy Ghost, the testimony he gives in them, concerning Jesus; and from *general* promises, make application of them to their own *particular* state and circumstances, as they may require; they would find upon numberless occasions that the Lord is speaking *in* them and *by* them, to the souls of his people, and in the sweetest and most endearing language. " I would rather have God's *Amen*, and his *Yea*, and *Verily*, (said a tried soul of old,) than the promise or oath of all the men upon earth." And so would every believer, when from long experience of God's fulfilment of his word and promises, he could *set to his seal that God is true.* But, if we never make use of God's promises; never exercise faith upon them; never bring them before the throne for payment; nor make memorandums, when they are paid; how shall we know their value, or God's love and faithfulness in their accomplishment?

Convinced of the importance of the thing itself, and with a view to direct the minds of God's people to the daily exercise of this grace of faith upon the word and promises of our Covenant God in Christ, I have here gathered out of the holy treasury, some sweet portion for gracious souls to feed on, from day to day. And so fully persuaded am I, of the preciousness of this employment, that I am confident to say, if the people of God would make it their uniform custom, morning by morning, with the first return of day, and, if possible, before the world hath power to break in upon the mind, thus to have recourse to God's word, and (as David said he did) *to hearken what the Lord God would say concerning him;* they would find, and perhaps frequently, before night, sufficient cause to bless God for his faithfulness in the accomplishment. Nay, sometimes indeed, they would discover the word to be so immediate and direct to the present moment, as if the Lord had left, for a while, the whole world, to draw nigh to them, in those visits of his love. Like the *Patriarch at Bethel*, they would be constrained to say, *Surely the Lord is in this place*, or in this word, *and I knew it not!*

It was thus holy men of old walked with God. They communed with the Lord, and the Lord with them, through the medium of his word. They made known their wants, and the Lord made known his grace. Prayers went up, and answers came down; and He *made all his goodness to pass before them.* In a more especial manner, they considered all the promises as their own. And they accepted of them, as given of the Lord with this express design, as if the Lord pledged himself by them to his people, that they might bring them before the mercy-seat, whenever they needed, and plead for payment. Hence they kept house, feasted, and lived joyfully upon them, when they had nothing else to live upon. And from this cause it was, that after a succession of many generations from father to son, they could, and did, appeal, to the uninterrupted experience of every preceding history, and left it upon record for the assurance and comfort of all that should come after, that *not one thing had failed of all the good things which the Lord had promised, but all was come to pass as it is this day.*

I cannot therefore but earnestly recommend to the gracious souls, for whom this little work is intended, similar conduct, that we may be the patient *followers of them who now through faith and patience inherit the promises.* And a method so short, so easy, and so practicable, as is here set forth, and which the most busy life, even among the labouring poor of our people, cannot find much difficulty in performing, will I trust be abundantly blessed of our gracious God. The labourer, who is straitened in time, and obliged sometimes to hasten to his work, without falling upon his knees in family prayer, may yet, even while putting on his clothes, look at the *Morning Portion;* and if unable to run through the observations, which follow the Scripture, may yet take with him the Scripture itself, and gather subject from it, under divine teaching, for prayer and praise, as he hastens on. And if this plan be constantly and invariably followed up, without the omission of a single morning, I venture to believe his diligence will be abundantly recompensed, upon numberless occasions, through life.

There is one advantage more, from the use of this work, which I detain the Reader, to mention, and which will be, I conceive, of no small importance, in making it blessed, if so be the Lord should dispose the minds of many gracious souls to the daily use of it. I mean, *the Communion of Saints.* This privilege of God's people, is much spoken of; but I rather fear not so much attended to, or regarded, as it ought. And yet, next to the rapture arising from communion with our glorious Head, what can open to more enjoyment, than communion, through Him, with the members of his mystical body? I cannot help telling, in this way, many precious souls, whom I love in the faith, and who I know love me, that I am looking forward to much spiritual enjoyment on this account, from our use of this little work, humble as it is. Not from my poor labours in the observations, which follow the Scripture; but from God's blessing on the Scripture itself. Let it be supposed, (what is very possible,) that many a true believer in Jesus, in different places, be led, in one and the same moment in the morning, to the perusal of the Morning Portion. Now, as the Scripture is the same; as the Almighty Spirit, who is the Author of that Scripture, the Quickener in prayer, and the Helper of the infirmities of his people in prayer, is the same; and as He, who leads out the minds of the people, at all times, and in all places, is the same; and his blessed work, in glorifying the Lord Jesus, is always the same; what can be more animating or delightful than the thought,

1*

that all so engaged, in one and the same Scripture, being under the same gracious influence, must necessarily be all looking up to the Lord Jesus, in one and the same moment; and, having fellowship with the Father, and with his Son Jesus Christ, have spiritual union also one with another, *as members of his body, of his flesh, and of his bones.* Hence, though far asunder from each other, in the body, and in numberless instances having never seen each other's face in the flesh, yet by virtue of the connexion with our spiritual Head, we truly participate in one and the same divine life, and enjoy the very sweet and distinguishing felicity, of *the Communion of Saints.*

I stop the Reader no longer than just to say, I humbly hope every truly gracious and awakened soul, who makes use of this Morning Portion, will not fail to connect with the use of it, a constant application to, and dependence upon, the Holy Ghost, as the Glorifier of the Father and of the Son; without whose work upon the heart, not a promise can we plead, not an argument can we use, not a grace can we exercise, even to the knowledge of our wants, or of the fulness of the Lord Jesus to supply them. But, my Brother, let me add, if your soul be warmed under the influence of the Holy Ghost, and while you read God's promise you find grace to convert that promise into a prayer, and when you have thus done act faith upon it, this will be to realize the mercy, and to make every promise your own. And oh! how truly blessed is it, when the believer thus proves that *all the promises of God in Christ Jesus are Yea and Amen, unto the glory of God by us.*

THE

POOR MAN'S MORNING PORTION.

JANUARY.

1st.—Jesus Christ; the same yesterday, and to-day, and for ever.—*Heb.* xiii. 8.

PRECIOUS truth to open the year with, and to keep constantly in view amidst all the fluctuating and changeable circumstances arising both within and without, and all around! My soul, meditate upon it: fold it up in thy bosom to have recourse to as may be required. Contemplate thy redeemer as he is here described. He is Jesus, thy Jesus, a Saviour, for he shall save his people from their sins. He is Christ also, God thy Father's Christ, and thy Christ; the Anointed, the Sent, the Sealed of Jehovah. He is the same in his glorious person; the same in his great salvation.—*Yesterday;* looking back to everlasting: *To-day;* equally so through all the periods of time: *For ever;* looking forward to the eternity to come. And, blessed thought! He is the same in his love, in the efficacy of his redemption; his blood to cleanse, his righteousness to justify, his fulness to supply grace here and glory hereafter. And what sums up the precious thought; amidst all thy variableness, thy frames, thy fears, doubts, and unbelievings, he abideth faithful. He is, he will be, he must be, Jesus. Hallelujah!

2.—Lord! let it alone this year also, till I shall dig about it, and dung it; and if it bear fruit, well; and if not, after that thou shalt cut it down.—*Luke* xiii. 8, 9.

Do I not behold the Lord Jesus here represented in his glorious office of our High-Priest and Intercessor? And is it thus, that he so mercifully pleads for the unawakened and unprofitable among his people? Pause, my soul! Was it not from the effects of his intercession, that the world itself was spared from instant destruction, when Adam first brake through the fence of God's law? Is it not now by the same rich grace that thousands are spared from year to year *in* Christ Jesus, before that they are called to the knowledge *of* Christ Jesus? Nay, my soul! pause once more over the view of this wonderful subject, and ask thyself, Was it not from the same Almighty interposition that thou was kept from going down to the pit, during the long, long period of thy unregeneracy, while thou wert wholly unconscious of it? Hadst thou died in that unconverted state, where must have been thy portion? And was it from thy gracious intercession, blessed Jesus, that I then lived, that I am now spared, and, after all my barrenness, that another year of grace is opening before me? Oh precious, precious Jesus! suffer me to be no longer unfruitful in thy garden! Do, Lord, as thou hast said. Dig about me, and pour upon me all the sweet influences of thy Holy Spirit, which, like the rain, and the sun, and the dew of heaven, may cause me to bring forth fruit unto God. And, Lord! if so unworthy a creature may drop a petition at thy mercy-seat for others, let the coming year be productive of the same blessings to all thy redeemed; even to my poor unawakened relations; and to thousands of those who are yet in nature's darkness. Oh! that this may be to them the acceptable year of the Lord!

3.—The year of my redeemed is come.—*Isaiah* lxii. 14.

YES! from everlasting the precise period of redemption was determined, and the appointed time of the vision could not tarry. Every intermediate event ministered to this one glorious æra, redemption by Jesus. The Church was in Egypt four hundred and thirty years, and in Babylon seventy. But we are told in the *former* instance, "the self-same night the Lord brought them forth with their armies, and the *latter* did not outstay the hour of their promised deliverance. So when the fulness of time was come, the Son of God came for the redemption of his people. And observe how graciously Jesus speaks of them: he calls them his redeemed. They were so in the covenant from everlasting; and when the time arrives for calling them by his grace, he claims them as the gift of his father, and the purchase of his blood. My soul, is this thy jubilee year? Art thou living as the redeemed of the Lord? If so, plead with thy redeemer for the hourly renewed visits of his love to thee, and for the year of redemption to all his unawakened.

4.—And when Abram was ninety years old and nine, the Lord appeared to Abram, and said unto him, I am the Almighty God : walk before me, and be thou perfect.—*Gen.* xvii. 1.

OUR old Bibles, in their margin, have retained the original *El Shaddai*, which we now read God Almighty, and marked it also God *All-sufficient ;* meaning, that Jehovah in covenant with Jesus as the Head of his people, is all sufficient in himself, and all sufficient for all their need in time and to eternity. He is God All-sufficient, or of many *paps*, many breasts of consolation (as some derive the word), for his faithful ones to suck at and draw from, in an endless supply. Here then, my soul, take this sweet title of thy Covenant God and Father in Christ Jesus for thy daily meditation, both at the opening and through all the periods of the coming year. And as even at old age the Lord still opened to Abraham this precious source for his comfort, so look up in Jesus and behold it as thine. And oh, my soul! do thou walk before him in the perfect righteousness of God thy Saviour, and thus daily keep up fellowship with the Father, and with his Son Jesus Christ.

5.—I am my beloved's, and his desire is towards me.—*Song* vii. 10.

YES, dearest Jesus ! I am truly thine, for thou hast dearly bought me with thy blood, and conquered me with thy grace. And now, through thy Spirit's teaching, I can and do discover that from everlasting thy desire was towards thy redeemed ones, and even when dead in trespasses and sins it was thy desire to quicken them into life, and bring them to thyself. And even now, notwithstanding all my backwardness to thee, thou restest in thy love, and thou art calling me by thy grace, and seeking continual fellowship in ordinances, and by thy word and providences; all which prove that thy desire is towards me. And as to the everlasting enjoyment of all thy church above, thy prayer to thy Father manifested thy desire, when thou saidst " Father, I will that they whom thou hast given me, be with me to behold my glory !" Are these the desires of my God and Saviour, my Husband, my Brother, my Friend ? And shall my heart be thus cold towards thee ? Oh ! for the reviving influences of thy Spirit, that I may cry out with the Church, " Let him kiss me with the kisses of his mouth ; for thy love is better than wine."

6.—For verily he took not on him the nature of angels,—*Heb.* vii. 10

CONTEMPLATE, my soul, the peculiar sweetness of that
grace which was in thy Jesus, when, for the accomplishment
of thy salvation, he passed by the nature of angels to take
upon him thy nature. There were but two sorts of transgressors in the creation of God; angels and men. But angels are left in everlasting chains, under darkness, to the judgment of the great day: and fallen, sinful, rebellious man,
finds grace of redemption. Had Jesus taken their nature,
would not this have been nearer to his own? Would not
their services have been vastly superior to ours? Would not
the redemption of beings so much higher in rank and intel-
lect, have opened a far larger revenue of praise to our adorable Redeemer? Pause over these thoughts, my soul, and
then consider therefrom how our Jesus, in his unequalled
condescension, hath thereby the more endeared himself to thy
love. And learn from hence, that if Jesus need not the service of angels, how is it possible that man can be profitable to
God. And the simple act of faith of a poor fallen sinner, in
believing the record that God hath given of his dear Son,
gives more honour to God than all the services of men or angels for ever. Mark this down as a blessed truth: Jehovah is
more glorified by thy faith and trust in him, than by all thy
works. Lord, give me this faith, that I may cleave to thee,
hang upon thee, follow thee, and never give over looking
unto thee, until mine eye-strings break and my heart-strings
fail, and then be thou " the strength of my heart, and my portion for ever!"

7.—One pearl of great price.—*Mat.* xiii. 46

GREAT indeed, and but One! for " Salvation is in no other;
neither is there any other name under Heaven given among
men, whereby we can be saved." My soul, hast thou considered Jesus in this precious point of view? Hast thou beheld him both in his divine and human nature, how unspeak-
ably glorious in himself, and how enriching to the souls of
his people? Art thou a spiritual merchantman, seeking
goodly pearls? and is Jesus the One, the only One, costly,
precious, and so infinitely desirable in thine eye, that thou
art willing so sell all, that thou wouldest part with millions
of worlds, rather than lose Christ? Hast thou found him in
the field of his Scripture, and dost thou ask how shall I buy?
Listen to his own most gracious words:—" I counsel thee to

buy of me gold tried in the fire, that thou mayest be rich."
Yes, thou generous Lord! I am come to buy of thee without
money and without price. For well I know, through thy
teaching, that neither the obedience of men or angels can
purchase the least title to thee, but thine own precious merits
and thine atoning blood. And now, Lord, possessing thee, I
possess all things: and will give up all beside, and part with
all, and forget all, since Jesus is mine, and I am his, in time
and to all eternity.

8.—Thou hast kept the good wine until now.—*John* ii. 10.

THE good wine of the gospel must be Jesus himself; for
He, and He alone, trod the winepress of his Father's wrath,
when the Lord bruised him and put him to grief. This is
the wine which, in Scripture, is said to cheer both God and
men ; for when God's justice took the full draught of it for
the sins of the redeemed, the Lord declared himself well
pleased. And when the poor sinner, by sovereign grace, is
first made to drink of the blood of the Lamb, he feels constrained to say, the Lord had kept the good wine until now ;
for never before had his soul been so satisfied. Oh, precious
Jesus! how sweet is the thought! Thy first miracle converted water into wine. Moses's ministry, under thy commission, was first manifested in turning water into blood.
Yes! dear Lord! when once thy grace hath wrought upon
the heart of a sinner, thou makest his most common mercies,
like water, to become richer than wine. Whereas the law,
which is the ministration of death as long as the poor sinner
continues under its power, make all his enjoyments to partake
of the curse. Oh! for continued manifestations of thy glory,
dearest Lord! Give me to drink of thy best wine, my beloved, " which goeth down sweetly, causing the lips of those
that sleep to speak."

9.—That will by no means clear the guilty.—*Exod.* xxxiv. 7.

PAUSE, my soul, over these solemn words! Will not Jehovah clear the guilty? And art thou not guilty? How
then wilt thou come before God, either now or hereafter?
Hearken, my soul, to what thy God hath also said :—" Deliver him from going down to the pit; I have found a ransom." Oh! soul-reviving, soul-comforting words! Yes, Jesus
became my surety, took my guilt, and bought me out of the
hands of the law and justice. God hath not therefore cleared the
guilty, but taken ample satisfaction on the person of the sin-

ner's surety. Hence now the double claim of justice and grace demand the sinner's pardon. Here then, my soul, rest thy present and thine everlasting plea. Keep up a daily, an hourly remembrance of it at the mercy-seat. While Jesus lives, and lives there as thine advocate, never doubt thy acceptance in the beloved. Guilty as thou art in thyself, yet spotless in him. The same God which made thy Jesus to be sin for thee, who knew no sin, makes thee the righteousness of God in him.

10.—My beloved is gone down into his garden, to the beds of spices, to feed in the gardens, and to gather lilies.—*Song* vi. 2.

WONDERFUL condescension! Jesus, the beloved of all his people, is indeed come down into his garden the Church! for he loves the sacred walks of a spot so near and so dear to him, which is at once the gift of his Father, and the purchase of his own most precious blood. Moreover, he hath gathered it out of the world's wide wilderness, and separated it as a sacred inclosure by his distinguishing grace. Surely then he will visit it! Yes; here he constantly walks: here he comes to observe the souls of his people as trees of his own right-hand planting. He is said to feed here: for the graces of his Spirit, which he calls forth into exercise, are more fragrant to him than all the spices of the East. And all the beauty and whiteness of the lily is not to be compared to the glory, loveliness, and sweet-smelling savour of the righteousness of Jesus, in which he beholds the souls of his redeemed as clad. And oh! here Jesus is gathering them to himself in all the different degrees of their growth, from the first moment of planting them in his garden, until he transplants them into the paradise of God. Art thou, my soul, in this garden of Jesus? Art thou rejoicing under his gracious hand? Are the dews of his ordinances, in this inclosure of thy Lord, dropping upon thee?

11.—I am the bright and morning star.—*Rev.* xxii. 16.

How oft, in some dark wintry morning like the present, have I beheld the morning star shining with loveliness, when all the other lights of heaven were put out! But how little did I think of thee, thou precious light and life of men! Thou art indeed the bright and Morning Star in the firmament of thy Church, thy word, and in the souls of thy redeemed. Henceforth, dearest Jesus, let the morning visit of this sweet Planet to our darkened earth remind me of thee, amidst all the gross darkness in which, by nature, we are surrounded. Sure pledge of day as this beneficent Star is, yet not more sure than thou in the day-dawn and day-star of prophecy which ministered to thy coming; and, in the twilight of grace upon the soul, the forerunner of a glorious day. Be thou my morning song, my noontide-joy, my evening meditation, and midnight light. Through all the wintry seasons of my pilgrimage shine forth, sweet Jesus, upon my soul. Oh! ye sons of sloth, ye children of darkness and of night, rouse from your beds of drowsiness, before the sleep of death seal up your eyes in everlasting darkness. Jesus, the Morning Star, now shines; and ere long Jesus, the Son of Righteousness, will appear, no more to go down, and all the sons of God will shout for joy!

12.—If thy brother be waxen poor, and hath sold away some of his possession, and if any of his kin come to redeem it, then shall he redeem that which his brother sold.—*Levit.* xxv. 25.

How poor and wretched was I before I knew Jesus! I had not only sold some of my possessions, but all. I was utterly insolvent, helpless, and ruined; one like the Son of Man redeemed me. But what a double blessedness was it to my soul, when I discovered that this Redeemer was so very near of kin to me that he was my brother. Hail, thou precious, precious Jesus! thou art, indeed, a "Brother born for adversity." Yes; blessed Jesus! thou art He whom thy brethren shall praise; and all thy Father's children shall bow down to thee. My soul, see to it that thou make the most of this relationship. Never, oh never, will thy Brother suffer his poor indigent relation to want any more, after that he hath thus redeemed both thyself and thy possession. Now do I see why it was the Church so passionately longed for Jesus under this tender character. "Oh! (said she,) that thou wert as my brother that sucked the breasts of my mother; when I should find thee without I would kiss thee, yea, I should not be despised."

13.—Master! where dwellest thou?—*John* i. 38.

Is this the earnest inquiry of my soul? Hear then the answer: "Thus saith the High and Lofty One, whose name is Holy, I dwell in the high and holy place; with him also that is of a contrite and humble spirit, to revive the spirit of the humble, and to revive the heart of the contrite ones." Pause my soul! Are these the qualities produced by grace in thine

2

heart? Jesus, Master, make me what thou wouldest have me
to be; and then come, Lord, agreeable to thy promises.
Thou hast said, My Father will come, and I will come, and
make our abode with him. And thou hast said, The Holy
Ghost shall come and abide with you for ever. What, my
soul! shall I indeed have such glorious personages for my
companions? Behold, Lord, the heaven, and the heaven of
heavens, cannot contain thee! Oh! for grace and a sanctity
of thought corresponding to such mercies, since our bodies
are the temple of the Holy Ghost which dwelleth in us!

14.—And she said to the king, it was a true report that I heard in mine
own land of thy acts, and of thy wisdom. Howbeit, I believed not
the words until I came, and mine eyes had seen it; and behold the
half was not told me.—1 *Kings* x. 6, 7.

IF the Queen of the South was so astonished in the view
of Solomon's wisdom, what ought to be thy surprise, my soul,
in the contemplation of Jesus, in whom are hid all the treasures of wisdom and knowledge? When thou didst first
hear of Jesus, and when constrained by necessity to come to
him, a poor, blind, ignorant sinner, how little didst thou conceive either of thyself or him! He told thee, indeed, all that
was in thine heart, and made thy very spirit, like her's, to
faint within thee, when he shewed thy sin and his salvation.
Surely then, and often since, even now hast thou been constrained to say, as she did, the half was not told thee by
others, of what sweet discoveries he hath made to thee of
himself. Think then, my soul, what holy surprise and joy
will burst in upon thee in the day when, at the fountain-head
of glory in his courts above, he will unfold all his beauty,
love, and wisdom; when thou shalt see him as he is, and
know even as thou art known!

15.—I was brought low and he helped me.—*Psalm* cxvi. 6.

IT is blessed sometimes that the streams of creature-comforts
should be dry, in order to compel us to go to the fountain-
head. When the fig-tree doth not blossom, and the fields
yield no meat, then a Covenant God is precious to fly to.
My soul! say, was not that assault of Satan sanctified, when
it brought Jesus thereby to thy rescue? Was not that cross
sweetly timed, when it tended to wean thee from the world?
And wouldest thou have been without that sickness, when
Jesus sat up by thee, soothed thee in thy languor, and made
all thy bed in thy sickness? Well was it for me that I was

brought low, or I should never have known in a thousand instances the help of my God. Oh then, my soul! like Paul, learn to glory in thy infirmities, that the power of Jesus may rest upon thee!

16.—And Hezekiah rejoiced, and all the people, that God had prepared the people; for the thing was done suddenly.—2 *Chron.* xxix. 36.

SWEET thought ever to keep in view, that it is the Lord that prepares the heart, and gives answers to the tongue. And, oh! how sudden, how unexpected, how unlooked-for, sometimes, are the visits of his grace! "Or ever I was aware (saith the Church) my soul made me like the chariots of Amminadib." Is my heart cold, my mind barren, my frame lifeless? Do thou then, dearest Lord, make me to rejoice in warming my frozen affection, making fruitful my poor estate, and putting new life into my soul. All I want is a frame of mind best suited to thy glory. And what is that? Truly, that when I have nothing, feel nothing, can do nothing, am worse than nothing, that then, even then, I may be rich in thee amidst all my own bankruptcy. This, dear Lord, is what I covet. And if thou withholdest all frames which might melt, or warm, or rejoice my own feelings, yet if my soul still hangs upon thee notwithstanding all, as the vessel upon the nail, my God and Jesus will be my rock, that feels nothing of the ebbings and flowings of the sea around, whatever be the tide of my fluctuating affections.

17.—My beloved standeth behind our wall. He looketh forth at the window, shewing himself through the lattice.—*Song.* ii. 9.

IT might be truly said, that it was behind the wall of our nature the Lord Jesus stood, when, by taking a body of flesh, he veiled the glories of his Godhead, during the days of his humanity. And may it not be as truly said, that it is still, as from behind a wall, all the gracious discoveries he now makes of himself are manifested to his people? For what from the dulness of our perception, the unbelief and the sins and infirmities of our nature, the most we see of our Jesus is but as through a glass darkly. But yet, my soul, how sweet are even these visits of his love, when we can get, though but a glimpse of the King in his beauty through the windows of ordinances, or the lattice of his blessed word. Oh! precious Jesus! let thy visits be frequent, increasingly lovely, and increasingly glorious, that the souls of thy people may increasingly delight in thee. Methinks I would lay

about the doors, and windows, and courts of thy house, and be
sending in a wish, and the fervent prayer of a poor beggar
who is living on thy bounty, that thou wouldest come forth to
my view and bless me with thy presence, until that all intervening mediums of walls and windows are thrown down, and
Jesus manifests himself to my longing eyes in all his glory.

18.—Therefore doth my Father love me, because I lay down my life
that I might take it up again.—*John* x. 17.

MARK, my soul, the precious cause thy Jesus here assigns
for the love of his Father. God the Father not only loves
God the Son as God, one with him in nature and in all divine perfections; but he loves him peculiarly because he
voluntarily undertook and accomplished by his death the
salvation of his people. Now then, my soul, make these
two sweet improvements from what Jesus hath here said.
First, think what must have been, and now is, the love of
thy God and Father to thee and every poor sinner, when he
truly loves his dear Son because he became the Saviour of
poor sinners. And, secondly, think what love Jesus hath
shown to poor sinners in thus manifesting his mercy in such
a way, and how dear they must be to the heart of Jesus,
which have made him dear in the sight of God. My soul!
never lose sight of this argument when thou goest to the
mercy-seat. Tell thy God and Father thou art come to ask
mercies in his name, and for his righteousness' sake, whom
the Father loveth on this very account. And oh! how very
dear should Jesus be to thee for his blood and righteousness,
who is dear to the Father for the same cause.

19.—As the new wine is found in the cluster, and one saith, Destroy it
not, for a blessing is in it; so will I do for my servant's sake, that
I may not destroy them all.—*Isaiah* lxv. 8.

IT is blessed to trace our mercies to the fountain head, and
to find them all folded up from everlasting in Jesus! What
was it that preserved our whole nature when blasted and
withered by the fall? Was it not because Jesus, the promised
seed, was in it? And what is it that preserves every individual among the children of God, during the dark season
of their unregeneracy, but the same precious cause? He
that looks on (and who is this but Christ himself?) amidst
all our perishing circumstances, by his powerful and all-prevailing intercession commands the destroyer not to touch his
people; for though in themselves loathsome, yet in Jesus are
they fair and lovely. My soul, learn hence thy security.

The whole cause for which thou wert preserved until called, and, when called, preserved through grace unto glory, both in conversion and in every after-act of God's dealings with thee, all refers itself to this one source—Destroy it not, there is a blessing *in* thee, though not *from* thee : Jesus is in thee, as the new wine is found in the cluster!

20.—What shall be done to the man whom the king delighteth to honour ?—*Esther* vi. 6.

NAY, my soul, ask thine own heart what shall be done to the God-man whom Jehovah, the King of kings, delighteth to honour? Oh! for the view of what John saw, and to hear what John heard, when he beheld heaven opened, and heard the innumerable multitude chanting Salvation to God and the Lamb! Lord, I would say, let every knee bow before him, and every tongue confess that Jesus Christ is Lord, to the glory of God the Father. And oh! most gracious Father, dost thou take delight that Jesus should be honoured? Is it thine honour when Jesus is honoured ; thy glory when Jesus is glorified? Oh! what wonderful encouragement is this to the faith and belief of a poor sinner ; that I not only praise my adorable Redeemer when I come to him for all things, and trust him for all things ; but these exercises of grace are as acceptable to God my Father, as they are honourable to God the Son. And this is the only way, and a blessed way it is indeed, by which a poor sinner can give glory to the Father, in believing the record which he hath given of his Son. Here, then, my soul, do thou daily be found in honouring the Glory-man, the God-man Christ Jesus, whom God the Father delighteth to honour.

21.—But for Adam there was not found an help meet for him.—*Gen.* xx. 20.

MY soul! mark what is here said, for sure it is a sweet Scripture. Amidst all the works of God, there was not one that could be found an help meet for man. The inferior creatures could indeed minister to his bodily comfort, but not to his soul. Eve herself, with all her loveliness, must have failed in this particular. Both the woman and her husband alike needed this help to the soul. How refreshing is the thought, and what a lovely view doth it give us of God's grace and mercy, that in the seed of the woman an help, in the fullest sense of the word, was found, both for time and eternity. Yes; blessed Jesus! in thee we trace this wonderous gift of God. Pause then, my soul! and add this thought to the

2*

vast account: The same love which fitted thee with an help
meet in a Saviour, hath fitted thee, and will continue to fit
thee, with the supply of all thy need. It were to be wished
that every child of God would never lose sight of this certain truth—that he must have the fittest station in life, the
fittest frame of mind and of body, the fittest yoke-fellow, the
fittest circumstances; in short, the fittest mercies and the
fittest trials; because every thing is made subservient to the
divine glory in Jesus. Sweet thought! He that spared not
his own Son, will, with him, freely give all things.

22.—They shall cry unto the Lord, because of the oppressors, and he
shall send them a Saviour, and a great one, and he shall deliver
them.—*Isaiah* xix. 20.

MARK, my soul, the sweet encouragement contained in
these words. Here is a cry—and it is the cry of the soul;
for it is directed unto the Lord. There is (as Elihu tells us)
a cry of nature under oppressions; but as this is not *to* God,
it is evident that it never came *from* God; for he tells us that
none of them saith, " Where is God my Maker, who giveth
songs in the night?" Job xxxv. 9. But when the Holy
Ghost convinceth of sin, and puts a cry in the heart by
reason of it, he convinceth also of the righteousness of Jesus.
Hence the difference of those cries is as wide as the East is
from the West. Mark therefore, my soul, this distinguishing
feature of grace; and see whether thy cries are *praying*
cries, and not *complaining* ones. And now observe what
follows. When poor sinners thus cry unto the Lord, he
shall send them a Saviour, and a great one. Who, but God
the Father, sent his Son to be the Saviour of poor lost sinners? Was not Jesus a Saviour indeed, and a great one?
Who, but He, could deliver the sinner from destruction!
And remark, further, the absolute certainty of the promise;
for it is said, He *shall* deliver them. Yes, blessed Jesus!
thy deliverance is sure; thy salvation certain. Thou hast
said, thy sheep shall never perish; neither shall any pluck
them out of thine hand. Pause now, my soul, over this
sweet verse. Surely in its bosom is folded up the sum and
substance of all the gospel. Here are all the Persons of the
Godhead, engaged for the salvation of every poor crying
sinner. Here is God the Holy Ghost, agreeably to his
blessed office, causing the sinner to feel the oppressions of
sin, and putting a cry in his heart, to the Lord, to be delivered from them. Here is God the Father answering that

cry, in mercy, and sending his Almighty Son to be the Saviour of the poor sinner. And here is Jesus the Saviour, and a great one, saving the poor sinner with an everlasting salvation. Shout then, my soul, and begin the song of Salvation to God and the Lamb.

23.—As sin hath reigned unto death, even so might grace reign through righteousness, unto eternal life, by Jesus Christ our Lord.—*Rom.* v. 21.

PAUSE, my soul, and put forth thy fullest thoughts in the contemplation of those two united sources of thy felicity, marked in this verse: the Father's eternal purpose, in the reign of grace; and the everlasting efficacy and infinite value of thy Jesus's righteousness, to eternal life. None but God himself can know the fullness and extent of either. I am persuaded, that angels of light can never entertain adequate conceptions of either. The eternal purpose of God hath bounded the reign of sin: it is but unto death. But those purposes give a further extent to the redemption from death and sin, by Jesus; for the glory of Christ's person, and the worth of his salvation, possess, in both, a vast overplus, a redundancy of merit, which brings the redeemed into favour and acceptance in Jesus, and with such a title to everlasting felicity as eternity itself can never exhaust—no, nor fully recompense or pay. Oh! for grace to contemplate the love of the Father, and of the Son, by this standard. Lord, I would be lost, I would be swallowed up, day by day in the unceasing meditation. Dearest, blessed, precious Jesus! give me to think of nothing else: to speak of nothing else; but, by faith, to possess in anticipation the joys of thy redeemed, until I come, through thee, and in thee, to the everlasting enjoyment of them, in thy kingdom of glory.

24.—And he shewed me Joshua the high-priest standing before the angel of the Lord, and Satan standing at his right hand to resist him. And the Lord said unto Satan, the Lord rebuke thee, O Satan: even the Lord that hath chosen Jerusalem, rebuke thee. Is not this a brand plucked out of the fire?—*Zech.* iii. 1, 2.

WHO shall say, how many such transactions as these are continually going on, for and against the people of God, in the court of Heaven, while we, upon earth, are unconscious either of our misery or mercy. The Holy Ghost was graciously pleased to have this made known to the church. And John had it again in commission to tell the church, that a song in heaven was sung at the expulsion of the devil from

heaven, because the accuser of the brethren was cast down.
My soul! doth he that first tempts thee, then become thine
accuser? Is he carrying on this practice, day and night, before God? And while Satan is thine accuser, is Jesus thine
Advocate? Oh! precious, precious Lord! how little hath
my poor ignorant and unthinking soul been meditating on
thee, in this thy merciful, sweet, and gracious office. Oh!
glorious thought! Now I see a blessedness in that Scripture which I have often read with indifference in times past.
"If any man sin, we have an Advocate with the Father,
Jesus Christ the righteous; and he is (for God my Father
hath set him forth so) the propitiation for our sins." Hail,
holy, wonderful Counsellor. Condescend, thou mighty
Pleader, still to take up my cause. Oh! may I behold thee
often in this high office! Oh, may I often hear thee with
the ear of faith, and my whole soul going forth in love towards thee, while thou art pointing to my poor soul, and
saying, " Hath not God the Father chosen this brand plucked
from the fire! Take away the filthy garments from him. I
have caused thine iniquity to pass from thee."

25.—This is a faithful saying, and worthy of all acceptation, that Christ
Jesus came into the world to save sinners.—1 *Timothy* i. 15.

HARK, my soul, to the proclamation from heaven! Is this
the faithful saying of a faithful God? Surely, then, thou
mayest well regard it; for it is for thy life. And if it be
worthy of *all* acceptation, it must be eminently so of *thine;*
for thou hast been a transgressor from the womb. But did
Jesus indeed come to save sinners? Yes! so the proclamation runs. Sinners, enemies to God. Jesus, it is said, received gifts for the rebellious, that the Lord God might dwell
among them. And with that tenderness which distinguished
his character, he said himself, that he came not to call the
righteous, but sinners to repentance. Well then, my soul,
upon this warrant of the faithful word of a faithful God, wilt
thou not so fully rely as to believe unto salvation? If any
inquiries arise contrary to this belief, let this be thine answer:
—Christ came to save sinners: that's enough for me; for I
am one. God's salvation is said to be for enemies: that is my
name by nature. Jesus received gifts for the rebellious: to
this character I plead also guilty. If men or devils would
endeavour to work unbelief in my heart, this is my answer:
Christ came to save sinners. Let those that never felt sin,
and consequently know not the need of a Saviour, stay and

argue the point as they may; my soul's eternal welfare is
concerned, and I will not lose a moment to close with the
heavenly proposal. Lord Jesus, thou waitest to be gracious!
The faithful saying of my God I accept on my bended knees.
It is, indeed, worthy of all acceptation, and, above all, of
mine. Here, while upon earth, will I proclaim thy praise;
and, in Heaven, the loudest of all voices must be mine, that
Christ came to save sinners, of whom I am chief.

26.—And they said one to another, Did not our heart burn within us
while he talked with us by the way, and while he opened to us the
Scriptures ?—*Luke* xxiv. 32.

Ought not the disciples of Jesus to do now, as the disciples
of Jesus did then? What but of Jesus should we speak of
by the way? Methinks the Lord's people, and especially
when coming from the Lord's house, should be distinguished
from the frothy conversation of mere carnal worshippers. I
would, by talking of Jesus, invite him to mingle with us, and
open to our understandings the Scriptures. I would therefore sometimes ask one, and another, when returning from
the house or the table of the Lord, How went the matter with
your soul to-day? I pray you tell me; was the King at
court? Did he receive petitions? Did he answer prayers?
Were you refreshed; were any healed; any comforted; any
made joyful, in his house of prayer? Surely we might hope,
by such edifying inquiries, each would help his fellow. And
He, of whom it is said the Lord hearkened and heard, when
of old the people of God were often talking one to another,
would again draw nigh, and make the heart burn with the
sweet manifestations of his love. But chiefly, blessed Master!
if I meet with none to ask whether they have seen the King
in his beauty, give me to taste of the sweet savour of thy
grace myself: come to me, Lord, in the refreshing, strengthening, heart-warming, soul-rejoicing, manifestations of thy
presence; for thy love is better than wine; and the very
crumb from under thy table is more delicious than the honey
and the honey-comb.

27.—He shall glorify me ; for he shall receive of mine, and shall shew
it unto you. John xvi. 14.

Some precious souls are at a loss to apprehend how the
Holy Ghost makes application of Jesus, and his benefits, to
his people. Hence they ask, How am I to know that the
righteousness of Jesus, and the blood of Jesus, are applied to

me? But be not thou, my soul, ignorant of so important a matter, on the clear apprehension of which thy daily comfort depends. Attend, my soul, to what thy Jesus saith in those precious words ; and, under the blessed Spirit's teaching, the matter will appear abundantly plain. He shall glorify me, saith Jesus. And doth not the Holy Ghost do this in every believer's view, when he gives the soul to see that all that vast extent of redemption blessings, which the Father treasured up in his dear Son for poor sinners, flow immediately from Jesus? And observe, the Holy Ghost doth not at first show the sinner that all result from the everlasting love and grace, and purpose of God the Father ; but he leads the sinner to view them, and receive them as the blessed fruits and effects of Jesus's meditation ; and then opens more fully the glory of the Father in the original design of them, in this precious way, from everlasting. This is indeed to glorify Jesus, and to glorify the Father in him. And how are these blessings applied? The scriptural answer is the best answer :—" He shall receive of mine," saith Jesus, " and show it unto you." And doth not that Almighty teacher do all this most sweetly and effectually, when, at any time, he so holds up the Lord Jesus, in all the glories of his person, and in all the beauties of his finished work, as to incline the sinner's heart so to behold the Saviour as to believe in him, and firmly to rely upon him? Is not the righteousness of Jesus received, and his precious blood applied, when the soul is led to the hearty and cordial assurance, that that righteousness is effectual to justify, and that blood to cleanse from all sin? Yes, precious Jesus! I praise thee for these blessings in thee. I adore thee, thou Holy Spirit, for thy divine teaching concerning them. And I glorify thee, thou Almighty Father, for thine abundant grace and mercy, in the gift of thy dear Son.

28.—As having nothing, and yet possessing all things.—2 *Cor.* vi. 10.

My soul, hast thou learnt this holy science? There are three blessed lessons the Holy Ghost teacheth on this ground. As, *first,* The believer is thoroughly emptied of himself. Art thou thus taught of God? Hast thou been led to see, to feel, to know, to be convinced that, after all thine attainments, after all thy long standing in the school of Jesus, thou hast nothing, canst do nothing, art worse than nothing ; and, literally, hast no more in thyself now to recommend thee to Jesus, than the first moment thou didst hear of his name? This is to have nothing. This is to be poor in spirit. *Secondly,* Dost thou possess all things in Jesus? Yes! if so be thou art living out of thyself wholly upon Him. And how is this known? Nothing more evident. When a sense of my emptiness endears to me his fulness; my poverty, his riches; my weakness, his strength; my sins, his righteousness: my guilt, his blood; I truly possess all things, as far as I approve what Jesus is to his people, and rest upon Him and the blessed fruits of his salvation, as God the Father designed him, who hath made him wisdom, righteousness, sanctification, and redemption, to his people. And there is a *third* precious lesson the Holy Ghost teacheth to the poor that have nothing, and yet possess all things; namely, so to possess Jesus himself, that he may not only make his poor ones rich in his riches, but be himself their treasure; so to supply them not only with what they need, but to be himself their fulness; not only to open to them light and life, but to be himself both their light and life; so to impart to them salvation, as to show them that he is himself their salvation: and, in short, so to give them present peace, and the assurance of everlasting happiness in his blood and righteousness, as to give them the perfect enjoyment that he is himself both their present and everlasting happiness, and their portion for ever! My soul! hast thou learnt, and art thou every day more and more learning these precious truths? Oh! then, look up to thy Jesus, and say with one of old, " Whom have I in heaven but thee; and there is none upon earth I desire beside thee. My flesh and my heart faileth; but thou art the strength of my heart, and my portion for ever."

29.—If the servant shall plainly say, I love my master, my wife, and my children, I will not go out free. Then his master shall bring him unto the judges; he shall also bring him home to the door, or unto the doorpost, and his master shall bore his ear through with an awl, and he shall serve him for ever.—*Exodus* xxi. 5, 6.

How sweet is Scripture explained by Scripture. Jesus saith, when sacrifice and offering under the law were both unprofitable, " Mine ears hast thou opened ;" or, as it might have been rendered, " Mine ears hast thou digged." Psalm xl. 6. And elsewhere :—" The Lord God hath opened mine ear, and I was not rebellious." Isaiah l. 5. The Apostle to the Hebrews decidedly explains this in reference to Christ. Heb. x. 5. And what was all this but to show the voluntary service of Jesus to the office and work of the Redeemer?

Was not Jesus, in all that high work, the servant of Jehovah ? Though he was in the form of God, and with him it was no robbery to be equal with God, yet he made himself of no reputation, and took upon him the form of a servant. And for whom did he this ? Was it not, in effect, saying, like the Jewish servant which was typical of him, " I love my Master, my Father, in the work of redemption ?" John xiv. 31.—" I love my wife, my church, my spouse." Song iv. 10.—" I love my children : behold I and the children whom thou hast given me." Isaiah viii. 18.—" I will not go out free." Oh ! precious Lord Jesus ! well might the Apostle say, " Husbands, love your wives, even as Christ loved the Church, and gave himself for it." Surely it was thy love, dearest Lord ! to thy Church, that moved thee to serve Jehovah, as Israel served for a wife ; and for a wife kept sheep. Hosea xii. 12. Oh ! for grace to love thee, and to serve thee for ever !

30.—That in the ages to come he might show the exceeding riches of his grace, in his kindness towards us, through Christ Jesus.—*Eph.* ii. 7.

PAUSE, my soul, and gather in all the powers of arithmetic, and try if thou art able to count what the exceeding riches of God's grace amount to. Think how great, how free, how sovereign, how inexhaustible, how everlasting ! All that a poor sinner hath in time, all that we can enjoy to all eternity, all is of grace. And what a title hath thy God chosen to be known by among his people, when, to make himself known more fully in Jesus, he stiles himself the God of all grace ! All grace ? Yes ; all grace, and all sorts and degrees of grace: pardoning grace, renewing grace, quickening grace, strengthening grace, comforting grace ; in short, all grace. And is all this treasured up in Jesus ? Oh! then, my soul, see that Jesus be thine, and all is thine. And mark this down as a sure unerring rule—as grace hath no source but in the Father's love, so the exalting that grace, in Jesus, is the Father's design in salvation. The brightest pearl in the Redeemer's crown, is that which shines with this inscription : " To the praise of the glory of his grace, wherein he hath made us accepted in the Beloved." Here, my soul, seek thy daily grace, more earnest than thy daily bread.

31.—What think ye that he will not come to the feast ?—*John* xi. 56.

Is this thy inquiry, my soul, when, at any time, thou art seeking Jesus in his word, in his ordinances, at his table?

Will he not come? Will Jesus not be there? Think how he hath dealt in times past. Did not Jesus rejoice, when the hour arrived for coming into the world for salvation? Doth he not rejoice, when coming to the heart of the poor sinner for conversion? And will he not come with joy, in all the renewed visits of his love? Besides—doth not Jesus know that it is a time of need to thee? And hath he not opened a way to the throne of grace, on purpose that his poor helpless children might come boldly to a throne of grace to obtain help, and find grace, in every time of need? Oh! then, mark it down as a sure thing, thy Jesus will be there. He spreads the feast, and he will be present. He waits to be gracious; waits to be kind to thee. Love is in his heart, and salvation in his hands. Hasten then to his house, to his table, to his bosom, to his heart; and say with the Church, " Come, my Beloved, and be thou like a roe, or a young heart, upon the mountains of Bether."

FEBRUARY.

1.—And they shall call his name Emmanuel; which, being interpreted, is, God with us.—*Matt.* i. 23.

My soul! hast thou never remarked what a peculiar beauty and sweetness there is in every name by which thy God and Saviour is made known to thee in his holy word? Surely, if nothing more had been intended by it, than to identify and prove his sacred Person, one name would have answered this purpose: evidently, therefore, somewhat of great importance is designed from his many names. And depend upon it, my soul, so much loveliness is there in every individual name of thy Jesus; and at one time or other, in thy walk of faith, so very much wilt thou need every one, and find the preciousness of every one, that thou wouldest not part with one of thy Redeemer's names—no, not for the world. This of Emmanuel, by which thou art commanded to call him, is a sweet one to endear him to thee. Had he not been Emmanuel, he could not have been Jesus; for none but God can save a sinner. And therefore he is called Emmanuel, which signifies, God with us. Hence therefore he is God. Put this down, as a glorious truth, in thy esteem. God in our nature. God

3

tabernacling in our flesh. God in us ; and God in our hearts,
the hope of glory. It is the Godhead of thy Jesus which
gives efficacy and value to every act of redemption. As God,
his righteousness is the righteousness of God to justify thee.
Mark that! His sacrifice to atone—His blood to cleanse—
His grace to bless. All these blessed acts of thy Jesus derive
efficacy to answer all their glorious purposes, because they
are the acts of God. And remark, my soul, yet further, that
all that yet remains to be fulfilled, in what he hath promised
concerning salvation ; in now pleading thy cause, and hereafter taking thee to glory: these cannot fail—because He
who hath promised is Emmanuel. Go on, my soul, one step
further, and remember that He, whom thou art to call Emmanuel, is also God in thy nature. Hence he is so very near
and dear, in all tender alliances, as to be bone of thy bone,
and flesh of thy flesh. My soul! never, never lose sight of
this most sweet and precious name of thy Jesus. Call him,
as thou art commanded, call his name Emmanuel.

2.—Seest thou this woman ?—*Luke* xvii. 44.

My soul! look at this woman at the feet of Jesus ; for thy
Jesus bids thee look, and gather instruction from the view as
well as the Pharisee. Behold how she wept, how she washed
the feet of Jesus, and anointed them with ointment. These were
sweet tokens of her love and adoration. But were these
the causes for which she obtained forgiveness? Oh! no.
Read what the Lord said to her:—" Thy faith hath saved
thee." Learn then, my soul, in what salvation lies. Love
may bring ointment to Jesus. Sorrow for sin, when grace is
in the heart, will cause tears to fall. But faith brings nothing ;
for it hath nothing. It casts itself wholly upon Jesus. Amidst
all its guilt, and fears, and tears, it is Jesus only to whom
faith looks. It is Jesus upon whom alone it depends. It hath
nothing to do with self; neither our own feelings, nor the exercise of our graces. These are blessed evidences of the
work of the Lord upon the heart: but they are not salvation.
It is Jesus, all precious, all glorious, all suitable Jesus! He
is the one blessed object of faith's joy, and hope, and pursuit,
and desire. And depend upon it, thy God and Father in
Christ Jesus is more pleased, more honoured by this simple
act of faith upon Jesus' glorious person and righteousness,
than by all the tears in the world ; when those tears lead us
to place a stress upon the *effects* of faith, instead of hanging
wholly upon the *cause*, in the glorious object, Jesus. Pause,

my soul, over this nice but proper distinction ; and this will be to find comfort always in Jesus. "Seest thou this woman ?"

3.—Who loved me, and gave himself for me.—*Gal.* ii. 20.

SEE, my soul, how Paul is for ever using Jesus, and feasting for ever upon him. Oh! seek grace to do the same. He saith Jesus loved him. Jesus the Son of God loved Paul. Now love, from any object, is valuable ; but from the first, and best, and greatest of all Beings, what invaluable love is this ? And who did Christ love ? "Why me," saith Paul ; "who was a blasphemer, a persecutor, and injurious." And how do you know, Paul, that Jesus loved you ? "He gave himself for me," saith Paul. Gave himself ? Yes! himself. Not his gifts only, not his grace, not his mercies, though all creation is his. And whatever he gave must have been an undeserved mercy ; for I merited hell, when he bestowed upon me heaven. "But even heaven, with all its glories, is nothing," saith Paul, " to what Jesus gave me ; for he gave himself for me." Oh! my soul, wilt thou not look up, wilt thou not be encouraged to hope, to believe, to hang upon Jesus, for the same. Oh! for faith to believe. Precious Jesus! thou Author and Finisher of faith, grant me this mercy. And while I read these sweet words concerning thee, who loved and who gave thyself for poor lost sinners, oh ! like Paul, and with the same assurance of faith, cause me to add—me, me ; Jesus loved me, and gave himself for me.

4.—The Comforter that should relieve my soul is far from me.—*Lament.* i. 15.

WHENCE is it, my soul, that those distressing thoughts arise ? Pause and inquire. Is the Holy Ghost the Comforter indeed withdrawn, when Jesus, thy Jesus, sweetly and graciously promised that he should abide for ever ? This cannot be. Is the righteousness of Jesus less ; or hath his blood, to atone and cleanse, lost its efficacy ? Oh! no. Jesus' righteousness, and Jesus' all-atoning propitiation, like the Almighty Author of both, must be eternally and everlastingly the same ; yesterday, and to-day, and for ever. Hath God thy Father forgotten to be gracious ? Oh! no. God thy Father proclaimed from heaven, that he is well pleased for his dear Son's righteousness' sake. And never, never shall a word gone out of the Lord's mouth be altered. From

whence then, my soul, is thy leanness, thy fears and despondency? Canst thou not discover? Oh! yes. It is all in
thyself, and thy unbelieving frame. Thou art looking to thyself, and not to all-precious Jesus! Thou wantest to feel
some new frame of thy own; some melting of heart, or the
like. And if thou couldest be gratified in this, then thou
wouldest go to Jesus with confidence; and there plead, as
thou thinkest, Jesus' name, and blood, and righteousness, for
acceptance. And doth the want of these feelings keep thee
back? Oh! fie, my soul, is this thy love, thy kindness, to thy
friend? Can any thing be more plain, than that thou art
making a part Saviour of thy feelings, and not a whole Saviour of thy Jesus? No wonder thou criest out, the Comforter is far from thee. For the Holy Ghost will teach thee,
that all comfort is only in Jesus. And mark this, my soul,
for all future occasions:—If thou wilt seek comfort in any-
thing out of Jesus, though it be in the sweetest frames,
as thou mayest think, of thine—Jesus, in mercy and love,
will put thy comforts out of thy reach. Oh! then come to
Jesus poor and needy, with, or without frames. Make him
all and in all; and He will be thy joy, thy comfort, and thy
portion for ever.

5.—In the hand of a Mediator.—*Gal.* iii. 19.

The hand of a mediator was the great blessing every enlightened son of Adam, from the fall, sighed after, and looked
for, in every approach to God. Hence the first transgressor,
for the want of it hid himself from the presence of God, amidst
the trees of the garden. Hence Israel cried out to Moses,
"Go thou near, and hear all that the Lord our God shall
say; but let not God speak with us, lest we die. And Job
longed for a Daysman (that is) a Mediator, that might lay
his hand on both parties. See then, my soul, thy privileges;
for thou hast a Mediator, and a glorious one indeed, in whose
mighty hand all thy concerns are eternally secured. "Ye
are come," saith the Apostle: he doth not say ye are coming; but, ye are come, "to Jesus the Mediator of the new
Covenant, and to the blood of sprinkling." Oh! then, in all
thy approaches, have an eye to Jesus. Put all thy affairs in
this glorious Mediator's hand. Remember he wears thy nature, pleads thy cause, takes up all thy concerns, and ever
liveth to make intercession for sinners; and therefore cast all
thy care upon him; for he careth for thee. And look to this
one grand thing—that all thy confidence and all thy joy ari-

seth wholly from Jesus's person and righteousness; not from any supposed graces, tears, repentance—nor even from faith itself, if viewed as an act of thine. Cast aside, as filthy rags, all that is thine; and never, no not for a moment, look at any thing as a procuring cause; but let Jesus have all thy confidence, all the glory, and thou wilt have all the comfort. Though Satan accuse, though conscience pleads guilty, God's broken law pronounceth condemnation, and justice demands the penalty; Jesus hath answered all, and is in the throne to see the issue. Oh! the blessedness of having all in the hands of a Mediator.

6.—The rich shall not give more, and the poor shall not give less, than half a shekel, when they give an offering unto the Lord, to make an atonement for your souls.—*Exod.* xxx. 15.

Pause, my soul, over this Scripture, and mark the graciousness of thy God and Father in the blessed truth conveyed in it. What, were all the souls of the redeemed charged equally alike in the account of God? Did God thy Father rate them thus? And did Jesus, thy precious Jesus! purchase all his redeemed with an equal price, when he bought them with his blood? If this be so, my soul, it must follow, that thou, a poor unworthy creature as thou art, overlooked as thou art by the great ones of the earth, and too frequently overlooking in thyself how precious every redeemed soul must be in Jesus' sight, cost as much to Jesus as the soul of Peter or of Paul, or any of the patriarchs, apostles or prophets. Oh! think of this; write it down on the tablets of thy remembrance. Will not this tend to endear Jesus yet more to thee, and bring home thy Father's love in the strongest affection? Add one thought more to this precious relation. If, to Jesus, thy redemption cost as much as any one of the redeemed in glory, think, my soul, after such a purchase, such a price, will he lose his property? will he forego what cost him so dear, and suffer one pearl of his mediatorial crown to be wanting? Add another sweet thought, my soul, to this delightful meditation. If, amidst the various inequalities of life, some poor and some rich, yet whatever difference was allowed or even expected in other offerings, according to the abilities of God's people; yet here, as a representation of the offering of the soul in Jesus' purchase, no one distinction was to be made; is it not plain that the redemption by Jesus is in him, and him only; and his righteousness unto all, and upon all, that believe; for

3*

there is no difference? Dearest Lord! may my soul never
lose sight of this blessed equality. Here thou art indeed, no
respecter of persons.

7.—Behold the Lamb of God!—*John* i. 36.

WHO is it calls upon thee, my soul, to this most gratifying
and enriching of all employments? Is it not God the Holy
Ghost, by the ministry of his servant John? And doth not
God thy Father do the same, by the ministry of his servant
Isaiah, when he bids thee behold Him, in whom his soul delighteth? And is not Jesus himself calling, again and again,
in the ministry of his word and ordinances, upon thy poor
forgetful heart, when he saith, "Behold me! behold me!
Look unto me, and be ye saved!" And wilt thou not obey
the sweet and gracious calls, on which all thy present peace
and everlasting happiness depend? Precious, precious Jesus!
Yes, my Lord! I would, methinks, so look unto thee, and
so behold thee, until my whole heart, and all its affections,
followed my eyes, and left not a thought behind for a single
object beside thee. I would eye thee, thou dear Redeemer,
as the Lamb of God! both where thou once wast, and where
thou now art, and follow thee whithersoever thou goest! I
would behold thee, as the Lamb of God, set up in the decrees
of eternity, from everlasting; for thou art the Lamb slain
from the foundation of the world. I would behold thee, set
forth in all the representations of thy redeeming blood, in the
innumerable sacrifices of the law, and in the Lamb of the
morning, and the Lamb of the evening, through the intermediate ages, to thy coming. I would behold thee, oh! thou
unequalled pattern of excelling meekness! when, in the days of
thy flesh, thou walkedst through the streets of Jerusalem; and
when, as a Lamb, thou wert led to the slaughter. I would eye
thee, oh! thou Lamb of God! until my eye-strings could hold
no longer, when as the lamb of God, and my soul's surety, thou
didst hang upon the tree, putting away sin, and satisfying
divine justice, by the sacrifice of thyself. And never would
I take off my eyes from thy cross, until called by thee to behold thee as the Lamb in the midst of the throne, where
thou art feeding thy church above, and dispensing blessings
to all thy church below. Yes, yes, blessed triumphant Lamb
of God! thou art the Lamb still. Change of place hath
made no change in thy nature, or thy love, or the efficacy of
thy redemption. Thou still appearest as a Lamb that has
been slain. And still thou bearest on thy glorified body, the

marks of thy redemption. Shall I not behold thee, then, dearest Jesus? Shall I not unceasingly behold thee, thus called upon by the Father, Son, and Spirit; and thus finding every thing that can satisfy my most unbounded desires, for time and for eternity? Help me, blessed Jesus! so to look, and so to live upon thee; and oh! do thou behold me, and bid me live, and make me thine own for ever.

8.—Who shall lay any thing to the charge of God's elect? It is God that justifieth. Who is he that condemneth? It is Christ that died; yea, rather, that is risen again: who is even at the right hand of God, who also maketh intercession for us.—*Romans* viii. 33, 34.

SEE, my soul, what a blessed security thou hast. Here is God justifying; Christ dying; the Holy Ghost raising the sinner's surety from the grave, as an evidence that the debt of sin is cancelled; and Jesus ever living to see the travail of his soul and be satisfied in the redemption of his people. What, then, shall rob thee of thy comfort, while thou art triumphing in thy Jesus? Sin shall not, for Jesus hath put it away by the sacrifice of himself. The law cannot; for thy Jesus hath answered all its just demands. Divine justice cannot; for God himself justifieth. Death and hell cannot; for Jesus hath conquered both. In short, all that stood in thy way, the Son of God hath removed. And wilt thou not, my soul, triumph in the great salvation of thy Jesus? Surely the poor debtor may walk as boldly before the prison door, as the king in his palace, when his debts are paid. No bailiff can touch him; no mittimus again confine him. If the Son shall make you free, you shall be free indeed. Triumph then, my soul! in the liberty wherewith thy Jesus hath made thee free; only be sure that all thy triumphs are in him. Let him have all the glory who hath wrought the whole redemption. Make thy Jesus all; for he hath done all for thee; and then sweetly repose thyself upon the person and work of thy Beloved. Let the adversary accuse, or opposition arise from without or within, yet, saith an apostle, here is the answer:—"God justifieth; for Christ died." Oh! how precious it is, after all the storms, and winds, and boisterous tossings, of law and conscience, to enter into that harbour which is Jesus. "We, which have believed," saith the apostle, "do enter into rest." He is indeed the rest, wherewith he causeth the weary to rest; and he is the refreshing.

9.—The Lamb that is in the midst of the throne shall feed them.—
Rev. vii. 17.

My soul! thou hast not forgotten what thou wert so lately
engaged in, a day or two since, at the call of God the Holy
Ghost, to behold the Lamb of God.   And art thou not still
looking at him, gazing upon him, feasting thine eyes, thine
heart, all thy affections upon him, and following him, in the
sweet contemplation, from his cross to his crown?   Come
then, my soul, harp again and again upon this blessed string;
for sure it is most blessed.   And remember, my soul, as thou
lookest, thy Jesus is in the *midst* of the throne—that is, the
very centre of it.   In Him dwelleth all the fulness of the
Godhead bodily.   For what is the Lamb of God, but God
revealing himself in him, to thee, my soul, and all his
people?   And remember, also, that the throne in the midst
of which thy Jesus is, in Scripture is called the throne of
God and the Lamb, on purpose to show thee that it is one
and the same.   And what is that throne, my soul, but a
throne of grace; a mercy-seat, a place for the poor and the
needy to approach, to obtain mercy, and find grace to help in
time of need?   Flee to it, my soul! haste! stay not: and
remember, as Jesus is in the midst of it, it is accessible every
way, and all around.   The poor timid believer, that fears to
go in front, may, like the woman in the gospel, who came
behind, touch but Jesus' garment: efficacy from the Lamb
is in every direction.   If Jesus was not there, it might be
alarming to approach; but, remember, the Lamb is there—
and he is the Lamb of God.   Sweet encouraging thought!
Come then, my soul, look to the Lamb.   See, by faith, how
he feeds the church which is above.   And will he not feed
the church below?   Oh! yes.   His flesh is meat indeed,
and his blood is drink indeed.   He is the heavenly Pelican,
that feeds his young with his blood.   And oh! what spiritual food, what divine food, what suitable food, what soul-
satisfying, soul-ravishing, soul-strengthening food!   Precious
Lamb of God! every thing in thee is food.   Feed my hungry soul, oh thou that art in the midst of the throne, and
send me not empty away.

10.—Unto you, therefore, which believe, he is precious.—1 *Pet.* ii. 7.

My soul! art thou anxious to know whether thou art a
true believer in Jesus?   Try it, then, by this mark, which
the Holy Ghost hath given by his servant the Apostle.   Do

you believe in Jesus for life and salvation? Yes, truly; if so be he is precious. Look at him, then. 1. Is Jesus precious in his person, precious in his work, precious in his offices, precious in his relations, precious in his whole character? 2. Do you know him so as to love him, to live to him, to rejoice in him, and to cast your whole soul upon him, for life and salvation? 3. Do you accept him as the Father's gift, the Sent, the Sealed, the Anointed, the Christ, of the Father? Is he so precious that there is nothing in him but what you love—nothing that you would part with? His cross is dear, as well as his crown? Afflictions with Jesus sweeter than prosperity without him? Pause over these questions. Recollect that there is nothing out of Jesus that can be truly satisfying. Thy dearest earthly friend, however sweet, hath yet some tinge, some alloy, of what is not sweet. But there is no mixture in thy Jesus: all is pure, and lovely, and transcendently glorious. He is, as one of old described him, a sea of sweetness, without a single drop of gall. And now, my soul, what sayest thou concerning Jesus? Is he precious to thee under all these, and a thousand more distinguishing excellencies? Say, if Jesus were to be bought, wouldest thou not sell all thou hast to buy? Were he to be sold, wouldest thou not rather lose thy life than part with him? Surely, then, he must be precious to thee: and as such, thou art a believer: for the Apostle has commanded us to say, that unto them which believe, he is precious. Take comfort then, my soul; He that is precious now, will be so for ever. Yes, precious Lord! there is none in heaven, or earth, I desire beside thee!

11.—Let mine outcasts dwell with thee, Moab: be thou a covert to them from the face of the spoiler.—*Isaiah* xvi. 4.

WHEN a man's ways please the Lord, he maketh even his enemies to be at peace with him. Moab was the sworn foe of Israel; but yet Moab shall be overruled to shelter and feed Israel. The world, like Moab, dislikes God's people: but as God's people must sojourn in the world, until the time comes for God to take them home, they shall be taken care of. " Let mine outcasts dwell with thee, Moab;" house them as travellers in an inn. See that they have a lodging. Let their bread be given, and their water sure. " They are poor; but they are my poor, saith our God. " They are outcasts; but they are mine outcasts." Oh! precious Jesus! I see thou wilt still own thy people. And wherefore is it, dearest Lord? Not for their worth, not for their deservings, not for their adherence to thee; but because thou hast loved them; because the Father hath given them to thee, and thou hast purchased their persons, redeemed them, and washed them, and made them thine. Grant, dearest Lord! that though we are constrained to dwell with Mesech, and to have our habitation among the tents of Kedar; though we are made as the filth of the earth, and the offscouring of all things—yet never, never may we forget our relationship to thee! Though outcasts, yet Jesus' outcasts. Be thou, Lord, our hiding place, our covert, in the midst of Moab; and so shall we be free from every spoiler: thou wilt be to us all we need—rivers of water in a dry place, and as the shadow of a great rock in a weary land.

12.—And the Lord shut him in.—*Gen.* vii. 16.

It was a sweet invitation to the patriarch Noah, when the Lord called him to the ark. Jehovah did not say, Go thou into the ark; but " Come." So saith Jesus to his people: " Come with me, from Lebanon, my spouse; with me, from Lebanon." Yes, precious Jesus! to be with thee is heaven; for thou thyself art the heaven of the soul. But observe further, my soul: when Noah had entered the ark, what kept him there? " The Lord shut him in." Yes! neither bolts nor bars were his security; but God himself, in his covenant engagements, kept him. The Patriarch could no more get out, than the unbelieving carnal throng (who, perhaps, hung about the ark when they saw the flood arise, and felt its power) could get in. Precious Jesus! and what is it keeps thy people now? Is it not thyself? Are not thy redeemed eternally secure in thee, and thy blood and righteousness, as Noah in the ark? Yes! thou who hast the key of all things; thou openest, and none shutteth; thou shuttest, and none openeth. In thee my soul is kept secure; for the Lord Jehovah hath shut me in; and I shall ride out all the storms and floods of sin and Satan, and Noah-like, rise above the fountains of the greatest deeps, being shut in in the ark Christ Jesus.

13.—Christ has redeemed us from the curse of the law, being made a curse for us.—*Gal.* iii. 13.

Pause, my soul, and contemplate the unspeakable mercies contained in those precious words! However little thou hast regarded them, yet they contain in their bosom the whole blessings of the gospel. It is to Jesus, in this one glorious act of his faith, should the sinner be continually looking. There, (the believer should say,) there hangs my hope, my joy, my confidence. Christ hath redeemed me from the curse of the law, being made a curse for me. Now, my soul, observe how Jesus accomplished this great mercy for thee. Whatever Christ redeemed the sinner from, he became *that* for him. In the act of redemption, by substituting himself in the sinner's place and room, he redeemed him from that place and room, by standing there himself. Hence, as the sinner stood before God, accursed by reason of sin; so Christ, by taking the sinner's sin upon himself, and standing in his stead to answer for it, was made a curse also. If, therefore, Christ will come under the law for sinners, that law will have as much to demand of him, as of sinners. If Jesus, from his boundless love and mercy, will take the sinner's curse upon himself, the law will speak as harsh to him as the sinner that is under the curse; and not only speak, but exact from him all that could be demanded from the sinner. Pause, my soul! And did Jesus, thy Jesus, thus stand, thus be considered; and was he made a curse for thee? Did he really, truly, suffer the cursed sinner's punishment, and die, the just for the unjust, to bring sinners unto God? Look to it then, my soul; he hath bought thee out, paid the full ransom, and taken away both sin, and the curse of sin, by the sacrifice of himself. Shout, my soul! shout salvation to God and the Lamb! Say, as Paul, " Christ hath redeemed us from the curse of the law, being made a curse for us."

14.—For where two or three are gathered together in my name, there
am I in the midst of them.—*Matt.* xviii. 20.

WHAT an encouraging declaration is this of our Jesus, to prompt the faithful to meet together on the Lord's Day; or, in short, any day, at all times, and all places. Observe, my soul, how sweet the Lord speaks:—" There am I in the midst of my people; not by my word only, not as represented in ordinances, not by the ministry of my servants, but I myself spiritually. The calls, the motions of grace felt in the heart, the tender tokens, the manifestations of my suitableness, fulness, all-sufficiency; these are all truly mine, which, by the influences of my Spirit, I communicate among you." Oh! precious, condescending Lord! now we see what it is that constitutes a true gospel church—even thy presence. Thou art the beauty and glory of it; and from thee alone all

power and efficacy is derived.   Thy churches are, indeed, as
thou hast taught, the golden candlesticks ; and thy ministers
are as stars in thy right hand.   But the candlesticks have no
light, until thou, by thy presence, enlighten them; neither do thy
servants, the ministers, hold forth the light of thy word pro-
fitably, until thou openest the heart, as thou didst poor Lydia's,
to receive the things delivered to the salvation of the soul.
Ye ministers of my God! draw all your comfort and encouragement, amidst all the difficulties you meet with, both from
within and without, in your sacred service, from this sweet
assurance of Jesus.   Whenever you go up to the assemblies
of God's people, hear the footsteps of your Master behind
you.   And ye who pant after sweet fellowship and communion with Jesus, seek it by the footsteps of the flock, beside
the shepherd's tents, where Jesus feeds his sheep.   Who
would be absent from that blessed place where Jesus comes
to bless?   And oh! what encouragement to the faithful to
bring with them their unawakened friends and relations, to
the assemblies which Jesus honours with his presence.
Surely He, who wrought salvation in our hearts, can work
the same in theirs.   No wonder, when such mercies Jesus
brings with him to his people, that the heart of David fainted to
go up to the house of the Lord, that he might see the power
and glory of Jesus, as he had seen it in the sanctuary.

15.—With purpose of heart they would cleave unto the Lord. *Acts* xi. 23.

My soul! art thou cleaving to thy Jesus?   It is a grand
thing so to do; and it must be from continued supplies of
grace, in Jesus, if thou art really doing it.   A few points
will show.   Is Jesus thy all?   Is he uppermost in all things?
Faith has for its one object Jesus.   Let a true believer be
wheresoever he may—at home, or abroad ; alone, or in company ; the closet, or the church—it is all the same, if he
really, truly, cleaves to the Lord with purpose of heart ;
there is a looking unto Jesus for all things, and in all things.
Again, if I cleave to the Lord, I shall do no one thing but
in his strength, and deliberately desire nothing but for his
glory.   The graces of the Holy Spirit, implanted in the souls
of the faithful, are fed and kept alive, and brought forth into
exercise, by the communications of Jesus.   My joy then is in
Jesus ; not in myself, not in what I feel.   These feelings of
mine may languish ; but while I cleave to the Lord, my spiritual joy will always be the same.   " From me," saith that
sweet Lord, " from me is thy fruit found !"   Once more—If

I cleave unto Jesus, shall I not find an increasing love for him, an increasing desire for him, and an increasing communion with him, from increasing knowledge of him, and of his love and preciousness? To be sure I shall. Well then, my soul, art thou indeed cleaving to him? Think how precious Jesus was, when first thou wast brought so savingly acquainted with him as to see thy need of him, and his suitableness and disposition to save thee. Dost thou think of these blessings less now? Oh! no. You love him more, because you know your need of him more, and therefore cleave to him the closer. Lastly, to add no more—Doth my soul truly cleave to Jesus? Why, then, I am loosening more and more from every thing beside. If Jesus hath my whole heart, then is the world and all creature idols thrown down. One Lord Jesus Christ is portion enough for a whole ransomed church of God to live upon to all eternity. In him there is portion enough for me. Oh! then, precious Lamb of God! be thou my portion; for in thee I have all things.

16.—Help, Lord! for the godly man ceaseth; for the faithful fail from among the children of men.—*Psalm* xii. 1.

My soul! art thou sometimes distressed in the recollection of the languishing state of Zion? Are faithful men, faithful ministers taken away from the evil to come? And dost thou sometimes at a mercy seat, feel thyself drawn out in fervent prayer, that the Lord would fill up the vacancies he is making by death, and raise up pastors after his own heart, and believers who love Zion, to supply their place? Take comfort, my soul; thy Jesus loves Zion; and she is still engraven on the palms of his hands, and her walls are continually before him. Jesus must have a church in the earth as long as the sun and moon endureth. Remember the reins of government are in Jesus' hands; and however the enemies of Zion, like wild horses, would ride over the children of Zion, Jesus puts his bridle in their jaws, and will turn them back by the way they came. Remember, also, that the care of the church is with Jesus. He saith himself concerning it; "I the Lord do keep it. I will water it every moment: lest any hurt it, I will keep it night and day." Blessed Jesus! I would say then, Zion is, and must be, safe. Die who may, Jesus lives; and to his church he saith, "Because I live, ye shall live also." Here then is enough for me, for the church, and for every child of God. My seed, saith Jesus, shall serve him. Hallelujah.

3

17.—Knowing that whilst we are at home in the body, we are absent
from the Lord ; we are confident, I say, and willing rather to be absent from the body, and to be present with the Lord.—2 *Cor.* v. 6, 8.

My soul! is this thy real language? Pause. Whilst
thou art at home in the body, how dark and dim, how few
and short are all the glimpses thou hast by faith of Jesus.
What from the workings of corruption, the claims of the
body, the concerns of the world, and the numberless, nameless, obstructions which surround thee, how little dost thou
know of Jesus. And wouldest thou desire for ever to live at
this distance? Think what the first view only of Jesus will
be, when thou art once absent from the body, and present
with the Lord! What holy transports will break in upon
the soul, when all the lines of love meet in one centre, to
manifest the Lord Jesus to thy view in his redeeming fulness!
If here below a single hour's enjoyment of thy Jesus,
through the medium of his word or ordinances, be so precious that no felicity on earth can equal, what must a whole
eternity be, in the full uninterrupted vision of God and the
Lamb? If, through the influences of thy blessed Spirit,
dearest Jesus! the tear of joy, and love, and praise, will here
fall in the contemplation of thy person and work, surely all
the flood-gates of the soul will open when I see thee as thou
art, and come to dwell with thee for ever. Oh! for grace,
then, to long for that blessed hour, when, absent from the
body, I shall be present with the Lord ; when I shall behold
thy face in righteousness, and shall be satisfied when I awake
with thy likeness.

18.—And I will make an everlasting covenant with them, that I will
not turn away from them to do them good ; but I will put my fear
in their hearts, that they shall not depart from me.—*Jeremiah* xxxii. 40.

Precious consideration to a poor exercised soul, that a Covenant God in Christ, hath not only engaged for himself, but
undertaken for his people also. God will not ; and his people
shall not. My soul! take a short view of the foundation of
this precious, precious promise. It is God's everlasting love,
everlasting grace, everlasting covenant. And remember, the
Author of it is not changeable as thou art. With Him is no
variableness, neither shadow of turning. Moreover, it is
purchased by the blood, sealed in the blood, and made eternally firm and sure in the blood and righteousness of Christ;
the everlasting efficacy of which is as eternal as the Author
of it. Neither is this all. There is an union with the Per

son of thy Jesus. The head without a body would be incomplete; and, united to his Person, the believer is interested in all his graces, fulness, suitableness, all-sufficiency: so that this preserves grace from perishing, because it is an everlasting spring. And Jesus lives to see it all complete. His intercession answers every want, and supplies every necessity. Neither is this all; for God the Holy Ghost sets to his seal in the heart, that God is true. His quickening, convincing, converting, manifesting grace, in the soul, in taking of the things of Jesus, and showing to the heart, becomes an earnest and pledge in assurance; and all tending to confirm, that God will not, and his redeemed ones shall not, turn away, but his covenant remain everlasting.

19.—The prisoner of Jesus Christ.—*Ephes.* iii. 1.

My soul! art thou a prisoner of Jesus Christ? See to it, if so, that, like the Apostle, thou art bound with Jesus' chains for the hope of Israel. They are golden chains. When Paul and Silas were fast bound in the prison, the consciousness of this made them sing for joy. Men have their prisons, and God hath his. But here lies the vast difference: no bars or gates, among the closest prisons of men, can shut God out from comforting his prisoners; and, on the contrary, nothing can come in to afflict Jesus' prisoners, when he keeps them by the sovereignty of his grace, and love, and power. Blessed Lord! look upon thy poor prisoner; and come in, dear Lord: with thy wonderful condescension, and do as thou hast said: sup with him, and cause him to sup with thee.

20.—I will say unto God, do not condemn me; show me wherefore thou contendest with me.—*Job* x. 2.

My soul! art thou at any time exercised with any trying dispensations? Doth thy God, thy Jesus, seem to hide his face from thee? Are his providences afflicting? Art thou brought under bereaving visitations? Is thy earthly tabernacle shaken by sickness? Are the pins of it loosening? Are thy worldly circumstances pinching? Is prayer restrained? Oh! refer thy state, my soul, be it what it may, to Jesus. Tell thy Lord, that, of all things, thy greatest dread and fear is, lest thou shouldest be mistaken concerning his love to thee. Say, as Job did, "Show me wherefore thou contendest with me." There is an Achan in the heart. Thy Jesus doth not withdraw for nothing. Love is in his

lips. Salvation fills the whole soul of Jesus. Fly to him,
then, my soul!   Say to him, Lord, make me what thou
wouldest have me to be. Oh! for a word, a whisper, of
Jesus. I cannot live without it. I dare not let thee go, except thou bless me.   Not all the past enjoyments, experiences, manifestations, will do me good, until thou again shine
in upon my soul. Oh! come then, Lord, Jesus! I fly to thee
as my God, my Saviour, my portion, my all. Never, surely,
wilt thou say to the praying seed of Jacob, Seek ye my face
in vain.

21.—Saw ye him whom my soul loveth?—*Song* iii. 3.

Is Jesus still the object of my soul's warmest affection; the
subject of all my thoughts, all my discourse, all my inquiry?
Oh! yes, my soul; whom else, in heaven or in earth, wilt
thou seek after but him!   Tell me, ye ministers of Jesus, ye
watchmen upon the walls of Zion, "saw ye him whom my
soul loveth?"   Ye followers of the Lamb, can ye show me
where Jesus feedeth his flock at noon?   Or rather, ye in the
upper regions, where the Son of God manifesteth himself in
the full glories of his Person; ye spirits of just men made
perfect, ye who have known, while sojourning here below,
what feeling of the soul that is, which, in the absence of
Jesus, is longing for his appearance; ye angels of light also,
ye who see him without an intervening medium—tell him, I
beseech you, how my soul panteth for his visits: tell him that
a poor pensioner, well known to my Lord, is waiting his
morning alms: nay, tell him that I am sick of love, longing
for a renewed view of his Person, his pardoning love, the
renewals of his grace. Jesus knoweth it all before you tell
him, and he will send his gifts and mercies—nay, he will
come himself; for he hath assured me of this: he hath said,
"If a man love me, my Father will love him, and we will
come and make our abode with him."   Behold, my soul, thy
Jesus is come!   I hear his well-known voice: he saith, "I
am come into my garden. Now will I hold him and not let
him go, and pray him not to be as a wayfaring man that
turneth in to tarry for a night, but abide with me until the
breaking of the everlasting day."

22.—Where the Spirit of the Lord is, there is liberty.—2 Cor. iii. 17.

What liberty, my soul, art thou brought into by thine
adoption into the family of God in Christ? Not from the
assaults of sin; for thou still carriest about with thee a body

of sin under which thou groanest. Not from the temptations of Satan ; for he is still levelling at thee many a fiery dart. Not from outward troubles ; for the world thou art still in, and findest it a wilderness state. Not from inward fears ; for thine unbelief begets many. Not from the chastisement of thy wise and kind Father ; for then many a sweet visit of his love, under the rod, would be unknown. Not from death ; for the stroke of it thou must one day feel ; though, blessed be Jesus, he hath taken out the sting in his blood and righteousness. What liberty then is it, my soul, thou enjoyest ? What hath the Spirit of the Lord, as a spirit of revelation discovering to thee the glory of Jesus, and thy interest in him, brought thee into ? Oh ! who shall write down the vast, the extensive account of thy freedom ? Say, my soul, hath not the sight of God's glory in Christ freed thee from the curse of the law, from the guilt of the law, from the dominion of sin, from the power of Satan, from the evil of unbelief in thine own heart, from the terrors of justice, from the alarms of conscience, from the second death ? Say, my soul, doth not the sight of Jesus dying for thee, rising for thee, pleading for thee, enlarge thy heart and loose thy bonds, and shake off all thy fetters and all thy fears ? Doth not Jesus in the throne give thee liberty to come to him, to call upon him, to unbosom thyself unto him, to tell him all thy wants, all thy necessities, and to lean upon his kind arm in every hour of need ? Shout, my soul ! and echo to the Apostle's words, " Where the spirit of the Lord is, there is liberty :" liberty to approach, liberty to plead, liberty to pray, liberty to praise and to adore the whole Persons of the Godhead, for having opened the prison-doors, and given thee freedom in Christ Jesus.

23.—Hath a nation changed their gods, which are yet no gods? But my people have changed their glory for that which doth not profit. *Jeremiah* ii. 11.

PAUSE, my soul, over these words ! Was it ever known that any nation changed their dunghill gods for others ? Such regard had they for whatever ignorance had set up, that the veneration never after ceased. But Israel, above every other nation of the earth, manifested folly, and even exceeded the most senseless and stupid of men. My soul ! dost thou not in Israel's folly behold thy own ? Was there ever one, when the Lord first called thee, less deserving ! A transgressor, as the Lord knew thee, from the womb ! and yet this did not prevent the Lord from calling thee. He loved thee because

4*

he would love thee: gave thee his Christ; gave thee his
Holy Spirit; gave thee the name, the privilege, the adoption, of a son. What returns hast thou made? How often
since hath thy backslidings, thy coldness, thy departures,
been like Israel? What vanity, what pursuit, what unprofitable employment, hath not at times been preferred to thy
God? Oh! how do I see my daily, hourly, continual need
of thee! thou art the hope of Israel and the Saviour thereof.
Keep me, Lord, near thyself; for without thee I am nothing!

24.—He that had gathered much, had nothing over; and he that had
gathered little had no lack.—2 Cor. viii. 15.

My soul! here is a delightful morsel for thee to feed upon
this morning. Thou art come out to gather thy daily food
as Israel did in the wilderness. Faith had no hoards. Thou
wantest Jesus now as much as thou didst yesterday. Well
then, look at what is here said of Israel. They went out to
gather—what? Why the morning bread: God's gift. Such
is Jesus, the bread of God, the bread of life. And as Israel
would have been satisfied with nothing short of this, so
neither be thou. And as Israel was never disappointed, so
neither wilt thou, if thou seek it in faith as Israel did. And
observe, they that gathered most had nothing over; so he
that gathered least had no lack. Yes, my soul! no follower
of Jesus can have too much of Jesus: nothing more than he
wants—nothing to spare. So the poorest child of God, that
hath the least of Jesus, can never want. The very touch of
his garment, the very crumb from his table, is his, and is
precious. Dearest Lord! give me a large portion, even a
Benjamin's portion. But even a look of thy love is heaven
to my soul.

25.—Who of God is made unto us wisdom, and righteousness, sanctification, and redemption.—1 Cor. i. 30.

What a sweet subject for my morning meditation is here!
Who is it, my soul, is made of God to thee these precious
things, but Jesus? And mark how they are made so!—I
am a poor ignorant creature, grossly ignorant by reason of
the fall. I knew not my lost estate, much less the way of
recovery. Here Jesus became to me wisdom. By his illu-
minating the darkness of my mind, he led me to see my ruin
and my misery. But this would never have brought me out
of it; for though I saw my lost estate, yet still I had no consciousness by what means I could be recovered. Here again

Jesus came to my aid, and taught me, that as I needed righteousness, he would be my righteousness, and undertake for me to God. But even after this was done, I felt my soul still the subject of sin; and how to subdue a single sin I knew not. Here Jesus came again, and gave me to see, that as he was wisdom to cure my ignorance, and righteousness to answer for my guilt, so he would be my sanctification also; purging, as well as pardoning and renewing, by his Spirit, my poor nature, when he had removed the guilt of it. Still I sighed for complete deliverance, and to make my happiness sure; and therefore Jesus came again, that, by his full redemption from all the evils of the fall, I might be made free; and therefore he became the whole together—wisdom, righteousness, sanctification, and redemption. And to stamp and seal the whole with the impression of God my Father, all that Jesus did he did by God's gracious appointment; for he was made of God to me all these, that all my glorying might be in the Lord. See to it, my soul, then, that this be all thy glory.

26.—As for me, I will behold thy face in righteousness. I shall be satisfied when I awake with thy likeness.—*Psalm.* xvii. 15

Is it refreshing to thee now, my soul, the least glimpse of Jesus' face; the smallest manifestation of the glories of his Person and of his work; and the very sound of his voice, in his word or ordinances? Think, then, what will be thy felicity in that morning of the eternal world, when, dropping thy veil of flesh, He, whom thou seest now by faith only, will then appear as open to thee as to the church above in glory! Pause, my soul, over the vast thought! What will be thy first sight of Jesus? What will be thy feelings, when, without any intervening medium, thou shalt see him face to face, and know even as thou art known? Precious Lamb of God! grant me grace to feel the blessedness of this first interview. Appearing, as I trust I shall, in thine own garments, and the robes of thy righteousness, and which thou hast not only provided for me, but put on, what will be the burstings forth of my heart, in the full view of the glories of thy Person, and the perfection of thy righteousness? Surely, Lord, when I thus behold thy face in righteousness, I shall be so fully satisfied, that the rest after which my poor soul, through a whole life of grace, since thou wert pleased to quicken me, hath been pursuing, will pursue no more. My immortal faculties will seek no more—will need no more. In thee, the whole

is attained. In thee, I shall eternally rest. Thou art the
everlasting centre of all happiness, glory, and joy. I shall
be so fully satisfied when I awake to this view, that here, in
thee, I shall be at home. And what is more, it will be an
everlasting duration, not only in happiness, but in likeness.
And as the coldest iron, put into the fire, partakes of the properties of the fire, until it becomes altogether heated and fiery
like it, so in thee, and with thee, thou blessed Jesus! cold as
my soul now is, I shall be warmed with thy love ; and from
thee, and thy likeness imparted, become lovely from thy loveliness, and glorious from thy glory! Precious, precious Jesus! is the hour near? Are thy chariot wheels approaching? Dost thou say, "Behold, I come quickly?" Oh! for
grace to answer—Even so come, Lord Jesus.

27.—He will be very gracious unto thee, at the voice of thy cry ; when
he shall hear it, he will answer thee.—*Isaiah* xxx. 19.

Mark, my soul, what is here said ; for every word in this
sweet Scripture tells. Thy God, thy Saviour, thy Jesus,
knows thy voice, hears thy cry, and will assuredly answer.
He will not only be gracious, but *very* gracious. He waits
to be gracious: waits the most suited time, the best time, the
praying time, the crying time ; for he times his grace, his
mercy, to thy need. And though thou knowest it not, yet so
it is: when his time is near at hand, which is always the best
time, he puts a cry in thine heart; so that the time of thy
cry, and the time for the manifestation of his glory, shall
come together. Is not this to be gracious—yea, very gracious.
So that while thou art looking after him, he is looking upon
thee. And before thou callest upon him, he is coming forth
to bless thee. Is not this very gracious? Now then, my
soul, make a memorandum of this for any occasions which
may hereafter occur. Put it down as a sure unerring truth :
—thy Jesus will be very gracious unto thee. Never allow
this promise to be called in question any more. Next, bring
it constantly into use. Faith, well-grounded faith in Jesus,
should always bring down general rules to particular cases
and circumstances, as the soul's experience may require.
Hence, when God saith he will be very gracious unto thee,
it is the act of faith to answer—If God hath said it, so it shall
certainly be. And therefore, as that gracious God, who
giveth the promise, giveth also the grace of faith to depend
upon the promise, the mercy is already done, and faith enters

upon the enjoyment of it. God's faithfulness and truth become the believer's shield and buckler.

28.—Leaning on Jesus' bosom.—*John* xiii. 23.

METHINKS I would contemplate for a while the privilege of this highly-favoured disciple John! Surely to sit at the feet of Jesus, to look up at his face, to behold the Lamb of God, and to hear the gracious words which proceeded out of his mouth, what should I have thought of this but a happiness unspeakable and full of glory? But the beloved Apostle leaned on Jesus' bosom! Oh! thou condescending Saviour! Didst thou mean to manifest, by this endearing token, how dear and precious all thy redeemed ones are in thy esteem? But stop, my soul! If John lay on Jesus' breast, where was it Jesus himself lay, when he left all for thy salvation? The disciple whom Jesus loved lay *upon* Jesus' bosom; but He whom the Father loved, lay *in* the bosom of the Father—nay, was embosomed there; was wrapt up in the very soul of the Father from eternity. Who shall undertake to speak of the most glorious state of the Son of God, before he condescended to come forth from the bosom of God for the salvation of his people? Who shall describe the blessedness of the Father and the Son in their mutual enjoyment of each other? Jesus, when he was in the bosom of the Father, had not emptied himself of his glory. Jesus had not been made in the likeness of sinful flesh. Jesus had not put himself under the law. He was not then a man of sorrows. He was not then acquainted with grief. He had not then exposed his face to shame and spitting; neither to poverty, temptation, the bloody sweat, and the cross. And did Jesus go through all these and more? Did Jesus leave the Father's bosom; and did the Father take this only begotten, only beloved son from his bosom, that John might lean on Jesus' bosom; and all the redeemed, like him, one day dwell with Jesus, and lean and rest in his embraces for ever? Oh! for hearts to love both the Father and the Son, who have so loved us; that we may be ready to part with all, and forsake all, and die to all, that we may live in Jesus and to Jesus, and rest in his bosom for ever.

MARCH.

1.—And his name shall be called Wonderful.—*Isaiah* ix. 6.

In the opening of the last month, the fragrancy of Jesus' name, as Emmanuel, gave a sweet savour to my soul. May He, whose name is as ointment poured forth, give a new refreshment to my spiritual senses this morning, in this name also as Wonderful; for surely every thing of Him, and concerning Him, of whom the Prophet speaks, is eminently so. But who shall speak of thy wonders, dearest Lord!—the wonders of thy Godhead, the wonders of thy Manhood, the wonders of both natures united and centred in one Person? Who shall talk of the wonders of thy work, the wonders of thy offices, characters, relations; thy miraculous birth, thy wonderful death, resurrection, ascension? Who shall follow thee, thou risen and exalted Saviour at the right hand of power, and tell of the exercise of thine everlasting priesthood? Who shall speak of the wonders of thy righteousness, the wonders of thy sin-atoning blood? What angel shall be found competent to proclaim the wonders of the Father's love in giving thee for poor sinners? What archangel to write down the wonders of thy love, in undertaking and accomplishing redemption? And who but God the Spirit can manifest both in the height, and depth, and breadth, and length, of a love that passeth knowledge? Is there, my soul, a wonder yet, that, as it concerns thee and thine interest in Him, whose name is Wonderful, is still more marvellous to thy view? Yes! oh thou wonderful Lord! for sure all wonders seem lost in the contemplation compared to that, that Jesus should look on me in my lost, ruined, and undone estate; for his mercy endureth for ever. Well might Jesus say, " Behold, I and the children whom thou hast given me are for signs and wonders." Isaiah viii. 18. Well might the Lord, concerning Jesus and his people, declare them to be as men wondered at. Zach. iii. 8. And blessed Lord, the more love thou hast shown to thy people, the more are they the world's wonder and their own. Precious Lord! continue to surprise my soul with the tokens of thy love. All the tendencies of thy grace, all the manifestations of thy favour, thy visits, thy love-tokens, thy pardons, thy renewings, thy mourning call, thy mid-day feedings, thy noon, thy evening, thy midnight grace—all, all are among thy wonderful ways of salvation; and all testify to my soul, that thy name, as well as thy work, is, and must be, Wonderful!

2.—For if there be first a willing mind, it is accepted according to that a man hath, and not according to that he hath not.—2 *Cor.* viii. 12.

SWEET thought this comfort to the soul under small attainments, "If there be first a willing mind." Surely Lord, thou hast given me this; for thou hast made me willing in the day of thy power. I feel as such, my soul going forth in desires after thee, as my chief and only good; though, alas! how continually do I fall short of the enjoyment of thee. I can truly say, "Whom is there in heaven, or upon earth, that I desire in comparison of thee!" When thou art present, I am at once in heaven; it makes a very heaven in my soul: thou art the God of my exceeding joy. When thou art absent, my soul pines after thee. And, truly, I count all things but dung and dross to win thee; for whatever gifts thou hast graciously bestowed upon me, in the kindness of friends, in the affections and charities of life, yet all these are secondary considerations with my soul. They are more or less lovely, as I see thy gracious hand in them; but all are nothing to my Lord. Is not this, dearest Jesus! a willing mind? Is it not made so in the day of thy power? But in the midst of this, though I feel this rooted desire in me after thee, yet how often is my heart wandering from thee. Though there is at the bottom of my heart a constant longing for thy presence, and the sweet visits of thy love, yet through the mass of unbelief, and the remains of indwelling corruption in my nature, which are keeping down the soul, how doth the day pass, and how often doth the enemy tempt me to question my interest in thee. Dearest Jesus! undertake for me. I do cry out, "When wilt thou come to me, though I am thus kept back from coming to thee?" When wilt thou manifest thyself to my soul, and come over all these mountains of sin and unbelief, and fill me with a joy unspeakable and full of glory? And doth Jesus, indeed, accept from the willing mind he hath himself given, according to what a man hath, and not according to what he hath not? Doth my Redeemer behold amidst the rubbish, the spark of grace he himself hath quickened? Will he not despise the day of small things? No! he will not. It was said of thee, that thou shouldest not break the bruised reed, neither quench the smoking flax. Mine, indeed, is no more. But yet Jesus will bear up the one, and kindle the other, until he send forth judgment unto victory. Peace then, my soul! weak as thou art in thyself, yet art thou strong in the Lord, and in the power of his might.

3.—That ye may be able to comprehend with all saints, what is the breadth and length, and depth, and height, and to know the love of Christ, which passeth knowledge.—*Ephes.* iii. 18, 19.

DID Paul pray that the church might be thus blessed? So should all faithful pastors. And there is enough in Jesus to call up the everlasting contemplation of his people. All the dimensions of divine glory are in Jesus. Who, indeed, shall describe the extent of that love which passeth knowledge? But, my soul, pause over the account. What is the breadth of it? Jesus' death reaches in efficacy to all his seed—all his children: to thee, my soul; for thou art the seed of Jesus. And though that death took place at Jerusalem near 2,000 years since, yet the efficacy of his blood, as from an high altar, as effectually washes away sin now, as in the moment it was shed. Remember, Jesus still wears the vesture dipped in blood. Remember, Jesus still appears as the Lamb slain before God! Indeed, indeed, Jesus was the Lamb slain from the foundation of the world. So that in *breadth*, it is broader than the sea, taking in all the seed of Jesus, through all ages, all dispensations, all the various orders of his people. Neither is the *length* of it less proportioned. Who shall circumscribe the Father's love, which is from everlasting to everlasting? Who shall limit Jesus' grace? Is he not made of God wisdom, righteousness, sanctification, and redemption? Is he not all this, in every office, every character, every relation? " Jesus Christ; the same yesterday, and to-day, and for ever !" And what is the *depth* of this love, but reaching down to hell, to lift up our poor fallen nature! And what is the *height*, but Jesus, in our nature, exalted far above all principalities, and powers, and might, and dominion, and every name that is named, not only in this world, but also in that which is to come ? Precious God of my salvation! oh! give me to see, to know, to entertain, and cherish, more enlarged views of this love, which hath no bottom, no bounds, no shore; but, like its Almighty Author, is from everlasting to everlasting. Shall I ever despond? Shall I ever doubt any more, when this Jesus looks upon me, loves me, washes me in his blood, feeds

me, clothes me, and hath promised to bring me to glory?
Oh! for faith to comprehend, with all saints, this love of
God, which passeth knowledge.

4.--How shall we sing the Lord's song, in a strange land?—*Psalm*
cxxxvii. 4.

METHINKS, my soul, this strange land is the very place to
sing the Lord's song in, though the carnal around understand it not. Shall I hang my harp upon the willow, when
Jesus is my song, and when he himself hath given me so
much cause to sing? Begin, my soul, thy song of redemption; learn it, and let it be sung upon earth, for sure enough
thou wilt have it to sing in heaven. Art thou at a loss what
to sing? Oh! no. Sing of the Father's mercy, in sending
a Saviour. Sing of Jesus' love, in not only coming, but dying for thee. Are the redeemed above now singing, " Worthy
is the Lamb that was slain?" Join in the chorus, and tell
that dear Redeemer, in the loudest notes, that he was slain,
and hath redeemed *thee* to God by his blood. Strike up thy
harp anew to the glories of redeeming grace, in that he not
only died for thee, but hath quickened thee to a new and
spiritual life. Add a note more to the Lord's song, and tell
the Redeemer, in thy song of praise, that he hath not only
died for thee, and quickened thee, but he hath loved thee, and
washed thee from thy sins in his own blood. Go on in thy
song, my soul; for it is the Lord's song. Sing not only of
redeeming love, but marvellous grace, for both are connected.
He that redeemed thee, hath all grace for thee. He hath
adopted thee into his family; hath made thee an heir of God,
and a joint heir with Christ. He hath undertaken for thee,
in all troubles, under all difficulties, to be with thee at all
times and all places, until he brings thee home to behold his
glory, that where he is, there thou mayest be for ever. And
are not these causes enough to keep thy harp always strung
—always in tune? And wilt thou not sing this song all the
way through, and make it the subject of thy continual praise
and love, in the house of thy pilgrimage? Moreover, the
several properties of the song are, in themselves, matter for
keeping it alive every day, and all the day. Think, my soul,
how free was this love of God to thee. Surely if a man de-
served hell and found heaven, shall he not sing? If I expected displeasure, and receive love—if I was brought low,
and one like the Son of Man helped me, shall I not say, as
one of old did, " He brought me out of the horrible pit, out

5

of the mire and clay; he hath put a new song in my mouth, even thanksgiving to our God?" If I think of the greatness of the mercy, of the riches of the mercy, of the sweetness of the mercy, of the all-sufficiency of the mercy; of the sureness and firmness, and everlasting nature and efficacy of the mercy—can I refrain to sing? No; blessed, blessed Jesus, I will sing, and not be afraid; for the Lord Jehovah is my strength and my song, and he is become my salvation. I will sing now, I will sing for evermore. In this strange land, in this barren land, in this distant land from my Father's house, I will sing, and Jesus shall be my song. He shall be the Alpha and the Omega of my hymn; and until I come to sing in the louder and sweeter notes of heaven, among the hallelujahs of the blessed, upon the new harp and new-stringed chords of my renewed soul, will I sing of Jesus and his blood, Jesus and his righteousness, Jesus and his complete salvation. And when the last song upon my trembling lips, with Jesus' name in full, shall be uttered; as the sound dies away, when death seals up the power of utterance; my departing soul shall catch the parting breath, and as it enters the presence of the court above, the first notes of my everlasting song will go on with the same blessed note to Him that hath loved me, and washed me from my sins in his own blood!

5.—Faint, yet pursuing.—*Judges* viii. 4.

SURELY what is said here, concerning the little army of Gideon, suits my case exactly. I know that in Jesus the victory is certain; but I know also, that I shall have battlings all the way. From the moment that the Lord called me out of darkness into his marvellous light, my whole life hath been but a state of warfare; and I feel what Paul felt, and groan as he groaned, under a body of sin and death; as sorrowful, yet rejoicing; as dying, but behold I live; as chastened, and not killed. Truly I am faint, under the many heavy assaults I have sustained; and yet through grace, pursuing as if I had met with no difficulty. Yes, blessed Jesus! I know that there can be no truce in this war; and looking unto thee, I pray to be found faithful unto death, that no man may take my crown! But, dearest Lord! thou seest my day of small things; thou beholdest how faint I am. Thou seest, also, how the enemy assaults me, and how the world and the flesh combat against me. While without are fightings, within will be fears. Yet, dearest, blessed Lord; in the Lord I have

strength; and how sweet is the thought, that though I have
nothing, though I am nothing, yet thou hast said, " In me is
thy help." Thou hast said, " The righteous shall hold on
his way; and he that hath clean hands shall wax stronger
and stronger." The worm Jacob, thou hast promised, shall
thresh the mountains. Write these blessed things, my soul,
upon the living tablets of thine heart, or rather beg of God
the Holy Ghost, the Remembrancer of thy Jesus, to stamp
them there for ever. He giveth power to the faint; and to
them which have no might, he increaseth strength. Even
the youths shall faint and be weary; and the young men
shall utterly fall. But they that wait upon the Lord shall renew their strength: they shall mount up with wings, as
eagles; they shall run, and not be weary; and they shall
walk, and not faint.

6.—And every one that was in distress, and every one that was in debt,
and every one that was discontented, gathered themselves unto him,
and he became a Captain over them.—1 *Sam.* xxii. 2.

My soul, was not this thy case when thou first sought after
Jesus? Thou wert, indeed, in debt, under an heavy load of
insolvency. Distress and discontent sadly marked thy whole
frame. Unconscious where to go, or to whom to seek, and
no man cared for thy soul. Oh! what a precious thought
it was, and which none but God the Holy Ghost could have
put into thine heart,—Go unto Jesus! And when I came,
and thou didst graciously condescend to be my Captain,
from that hour how hath my soul been revived. My insolvency thou hast taken away; for thou hast more than paid
the whole demands of the law; for thou hast magnified it and
made it honourable. My distress under the apprehension of
divine justice thou hast removed; for God's justice, by thee,
is not only satisfied, but glorified. My discontent can have
no further cause for exercise, since thou hast so graciously
provided for all my wants, in grace here, and glory hereafter.
Hail! thou great and glorious Captain of my salvation! In
thee I see that Leader and Commander which Jehovah, thy
Father, promised to give to the people. Thou art indeed,
blessed Jesus! truly commissioned by thy Father to this very
purpose, that every one that is in soul-distress, by reason of
sin, and debtors to the broken law of God, may come unto
thee, and take thee for their Captain. And truly, Lord, thy
little army, like David's, is composed of none originally but
distressed souls. None would take thee for his Captain

whose spiritual circumstances are not desperate. None but the man whose heart hath felt distress, by reason of sin, and is sinking under the heavy load of guilt, will come under thy banner. Oh! the condescension of Jesus to receive such, and be gracious unto them. Oh! that I had the power of persuasion, I would say to every poor sinner, every insolvent debtor, every one who feels and knows the plague of his heart—Would to God you were with the Captain of my salvation, he would recover you from all your sorrow. Go to him, my brother, as I have done; he will take away your distress by taking away your sin. He will liberate you from all your debt by paying it himself. He will banish all discontent from the mind, in giving you peace with God by his blood. Yes! blessed, almighty Captain! thou art indeed *over* thy people, as well as a Captain *to* thy people. By the sword of thy spirit, which is the word of God, thou workest conviction in our hearts; thou makest all thine enemies fall under thee; thou leadest thy people on to victory, and makest them more than conquerors through thy grace supporting them. Lord, put on the military garments of salvation on my soul, and the whole armour of God, that under thy banner, I may be found in life, in death, and for evermore.

7.—They shall hunger no more.—*Rev.* vii. 16.

My soul! contemplate for a moment, before thou enterest upon the concerns of time and sense in the claims of the world, the blessed state of the redeemed above. They are at the fountain head of happiness, in their station, in their service, in their society, in their provision, in their everlasting exemption from all want, and, above all, in the presence of God and the Lamb. "They shall hunger no more." Sweet thought. Let me this day anticipate as many of the blessed properties of it as my present state in Jesus will admit. If Jesus be my home, my residence, my dwelling-place, will not the hungerings of my soul find supply? Yes! surely. A life of faith on the Son of God, is a satisfying life under all the changes of the world around. Finding Jesus, I find sustenance in him, and therefore do not hunger for aught besides him. "Thou art my hiding-place," said one of old; and my soul finds occasion to adopt the same language. And He that is my hiding-place, is also my food and my nourishment. In Jesus there is both food and a fence; there is fruit as well as a shadow; and the fulness of Jesus needs vent in the wants of his people, for the pouring forth of his all-sufficiency. My soul! cherish this thought to the full. If thy hunger be really for Jesus, and him only, then will thy hunger be abundantly supplied in his communication. As long as I look at my wants, without an eye to Jesus, I shall be miserable. But if I consider those wants, and that emptiness purposely appointed for the pouring out of his fulness, they will appear as made for the cause of happiness. Jesus keeps up the hungering that he may have the blessedness of supplying them; he keeps his children empty that he may fill them, and that his fulness may be in request among them. So far, therefore, is my hungering from becoming a source of sorrow, it furnisheth out a source of holy joy. I should never be straitened in myself, when I am not straitened in Jesus. Nay, it would be a sad token of distance from Jesus if a sense of want was lessened. While on the other hand, the best proof I can have of nearness to Jesus, and living upon him, is, when my enjoyment of Jesus discovers new and increasing wants, and excites an holy hungering for his supplying them. By-and-by I shall get home, and then, at the fountain-head of rapture and delight, all hungering and wants will be done away in the full and everlasting enjoyment of God and the Lamb!

8.—From this day will I bless thee.—*Haggai* ii. 9.

MY soul! what day is the memorable day to thee from whence commenced thy blessing? No doubt from everlasting the Lord hath blessed his people in Jesus. But the commencement of thy personal enjoyment of those blessings, was at the time the Lord graciously laid the foundation of his spiritual temple in thee; the blessed, the gracious, the auspicious, the happy day, when the Lord made thee willing in the day of his power! Oh! blessed day, never, never to be forgotten! A day of light; when the light of Jesus first broke in upon me. A day of life; when the Lord Jesus quickened my poor soul, which before was lying dead in trespasses and sins. A day of love; when his love first was made known to my soul, who so loved me as to give his dear and ever-blessed Son for me: and His love was sweetly manifested, who so loved me as to give himself for me. A day of the beginning of victory over death, hell, and the grave. A day of liberty; when the Lord Jesus opened my prison doors and brought me out. A day of wonder, love, and praise; when mine eyes first saw the King in his beauty, and my whole soul was overpowered in the contemplation of

5*

the grace, the glory, the beauty, the loveliness, the suitable-ness, the all-sufficiency, of his glorious Person and his glo-rious work. A day! oh what dear name shall I term it to be? A day of grace, a jubilee, a salvation day ; the day of my espousals to Jesus, and of the gladness of my Redeemer's heart. And, my soul, did thy God, did thy Jesus, say, that from that day he would bless thee? And hath he not done it? Oh! yes, yes; beyond all conception of blessing. He hath blessed thee in thy basket and thy store. All the bles-sings, even in *temporal* mercies, which were all forfeited in Adam, are now sweetly restored, and blessed, and sanctified, in Jesus : nay, even thy very crosses have the curse taken out of them by thy Jesus; and thy very tears have the spiced wine of the pomegranate. And, as to *spiritual* blessings, God thy Father hath blessed thee with all in his dear Son. Thy Father hath made over himself, in Jesus, with all his love and favour. And Jesus is thine with all his fulness, sweetness, all-sufficiency. And God the Spirit, with all his gracious influences and comforts. And the present enjoy-ment of these unspeakable mercies becomes the sure earnest of blessings which are *eternal.* Jesus himself hath declared, that it is the Father's own gracious will that he should give eternal life to as many as the Father hath given him; and therefore eternal life must be the sure portion of all his re-deemed. He that believeth in the Son, hath indeed everlast-ing life; and Jesus will raise him up at the last day. Pause, my soul! and view the vast heritage to which thou art begot-ten from the day of thy new birth in Jesus. Oh! most gra-cious Father! let me never lose sight of those sweet words, nor the feeling sense of my interest in them, in which thou hast said, " From this day will I bless thee."

9.—But now in Christ Jesus, ye, who sometimes were far off, are made nigh by the blood of Christ.—*Ephes.* ii. 13.

OF all the vast alterations made upon our nature by grace, that which is from death to life seems to be the greatest. I do not think the change would be as great, if Jesus were to make a child of God, after his conversion, at once an angel, as when by his blessed Spirit, he quickens the sinner, dead in trespasses and sins, and brings him into grace. My soul! contemplate the sweet thought this morning, that it may lead thee, with thy hymn of praise, to all precious Jesus! First then, my soul, think *where you then stood*, before this vast act of grace had quickened you. You stood on the very con-

fines of hell—unawakened, unregenerate, uncalled, without
God, and without Christ. Supposing the Lord had not
saved you; supposing a sickness unto death had, by his command, taken you; supposing that any one cause had been
commissioned to sign your death-warrant while in this state;
where must have been your portion? And yet consider,
my soul, how many nights and days did you live in this unconscious, unconcerned state! Oh! who, in this view of the
thought, can look back without having the eye brim-full of
tears, and the heart bursting with love and thankfulness?
Go on, my soul, and contemplate the subject in another point
of view; and pause in the pleasing thought, *where you now
stand*. "You are now," saith the Apostle, "made nigh by
the blood of Christ." You that was an enemy to God by
wicked works, yet now hath he reconciled in the body of his
flesh, through death, to present you holy, and unblameable,
and unreproveable, in his sight. And now, my soul, if
death should come, it is but the messenger to glory. Precious,
blessed thought. And oh! how much more precious blessed
Jesus, the Author of it! Advance, my soul, one step more
in this sweet subject, and pleasingly consider, *where you soon
shall be*. Paul answereth, "*So shall we be ever with the Lord.*"
Ever with the Lord! Who can write down the full amount
of this blessedness? Ever with the Lord! *Here* we are, *in
Jesus*, interested in all that belongs to Jesus: but *there*, we
shall be also *with Jesus*. *Here* we see him but as through a
glass darkly: but *there*, face to face. *Here* even the views we
have of him, by faith, are but glimpses only—short and rare,
compared to our desires: but *there*, we shall see him in reality,
in substance, and unceasingly the precious, glorious, God-
man Christ Jesus. *Here* our sins, though pardoned, yet dim
our view, by reason of their effects: *there* we shall for ever
have lost them, and see and know even as we are known. And
have these blessed changes taken place in my soul; and all
by thee, thou gracious, precious, Holy One of Israel? Oh!
for grace to love thee, to live to thee, to be looking out for
thee, dearest Jesus! that I may be counting every parting
breath, every beating pulse, as one the less, to bring me
nearer and nearer to Jesus, who is my everlasting home, and
will, ere long, be my never-ceasing portion and happiness in
eternity. Hallelujah.

10.—And hast feared continually every day, because of the fury of the oppressor, as if he were ready to destroy; and where is the fury of the oppressor ?—*Isaiah* li. 13.

PAUSE, my soul, over those sweet expostulating words of thy God. Wherefore should the fear of man bring a snare? How much needless anxiety should I spare myself, could I but live, amidst all my changeable days and changeable circumstances, upon my unchangeable God. Now, mark what thy God saith of thy unreasonable and ill-grounded fears :— " Where is the fury of the oppressor ?" Can he take from thee thy Jesus? No! Shouldest thou lose all thy earthly comforts, Jesus ever liveth, and Jesus is thine. Can he afflict thee if God saith no? That is impossible. Neither men nor devils can oppress without his permission. And sure enough thou art, thy God and Saviour will never allow any thing to thy hurt; for all things must work for good. And canst thou lessen the oppressor's fury by anxious fears? Certainly not. Thou mayest, my soul, harass thyself and waste thy spirits, but never lessen the fury of the enemy thereby. And wherefore, then, shouldest thou crowd the uncertain evils, and the *may be's* of to-morrow, in the circumstances of this day's warfare, when, by only waiting for the morrow, and casting all thy care upon Jesus, who careth for thee, his faithfulness is engaged to be thy shield and buckler? Peace then, my soul, thou shalt be carried through this oppression, as sure as thou hast been through every former ; for Jesus is still Jesus, thy God, and will be thy guide even unto death.

11.—And behold, there came a leper and worshipped him, saying, Lord ! if thou wilt, thou canst make me clean. And Jesus put forth his hand and touched him, saying, I will ; be thou clean. And immediately the leprosy was cleansed.—*Matt.* viii. 2, 3.

BEHOLD, my soul, in the instance of this leper, thine own circumstances. What he was in body, such wert thou in soul. As his leprosy made him loathsome and offensive before men, so thy polluted soul made thee odious in the sight of God. He would not have sought a cure, had he not been conscious of his need of it. Neither wouldest thou have ever looked to Jesus, had he not convinced thee of thy helplessness and misery without him. Moreover, he would not, though convinced how much he needed healing, have sought that mercy from Jesus, had he not been made sensible of Jesus' ability to the cure. Neither wouldest thou ever have come to Jesus, hadst thou not been taught who Jesus is, and how fully competent to deliver thee. The poor leper did not doubt whether Jesus was able; though he rather feared that ability might not be exercised towards him. His prayer was, not if thou art *able;* but, " Lord, if thou *wilt,* thou canst make me clean." Now here, my soul, I hope thy faith, through grace, exceeds the Jewish leper. Surely thou both knowest Jesus' power and Jesus' disposition to save thee. Unworthy and undeserving as thou art, yet his grace is not restrained by thy undeservings, no more than it was first constrained by thy merit. His love, his own love, his free love, is the sole rule of his mercy towards his children, and not their claims; for they have none, but in his free grace and the Father's everlasting mercy. Cherish these thoughts, my soul, at all times, for they are most sweet and precious. But are these all the blessed things which arise out of the view of the poor leper's case? Oh! no; the most delightful part still remains in the contemplation of Jesus' mercy to the poor petitioner, and the very gracious manner the Son of God manifested in the bestowing of it. He not only healed him, and did it immediately, but with that tenderness which distinguished his character and his love to poor sinners, Jesus put forth his hand and touched him: touched a leper. Even so, precious Lord! deal by me. Though polluted and unclean, yet condescend to put forth thine hand and touch me also. Put forth thy blessed Spirit. Come, Lord, and dwell in me, abide in me, and rule and reign over me. Be thou my God, my Jesus, my Holy One, and make me thine for ever?

12.—Followers of them who, through faith and patience, inherit the promises.—*Heb.* vi. 12.

How gracious is the Holy Ghost, in not only holding forth to the people of Jesus the blessedness and certainty of the promises, but opening to our view multitudes, who are now in glory, in the full enjoyment of them. My soul! dost thou ask how they lived, when upon earth in the full prospect, before that they were called upon to enter heaven for the full participation of them? Hear what the blessed Spirit saith concerning it in this sweet Scripture. It was through faith and patience. Now observe how these blessed principles manifested themselves. Another part of Scripture explains —" They all died in faith, not having received the promises; but having seen them afar off, and were persuaded of them,

and embraced them. Now this is the whole sum and substance of the believer's life: he *sees them afar off*, as Abraham
did the day of Christ—as David, who had the same enjoyment in a believing view, with which his whole soul was
satisfied ; for he saith, it was all his salvation and all his desire ; a covenant which he rested upon, as ordered in all
things, and sure. Pause, my soul, over this, and ask within,
are your views thus firmly founded ? What, though the day
of Christ's second coming be far off, or nigh, doth thy faith
realize the blessed things belonging to it as certain, and as
sure as God is truth ? Pause, and see that such is thy faith
—then go on. The faithful, who now inherit the promises, and
which the Holy Ghost bids thee to follow, not only saw with the
eye of faith the things of Jesus afar off, but *were persuaded of
them ;* that is, were as perfectly satisfied of their existence
and reality, as if they were already in actual possession.
Pause here again, and say, is this thy faith ? Are you perfectly persuaded that God was in Christ, reconciling the
world to himself, not imputing their trespasses unto them ?
Are you convinced that it is God's design, God's plan, God's
grace, God's love, God's mercy, in all that concerns Jesus ?
Art thou convinced that God's glory is concerned in the
glory of Jesus, and that every poor sinner gives glory to God
in believing the record that God hath given of his Son ? Dost
thou, my soul, believe heartily, cordially, fully, joyfully believe, these precious things; nay that, in fact, it is the only
possible way a poor sinner can give glory to God, in looking
up to him as God, in giving him the credit of God, and
taking his word as God, concerning his dear Son Jesus
Christ. Dost thou, my soul, set thy seal to these things ?
Then art thou *persuaded of the truths of God*, as the patriarchs
were *who saw them afar off.* Once more—the faithful, whom
the Holy Ghost calls upon thee to follow, *embraced them also*,
as well as were persuaded of them. They clasped *by faith*,
Jesus in their arms, as really and as truly as Simeon did *in
substance.* Their love *to* Jesus, and their interest *in* Jesus,
their acquaintance by faith *with* Jesus, were matters of certainty, reality, delight ; and their whole souls were, day by
day, so familiarized in the unceasing meditation, that they
walked by faith with Jesus while here below, as now, by
sight, they are with him above in glory. Pause, my soul !
Is this thy faith ? Then, surely, Jesus is precious, and thou
art indeed the follower of them who now, through faith and
patience, inherit the promises. And ere long, like them,

thou shalt see him whom thy soul loveth, and dwell with him for ever.

13.—O thou of little faith, wherefore didst thou doubt ? *Matt.* xiv. 31.

My soul! how sweet is it to eye Jesus in all things, and to be humbled in the recollection of his compassions to thy unaccountable instances of unbelief, after the many, nay continued, and daily experiences which thou hast had of his love and faithfulness. And doth thy Jesus speak to thee this day, in those expostulating words. "Oh thou of little faith, wherefore didst thou doubt?" What answer wilt thou return? Is there any thing in thy life to justify, or even to apologize, for doubting? Look back—Behold thy God and Father's grace, and mercy. and love! A Saviour so rich, so compassionate, so answering all wants, in spirituals, temporals, and eternals! A blessed Spirit, so condescending to teach, to lead. and by his influences, to be continually with thee! Surely a life like thine, crowded with mercies, blessings upon blessings, and one miracle of grace followed by another—wherefore shouldest thou doubt? What shall I say to thee, oh thou that art the hope of Israel, and the Saviour thereof! Lord give me to believe. and help thou mine unbelief. I beseech thee, my God and Saviour, give me henceforth faith to trust thee when I cannot trace thee: give me to hang upon thee when the ground of all sensible comforts seems sinking under my feet. I would cling to the faithfulness of my God in Christ, and throw my poor arms around thee, thou blessed Jesus! when all things appear the most dark and discouraging. And thus, day by day, living a life of faith and whole dependence upon thy glorious Person and thy glorious work, pressing after more sensible communion with thee, and more imparted strength and grace from thee, until at length, when thou shalt call me home from a life of faith to a life of sight—then, precious Jesus! would I say to thee, with my dying breath, "Oh present me, washed in thy blood and clothed in thy righteousness, among the whole body of thy glorious church, not having spot or wrinkle, or any such thing, but that I may be without blame before thee in love."

14.—And for their sakes I sanctify myself.—*John* xvii. 19.

Let thy morning thoughts, my soul, be directed to this sweet view of thy Saviour. Behold thy Jesus presenting himself as the Surety of his people before God and the Father.

Having now received the call and authority of God the
Father, and being fitted with a body suited to the service of
a Redeemer, here see him entering upon the vast work, and,
in those blessed words, declaring the cause of it—*I sanctify
myself.* Did Jesus mean that he made himself more holy for
the purpose ? No, surely ; for that was impossible. But by
Jesus' sanctifying himself, must be understood (as the Naza-
rite from the womb, consecrated, set apart, dedicated to the
service to which the Father had called him) a voluntary
offering—an holy unblemished sacrifice. And observe for
whom : *for their sakes ;* not for himself, for he needed it not.
The priests under the law made their offerings, first for themselves, and then for the people. But such an High-Priest
became us, who is holy, harmless, undefiled, separate from
sinners, and made higher than the heavens; and who needed
not daily, as those high priests, so to offer. For the law
maketh men high-priests which have infirmity ; but the Son
is conceecrated for evermore. My soul ! pause over this view of
thy Jesus ; and when thou hast duly pondered it, go to the
mercy-seat, under the Spirit's leadings and influences, and
there, by faith, behold thy Jesus, in his vesture dipped in
blood, there sanctified, and there appearing in the presence
of God for thee. There plead the dedication of Jesus ; for it
is of the Father's own appointment. There tell thy God and
Father (for it is the Father's glory when a poor sinner glo-
rifies his dear Son in him) that He, that Holy One, whom
the Father consecrated, and with an oath confirmed in his
high-priestly office for ever, appeareth there for thee. Tell
God that thy High-Priest's holiness and sacrifice was altogether holy, pure, without a spot ; and both his Person, and
his nature, and offering, clean as God's own righteous law.
Tell, my soul, tell thy God and Father these sacred solemn
truths. And while thou art thus coming to the mercy-seat,
under the leadings of the Spirit, and wholly in the name and
office-work of thy God and Saviour, look unto Jesus, and
call to mind those sweet words, for whose sake that Holy
One sanctified himself ; and then drop a petition more before
thou comest from the heavenly court : beg, and pray, and
wrestle, with the bountiful Lord, for, suited strength and
grace, that as, for thy sake, among the other poor sinners of
his redemption-love, Jesus sanctified himself, so thou mayest
be able to be separated from every thing but Jesus ; and as
thy happiness was Christ's end, so his glory may be thy first
and greatest object. Yes, dearest Jesus ! methinks I hear

thee say, thou shalt be for me, and not for another : so will I be for thee. Oh! thou condescending, loving God! make me thine, that whether I live, I may live unto the Lord ; or whether I die, I may die unto the Lord ; so that living or dying I may be thine.

15.—Then went King David in, and sat before the Lord. And he said, Who am I, O Lord God! and what is my house, that thou hast brought me hitherto ? And is this the manner of man, O Lord God? —2 *Sam.* vii. 18, 19.

THE language of David, under the overwhelming view he had of divine goodness as it concerned himself, is suited to the case of every child of God, as he may trace that goodness in his own history. Surely every awakened soul may cry out, under the same impressions, " Who am I, O Lord God! and what is my house, that thou hast brought me hitherto ?" My soul! ponder over the sweet subject as it concerns thyself. Behold what manner of love the love of God is from the manner of man! View it in each Person of the Godhead! What is the highest possible conception any man can have of the love of God our Father to us? Was it not when, as an evidence of the love he had to our nature, he put a robe of that nature, in its pure and holy state, upon the Person of his dear Son ; when he gave him a body in all points such as ours, sin only excepted, that he might not only in that body perfect salvation, both by his obedience and death, but also that he might be our everlasting Mediator for drawing nigh to the Godhead, first in grace, and then in glory ? Tell me, my soul, what method, in all the stores of Omnipotency, could God thy Father have adopted to convince thee of his love, as in this sweet method of his wisdom. God intimates, by this tender process, that he loveth the human nature which he hath created. And though, to answer the wise measures of his plan of redemption, he hath not as yet taken all the persons of his redeemed up to his heavenly court, yet he will have their glorious Head, their representative, there, that he may behold Him, and accept the whole church in Him, and love them and bless them in Him, now and for ever. Oh! my soul! if this view of thy Father's love was but always uppermost in thine heart, what a ground of encouragement would it for ever give thee, to come to thy God and Father in him and his mediation ; who, while he is One in the divine nature, is One also with thee in the human, on purpose to bid thee come. And as for thee, thou blessed

Jesus! thy love and thy delights were always with thy
people. From everlasting thy tendencies of favour have
been towards them; thine whole heart is ours. All thy
grace, in being set up as the Covenant-head for us; and all
the after-actings of the same grace in time; all that thou
didst then, and all that thou art doing now—all, all testify
the love of our Jesus. And may I not say to thee, thou dear
Redeemer! as David did—"Is this the manner of man, O
Lord God?" Yes! it is; but it is of the glory-man, the
God-man Christ Jesus; and no less thou Holy Spirit, whose
great work is love and consolation. What a thought is it to
warm my soul into the most awakened contemplation and
delight in the view of thy love, that though thou art of purer
eyes than to behold iniquity, yet dost thou make the very
bodies of the redeemed thy temples, for thine indwelling residence. My soul! do as David did! go in before the Divine
Presence; fall down and adore in the solemn thought—
"Who am I, O Lord God! and what is my Father's house?"

16.—The man will not be in rest, until he have finished the thing this
day.—*Ruth* iii. 18.

BEHOLD, my soul, in this scripture history, some sweet
features by which the disposition of Jesus' love, and the
earnestness in his heart to relieve poor sinners, is strikingly
set forth. When a poor sinner is made acquainted with the
Lord Jesus, hath heard of his grace, goes forth to glean in
his fields; at the ordinances of his house, and under the
ministration of his word, lays down at his feet, and prays to
be covered with the skirt of his mantle; Jesus not only takes
notice of that poor seeking sinner, but gives the poor creature to know, by some sweet and secret whispers of his Holy
Spirit, that he is not unacquainted with all that is in his heart.
And when such have lain long, and earnestly sought, even
through the whole night of doubt and fear, until the morning
of grace breaks in upon the soul, yet may they be assured
the God-man Christ Jesus will not rest until he hath finished
the thing. It is one of the most blessed truths of the gospel,
(and do thou, my soul, see to it, that it is written in thy best
and strongest remembrance to have recourse to, as may be
needed, on every occasion,) that a seeking sinner is not more
earnest to see Jesus, and enjoy him, than Jesus is to reveal
himself to that seeking sinner, and form himself in the sinner's heart the hope of glory; for Jesus will not, cannot,
cease his love to poor sinners, until the object for which he

came to seek and save them is fully answered. And it is a thought, my soul, enough to warm thy coldest moments, that all the hallelujahs of heaven cannot call off thy Jesus' attention from the necessities of even the poorest of his little ones here upon earth. In every individual instance, and in every case, Jesus will not rest until that he hath finished the thing, as well in the hearts of his people as in the world, when he finished the work his Father gave him to do. Yes! Jesus will not rest until the last redeemed soul is brought home to glory. Precious consideration! how ought it to endear yet more the preciousness of the Redeemer!

17.—Wherein ye greatly rejoice, though now for a season, if need be, ye are in heaviness through manifold temptations.—1 *Pet.* i. 6.

My soul! it is too difficult a task for flesh and blood, but it is among the most blessed triumphs of grace, to glory in tribulation, that the power of Jesus may rest upon the soul. Pause over the subject, and see whether in the little exercises of thy life, such things are among thine experiences. A soul must be truly taught of God the Father; truly acquainted with Jesus, and living near to him! and truly receiving the sweet and constant influences of the Holy Ghost: when, in the absence of the streams of all creature comforts, he is solacing himself at the fountain-head; and amidst all the fiery darts of temptations! But, my soul, if this be thy happy portion, thou must have acquired it in the school of grace. There are some precious marks by which thou wilt ascertain these things. As first—I must see that the manifold temptations, be they of what kind or number they may, are in the permissions of Jesus. I must trace the footsteps of Jesus in them, the hand of Jesus directing me through them, the voice of Jesus I must hear in them; and, in short, his sacred person regulating and ordering all the several parts of them. If I see his love, his wisdom, his grace, his good-will, in all the appointment; whatever heaviness the temptations themselves induce, there will still be cause left for joy—yea, for great joy. Moreover, it will be an additional alleviation to soften their pressure, if, through the whole of their exercise, the soul be enabled to keep in view, that God's glory, and my soul's happiness, will be the sure issue of them. If I can realize Jesus' presence, as I pass through them, and interpret with an application to myself that blessed promise, in which the Lord saith, "I know the thoughts I think towards you, saith the Lord, thoughts of peace, and not of evil, to give you an expected end;" these mercies, mingled with the trial, will sweeten and almost take away all its bitter. And lastly, to add no more— If, my soul, the Holy Ghost should lead out thine whole heart upon the person of Jesus during the conflict, and, by making thee sensible of thy weakness, to take shelter in him, and to lean altogether upon his strength; so that thou art able to believe and to depend upon the fulfilment of his promise, when, to the eye of sense, there doth not seem a way by which that promise may be fulfilled; these are foundations for rejoicing, and of great rejoicing too; because they are all out of thyself and centred in Him, with whom there is no possibility of change. These are, like the *Michtams* of David, precious, golden things. For this is to live upon Jesus, to rejoice in Jesus, and to find in him a suited strength for every need. Blessed will be these exercises, my soul, if thou art enabled thus to act under manifold temptations.

18.—And Israel strengthened himself, and sat up in the bed.—*Gen.* xlviii. 2.

THIS was an interesting moment in the life, or rather the death, of the patriarch, and may serve, my soul! to show what ought to be the conduct of the believer in his last, expiring hours. The imagination can hardly conceive any situation equally momentous, in every point of view, both as it concerns a faithful God, a man's own heart, and the church the dying saint is going to leave behind. What can form a more lovely sight than a dying saint, sitting up in the bed, (if the Lord permits the opportunity,) and recounting, as Jacob did, the gracious dealings of the Lord, all the way along the path of pilgrimage—" The God which fed me," said Jacob, " all my life long unto this day: the angel (and who was this but Jesus?) which redeemed me from all evil." Pause, my soul! Anticipate such a day. Figure to thyself thy friends around thee, and thou thyself strengthened, just to sit up in the bed, to take an everlasting farewell. What hast thou to relate? What hast thou treasured up of God's dealings with thee, to sweeten death in the recital, to bless God in the just acknowledgment, and to leave behind thee a testimony to others of the truth as it is in Jesus? My soul, what canst thou speak of? What canst thou tell of thy God, thy Jesus? Hast thou known enough of him to commit thyself into his Almighty hands, with an assurance of salvation? Pause! Didst thou not in the act of faith, long since, venture thyself upon Jesus for the whole of thy everlasting welfare? Didst thou not, from a perfect conviction of thy need of Jesus, and from as perfect a conviction of the power and grace of Jesus to save thee—didst thou not make a full and complete surrender of thyself, and with the most perfect approbation of this blessed plan of God's mercy in Christ, to be saved wholly by him, and wholly in his own way, and wholly to his own glory? And, as such, art thou now afraid, or art thou now shrinking back, when come within sight almost of Jesus' arms to receive thee? Oh no! blessed be God! this last act of committing thy soul is not as great an act of faith as the first was; for since that time thou hast had thousands of evidences, and thousands of tokens in love and faithfulness, that thy God is true. Sit up then, my soul, and do as the dying patriarch did, recount to all around thee thy confidence in the Son of God, who hath loved thee, and given himself for thee. Cry out as he did, "I have waited for thy salvation, O Lord." And as this will be the last opportunity of speaking a word for God, testify of his faithfulness, and encourage all that behold you to be seeking after an interest in Jesus, from seeing how sweetly you close a life of faith before you begin a life of glory; in blessing God, though with dying lips, that the last notes which you utter here below, may be only the momentary interruption to the same subject in the first of your everlasting song—"*To him that hath loved you, and washed you from your sins in his blood.*"

19.—Oh that I knew where I might find him, that I might come even to his seat! I would order my cause before him, and fill my mouth with arguments. Will he plead against me with his great strength? No; but he would put strength in me.—*Job* xxiii. 3, 4, 5.

My soul! are these thy breathings? Dost thou really long, and, like David, even pant, to come before the throne of grace? Art thou at a loss how to come, how to draw nigh? Wouldest thou fill thy mouth with arguments, and have thy cause so ordered as to be sure not to fail? Look to Jesus? Seek from him the leadings of the Spirit? And while thine eye is steadily fixed on thy Great High-Priest within the vail still wearing a vesture dipped in blood, see to it that thy one great plea is for a perfect and complete justification before God and thy Father, upon the sole footing of righteousness. Yes, my soul! plead earnestly, heartily, steadily; and, like Jacob wrestling with God, upon the sole footing of righteousness. Wouldest thou fear on this ground? Yes! thou

wouldest have cause enough to fear and tremble, if thy plea
was with the least reference to any righteousness of thine.
But, my soul, remember it is Jesus' righteousness, and his
only, with which, like Job, thy mouth must be filled with arguments. This is the strength thy God and Father will put
in thee: and it is a strength of Jehovah's, founded in his
justice. As a poor guilty sinner, thou couldest have nothing
to plead but free grace and rich mercy. But when thou
comest in Jesus, thy Surety's righteousness, thou mayest appeal, and art expected so to do, to God's holiness and his
justice also. Oh! how sweet the assurance, how unanswerable the plea, how secure the event! Jesus hath fulfilled the
law—Jesus hath paid the penalty of justice; and God hath
promised to pardon and bless his seed, his redeemed in him.
Hence the apostle Paul, in the contemplation of death and
judgment, while looking at his everlasting security in Jesus,
cries out—"Henceforth there is laid up for me a crown of
righteousness, which the Lord, the righteous Judge, shall
give me at that day; and not to me only, but unto all them
that love his appearing." Behold then, my soul, thy vast
privilege; and when, like Job, thou art desiring to approach
a throne of grace now, or looking forward to a throne of
judgment hereafter—never, never for a moment forget that
this is the way, and the only way, (for a blessed sure way it
is,) of maintaining communion with God in Christ. Thy
God, thy Father, will not plead against a righteousness of
his own appointing; but he will put Jesus, his strength, in
thee. Hallelujah.

20.—Thine eyes shall see the King in his beauty.—*Isaiah* xxxiii. 17.

Who, my soul, but Jesus could be intended by this sweet
promise? And who is beautiful and lovely in thine eyes but
him? There was no beauty in him, while thou wert in a
state of unrenewed nature, that thou shouldest desire him;
neither can any man truly love him, until that a soul is made
light in the Lord. Is Jesus then lovely to thee? Hast thou
seen him? Dost thou now know him, love him, behold him,
as altogether fair, and the chiefest among ten thousand? Then,
surely, this promise hath been, and is, continually fulfilled in
thy experience. Hast thou so seen him, as to be in love with
him, and to have all thine affections drawn forth toward him?
Dost thou, my soul, so behold him, as to admire him, and love
him, above all; and so to love him, as never to be satisfied
without him? Moreover—hast thou seen this King in his

beauty, in his fulness, riches, and suitableness, to thee as a Saviour? Surely, blessed Jesus! there are not only glorious, precious excellencies in thee, and thine own Divine Person, which command the love and affection of every beholder, as thou art in thyself; but there is a beauty indeed in thee, considered as thou art held forth by our God and Father, in all thy suitableness to thy people. In thy beauty, blessed Lord, there is to be seen a fulness of grace, and truth, and righteousness, exactly corresponding to the wants of poor sinners— thy blood to cleanse, thy grace to comfort, thy fulness to supply; in thee, there is every thing we can want—life, light, joy, pardon, mercy, peace, happiness here, glory hereafter. And do I not see thee, thou King in thy beauty! indeed, when I behold thee as coming with all these for my supply? So that, under the enjoyment of the whole, I feel constained to cry out, with one of old, "I will love thee, O Lord, my strength. The Lord is my strength and my song; and he is become my salvation." Neither is this all: for in beholding the King in his beauty, I behold him also in his love. Yes, blessed Lord! thou art indeed most beautiful and lovely; for thou hast so loved poor sinners as to give thyself for them; and the conscious sense that our love to thee did not first begin, but thine to us was the first cause for exciting ours, and the shedding forth that love in our hearts, by thy blessed Spirit, first prompted our minds to look unto thee, makes thee lovely indeed. And now, Lord, every day's view of thee increaseth that love, and brings home thy beauty more and more. The more frequent thou condescendest to visit my poor soul, the more beautiful dost thou appear. Every renewed manifestation, every view, every glimpse, of Jesus, must tend to make my God and King more gracious and lovely to my soul, and add fresh fervour to my love. Come then, thou blessed, holy, lovely One, and ravish my spiritual senses with thy beauty, that I may daily get out of love with every thing of created excellency, and my whole soul be filled only with the love of Jesus; until, from seeing thee here below, through the mediums of ordinances and grace, I come to look upon thee, and live for ever in thy presence, in the full beams of thy glory in thy throne above.

21.—Truly our fellowship is with the Father, and with his Son Jesus Christ.—1 *John* i. 3.

PRECIOUS, blessed consideration! Art thou, my soul, at this time in the full enjoyment of it? Pause over the inquiry.

Sometimes for the want of this search of soul, and the neglect of it, deadness, or at least leanness, creeps in. Say then, my soul, how art thou dealing with thy God; and how is thy God dealing with thee? When were his latest manifestations? When did he take thee to his banqueting-house; or, when didst thou sit under his shadow? Hast thou very lately heard his voice, saying, "Fear not, I am thy salvation?" The discovery of these things are among the sweetest exercises which flow from the indwelling Spirit. Go on further in the inquiry—How art thou seeking with thy God? When hadst thou fellowship and communion with the Father, and with his Son, Jesus Christ? What petitions hast thou now awaiting for answers from the heavenly court? What grateful acknowledgements have lately gone up for mercies received? How is thine acquaintance there advancing? How art thou growing in grace, and in the knowledge of thy Lord and Saviour Jesus Christ? If these things are neglected by thee, will not a strangeness between thy God and thee come on; such as is induced by earthly friendships, when absence and time, where there is no correspondence kept up, wears out remembrance? My soul! rouse up and consider the vast importance of keeping up constant intercourse with thy God and Saviour. Precious Jesus! do thou keep the flame of love alive; manifest to my soul the certainty and reality of my union with thee, thou sweet Saviour, by causing this blessed communion to be constant, unceasing, and full of divine communications. Let thy Spirit call forth in me the exercise of the graces he hath planted; and do thou come forth in refreshing manifestations of love; so that, while prayers go up, blessings may come down; and while thou art graciously saying, "Seek ye my face," my heart may say unto thee, "Thy face, Lord, will I seek." Oh the blessedness of such a life! to break the power of sin; to revive and strengthen the spirits; to open and enlarge to my view the discoveries of thy Person, thy glory, thy riches, thy suitableness, thine all-sufficiency! If, dearest Jesus! thou wilt mercifully keep this fellowship, this partnership, alive in my soul, how will my poor soul be living upon thee, and with thee; and how shall I be exchanging with thee all my leanness, poverty, wretchedness, and weakness, for thy fulness, riches, righteousness, and strength. Come then, Lord Jesus! and until the day break, and the shadows flee away, "turn, my beloved, and be thou like a roe, or a young hart, upon the mountains of Bether!"

22.—Thus saith the Lord ; I remember thee, the kindness of thy youth, the love of thine espousals, when thou wentest after me in the wilderness, in a land that was not sown.—*Jeremiah* ii. 2.

PAUSE, my soul, over this condescending token of God's love to Israel, and see whether it doth not hold forth to thee a blessed portion for thy encouragement. Israel had been most undeserving ; but yet the Lord would put Israel in remembrance, by assuring his people that he remembered their love. When God first formed Israel into a people—when he led them into the wilderness, and married Israel, they sung the praise of Jehovah in their love songs, on the day of their espousals. " Now," saith the Lord, " I remember thee in these things ; for these were tokens of affection, when thou wentest after me, in following the pillar of cloud through the desert ; in trusting to a harvest, though as yet the land was not sown." And may I, blessed Lord, sweetly interpret this precious portion with application to myself, as though my God so spake to me of the day of my espousals ? Doth my God and Saviour remember me in the first awakenings of his grace, when at the first mention of his name, my soul made me like the chariots of Amminadib? Well, then, may my soul remember thee, oh thou God of my salvation ? The saviour of thy past love and past experiences gives now, at this moment, new delight to my soul, and awakens new desires of communion with my God. The very recollection of what I then was, and how thou calledst me, and made my time a time of love ; and how thou passedst by, and didst bid me live, and didst cleanse me, and take me home, and betrothedst me to thyself, and made me thine for ever; the very thoughts refresh my soul now ; and these former experiences drive away present distresses and despondency ! How is it my soul, with thee now ? Art thou less in frame—less in love ? Hast thou not the same earnest liking to Jesus now, as then ? Is the strength of thy love, and desires, and delights, abated ? Look at this blessed Scripture. Hear what God saith to Israel, in a time of Israel's coldness. See how God's love was not changed, though Israel's was so abated. Art thou, my soul, conscious of the same ? Art thou lamenting it ; desiring, waiting for some renewed token of thy Jesus' love ? Is his name, his Person, his righteousness, still precious ? Dost thou wait but for the whispers of his grace ? See, here it is —" I remember, though thou hast forgotten, the day of thine espousals !" Oh ! the wonderful condescension of the Son of God ! Behold, my soul, how, in this very way, how prepar-

ing thine heart for the renewings of his love, and his sweet
manifestations towards thee! Oh! cry out with the church
of old, under similar circumstances, " Draw me; we will
run after thee." Unless thou drawest, Lord, the distance will
remain; but the desire of being drawn shows the earnestness
for union. Lord, I beseech thee, do this; bring me near to
thyself, to thine everlasting embraces: then shall I run, nay,
even flee to my beloved, and will hang upon thee as the
vessel hangeth on the nail, and dwell, and remain, with thee
for ever.

23.—By his own blood he entered in once into the holy place, having
obtained eternal redemption for us.—*Heb.* ix. 12.

PONDER, my soul, these solemn expressions concerning
thy Jesus. Mark, in them, their vast contents. Jesus, as a
Prophet, hath revealed his salvation: as a Priest, he alone
hath procured it, and offered it up to God and the Father:
and, as a King, he ever lives and reigns to see its efficacy
fully accomplished in all his redeemed, being made partakers
of it. Behold in this his priestly office, both as an High-
Priest and as the Sacrifice, what he hath wrought, and what
he hath accomplished; even eternal redemption. Mark, my
soul, the several volumes of mercy comprised in it. *First*—
Of man's revolt from God. *Secondly*—The deadly breach
by reason thereof. *Thirdly*—The proclamation from Heaven,
of God's determined purpose to take vengeance of sin.
Fourthly—Man's total inability to appease the divine wrath,
either by doing or suffering. *Fifthly*—Divine grace, in the
love of the Father, permitting a substitute, competent to do
this great act of salvation, for men; and appointing and con-
stituting no less a Person than his dear Son to the accomplishment of it. *Sixthly*—Jesus, the Son of God, voluntarily
giving himself an offering and a sacrifice for sin, and by that
one offering of himself, once offered, for ever perfecting them
that are sanctified. *Seventhly*—Having thus accomplished
the purpose of salvation upon earth, Jesus is now by his own
blood entered into the holy place, to make the whole effectual
by the exercise of his priestly office in heaven. And *lastly*,
to add no more—God accepting and confirming his perfect
approbation of the whole, and now proclaiming peace on
earth, good-will towards men. Ponder over these grand,
these glorious, these momentous subjects, my soul, this day!
Take them about with thee wheresoever thou goest; fold

them in thy bosom; write them on the tablets of thine heart; let them arise with thee, and lay down with thee. And, in all thine approaches to the mercy-seat, behold Him, and let him never be lost to the view of the eye of faith, by whom the whole is wrought, and of whom this sweet Scripture speaks; who "by his own blood entered in once into the holy place, having obtained eternal redemption for us."

24.—I in them, and thou in me, that they may be made perfect in one *John* xvii. 23.

THINK, my soul, to what a trancendent honour, to what a state of unspeakable happiness, the truly regenerated believer in Jesus is begotten. Who shall declare it; what heart shall fully conceive it! Mark, my soul, how graciously thy Redeemer hath pointed it out, in those sweet words. Observe the foundation of the whole, in that glorious mystery of union between the Father and the Son. This is at the bottom of all our mercies, and becomes the source and spring of every other. "*Thou in me,*" saith Jesus; not only as One in the nature and essence of the Godhead, in a sameness of nature, of design, of will, of perfections, and in all the attributes which constitute the distinguishing properties of Jehovah; but peculiarly as Mediator, the Head of his church and people, in communicating all the fulness of the Godhead to dwell bodily in Jesus as the Glory-man, the God-man, the Anointed of God. Thus, being one with Christ, and dwelling in Christ, in such a way and manner as the Godhead never did, and never can, dwell in any other. And as Jesus is thus One with the Father in the essence of the Godhead, and all Father in him, dwelling in him, and being in him, in the work of redemption, as Mediator—so is Jesus One in the nature of the manhood, with all his mystical members. "*I in them,*" saith Christ, "as thou art in me." Jesus is the Head of his body the church, and he is their fulness; and they members of his body, of his flesh, and of his bones. Hence result the blessed effects which his redeemed all derive from him, *that they may be made perfect in one.* Sweet and precious thought! In Jesus they are made perfect. From him they derive perfection. As one with him, they are counted and beheld perfect before God; and by him they will be found so to all eternity. And what particularly endears this view, this lovely view, of the believer's perfection in Christ Jesus, is this; that every individual member of Jesus' mystical body, is all alike equally interested in this perfection in Jesus. For as it is from the same Spirit dwelling in them all, that they are quickened to this spiritual life in Christ Jesus, and are all of them made living members, and united to Jesus, their own glorious Head; so there must be an equally near and dear union to Jesus, and to one another. Delightful consideration! As the Apostle reasons upon another consideration, " The eye cannot say to the hand, I have no need of thee; nor the foot say, because I am not the hand, I am not of the body." In Jesus they are all one; neither can any touch the least of his people, no more than the apple of his eye, without touching him. Is it so, my soul? And art thou one with Jesus, one with the glorious Head, one with the precious Members? Hast thou communion in all that concerns Christ; communion and interest in his Person; communion in his righteousness; communion in his life, in his death, in his resurrection, in his church, in his people, in his ordinances, in all that concerns Jesus! Oh! then, rest assured that thou shalt have an everlasting communion, and nothing shall separate thee from Jesus—neither in time nor to all eternity. Go down, my body, go down to the grave with this perfect confidence— that if the Spirit of him that raised up Jesus from the dead dwell in you, he that raised up Christ from the dead shall also quicken your mortal body, by his Spirit that dwelleth in you.

25.—The mercy promised.—*Luke* i. 72.

THE mercy promised! Why, God graciously promised many mercies, and most faithfully and fully performed them. Yes! every thing out of hell may well be called a mercy. Every child of Adam beareth about with him, day by day, tokens of God's mercy. The air we breathe, the garments we put on, the food we eat; all the comforts, conveniences, enjoyments of life; these are all mercies. But none of these are what the sweet portion of the morning points at. It is here a particular, a special, one specific mercy. And who can this mean, my soul, but Jesus, thy Jesus? He is indeed the mercy promised; the first mercy, the first promise; the first, best, and comprehensive gift of God in the Bible. He is indeed the mercy of mercies, the first-born, the sum and substance of every other. He is essential to make all other mercies really and truly mercies; for, without him, they ultimately prove injurious. He is essential to put a sweetness, to give a relish, a value, an importance, to every other. Where Jesus is, there is mercy; where Jesus is not, what can profit? My soul! hast thou considered this? Dost thou know it? Is Jesus thine? Is this mercy promised, really, truly given to thee? Hast thou taken him home to thine house, to thine heart? Pause! If it be so, how dost thou value him, know him, use him, live to him, walk with him, hope in him, rejoice in him, and make him thine all? Hast thou received him as a free mercy, an undeserved mercy? Hast thou accepted him as so seasonable a mercy, that, without him, thou wouldest have been undone for ever? Is he now so truly satisfying to thee in all thy desires, for time and for eternity, that thou canst bid adieu to every enjoyment if needful; and, looking up to Jesus, canst truly say, " Whom have I in heaven but thee? and there is none upon earth that I desire beside thee!" Oh! my soul! if this be thy portion, then hast thou a Benjamin's portion indeed! God thy Father hath given thee indeed the mercy promised; and Jesus is, and will be, thy mercy, and the mercy of all mercies, to all eternity. Amen.

26.—Thy lips, O my spouse, drop as the honey-comb.—*Song* iv. 11.

WHILE Jesus is so precious to his people, that they seek him in every thing that is lovely, and indeed can discover nothing to be lovely until they have found Jesus in it, what an endearment is it to the soul of a believer, when he discovers Jesus looking upon him, eyeing him, and even commending Jesus' own graces, which he hath imparted to the soul, brought out into exercise again by the influences of his own holy Spirit. My soul! canst thou really be led to believe that Jesus is speaking to his church, to his fair one, his spouse, to every individual soul of his redeemed and regenerated ones, in those sweet words of the Song? Doth Jesus, the Son of God, call thee his spouse; and doth he say thy lips drop as the honey-comb? Pause, my soul, and ponder over these gracious words of thy God. By thy lips, no doubt, Jesus means thy words; of which Solomon saith— " Pleasant words are as an honey-comb, sweet to the soul, and health to the bones." Prov. xvi. 24. Do thy lips drop in prayer, in praise, in conversation, in Christian fellowship, in ordinances, and in all the ordinary intercourse of life? Is Jesus thy one theme; his name, his love, his grace, his work, his salvation; what he hath done, what he hath wrought; how he hath loved, how he hath lived, how he hath died, how he now lives again to appear in the presence of God for his people; and to give out his fulness, his mercies, his treasures; in visits, in manifestations, and the ten thousand numberless, nameless, ways by which he proves himself to be Jesus? Do thy lips, my soul, drop in these topics when thou walkest by the way, when thou liest down, when thou risest up; and when thou goest in before the presence of God, in the public worship of the temple, or the private closet where no eye seeth thee but Him that seeth in secret? And doth thy Jesus really mark these things? Doth he condescend to notice his poor creature, and to esteem these droppings as the sweetness of the honey? Precious God! precious Jesus! what a love is here. Oh! for grace, for love, for life, for every suited gift of my God and Saviour; that my lips, from the abundance of the heart, may drop indeed as the honey-comb—sweetly, freely, not by constraint, except the constraint of thy love; but constantly, unceasingly, for ever, as the drops of the honey-comb which follow one another; that prayer may follow praise, and praise succeed to prayer; and that there may be a succession in magnifying and adoring the riches of grace; that the name of Jesus may be always in my mouth; and from that one blessed source, that Jesus lives in my heart, and rules, and reigns, and is ormed there the hope of glory.

27.—The trumpet of the jubilee.—Levit. xxv. 9.

My soul! pause over the subject of the jubilee trumpet; for surely much of gospel was proclaimed by it. It should seem that there were *four* distinct and special sounds of the trumpet in the camp of Israel. The trumpet of *memorials* so called, (Levit. xxiii. 24,) was blown on the occasion of the new moon, calling the people to the joyful assembly, Psalm. lxxxi. 3. There was also the *fast* trumpet, of which the prophet speaks, Joel ii. 1. Besides these, the *war* trumpet gave a certain sound to prepare to battle, 1 Cor. xiv. 8. And this of the *jubilee*, which differed from all. And although the jubilee trumpet was never heard but once in fifty years, yet so sweet and so distinguishing was the sound, that no poor captive, among the servants in the camp of Israel, was at a moment's loss to understand its gracious meaning. Say, my soul, is not the gospel sound, when first heard by the ear of faith, precisely the same? When pardon was first proclaimed to thee by the blood of Christ, and the day of his atonement so manifested to thy spiritual senses, that the captivity of sin and Satan lost their powers upon thee, was not this indeed the jubilee trumpet, and the acceptable year of the Lord? Hast thou heard this joyful sound? Hath the Son of God made thee free? Hath Jesus caused thee to return to thy long-lost, long-forfeited, inheritance? And wilt thou ever forget the unspeakable mercy? Hail! thou Almighty Deliverer, thou Redeemer of thy captives! I had sold my possession, sold myself, for nought; and thou hast redeemed it for me again without money. I had sold it indeed, but could not alienate it for ever, because the right of redemption was with thee. Yes, blessed Jesus! thou art He whom thy brethren shall praise. Thou art the next of kin, the nearest of all relations, and the dearest of all brothers! And thou hast redeemed both soul and body, both lands and inheritance, by thy blood; and so redeemed the whole, as never more to be lost again or forfeited for ever. And now Lord, thy jubilee trumpet sounds; and the proclamation of the everlasting gospel is heard in our land, to give liberty to the captive, sight to the blind, to bring the prisoners out of the prison, and them that sit in darkness out of the prison house! Oh! cause me to know the joyful sound, and daily to walk in the light of thy countenance. Cause me, by the sweet influences of thy spirit, to live in the constant expectation of the year of the everlasting jubilee, when the trumpet of the archangel shall finally sound, and all thy redeemed shall then return to Zion, with songs of everlasting joy upon their heads; when they shall obtain joy and gladness, and sorrow and sighing shall flee away. Hallelujah!

28.—For where a testament is, there must also of necessity be the death of the testator; for a testament is of force after men are dead, otherwise it is of no strength at all whilst the testator liveth.—*Heb.* ix. 16, 17.

BEHOLD, my soul, how graciously the Holy Ghost hath here represented the necessity of Jesus' death, in order that the testament or will he left behind him, might have the intended effect; and all the benefits and blessings he bequeathed in it to his people, might be fully paid and made over to them for their present peace and everlasting happiness. Now, my soul, mark down, for this day's special meditation, the many precious things here contained. Observe how very accommodating the Holy Ghost is, to explain to thee divine things, by the similitude of human transactions. As a man makes his will, so Jesus made his. As what a man gives is altogether a free and voluntary act, so Jesus was not constrained by what he gave in his blessed will; but the whole was the result of his own free, gracious, and everlasting love. And as a man must die before his will can be put in force, so Jesus must, and did die, that his testament and will might have the full effect also. But there is one sweet point more to be taken into this account, in which, my soul, thy Jesus hath infinitely surpassed all men in this article of their wills. When a man dies, he appoints by will an executor, to whom he must trust the management of all his effects after his decease : and should this executor prove unfaithful, his best designs for those he loved, when living, may all fail of the end when he is dead. Now here lies the sweetness of Jesus' will :—He not only made the will, but he himself will see it fully executed ; for as he died once, in order that by his death his will might be confirmed, so he ever liveth to see the whole of his blessed gifts and legacies paid. Precious, precious Jesus! how sure then is thy will, and the certainty of every tittle of it being fulfilled. Now, my soul, there are two grand things which concern thee to inquire concerning the will of the Lord Jesus. The first is, whether thou hast any interest in it ? And the second is, what the Lord Jesus hath left behind him ? Recollect, my soul, that in this instance, as in the former, when men make their wills, it is to dispose of their effects to their relations, their friends, their families. Jesus also hath his relations, his friends, and his family. Yes! thou dear Lord! thou condescendest to call thy people thy spouse, thy brethren, thy children, thy jewels, thy redeemed ! My soul ! dost thou claim relationship to Jesus? Canst thou prove, or hast thou proved, his will ? Is Jesus thine husband ? Hath he betrothed thee to himself? Again—Hast thou the marks of a child in God's family ? Art thou born again ? Again—if you are his, then hast thou his Spirit ; for he that is joined to the Lord is one Spirit. If you are a child of God, and a joint-heir with Christ, then art thou under his divine leadings ; for as many as are led by the Spirit of God, they are the sons of God. If thou hast these marks of relationship, thou mayest safely look for his gifts. Surely Jesus hath remembered in his legacies his spouse, his children. And oh ! what an inventory wilt thou find, my soul, under the *second* inquiry, when thou hast fully proved the first! Oh! what legacies, what gifts, what an inheritance, art thou entitled to by the will of Jesus! All temporal blessings, all spiritual blessings, all eternal blessings! Pardon, mercy, peace, in the blood of his cross; the sweet enjoyment of all providences in this life, and the sure possession of everlasting happiness in that which is to come! Oh! how true was it, my God and Saviour, when thou didst say, "I will cause them that love me to inherit substance!"

29.—The precious ointment upon the head that ran down upon his beard, even Aaron's beard, that went down to the skirts of his garment.—*Psalm* cxxxiii. 2.

My soul, behold, in the anointing here set forth of the Jewish high-priest, a type of His anointing who is a Priest for ever, and a Priest upon his throne; and while looking at Aaron, say, as the Lord Jesus did upon another occasion concerning Solomon, "a greater than Aaron is here." It is sweet, very sweet, and very profitable, to behold the old church shadowing forth the new, and the law ministering to the gospel. Yes, blessed Jesus! I behold in Aaron, and in the precious ointment poured forth upon his head, thus running down to the skirts of his garments, the beautiful representation of that fulness of the Spirit, which was poured out on thee without measure; that from thee the communication might flow down to the poorest, the humblest, the lowest of thy members, even to the very skirts of thy clothing. It pleased the Father that in thee should all fulness dwell; that of that fulness all thy people might receive, and grace for grace. And by virtue of our interest in thee, and union with thee, all thy people do richly partake of communion in all thy benefits, blessings, mercies. The sun shines not to itself, nor for itself, but to impart light and life to others: so dost thou, the Son of Righteousness, shine forth in all thy glory, not for thyself, but to bless, and enliven, and give out of all thy grace and fulness, every suited blessing, according to the measure of the gift of Christ. "My soul! bring home these precious truths to the conviction of experience. Was Jesus, indeed, anointed for his people? Was grace poured into his lips? Was he, like Aaron, so installed into the office of the priesthood, and the Holy Spirit so immeasurably communicated to him, on purpose that all his little ones should partake of this unspeakable gift of God? Did God

7*

the Father say to Jesus, "I will pour my Spirit upon thy
seed, and my blessing upon thine offspring?" Well then, my
soul, hast thou partaken of the Holy Spirit? Hast thou
communion with Jesus in all that concerns thy salvation?
A child of God, a joint-heir with Christ, and a soul begotten
of the Holy Spirit, hath interest and communion in all that
belongs to Jesus, as the great Head and Mediator of his
church; interested in his person, interested in his work, interested in his righteousness, in his life, in his death, in his
resurrection, in his everlasting priestly office, and in his
everlasting glory. What saith my soul to these things? Go,
my soul, go this morning, go in the strength of this interest,
and look at a throne of grace, within the vail, whither thy
fore-runner is for thee entered; behold thy glorious Aaron,
wearing the priestly vestments still, and having all grace, all
fulness; waiting to be gracious, and to impart of that fulness to thy necessities; and having received gifts for men,
yea, for thee, the most rebellious, that the Lord God might
dwell among them. Lord, proportion thy mercies to my
wants; and, as the day is, so let the strength be.

30.—So then with the mind I myself serve the law of God; but with
the flesh the law of sin.—*Romans* vii. 25.

Is this thy language, my soul? Hast thou learnt with
Paul, with Job, with Isaiah, and all the faithful gone before,
to loath thyself in thine own sight? Dost thou groan, being
burdened with a body of sin which drags down the soul?
Pause over this view of human nature. In the first place—
think, my soul, what humbling thoughts such a state of corruption ought to induce. Though the mind be regenerated,
though with the mind the believer serves the law of God,
delights in the law of God, loves the law, and would make
it the subject of devout meditation all the day; yet such is
the body of sin, the flesh, with its affections, and appetites,
and desires, that it draws away the attention, imperiously
puts in its claims, and rises up in rebellion continually. And
are the souls of God's children thus exercised, thus afflicted,
in the struggles between the different motions of grace, and
corruption from day to day? Yes! such is the state, such
the uniform experience of God's people in all ages. Paul
thus complains, though he had been so highly sanctified.
Perhaps there never was a child of God brought into closer
and more intimate communion with God. He had been

caught up to the third heaven, and heard unspeakable words. He had laboured more than all the apostles. He had been converted by a miracle from heaven, and by the immediate call of the Lord Jesus personally to him. But yet this highly favoured servant of the Lord, this blessed apostle, who was continually flying on the wings of zeal and love in the service of his master, even he, with his flesh, he tells us, served the law of sin; nay, he felt and discovered a law of sin in his members, warring against the law of his mind, and bringing him into captivity to the law of sin which was in his members; and under a deep distress of soul he cried out —"O wretched man that I am, who shall deliver me from the body of this death?" Is it so then, my soul, with thee also? Dost thou discover the same in thy experience? Dost thou feel the rebellions of sin rising up within thee? Dost thou detect thine heart, wandering even in the moment of solemn exercises; and, in short, thine own body, the worst and greatest enemy thou hast to contend with? Oh! then, learn from hence what humbling views oughtest thou to have of thyself, and to lay low in the dust in consequence thereof before God. When thou hast fully contemplated this state of a fallen nature, let thy next improvement of this subject be to endear the Lord Jesus to thee, my soul, more and more; to fly out of thyself, to fly to Jesus, to take refuge in him and his great salvation; from even thyself, with all that body of sin and death, under which thou thus continually groanest; and to derive herefrom a daily and hourly conviction yet more strong and unanswerably conclusive, that nothing but the blood of Jesus can cleanse, nothing but the righteousness of Jesus can save and justify a sinner. Say as Paul did, when from the bottom of his heart that soul-piercing question arose, "Who shall deliver me from the body of this death? I thank God through Jesus Christ our Lord."

31.—Having a desire to depart, and to be with Christ.—*Phillipp.* i. 23.

My soul! thou hast not, I hope, dismissed the solemn thoughts opened to thy view by the Scripture of yesterday. Surely, since that last morning, thou hast had but too many renewed occasions to feel the truth of it. Sin is not only present *with* thee at all times, but *in* thee, and as inseparable from thy unrenewed part, as the shadow from the substance. Thou knowest this, thou feelest it, thou groanest under it; and the consciousness of it is, in itself, enough to make thee go humbly all thy days. All other afflictions are nothing to this affliction: this, like the ocean compared to rivers, surpasseth and swalloweth up all. It is indeed a soul-supporting thought, (and, blessed be God, thou feelest the sweetness of it,) that under all, and in all, Jesus is thy hope. And while sin is always present with thee, Jesus, thy Advocate and Propitiation, is present for thee with the Father. But though in Him and his righteousness accepted and secure, yet the consideration how much thy daily short-comings and transgressions dishonour God, and deprive thee of comfort here, is matter sufficient to make thine eyes run down with water, and thine heart continually to mourn before the mercy-seat. And will these things always be the same whilst thou carriest about with thee this body of sin? Shall this perishing part of thine be always so unfavourable to the sweet and gracious desires of the soul? Shall I never, never truly and uninterruptedly enjoy Jesus, until the body is dissolved, and the dust returns to the earth, out of which that part of my nature was taken? Pause, my soul, and say—Hast thou not then a desire to depart, and to be with Christ? Is not the grave, in this view, not only made bearable, but even desirable—nay, even pleasant? What! shall I never be wholly free from sin, until that I am wholly freed from the body? Shall I never be secure of sweet enjoyment with Jesus in ordinances, in retirement, in prayer, in praise, until that I drop this body of sin? And wouldest thou not, my soul, gladly part with such a partner, near and dear as it is, if this partner, in its present state, so dreadfully robs thee of thy most precious enjoyments? It is true, death in itself is not desirable; but if only by dying thou canst enjoy Jesus; and if only by dying this body will lose its corruptions; if the grave hath a commission from thy Jesus to destroy that part only of thy body which is corrupt, and, at the same time, to act as a preserver of that part which Jesus, at the last day, will raise up to glory; if Jesus hath assured thee that, though worms destroy thy corrupt part, yet thine eyes, even thy bodily eyes, when raised up by Jesus a glorified body, shall see God; and if thy body, thus raised up and reanimated, shall then be not only wholly freed from all corruption, but equally disposed as the soul to praise thy God and Saviour for ever and ever, and both soul and body united as dear friends in this blessed service; oh! then, from henceforth never, my soul, look at death any more but as thy kind friend. It is to die to sin; but it is to live to Jesus. It is to be dead to all things but Jesus, that Jesus may be all things in life for ever. Oh! then, for this desire to depart, and to be with Christ.

APRIL.

1.—And this is his name whereby he shall be called—THE LORD OUR RIGHTEOUSNESS.—*Jeremiah* xxiii. 6.

BEGIN this month, my soul, with contemplating thy Jesus, in this glorious distinction of character; and beg of God the Holy Ghost, who hath here declared that, under this character, Jesus shall be known and called, that every day through the month, and through the whole of life, thou mayest find grace and strength so to know and so to call Jesus, as to be everlastingly satisfied that thou art made the righteousness of God in him. And first, my soul, consider who and what this Holy One is. He is the Lord Jehovah. In the glories of his *essence*, he is One with the Father. In his *personal* glories, he is the Lord thy Mediator. And in his *relative* glories, he is thy righteousness. For, by virtue of his taking thy nature, what he is as Mediator and as the Surety of his people, he is for them. Pause over this blessed view, and then say, what can be more blessed than thus to behold Jesus as what he is in himself *for* his people? Look at him again, my soul, and take another view of him in his loveliness; in what he is *to* his people. This precious Scripture saith, that he is the Lord *our* Righteousness; that is, by virtue of his Godhead he is our Righteousness, in such a sure way, and with such everlasting value and efficacy, as no creature could be. The righteousness his redeemed possess in him, and have a right in him, and are entitled to in him, is the righteousness of God; and therefore impossible ever to be lost, and impossible ever to be fully recompensed in glory. Sweet and blessed consideration! it seems too great to be believed. And so it would, indeed, if the authority of Jehovah had not stamped it, and made the belief of it the first and highest act of a poor sinner's obedience. And, observe, my

soul, yet further, there is this blessed addition to the account
—*he shall be called so.* By whom? Nay, by every one that
knows him. The poor sinner shall call him so, who is lead
to see and feel that he hath no righteousness of his own; he
shall call Jesus his Lord, his Righteousness; he shall *call him*
so to others, he shall call *upon* him for himself; he shall be
that true Israelite, that very One whom the Prophet describes
—" Surely shall one say, in the Lord have I righteousness
and strength." The redeemed upon earth, the redeemed in
heaven, the church of the first-born, shall call him so. The
whole army of patriarchs, and prophets, and apostles, all
shall know Jesus, as the Lord our Righteousness. Nay, God
himself, our Father, shall call his dear Son by this glorious
name; for it is He who hath constituted and appointed him
as the Lord our Righteousness. And that Jesus is our Righteousness is from this very cause, " that he is made of God to
us wisdom and righteousness, sanctification and redemption,
that he that glorieth may glory in the Lord." Now, my
soul! what sayest thou to this sweet view of Jesus in this
most precious Scripture? Is not this name of Jesus most
grateful to thee, as ointment of the richest fragrancy poured
forth? Can any name be as sweet and delightful to one convinced, as thou art, that all thy righteousness is as dung and
dross, as the name of Jesus—the Lord our Righteousness?
Witness for me, ye angels of light, that I renounce every
other; and from henceforth will make mention of his righteousness, and his only. Yes, blessed Jesus! my mouth shall
daily speak of thy righteousness and salvation; for I know
no end thereof.

2.—And Aaron shall lay both his hands upon the head of the live goat,
and confess over him all the iniquities of the children of Israel, and
all their transgressions in all their sins, putting them upon the head
of the goat, and shall send him away by the hand of a fit man into
the wilderness. And the goat shall bear upon him all their iniquities,
unto a land not inhabited.—*Levit.* xvi. 21, 22.

PAUSE, my soul! and behold the tender mercy of thy God,
in thus causing to be represented to the church of old, by so
striking a service, that grand and most momentous doctrine
of the gospel, which, in after ages of the church, was fully
set forth and completed when Jehovah laid upon our Lord
Jesus Christ the iniquities of his people. And do, my soul,
attend to those several most interesting points here graciously
revealed. As first—This was the express command of God.

Yes! who but God could transfer, or permit a change of persons in the transferring of sin? This is one of the most blessed parts of the gospel, that when Jesus bore our sins in his own body on the tree, it was by the express will and appointment of Jehovah. The Lord Jesus took not those sins on himself; but the Lord laid on him the iniquity of us all. Mark this down in strong characters. Then next consider— that as Jesus had a transfer of all the sins of his people, consequently they were no longer upon the people from whom they were transferred. Here faith finds full scope for exercise, in giving God the credit due to God. The sending away the goat was intended to represent the full remission of sins; and by the goat bearing them away to a land not inhabited, intimated that those sins should never be seen or known any more, according to that precious Scripture of the Holy Ghost by the prophet: "*the iniquity of Israel shall be sought for, and there shall be none; and the sins of Judah, and they shall not be found.*" Jerem. l. 20. And there is one sweet thought more, not to be overlooked in this blessed Scripture, concerning those sins. Observe, my soul, the particularity of the expression. The confession of Aaron, the great high-priest, was not only of all the iniquities of the children of Israel, but of all their transgressions *in* all their sins. Pause, my soul, over this view, and recollect that there are many, and sometimes very heinous and aggravated, circumstances of transgression in thy sins. Now what a sweet thought of relief to thy mind is it, under particular and galling circumstances of sin, to behold thy Jesus bearing thy sins, and all the transgression of all thy sins. The Lord caused *to meet in him,* as the passage might have been rendered, the iniquities of us all. Isaiah liii. 6. Jesus was made the common receiver, the drain, the sink, into which all the sins, and every minute and particular sin was emptied. He shall drink of the brook in the way, said the Holy Ghost, Psalm cx. 7. Was not this the black, the filthy brook of *Cedron,* into which all the filth from the sacrifices of the temple were emptied? Here it was Jesus passed, when, in the night of his entering on his passion, he went into the garden. Look on this, my soul, and see where it doth not strikingly, though solemnly at the same time, set forth Jesus bearing all and every particular transgression in all thy sins. One thought more. The goat, thus laden with all the sins of the people, was to be sent away by the hand of some fit man into the wilderness. As none but Jesus could be competent to bear sins,

so none but Jesus could be fit to bear them away into a land
of everlasting forgetfulness. It doth not lessen the beauty of
this blessed Scripture in the representation here made, in Jesus being set forth under two characters; for he is so in many.
None but Jesus can indeed accomplish all; he is the High-
Priest, the Altar, and the Sacrifice, through all the law; and
he is the fit man here represented, as well as the burden-
bearer of sin. Hail, thou Great High-Priest! Blessed for
ever be thou who hast borne away all the sins of thy people
into a land not inhabited. Thou hast crossed out, in God's
book of account, each and every individual sin, and the transgression of all our sins, in the red letters of thy blood; and
never shall they appear again to the condemnation of thy
people.

3.—A man of sorrows, and acquainted with grief.—*Isaiah* liii. 3.

My soul! there is one feature in thy Redeemer's character which in the unequaled abasement of his person, demands
thy constant contemplation. I fear it hath not been considered by thee as it ought. And yet it is so sweetly accommodating and lovely that the more thou beholdest thy Jesus
in this tender light, the more endeared he must appear to
thee. The prophet, under the Holy Ghost, hath here in a
few words sketched the outlines of it—" *A man of sorrows,
and acquainted with grief.*" It was most essential that Jesus
should be all this, because it belonged to the curse which he
became for his people, when he offered himself as their
surety. You will remember, my soul, the curse which God
pronounced upon the earth, and man's passage through it,
when he broke the divine law. The ground was cursed;
the produce of it was to be thorns and thistles; in sorrow,
and in the sweat of the brow was man to eat bread; and, at
length death was to close his life. Now it behoved Him who
undertook to remove the curse. to bear that curse before the
removal of it, and, as such, it behoved Jesus to be a man of
sorrows, and acquainted with grief. Hence all these seized
on the Lord Jesus, in the first moment he assumed our nature. And though he had no sin in his nature, not being
born in the ordinary way of our nature, yet, as a Surety, he
was at once exposed to all the frailties, in the sinless sorrows,
and travails and labours of it. This sentence would not have
been fulfilled had not Jesus eat bread in the sweat of his brow.
So interesting a part, therefore, was it in Christ's life, that he

should labour in a common occupation, that this part of the curse might not go by without being accomplished. And how eminently, my soul, was this part indeed fulfilled, when, in the garden, the sweat of his brow, was drops of blood! How full of thorns and thistles was the earth to Jesus, may be in some measure considered, when we behold him in the unequaled sorrows of the opposition he met with from the world, the unkindness of friends, the malice of enemies. The thorny crown put upon his sacred head was little considered by those that put it: but yet it was in reality crowning him Lord of sorrow and grief, beyond all men that were ever exercised with affliction. So great indeed was the continued load he bore of grief, and so much did it tend to waste and wear the spirits, that according to the expression of the Jews to him—*thou art not yet fifty years old*, evidently proved that he had the visage of one of fifty, when only thirty. And it is remarkable, though we are told that Jesus rejoiced in spirit, yet we never read that he was once seen to laugh during his whole life. Precious Jesus; enable me ever to be looking unto thee, thou meek and lowly Lamb of God; and may I never lose sight of this sweet part of thy character also, that whilst thou didst bear our sins, so didst thou carry our sorrows; and in fulfilling the law, didst take away the curse also, when in sorrow thou didst eat bread all the days of thy life.

4.—A place called Gethsemane.—*Matt.* xxiv. 36.

My soul; let thy morning meditation be directed to the garden of Gethsemane; that memorable spot, sacred to the believer, because so much beloved and resorted to by Jesus. Here Jesus oft came with his disciples. And here, my soul, do thou often take the wing of faith, and flee in devout contemplation. Was this place dear to thee, thou precious Redeemer? And was it not because here thou didst enjoy the sweetest refreshings in communion with the Father? Was it not because here thou knewest would begin the conflict and the agony, in which the great business for which thou camest on earth would be accomplished? Didst thou abide here, Lord, a whole night, after a day's constant preaching to the people, the week only before thy crucifixion? (See Luke xxi. 37,) and when the night was passed, didst thou again repair to the temple to the same employ? Was Gethsemane dear to Jesus? Was here his favorite haunt? And

8

shall not my soul delight to be often here in solemn meditation? Will not my Lord lead me there, and going with me
there, sweetly speak to me there? that while in imagination I tread the sacred ground, my soul may view the several
spots, and say,—*Here* it was, perhaps, my Redeemer was
withdrawn a stone's cast from his disciples that the powers of
darkness might more furiously assault his holy soul! And
here the angel stept from heaven to strengthen him; and
here the Lord Jesus was in his agony, when the sweat of his
body forced through all the pores great drops of blood, falling
down to the ground! Is this Gethsemane? and why Gethsemane? The Jews called it *Ge-hennom*, or Hell; for here
it was Josiah burnt the idol-vessels. 2 Kings xxiii. 4, 5, 6, 10.
And it is the same as Tophet, the only word the Jews used
for hell after their return from the Babylonish captivity.
The field of Cedron was indeed a dark and gloomy place;
and by its side ran the foul and black brook which Jesus
passed over when he went into Gethsemane. Here David
of old went mourning and lamenting, when Ahitophel, like
another Judas, betrayed him, and his life was sought after.
2 Sam. xv. 28. And here the son of David passed also,
when the man of whom David by the spirit of prophecy spake,
(Psalm xli. 9,) which eat bread with Jesus, lifted up his heel
against him. And was this Gethsemane the favoured spot
of Jesus, because here he had so sweetly enjoyed communion
with his Father, and because here he should encounter the
powers of darkness? Learn then, my soul, from thy Jesus,
where thou oughtest to seek grace in a refreshing hour, to
comfort a trying hour. Say, my soul, where should be thy
dying place, but where thy God hath most blessed thy living
place? There, Jesus, make my seasons (if it needs be) of
conflict, where thou hast sanctified and made blessed by thy
Bethel visits. And was a garden the favoured spot of Jesus?
Yes! It was in a garden the first Adam lost himself and
his posterity; there, then, Jesus will recover the forfeited inheritance. Did the devil begin in Eden to ruin man? Why,
then, in Gethsemane Jesus will begin to conquer hell for
man's recovery. Did Satan, from the garden, bind and carry
captive the first Adam? Then from a garden also shall he
cause to be bound, and carried away to the cross, the second
Adam, that he, by death, might destroy him that had the
power of death—that is, the devil, and deliver them who,
through fear of death, are all their lifetime subject to bondage.
Solemn Gethsemane! awful, but hallowed spot; here would

I often come: here contemplate Jesus, my blessed surety, groaning yet conquering; pressed under all the hellish malice of the devil, yet triumphing over all; deserted by his disciples, sweating a bloody sweat, sustaining the wrath of offended justice, drinking the cup of trembling! Is this Gethsemane! Oh, thou Lamb of God! thou Pascal Lamb! here oft bring me: here show me thy loves! and as thy joys were here turned into sorrows, give me to see how the curses which I deserve, but which thou didst endure, were converted into blessings, and that by thy stripes I am healed. Hail, sacred Gethsemane!

5.—Being in an agony.—*Luke* xxii. 44.

My soul! art thou still in Gethsemane? Look at Jesus once more: behold him in his agony; view him in his bloody sweat, in a night of cold, and in the open air, when we are told that the servants in the high-priest's hall were obliged to make a fire of coals to warm themselves. In such a night was thy Jesus, from the extremity of an anguish in his soul by reason of thy sins, made to sweat great drops of blood. Look at the Lord in this situation, and as the prophet by vision beheld him coming up with his dyed garments, as one that had trodden the wine-fat; so do thou, by faith, behold him in his bloody sweat when, from treading the wine press of the wrath of God, under the heavy load of the world's guilt, his noble raiment was stained with blood. Sin first made man to sweat, and Jesus, though he knew no sin, yet taking out the curse of it for his people, was made to sweat blood! Oh! thou meek and holy lamb of God; methinks I would, day by day, attend the garden of Gethsemane by faith, and contemplate thee in thy agony. But who shall unfold it to my wondering eyes, or explain all its vast concern to my astonished soul. The evangelists, by their different turns of expression to point it out, plainly show that nothing within the compass of language can unfold it. *Matthew* saith the soul of Jesus was *exceeding sorrowful, even unto death.* Matt. xxvi. 38. The sorrows of hell, as is elsewhere mentioned, encompassed him. Psalm xviii. 5. My soul! pause over this. Was Jesus' soul thus sorrowful, even with hell-sorrows, when, from the sins of his people charged on him, and the penalty exacted from him as the sinner's surety, the wrath of God against sin, lighting upon him, came as the tremendous vengeance of hell? *Mark* describes the state of the Lamb of God as *sore amazed*. The expression signifies an horror of mind ; such a degree of fear and consternation as when the hairs of the head stand upright through terror of mind. And was Jesus thus agonized, and for sins his holy soul had never committed, when standing forth as the surety for others ? *John's* expression of the Redeemer's state, on this occasion is, that *his soul was troubled.* John xii. 27. The original of this word, troubled, is the same as the *Latins* derive their word for hell from. As if the Lord Jesus felt what the prophet had said concerning *everlasting burnings*, Isaiah xxxiii. 14. "My heart," said that patient sufferer, "is like wax; it is melted in the midst of my bowels." Psalm xxii. 13. Hence Moses, and after him Paul, in the view of God's taking vengeance on sin, describes him under an awful account—*Our God is a consuming fire*. Deut. iv. 24. Heb. xii. 29. Beholding his Father thus coming to punish sin, in his person, Jesus said—*my iniquities have taken hold upon me, therefore my heart faileth me*, Psalm xl. 12. And *Luke* folds up an account of Jesus *being in an agony ;* such a labouring as implies an universal convulsion : as dying men, with cold clammy sweats ; so Jesus, scorched with the hot wrath of God on sin, sweated in his agony clots of blood ? My soul, canst thou hold out any longer ? Will not thy eye-strings and heart-strings break, thus to look on Jesus in his agony ? Oh ! precious Jesus ! were the great objects of insensible, inanimated nature, made to feel as if it took part in thy sufferings, and am I unmoved ? Did the very graves yawn at his death and resurrection ? and were the rocks rent, while my tearless eyes thus behold thee ? Oh, gracious God I fulfil thy promise by the prophet, that I may look on him whom I have pierced, and mourn as one that mourneth for his only son, and be in bitterness as one that is in bitterness for his first born.

6.—Jesus knowing all things that should come upon him, went forth, and said unto them, Whom seek ye ? They answered him, Jesus of Nazareth. Jesus saith unto them, I am he. And Judas also, which betrayed him, stood with them. As soon as he had said unto them, I am he, they went backward and fell to the ground.—*John* xxviii. 4, 5, 6.

WHAT a glorious Scripture is this I Ponder it well, my soul ; for of all the miracles of thy Jesus, there is not one more sweet and satisfactory to contemplate. Yesterday thou wert looking at thy Redeemer under a heavy cloud. Look

at him as he is here represented, for he is still, in this transaction, in the same garden of Gethsemane ; and behold how
the Godhead shone forth with a glory surpassing all description. Observe what a willing sacrifice was Jesus. He knew
the hour was come ; for he had said so. He doth not wait
to be taken, and by wicked hands to be crucified and slain ;
but he goeth forth to surrender himself. Yes ! Jesus did not
go to the garden of Gethsemane for nothing : he knew Judas
would be there : he knew the powers of darkness would be
there: he knew how his whole soul would be in an agony ;
but there Jesus would go. He had said at the table to his
disciples, " Arise, let us go hence." Precious, precious
Jesus ! how endearing to my poor soul is this sweet view of
thy readiness and earnestness to become a sacrifice for the
sins of thy people. Thou hadst this baptism, Lord, to be
baptized with ; and how wast thou straitened until it was
accomplished ! There was a time, dear Lord, when the
multitudes sought for thee to make thee a king, so convinced
were they, for the moment, who thou wert ; and then thou
didst hide thyself from them. But now, when thine enemies
come to make thee king with a crown of thorns, and to nail
thy sacred body to the cross, thou didst hasten to meet them.
Well might the Prophet say, thou wentest forth for the salvation of thy people ! Look at this scripture again, my soul.
" Whom seek ye ?" said Jesus. Did they not know him ?
It was a light night, most probably, for the moon was then at
the full: beside, the seekers of Christ had lanterns and
torches. How was it they did not know him ? Didst thou
for the moment, dearest Lord ! do by them as thine angels at
the gate of Lot by the Sodomites, so cause their eyes to be
holden that they should not know thee ? Was there somewhat of a miracle in this also ? But, my soul, behold the
wonder of wonders that followed : no sooner had Jesus said
to their inquiry, Whom seek ye ? " I am he," than they
went backward and fell to the ground. Was there indeed
some sudden overpowering emanation of the Godhead, breaking through the vail of Jesus's flesh, which induced this
effect ? Was it ever known, ever heard of, in any age or
period of the world, of such an effect before ? Supposing all
the monarchs of the earth, with the mightiest armies of men,
could be assembled together, how should such an event be
induced by the breath of their mouth ? Contemplate this,
my soul ! again and again. Rejoice, my soul ! in this view
of thy Saviour; for never, surely, was a greater miracle of

8*

thy Redeemer's wrought: and remember how soon it took place after his agony. Never go to Gethsemane in meditation, without taking the recollection of it with thee. Behold the Man ; behold the God ! Here was nothing exercised by Jesus ; no weapon, no threat, no denunciation, no appeal to the Father. Jesus only simply said, "I am he," and they fell to the earth. Precious Jesus! what a volume of instruction doth it afford. If such was the effect in the day of thy flesh, how sure is that Scripture concerning the day of thy power, in which it is said, "The Lord shall consume the wicked with the breath of his mouth, and destroy them with the brightness of his coming." 2 Thess. ii. 8. And if, my soul, there was such power in the word of thy Saviour, when he only said to his enemies, "I am he," why shouldest thou not feel all the sweetness and gracious power of his love, when he saith, "Fear not, I am he," behold I am with thee: it is I, be not afraid." Ponder, my soul, in this view also, the awful state of a soul hardened by sin. The enemies of Jesus, though they fell to the ground at his mere word, felt no change, no compunction at the display of it. Judas also was with them. Yes! he fell also ; but Satan had entered into him, and a reprobate mind marked him as the son of perdition. Oh! precious Jesus! how fully read to thy people, in every part of thy word, is the solemn truth, that grace makes all the difference between him that serveth God, and him that serveth him not. Oh! keep me, Lord, and I shall be well kept; for unto thee do I lift up my soul.

7.—He hath poured out his soul unto death.—*Isaiah* liii. 12. ,

My soul! from the garden to the cross, follow Jesus! Behold him apprehended and hurried away, both to judgment and to death. He who struck to the ground the band that came to take him, might surely, by the same breath of his mouth, have struck them to hell, and prevented his being apprehended by them. But one of the sweetest and most blessed parts of Jesus' redemption of his people, consisted in the freeness and willingness of his sacrifice. Yes! thou precious Lamb of God! no man (as thou thyself hadst before said) had power to take thy life from thee ; but thou didst lay it down of thyself: thou hadst power to lay it down, and thou hadst power to take it again. Delightful consideration to thee, my soul! Now, my soul, let this day's meditation be sacred to the view of thy Redeemer, pouring out his *soul* unto

death. And to-morrow, if the Lord gives thee to see the
morrow, let the solemn subject of thy study be the sufferings
of Jesus in his *body*. Pause, then, my soul, and call up all
the powers of thy mind to the contemplation of what the
scripture teacheth, concerning thy Redeemer's pouring out
his soul unto death. Seek the teachings of the Holy Ghost
in this solemn and mysterious subject. The original curse
pronounced on the fall, which Jesus took upon himself, and
came to do away, contained somewhat vastly great. For as
the blessing promised to obedience, *do this and thou shalt live*,
certainly meant somewhat much greater than mere animal
life, and implied sweet fellowship and communion with God;
so the curse to disobedience, *dying thou shalt die*, as plainly
intimated much more than the mere return of the body to the
dust out of which it was taken; it meant what in Scripture
(Rev. xx. 6.) is called the *second death*, meaning hell and
everlasting misery. Hence, in the recovery of our lost and
fallen nature from this awful state, when Jesus undertook the
salvation of his people, he was to sustain all that was our
due; and in the accomplishment of this, he not only died in
his body, but he poured out his soul unto death. As the
sinner's Representative, and the sinner's Surety, he bore the
whole weight and pressure of divine justice due to sin; according to what the Holy Ghost taught—"Indignation and
wrath, tribulation and anguish, upon *every soul* of man that
doeth evil." Rom. ii. 9. Not that the Redeemer needed, in
the accomplishment of this, to go down into hell to suffer the
miseries of the damned; for when the avenging wrath of God
came upon him, he endured it here. The wrath of God may
be sustained in earth as well as hell; witness the evil spirit
that is called the prince of the power of the air, Ephes. ii. 2;
for wherever the apostate angels are, they still endure divine
wrath. Hence, when the Lord Christ poured out his soul
unto death by reason of the extremity of his soul's sufferings,
and soul's travail for his redeemed, he sustained all this as
the sinner's Surety, in becoming sin and a curse, to feel and
suffer all that was the sinner's due. Oh! who shall say,
what heart shall conceive, the greatness and extensiveness of
thy sufferings, precious, precious Lamb of God? Oh! who
shall undertake fully to show the infinite suitableness of Jesus to every poor humble convinced sinner, in delivering him
from the wrath to come? Here, my soul, fix thine eyes;
here let all thy powers be employed in the unceasing contemplation, while beholding Jesus, thy Jesus, pouring out his

soul unto death ; while numbered with the transgressors, and bearing the sin of many, and making intercession for the transgressors.

8.—He humbled himself, and became obedient unto death, even the death of the cross.—*Philipp.* ii. 8.

My soul ! dost thou not feel, at every step towards Calvary, somewhat of the angel's words, when he cried "One woe is past, and behold there come two woes more hereafter !" Rev. ix. 12. Surely never was there a manifestation of the holiness of Jehovah, nor the utter detestation of God against sin, as was set forth in the crucifixion of Jesus. Would men, would angels, see what sin really is, let them go to the cross of Jesus. The casting rebellious angels out of heaven ; the curse pronounced upon the earth ; the drowning the old world by water ; the burning Sodom by fire ; nay, the millions of miseries among men, and the unquenchable fire of hell ; though all these may make the souls of the awakened exclaim against sin, yet all these are slight and inconsiderable things, compared to the wrath of God poured out upon the person of God's own Son, when he died the accursed death of the cross. My soul, take thy stand this day at the foot of the cross. Behold the Lamb of God ! There see divine justice more awfully displayed than it would have been in the everlasting ruin of all creation. And oh ! may it be thy portion, my soul, while looking unto Jesus, to say as Paul did—"I am crucified with Christ, nevertheless I live ; yet not I, but Christ liveth in me ; and the life which I now live in the flesh, I live by the faith of the Son of God, who loved me, and gave himself for me." But, my soul, while thou lookest up to Jesus hanging on the painful tree, contemplate the sufferings of the Lord Jesus in his sacred body. The death of the cross was a violent death ; for as there was no sin in Jesus, there could not have been those seeds of death, which, in all the race of Adam are found to bring forth fruit unto death. Precious thought this, even in the moment of beholding Jesus' life taken by violence. Had Jesus not died by a violent death, he would have been no sacrifice ; for that which died of itself naturally, could not by the law have been offered to God. The death of Jesus was also a cursed death ; for it is written, "Cursed is every one that hangeth on a tree." Behold, my soul, thy Lord thus lifted up as a spectacle between heaven and earth, as if cursed and despised both of God and man. The death of Jesus was a *painful* death, in which many deaths were, as it were, contained in one. The nails driven through the most feeling parts of the hands and feet, and the body stretched forth on the transverse timber, in this manner the cross, with the Lord Jesus fastened upon it, was lifted up in the air, until the bottom fell into its socket, which suddenly shook the whole and every part of his sacred body: and thus the whole weight hanging on his pierced nailed hands, the wounds in both hands and feet, by degrees, widened as he hung, until at length he expired in tortures. Precious, precious Redeemer! was it thus thou didst offer thy soul an offering for sin? Was there no method in all the stores of Omnipotency, for satisfying divine justice, but by thy holy, harmless, undefiled body dying the violent, cursed, painful death of the cross? Oh! by the crimson fountain of thy blood, which issued from thy pierced side, enable me to sit down, day by day, until I find my whole nature crucified with thee in all its affections and lusts. Let there be somewhat, dearest Lord, of an holy conformity between my Lord and me: and if Jesus died *for* sin, may my soul die *to* sin; that by mortifying the deeds of the body I may live: and by carrying about with me always the dying of the Lord Jesus, the life also of Jesus may be made manifest in my mortal body.

9.—Then said Jesus, Father, forgive them, for they know not what they do.—*Luke* xxiii. 34.

My soul! art thou still taking thy stand at the foot of the cross? Art thou still looking up to Jesus? If so, listen now to his voice. There were seven expressions of Jesus which were the last words that he uttered on the cross. The last words of dying friends are particularly regarded: how much more the last words of the best of all Friends, even the dying Friend of poor lost perishing sinners. Those which I have chosen for the portion of the day were the first; and they contain the strong cry of Jesus to his Father for forgiveness to his murderers. And what endears those expressions yet more to the heart, are, that they are not only the first upon the cross, but they are wholly, not for himself, but the people. During the whole painful process of suffering, when they scourged him, crowned him with thorns, smote him with their hands, and mocked him, we hear no voice of complaint. "He was led as a lamb to the slaughter, and as a sheep be-

fore her snearers is dumb, so he opened not his mouth."
Precious, meek Lamb of God! But now, when lifted up on
the cross, Jesus broke silence, and cried out, " Father, forgive them, for they know not what they do." Pause, my
soul! Look again at the cross. Was not Jesus now entered
upon his high-priest's office? Was not the cross as the altar
from whence the sacrifice was offered? Was not Jesus himself the Sacrifice? And was not Jesus the Sacrificer? Might
not the pale, the dying, whitened visage of Jesus, be compared to the white ephod of the high-priest; the streaming
blood, flowing over his sacred body from the several wounds,
as the incense of his censer; and the dying sweat of his holy
frame, like the smoke ascending with the sweetest savour before God? As the arms of Jesus when he thus prayed, were
stretched forth on the cross, so the high-priest spread forth
his hands, when burning the incense for sacrifice, in pleading
for the people. Hail, thou glorious High-Priest! in this the
humblest moment, and the most powerful of thine intercession.
Surely every wound of thine, every look, every feature, every
groan, pleaded with open mouth this gracious intercession for
forgiveness of sinners. Lord; was I not included in the
prayer? Was not the eye of Jesus upon me in the moment
of this all-prevailing advocacy? Oh! ye, of every description and character, that still sit unconcerned and unmoved at
this cry of the Son of God, is it nothing to you, all ye that
pass by? Think, my poor unawakened brother, how justly
that voice might have been heard for all the enemies of Jesus
—" Depart from me, ye cursed ;" when the tender language
of Jesus was, " Father, forgive them, for they know not what
they do." And think, moreover, that the same gracious
voice is still heard in heaven, and of the same blessed force
and efficacy as ever; for while our sins are calling for judgment, the blood of Jesus calls louder for mercy. Dear Lord!
let this first cry of thine upon the cross, be the first and last
of all my thoughts under every exercise and temptation of
sin and Satan—" Father, forgive them, for they know not
what they do."

10.—When Jesus therefore saw his mother and the disciple standing by
    whom he loved, he saith unto his mother, Woman, behold thy Son.
    Then saith he to the disciple, Behold thy mother.—*John* xix. 26, 27.

THIS was the second among the dying words of the Lord
Jesus; and, no doubt, of high importance in their full sense

and meaning: not simply to recommend Mary to the care of the beloved Apostle John, but probably of greater moment in reference to the church of Jesus at large. My soul; is it not very certain that the Lord Jesus knew all the events which would take place in all generations of his people? And, as such, did not Jesus perfectly well know also that the time would come when divine honours would be offered to Mary? These points cannot be disputed. Well, then, is it not worthy the closest observation, that Jesus, both in this place and upon all other occasions, when speaking of Mary, called her woman? Why so? if as Jesus knew that there would be some who would pray to her, and call her Mother of God, by which name the Holy Ghost never distinguished her, neither the Lord Jesus himself; could there have been a more decided method adopted than this to discountenance such idolatry, than when Jesus, in his dying moments, called Mary only woman? Besides, was it not on another account, that as Jesus was to be the seed of the woman which was promised to bruise the serpent's head, such a dying testimony might serve instead of a thousand witnesses in proof of the confirmation of the fact: and Mary's song might be the song of thousands—" My soul doth magnify the Lord, and my spirit hath rejoiced in God *my Saviour.*" But when we have thus attended to the second cry of Christ upon the cross in reference to those sweet points, do thou my soul remember also how tenderly those expressions of thy Lord recommend all the endearing affections of love and regard through all the members of Christ's mystical body. To behold our mother, or to behold our sons, are only different expressions to intimate that all true believers in Jesus are members of one another and of his body, his flesh, and his bones? And as it was by our Lord himself in this life, so is it with all his redeemed, both in this life and in that which is to come; they who do the will of his Father, which is in heaven, the same are Christ's brethren, and sisters, and mother.

11.—And Jesus said unto him, Verily I say unto thee, to-day shalt thou be with me in paradise.—*Luke* xxiii. 43.

My soul! hear the gracious words of thy Jesus. This was the *third* cry of the Redeemer on the cross. And oh! how full of grace, rich, free, unmerited, unexpected, unlooked-for grace, to a poor, lost, perishing sinner, even in the very moment of death. Let the self-righteous pharisee behold this example of redeeming love, and wonder, and be confounded. Surely no one will venture to suppose that this man's good works were any recommendation, when the poor wretch was dying under the hands of justice. What was it then that saved him but the complete salvation of Jesus? The Son of God was offering his soul on the cross a sacrifice for sin, and, being between two notorious sinners, gave a rich display of the sovereignty of his grace and his love to poor sinners; and, in confirmation, snatched this one as a brand from the burning—took him from the very jaws of hell, and that very day led him in triumph to heaven, thereby manifesting to every poor sinner in whose heart he puts the cry for mercy, that that cry shall never be put forth in vain. And mark, my soul, how powerfully the grace of the Lord Jesus wrought upon this man. He and his companion both knew that before night they would both be in eternity. The thought affected neither: they joined the rabble in insulting Jesus. Save thyself, and us, was the language of the heart of both, until the grace of Jesus wrought on this man's mind, and changed the reviler into an humble suitor. What could there be in Jesus thus to affect him? Jesus hung upon the cross like a poor Jew. Jesus had been always poor, and never more so than now. And yet, in the midst of all these surrounding circumstances, such a ray of light broke in upon this man's mind, that he saw Jesus in all his glory and power, acknowledged him for a King, when all the disciples had forsook him and fled, and prayed to be remembered by him when he came into his kingdom. Precious Lamb of God! bestow upon me such a portion of thy grace as, under all the unpromising circumstances around, may call forth the like conviction of thy power and my need. And oh! that this pattern of mercy might be reviewed by thousands of poor perishing, dying sinners. Methinks I would have it proclaimed through all the public places of resort, through all the haunts of licentiousness, among the numberless scenes of hardened sinners who fear that they have sinned beyond the possibility of forgiveness. Oh! look at this example of Jesus' love, ye that are going down to the grave full of sin and despair; behold the thief, behold the Saviour! And oh! for a cry of grace like that of the dying malefactor— "Lord, remember me when thou comest into thy kingdom;" and Jesus' gracious answer—"To-day shalt thou be with me in paradise."

12.—And about the ninth hour, Jesus cried with a loud voice, saying Eli, Eli, lama sabachthani? that is to say, My God, my God, why hast thou forsaken me?—*Matt.* xxvii. 46.

MARK, my soul! Jesus had hung upon the cross now for six hours. Think what agonies he sustained both in soul and body. The fury of hell had broke out upon him, and in the cruelties of the men around him, exercised upon his sacred person, manifested how extensive that fury was. But had this been all, had God the Father smiled upon him, had the cup of trembling been taken away, some alleviation would have taken place in Jesus' sufferings; but so far was this from being the case, that the heaviest load of sorrow his holy soul sustained, was the wrath of the Father due to sin, as the sinner's Surety. Angels, no doubt, looked on. All heaven stood amazed. And, at length, overpowered with the fulness of sorrow and anguish of soul, the dying Lamb cried out, " My God, my God, why hast thou forsaken me?" Pause, my soul, while thou hearest in the ear of faith, still vibrating in the air, the dolorous cry, and conceive, if it be possible, what the holy, harmless, undefiled Jesus felt, when such expressions of exquisite terror and distress were forced from his dying lips. What forsaking of Jesus was this by God his Father? Not the dissolving of the union between them: not the withdrawing the arm of his strength; for Jesus still calls him, "Eli, Eli," that is, my strong one: not that he left him to himself; neither that his love for Jesus was lessened: but it was the withdrawing or withholding those sweet manifestations whereby he had sustained the human nature of Jesus through the whole of his incarnation. It was beholding Jesus in this solemn season as the sinner's Surety; and, as such, it was a punishing desertion, implying that, as Jesus stood, or rather hung, with all the burden of our sin, he was so deserted for that time as we, out of Jesus, deserve to be forsaken for ever. The cry of Jesus, the shriek of his precious soul, under this desertion, represented the everlasting shrieks of them that are cast out of God's gracious presence to all eternity. Here pause again, my soul. And wouldest thou have howled in this endless, pitiable cry for ever, had not Jesus uttered it for thee once? And art thou, by virtue of it, saved from this wrath to come? Hath Jesus both borne thy sins, carried thy sorrows, and been forsaken of his Father, that thou mightest enjoy his presence and favour for ever? My soul, what wilt thou render to the Lord for all his benefits? Wilt thou not take the cup of salvation and

9

call upon the name of the Lord now thy Jesus hath for thee
taken the cup of trembling, and drank all the dregs of it?
Precious, precious Redeemer! may I never, never lose sight
of thee in this part of thy sufferings also; and especially eye
thee still more when my soul is under the hidings of God's
countenance.   Let me recollect, dearest Lord! that thou hast
been forsaken *before* thy people and *for* thy people; and here,
as in all other instances, thou hast the pre-eminence, so as to
sanctify even our momentary desertions to our good and to
thy glory.   Yes, precious Lord! such are the blessed effects
of thy desertion, that hence my soul learns, my God still sup-
ports, though my God may withhold his comforts.   Jesus
was forsaken for ever.   And grant me, dearest Lord! from
thy bright example, to cast myself wholly upon thee, as thou
didst upon thy Father, when all sensible comforts fail, convinced that thou art the strength of my heart and my portion
for ever!

13.—After this Jesus, knowing that all things were now accomplished,
that the Scriptures might be fulfilled, saith, I thirst.—*John* xix. 28.

AFTER this, that is, I conceive, (though I do not presume to
mark the very order in which the Lord Jesus uttered his
loud cries upon the cross,) after his complaint of desertion:
for whether this was the *fourth* or the *fifth* of the seven last
words of the Redeemer, I dare not determine; yet the words
themselves were highly important, and significant of great
things, in reference to Jesus and his people.   Jesus thus cried
that the scriptures might be fulfilled, it is said; for it had been
prophesied of him, that gall was given him to eat—and, when
thirsty, vinegar to drink, Psalm lxix. 21.   And the soldiers,
unconscious what they did of fulfilling this very prophecy,
gave him spunge dipped in vinegar.   But, my soul, was it
the thirst of the body thy Jesus complained of?   I think not.
He had before declared, at his last supper, that he would
drink no more of the fruit of the vine, until the day he drank
it new in the kingdom of his Father.   What could be then
the thirst of Jesus, but the thirst of his soul for the accomplishment of redemption *for* his people, and the accomplishment of
redemption *in* his people.   He thirsted with an holy vehement thirst for the everlasting salvation of his ransomed, and
seemed to anticipate the hour, by this expression, when he
should see the travail of his soul, and be satisfied.   But did
not Jesus also in this hour, as bearing the curse and wrath

of God for sin, thirst in soul with that kind of thirst which, in hell, those who bear the everlasting torments of condemnation feel, when they are under an everlasting thirst which admits of no relief? That representation the Lord Jesus gives of this state, in the parable of the rich man's thirst, serves to afford a lively but alarming view of such superlative misery. Oh! that those who now add drunkenness to thirst, would seriously lay this to heart. Did God suffer his dear Son, to whom sin was but transferred, and not committed by him— did he suffer him to cry out under this thirst; and what may we suppose will be the everlasting cry of such as not only merit his wrath for sin, but merit yet more, his everlasting wrath for refusing redemption by Jesus, who thirsted on the cross to redeem sinners from endless thirsting in despair and misery? My soul! did Jesus thirst for thee? Were his dying lips parched, and his soul made deeply athirst for thy salvation? And shall not this thirst of thy Redeemer kindle an holy thirst in thee for him, and his love, and his great salvation? Wilt thou not now this morning, anew, look up by faith to the cross, and to the throne, and catch the flame of love from his holy, loving, longing, languishing eyes, unti-all thy powers go forth in vehement desires, like him of old, crying out—" As the hart thirsteth for the water-brooks, so longeth my soul after thee, O God. Let him kiss me with the kisses of his mouth; for thy love is better than wine."

14.—When Jesus therefore had received the vinegar, he said, It is finished.—*John* xix. 30.

PERHAPS these words formed the *sixth* cry of the Lord Jesus on the cross. The glorious close of all his sufferings was now arrived; and, full of these high ideas which occupied his holy mind, he cried out, " It is finished." What is finished? Redemption work is finished. All the long series of prophesies, visions, types, and the shadow of the good things to come, which pointed to Jesus, and redemption by him, were now finished in their accomplishment. The law was finished in its condemning power; and the gospel commenced its saving influence. Jesus, by that one sacrifice now offered, had for ever perfected them that were sanctified. The separation between Jew and Gentile was now finished, and done away for ever. Jesus had now gathered together in one all the children of God which were scattered abroad. The iron reign of sin and Satan, of death and hell, were now broken in pieces by this Stone cut out of the mountain without hands; and life and immortality, pardon, mercy, and peace, were brought to light, and secured to the faithful, by this finished redemption of the Lord Jesus Christ. The peace, the love, the favour of God the Father, was now manifested, and that spiritual kingdom of the Lord Jesus, which shall have no end, was from this moment set up in the hearts and minds of his people. The sure descent of the Holy Ghost was now confirmed; and the Lord Jesus already, by anticipation, beheld his Israel of old, and his Gentile church, as well as Ethiopia and the multitude of the isles, stretching forth their hands unto God. With these and the like glorious prospects the mind of Jesus was filled; and having received the vinegar, as the last prophecy remaining then to be completed, he cried out, " It is finished." My soul! never let these precious, precious words of Jesus depart from thy mind. Do by them as Moses commanded Israel concerning the words he gave them; let them be in thy heart and in thy soul: bind them as a sign upon thine hand, and let them be as frontlets between thine eyes. Tell thy God and Father what thy Jesus has told thee—" It is finished." He hath finished redemption *for* thee; and He will finish redemption *in* thee. He hath destroyed death, hath satisfied and glorified the law, taken away the curse, made full restitution for sin, brought in an everlasting righteousness, and opened the glorious mansions of the blessed as the home and rest of all his people. Oh! my soul, let these dying words of thy Jesus be made by thee as an answer to all thy prayers, and begin that song to the Lamb, which, ere long thou wilt fully and loudly sing among the church above—Worthy is the Lamb that was slain; for thou wast slain, and has redeemed us to God by thy blood.

15.—And when Jesus had cried with a loud voice, he said, Father, into thy hands I commend my spirit; and having thus said, he gave up the Ghost.—*Luke* xxiii. 46.

My soul! ponder well these last of the last seven words of thy God and Saviour, which he uttered on the cross; for surely they are most sweet and precious, and highly interesting, both on thy Saviour's account and thine own. And first remark the *manner* in which the Lord Jesus thus breathed out his soul: not like a man spent and exhausted, after hanging so many hours on the cross, faint with loss of blood, and

such agonies of soul as never one before endured ; but it was
with a loud voice, thereby proving what he had before declared—" No man taketh my life from me ; I have power to
lay it down ; I have power to take it again." Precious Jesus !
how sweet this assurance to thy people. But wherefore cry
with a loud voice ? A whisper, nay, a thought of the soul
only, if with an eye of communication to God the Father,
would have been sufficient, if this had been all that was intended.   Wherefore then did Jesus cry with a loud voice ?
Was it not that all in heaven, and all in hell, might hear ?
Did not angels shout at the cry ?   Did not the spirits of just
men made perfect among the faithful gone to glory in Jesus'
name, hear and sing aloud ?   Did not all hell tremble when
Jesus thus cried aloud, conscious that the keys of the grave,
and death, and hell, were now put into his Almighty hand ?
Oh, precious, precious Jesus ! was this among thy gracious
designs for which, when thou wert retiring from the bloody
field of battle, as a conquerer, thy loud voice shouted Victory ?
And was there not another sweet and gracious design in this
loud cry, oh thou blessed Jesus ?   Didst thou not intend
thereby that poor sinners, unto the ends of the earth, might,
by faith, hear, and believe to the salvation of their souls ?
Didst thou not, dearest Lord ! when bowing thy sacred head,
as if to take a parting look of the disciple and the Marys, at
the foot of the cross, and beholding them as the representa-
tives of all the members of thy mystical body, didst cry with
a loud voice, that all with them might behold thy triumphs,
and rejoice in thee their glorious Head ?   Yes, Lamb of
God ! we adore thee in this glorious act ; for we do accept it
as it really is, the act of our one glorious Head. In this solemn committing of thy Spirit to the Father, we consider our
spirits also as committed with thee, and by thee. My soul !
mark this down carefully in the inmost tablet of thine heart.
In all this, blessed Jesus ! thou wert, and art, our Head.
Thou didst, to all intents and purposes, take every individual
believer of thine as a part of thyself, and by this act didst
commit, with thyself, the whole into thy Father's hands, to
be kept until the hour of their dropping their bodies, then to
be united to thee for ever.   Oh ! precious Jesus ! oh precious
mercy of our Jesus, how safe, how eternally safe and secure,
are all thy redeemed !   Well might thine Apostle say, " No
man liveth to himself, and no man dieth to himself ; for in
Jesus his people ever live, and in Jesus they securely die."
Henceforth, dear Lord ! let me know myself to be already
9*

committed with thee, and by thee, into the hands of my God
and Father in Jesus, and when the hour cometh that the cas-
ket, in which that precious jewel, my soul, now dwells, is
opened for the soul to take her departure, oh then for faith,
for lively, active, earnest faith, to follow the example and to
adopt the very language, of my God and Saviour, and to
cry out—Lord Jesus, into thy hands I commend my spirit ;
for thou hast redeemed me, O Lord, thou God of truth !

16.—There laid they Jesus.—*John* xix. 42.

My soul ! it is usual for the relations and friends of those
that are deceased to attend the funeral. Art thou a friend, a
relation of Jesus ? Oh ! yes ; I trust thou art. He was, and
is, the dearest of all friends, the nearest of all relations. He
is at once all and every one—the Father, the Husband, the
Brother. The invitation is therefore sent to thee, personally
to *thee*. Every voice of affection calls thee to the tomb of
Jesus, saying, " Come, see the place where the Lord lay."
And if, like Mary Magdalene, from more abundant love, thou
art asking, " Where have they laid him ?"—the answer immediately is returned, Come and see. Yes, thou dear Redeemer ! by that faith thou hast graciously given me, I will
come and see. Let my faith take wing, and light down in
Joseph of Arimathea's garden, and behold the place where
the Lord lay. Was this the memorable spot ? Did Jesus lay
here ? Did he here make (according to the ancient prophecy
foretold of him) his grave with the wicked and with the rich
in his death, because he had done no violence, neither was
any deceit in his mouth ? Here let me look ; here let my
soul wander in contemplation ! Oh ! what a marvellous
sight to behold Jesus thus lain in the grave ! Surely we may
cry out, as the church did in the view, " My beloved is white
and ruddy." Never did death so triumph before. Never
did the grave receive and hold such a prisoner. But, my
soul, behold also, in the view, how Jesus triumphed even in
death. It was through death he destroyed him that had the
power of death—that is, the devil, that he might deliver them
who, through fear of death, are all their life-time subject to
bondage. And what saith Jesus to my soul from the grave ?
Fear not, I have the keys of death and the grave : fear not
to go down to the Egypt of the grave ; I will go with thee,
and will surely bring thee up again from thence. And observe, my soul, as the grave could not detain thy Lord, thine

Head, a prisoner ; so neither can the grave beyond the appointed time, detain any of his members. And as the union between the Godhead and the manhood in Jesus was not broken off by death, so neither can the union between Jesus and his people be interrupted by death. The covenant of redemption, the union of Jesus with his people, the love of God in Christ to the souls and bodies of his redeemed, all these rot not in the grave : nay, where sin is taken out, the very enmity of the grave is slain : and though it acts as a devourer of our corrupt bodies, yet it acts as a preserver also of the refined part, that the dust and ashes of his saints Jesus may visit, and manifest his care over from day to day. Precious Lord ! here then, as in every thing, thou hast the pre-eminence. Thou hast gone before : thou hast sweetly perfumed the grave by having lain there. And where should the dying members be but where their living Head hath been before ? Hence, then, my soul, take comfort, and fear not when thy partner the body is called upon to go down to the grave. When the soul flies to Jesus in heaven, the body will sweetly rest in Jesus till summoned from the grave. Thy God, thy Jesus, hath the appointment for thy departure ; both the place where, the time when, and the manner how, are all with him. He hath the keys both to open the door of death, and to open the kingdom of heaven. Leave all then with him. Frequently, by faith, visit his sepulchre, and behold where they laid him. And in the triumphs of thy Jesus, as thine head, already take part, as a member of his body, crying out with the Apostle, " O death, where is thy sting ; O grave, where is thy victory ? God be praised who giveth us the victory, through our Lord Jesus Christ."

17.—The Lord is risen indeed.—*Luke* xxiv. 34.

LET thy meditations, my soul, this morning be sweetly exercised upon thy risen and exalted Saviour. For if thy Lord be indeed risen, then will it undeniably follow, that as he died for our sins, so he arose for our justification, and is thereby become the first fruits of them that sleep. Beg of God the Holy Ghost to lead thee into the devout contemplation and enjoyment of this soul-reviving subject. Trace the testimonies of this wonderful event, until, from being overpowered in the vast assemblage of witnesses, thou art prompted to cry out in the same language, " The Lord is risen indeed." And surely never was there any one fact so fully, so clearly, and so circumstantially confirmed. It hath the united testimony of heaven and earth; of angels and men; of the living and the dead; of friends and foes; and God himself confirming it in the midst of his people, by sending down the Holy Ghost agreeably to the promise of Jesus at the day of Pentecost. Review these things in order. *First*, heaven gave in its evidence in those supernatural signs, which issued in the morning of Jesus' resurrection; for we are told that an angel descended from heaven, and rolled back the stone from the door of Jesus' sepulchre, and sat upon it. And, *secondly*, earth gave her testimony also to the same, by the convulsions sustained at his approach—there was a great earthquake. And then again, as angels came to inform the pious women who waited to embalm the sacred body of Christ, that Jesus was risen; so the testimony of multitudes among men gave equal attestation to this glorious truth. For beside the many separate and distinct appearances Jesus made to numbers, he appeared to above five hundred brethren at once, by way of confirming the undoubted fact. The *living*, who ate and drank with him after he arose from the dead, surely could not be mistaken. And the *dead*, which arose from their graves, as if to celebrate the glories of his resurrection, in which they took part, came forth, when the sepulchres yawned at the triumph of Jesus, and went into the holy city and appeared unto many. And not only the friends of Jesus, but the foes of Jesus, became undesignedly the witnesses of this great truth: for by attributing his resurrection to the disciples' stealing away his body, they positively prove that the body of Christ remained not in the sepulchre. And that the poor timid disciples, whose meetings were all in secret, for fear of the Jews, should project such a scheme as to take away the body, which the Roman soldiers were purposely placed to secure, is not to be equalled in folly in the very idea, unless by that other part of the childish story, that the body was stolen while the guard slept; and so the testimony, it should seem, to this tale, is the testimony of men sleeping! Here, then, my soul, in devout contemplation, take thy stand at the door of the sepulchre of thy Jesus, and ponder over such a multitude of witnesses who all cry out, with one voice, as the angels did to the astonished women, "He is not here; for he is risen, as he said. Come, see the place where the Lord lay." And oh! thou dear Redeemer! do thou, while my soul is pondering these things, do thou draw nigh, as thou didst to thy disciples on the morning of thy resurrection,

and sweetly commune with me of all these blessed truths
concerning thyself; lead me, by faith, through all the precious subject, from the sepulchre to thine house of prayer, to
the ordinance and thy table, from thy cross to thy crown;
and cause my whole heart to burn within me, while thou art
talking to me by the way, and while thou art opening to me
the Scriptures. Then shall I truly rejoice that my Lord is
indeed risen from the dead, and my soul is risen with him,
from dead works to serve thee the living and true God.

18.—And declared to be the Son of God with power; according to the
Spirit of Holiness, by the resurrection from the dead.—*Romans* i. 4.

Do not, my soul, hastily pass away from this most precious subject of thy Lord's resurrection. It is an inexhaustible
theme, and will be among thy felicities in eternity. Yesterday, thou didst but barely consider the fact. Let this day
occupy thy thoughts on another sweet portion of it, in beholding how Jesus effected it by his own power and Godhead. He had said before, that he had power to lay down
his life, and power to take it again. And he had told the
Jews to destroy the temple, by which he meant the temple of
his body, and he would raise it again in three days. He had
proclaimed himself to be the resurrection and the life: and
here he proved it, when he was declared to be the Son of
God with power; according to the Spirit of holiness, by his
resurrection from the dead. Now, then, pause over this glorious view of Him who was thus proved to be one with the
Father, and who, at the same time, was one in thy nature,
bone of thy bone, and flesh of thy flesh. Beautiful and comprehensive is the expression : declared to be the Son of God;
for who but God could accomplish such an event? And by
the Spirit of holiness he was equally declared to be not liable
to corruption; for, as God's Holy One, it was impossible that
his flesh should see corruption. Psalm xvi. 10. And the
Holy Ghost again, by Peter the Apostle, explains it when he
saith, " Christ was put to death in the flesh, but quickened in
the Spirit." 1 Pet. iii. 18. The flesh here means his human
nature; and the quickening by the Spirit (being what is
called the antithesis, that is, the opposite to flesh) means his
own Spirit, his own power and Godhead; similar to what is
said in the Hebrews concerning the offering of Jesus, that
through the Eternal Spirit he offered *himself*, Heb. ix. 14.—
meaning, that his Godhead gave dignity and value to the

offering of his body for the sins of his people. Ponder this blessed truth, my soul ; for it is most blessed, and of much greater importance than at the first view of the words, it may strike you. Behold in it, that it was the Godhead of Jesus by which thy Jesus triumphed over death and the grave. The Father's hand was in it most certain, as it was in all the other acts of redemption ; for the Holy Ghost taught the church, by Paul, that God had raised up the Lord. 1 Cor. vi. 14. And manifested by this, saith the Holy Ghost, that he was the God of Peace, in bringing again from the dead the Lord Jesus Christ. Heb. xiii. 20. And the Holy Ghost had his almighty hand in the same ; for it is the Spirit that quickeneth ; and hence Christ is said to have been justified in the Spirit. 1 Tim. iii. 16. But while we are taught by these Scriptures, and others to the same purport, to behold both the Father and the Holy Ghost acting in the resurrection of Jesus—by this, and others of the same kind, we are taught to view the Godhead in Christ as the cause of his resurrection. For if Jesus had been raised by the power of the Father and the Holy Ghost only, how would he have been declared to be the Son of God by his resurrection ? For, in this case, nothing more would have been manifested in his resurrection than in the resurrection of others ; for it is by the power of God that the dead are to be raised. Hence, my soul, behold the vast importance of this great point in the resurrection of thy Lord : and never lose sight of this blessed truth, that thy Jesus, who is thy resurrection and thy life, arose himself by this self-quickening principle. Behold, in this point of view, what a glorious truth is the resurrection of Jesus. And what a lovely promise did the Lord, by the Prophet, give to all the people of God concerning this, ages before this glorious event took place—" Thy dead men shall live ; together with my dead body shall they arise. Awake and sing, ye that dwell in the dust ; for thy dew is as the dew of herbs, and the earth shall cast out her dead." Isaiah xxvi. 19.

19.—Who was delivered for our offences, and raised again for our justification.—*Romans* vi. 25.

My soul, thou must not yet dismiss—no, nor ever dismiss, the sweet and precious subject of thy Lord's resurrection. One part of it thou hast not yet scarce glanced at ; and yet it is such a one as thine everlasting safety, and thy justification before God, depends upon. "For," as the Holy Ghost hath said, by the mouth of his servant, the Apostle, "if Christ be not risen, then are believers yet in their sins." 1 Cor. 15, 17. See to it then, my soul, that what this sweet Scripture of the morning saith be true, that Jesus was delivered for thine offences, and was raised again for thy justification. While Jesus was on the cross, and when Jesus was taken down and laid in the grave, the payment and the ransom for sin was then discharging. Jesus was then truly delivered for our offences. And when he arose from the dead, then the poor sinner, for whom he was delivered, and for whom he died, was truly justified before God ; for thereby proof was made that the debt was paid, the receipt given, and God, in confirmation of it, styled himself by a new name, even the God of Peace, in bringing again from the dead, our Lord Jesus Christ, as the great Shepherd of his sheep, through the blood of the everlasting covenant. Hence the resurrection of Jesus was like going into the presence of God to cancel the bond, the hand-writing of ordinances, that was against us. It was as if Jesus gave this testimony in his glorious resurrection, that both sin and death had now lost their retaining power ; the dominion of both were for ever done away, and all true believers in Christ might join the Apostle's song—"Who shall lay any thing to the charge of God's elect ? It is God that justifieth ; who is he that condemneth ? It is Christ that died—yea rather, that is risen again, who is even at the right hand of God, who also maketh intercession for us." My soul, be sure to keep this in constant view, when, at any time, thou art meditating on the death and resurrection of Jesus : and let both be thy daily meditation. Think how truly blessed, how truly happy, how present, and everlastingly secure, must those souls be who are interested in the death and in the resurrection of the Lord Jesus. By the one he hath purchased their pardon, and by the other, he had justified their persons ; so that, when law and justice present their charge against them, this is the unanswerable plea,—Jesus was delivered for our offences, and raised again for our justification. Oh! dearest Lord! grant me daily and hourly to be bringing into all my spiritual enjoyments the sweet sense and consciousness of being thus interested, justified, and secured. Give me a present right and title, that I may live upon it ; and by and by, when thou shalt call me home, then, O Lord, present me finally and fully, once for all, as made comely in thy comeliness, clothed in thy righteousness, and fully prepared, both in soul and body, for everlasting happiness and glory among them that are sanctified.

20.—Now is Christ risen from the dead, and become the first fruits of them that slept —1 *Cor.* xv. 20.

ONE view more, my soul, while thou art meditating upon this delightful subject of thy Redeemer's triumph over death and the grave, and now look at Jesus' resurrection as a sure pledge and confirmation of thine own. Did Jesus' holy body arise? Then so shalt thine, sinful and polluted as it now is, but then made a glorified body by virtue of thy union with him. For so saith the Holy Ghost, by his servant the Apostle, "He shall change our vile body, that it may be fashioned like unto his glorious body. For if the Spirit of him that raised up Jesus from the dead, dwell in you, he that raised up Christ from the dead, shall also quicken your mortal bodies by his Spirit that dwelleth in you." Phil. iii. 21. Rom. viii. 11. Pause then, my soul, and rejoice in this glorious and transporting doctrine. As sure as Jesus arose, so sure shall all his people : for Jesus arose as the first fruits. Jesus arose, not as a private person, but as the public head. Never call to mind the resurrection of Jesus, but be sure to connect always with it this blessed view of the subject—every redeemed believer is part of Christ's body. And as we are by nature part of the first Adam, and die, from our union and connexion, and being of the same nature with him ; so, by grace, being part of Christ's mystical body, who is called in Scripture, particularly on this account, the second Adam, his people are interested in all that concerns him, and because he liveth, they must live also. Hence he is called the first fruits, the first born from the dead. And as all the after fruits of the harvest follow the first fruits ; so the saints, born again of God, follow the first born from the dead to glory. Oh! heart-reviving subject! The eyes that now read these lines, and the hand that now writes them, if a part of Christ's mystical body by regeneration, must assuredly be a part in the resurrection. In the eye of the law, they are one. Jesus is the head of his body the Church : and how incomplete in glory would be that glorious head without the whole and every individual member of his fair one, his spouse, which he hath betrothed to himself for ever. Shout then, my soul! and shout aloud, and say with Job— "Though after my skin, worms destroy this body, yet in my flesh shall I see God." My flesh shall moulder indeed in the dust, and see corruption. And so would I have it to be. Vile and polluted as it now is, and fighting as it now doth against my soul's desires and affections, methinks, I would not, if it were possible, take it with me to heaven as it now is. But when Jesus shall change this vile body, and have fashioned it like unto his glorious body, then it will be without spot or wrinkle, or any such thing ; and then soul and body united together in love, and both united to the Lord, will form one united object to praise and glorify God, Father, Son, and Holy Ghost, to all eternity ! My soul, dwell upon these things; give thyself wholly to them ; and as thou believest that Jesus died and rose again, so equally believe also, that all they that sleep in Jesus will God bring with him. For this the Apostle had in commission from the Lord, to tell all true believers that when Jesus shall descend from heaven, with a shout, with the voice of the archangel, and with the trump of God, the dead in Christ shall arise ; and then they which remain unto the coming of the Lord, shall be caught up together with them to meet the Lord in the air, and so shall they ever be with the Lord. Oh! for grace to comfort one another with these words.

21.—The glory which thou gavest me I have given them, that they may be one, even as we are one.—*John* xviii. 22.

THOSE are sweet views of Jesus which point to our oneness and union with him, by which alone we derive an interest in him, and are made partakers both in his grace and glory. By virtue of this it is, that the glory the Father gave Jesus, as Mediator, all his people are interested in, and truly enjoy. For though, like the heir of the kingdom, when an infant, the babe is unconscious of his dignity, yet is not the less entitled to his high birth and rank ; so the seed of Jesus, while in this childhood of existence, though they do not live up to their high privileges through the weakness of their faith, yet their claim in Jesus is not the less. Jesus hath given them the glory of being brought within the covenant; the glory of redemption ; the glory of the Holy Ghost's gifts and influences ; and, in short, all the glory which a state of grace implies, and which is the earnest of the future fulness of glory. And, my soul! dost thou ever pause over this account of present glory as if thou didst now truly know thine interest in and enjoyment of it? Look at it only under these *two* considerations, and then bow down under a sense of it in the dust before God. In the first, put forth thy utmost faculties to calculate that glory which, if thou art one of Jesus' redeemed people, thou now truly hast in having union with Christ! Who shall undertake to describe that glory imparted to a poor worm of the earth, who is brought into union with God's dear Son? Paul speaks of it as an high privilege, when he said, " Ye are come to an innumerable company of angels." But what is the society of angels, compared to an union with Jesus? Moreover, angels have no such privilege: for while Jesus is to them their Lord and Sovereign, and governs them by his supreme command, yet is he not to them as he is to his church, the glorious head of that church, which is his body, and by which he perpetually communicates to all his members a source of gracious and glorious influences, according to what he hath said, " Because I live, ye shall live also." Hence what the Redeemer said to the Father is explained on this sure testimony —" The glory thou gavest me I have given them, that they may be one, even as we are one." Look at the subject under *another* consideration. Hath not Jesus given present glory to all his redeemed in that communication which is perpetually passing and repassing between him and them, by virtue of this oneness, and unity, and interest, into which they are actually brought? My soul! what saith thine experience to this precious truth? Dost thou really and truly partake of what is Jesus'; and doth he not really and truly partake of what is thine? Is there not an exchange, a barter, a fellowship, carried on between thy glorious head and thyself? Surely thou hast communion in whatever belongs to Christ as Mediator, in his righteousness, in his grace, his redemption, his glory. And doth not Jesus manifest continual tokens that he takes part in all that concerns thee; thy sorrows, thy wants, thine afflictions? Was it not said of him, ages before his incarnation, when speaking of his people, "in all their affliction he was afflicted?" And is it not said now, that whosoever toucheth his people, touched the apple of his eye? Oh! unparalleled grace! Oh! matchless love! that the Son of God should thus manifest his affection. What will you call this, my soul, but what thy God and Saviour hath called it—the glory which the Father gave him he hath given to his people? And all this on purpose to prove that they are one with him. Hallelujah!

22.—Wheresoever the carcase is, there will the eagles be gathered together.—*Matt.* xxiv. 28.

MY soul! these are the words of Jesus, none of which should be suffered to fall to the ground. No doubt much instruction is contained in this passage. An eagle is a bird of prey: and Job saith that the eagle hasteth to the prey as the swift ships. Job ix. 26. In all birds of prey there is great sagacity, a vast quickness of scent to smell their proper food afar off; and thus natural instinct, added to a rapacious appetite, compels those creatures to fly swift to their prey, and to devour the carcase. Is there nothing in all this that suits thee, my soul? Oh! yes. If Jesus hath given thee a real principle of life in himself, which becomes a spiritual quickening from day to day, and from one hour to another, thy hungering and thirsting for Jesus will be as earnest and as importunate as the instinct of nature in those birds for daily food. Pause, my soul, and say—is it so? Dost thou seek after Jesus in his ordinances, in his word, in retirement, in meditation, in prayer, in providences, and, in short, in all the various ways by which thou mayest enjoy him, as a famished bird would hasten to its prey? If Jesus be indeed the one blessed object of thy desire, will not this be manifested by the earnestness of thy desires? Did David long for the waters of Bethlehem when thirsty? Did he declare, that as the hart panted for the water-brooks, so he longed for the enjoyment of God? Here then, my soul, mayest thou learn how to estimate the real standard of thy affections to thy Jesus. Oh! for grace to have the soul exercised day and night, and never, never to give over those longings, like pregnant women, until the full desires of the soul in Jesus, and upon Jesus, be fully gratified. Methinks, as the eagles gather together unto the carcase, so should believers be found feasting upon Jesus. In Jesus, and his glorious excellencies, every thing is suited to the wants of the believer: his name, his person, his work, his blood, his righteousness; every perfection, every promise, every experience we have had in him, in times past, becomes food to the soul. So that the spiritual cravings of the soul, when the soul is in health and strength, like the natural cravings of the bird of prey, act like the same instinct to lead to and to feed upon Jesus. See then, my soul, whether this morning thou art risen with a keen appetite for Jesus. Surely thou hast tasted that the Lord is gracious in times past. And if thou art in health of soul, wilt thou not as much hunger again for

this heavenly food, as the body of an healthy man craves for
his morning meal?   Oh! blessed Lord! give me this appetite.   Excite an hungering in me for thee.   Let it be for
thyself; not for thy gifts only, not for thy graces only, sweet
as these are ; but, blessed Jesus, let it be for thyself.   And let
this desire be continual ; every day, and all the day.   And
let it be wholly to thee, in all that belongs to thee : I mean,
after every thing in Jesus ; thy cross, if needful, as well as
thy crown ; a love to thy precepts as well as thy promises.
And oh ! let this desire be so insatiable, so earnest, so unceasing, that nothing I have of thee may so satisfy me that I
should long no more after thee ; but, rather, provoke my
soul's appetite, and tend but to inflame my heart in longings
more and more, till, from tasting of thee here below, thou
bringest me to the fountain-head of enjoyment above, where
my longing eyes and longing soul shall feast upon Jesus and
his love for ever and ever.   Amen.

23.—For to this end Christ both died, and rose, and revived, that he
    might be Lord both of the dead and living.—*Romans* xiv. 9.

AND was this the cause, dearest Jesus ! of all thy sufferings, that thou mightest be the universal monarch on thine
eternal throne ?   Then bend thy knee, my heart, and all the
affections of my soul, and hail thy Jesus Lord of all !   Now,
Lord, I see, through thy blessed teaching, though a fool, and
slow in heart to believe all that the prophets have spoken—
now I see how expedient it was that Christ should suffer, and
should enter into his glory.   Yes! thou art, indeed, Lord
both of dead and living—the dead to raise, even the dead in
trespasses and in sins ; and the living, to live in them, and rule
and guide them.   And as thou art Lord both of dead and
living, so, precious Jesus ! wilt thou be Lord over all the
dead and lifeless affections of thy redeemed.   Surely, Lord
Jesus, my soul may well believe this ; for if, when upon the
cross, thou didst conquer death, now thou art upon the throne,
every power must be put beneath thy feet.   Shout then, my
soul ! shout all ye followers of the Lord! never more let
dead frames, or dying affections, or unbelief, or all the temp
tations of Satan, cast us down.   Is not Christ upon the throne ?
And is he not Lord both of dead and living ?   And hath not
this Almighty Lord both of dead and living, power to save,
power to quicken dead sinners, and comfort living saints ; to
give grace to the weak ; and to them that have no might, to

increase strength? Hath he not power to kindle anew his own graces that he first planted ; to bring back again wanderers, to reclaim the long-lost backsliders, to soften hard hearts, to bind up broken hearts, to justify the guilty, to sanctify the filthy, to adopt orphans, to bless the fatherless, to be gracious, and kind and merciful—in a word, to be Jesus? For in that one word is summed up all! Oh! blessed Master! oh for an heart to love thee, to live to thee, to walk with thee, to rejoice in thee, to be always eyeing thee on thy throne ; and never, never to lose sight of thee, my glorious, risen, and exalted Saviour! in this sweet and endearing point of view, in which thy servant the Apostle hath here represented thee ; that it was for this end, as well as a thousand other blessed purposes, that Christ both died, and rose, and revived, that he might be Lord both of dead and living. Hallelujah! Amen.

24.—The breaker is come up before them ; they have broken up, and have passed through the gate, and are gone out by it ; and their king shall pass before them, and the Lord on the head of them.—*Micah*. ii. 13.

PAUSE, my soul, over this precious scripture, and ask thine own heart who this almighty Breaker can be, except the Lord Jesus Christ; for he, and he alone, answers to such a divine character. Was it not he which came up as the Breaker from everlasting, when, in the council of peace, the divine decree was broken open, and the Son of God stood forth the sinner's Surety? Was it not he whom John saw by vision, who alone was found worthy in heaven to open the book, and loose the seals thereof? Was it not the same precious Holy One who, when in the volume of the book it was found written of him, that he should fulfil the law of Jehovah for sinful man, cried out, " Lo! I come?" And was it not Jesus, even thy Jesus, my soul, that in the fulness of time came up as the Breaker, to break down the dreadful bar of separation which sin had made between God and man, and to open a new and living way for the sinner to God by his blood? And when he had broken down the fence sin had made in disobedience to the divine law ; the accusations of Satan ; the dominion of death and the grave, by sustaining the whole weight and burden of all in his own precious Person ; did he not, as the almighty Breaker, burst asunder the bars of death, and prove himself thereby indeed to be this almighty Breaker, in such a palpable evidence, that it was impossible his holy soul could be holden by it? And hath he not broken through all intervening obstacles, ascended up on high, led captivity captive, entered into glory, and there ever liveth and appeareth in the presence of God for us? Is not Jesus then this almighty Breaker? But, my soul, look yet further. It is said also, in this blessed Scripture, that the Breaker is not only come up before them, (that is, his people,) but that "they have broken up, and have passed through the gate, and are gone out by it; and their king shall pass before them, and the Lord on the head of them." And so they are, if so be this almighty Breaker hath broken down the strong holds of sin and Satan in which they lay bound; broken down the natural hatred and enmity of their own heart against God and his Christ in which they were born, and in which they lived, and must have died, but for his sovereign grace manifested in them and towards them; burst open the prison doors of Satan, and broke off his cursed chains, and brought them out; if these things are wrought and accomplished in the people, may they not be said, in his strength, to have broken up and have passed through the gate of Satan's dominions, and are gone out by it into the glorious liberty of the sons of God? Is it so, my soul, in thy experience? Dost thou indeed know Jesus for thy almighty Breaker, by such sweet and precious tokens of his love and power? Hath thy King passed thus before thee, and thy Lord on the head of thee? Oh! then, be ever on the look out for all the renewed visits of his grace, in which he still acts as thine almighty Breaker, in breaking down all the remaining obstacles which thy unbelief, and fears, and doubts, are continually raising up against thy own happiness, in his precious manifestations. Look up to him daily, hourly, minutely, if possible, that he may break down all the remains of indwelling corruption in thy nature, by which these fears and this unbelief gets holdfast in thy soul; and be often on the look out also for that glorious day of God, when this almighty Breaker shall finally and fully come, and break through the clouds to judgment, to break down every remaining evil that keeps thee now from the everlasting enjoyment of thy Lord. Hasten, blessed Jesus! come, my Beloved! and, with a glory infinitely surpassing all conception, manifest thyself as the almighty Breaker, in this full display of thy sovereignty and power. And then, as Samson (thy type in this instance) carried with him the gates of his prison, so wilt thou break up and carry away all the gates of thy people's graves, and take all thy redeemed home with thee to glory, that where thou art, there they shall be also. Hail, thou almighty Breaker! Jesus omnipotent reigneth!

25.—And the apostles said unto the Lord, Increase our faith.—*Luke* xvii. 5.

DID the apostles need so to pray? Then well may I. Oh! thou great Author and .Finisher of our faith! I would look up to thee, with thankfulness, that thou hast granted even the smallest portion of faith to so unworthy a creature as I am. Surely, my soul, it is as great a miracle of grace that my God and Saviour should have kindled belief in thy strong heart, amidst all the surrounding obstructions of sin and Satan which lay there ; as when the miraculous fire from heaven, in answer to the prophet's prayer, came down and consumed the wetted sacrifice. I praise thee, my God and King, this day, in the recollection of this unspeakable, unmerited mercy. And though this faith in my heart still be but as a grain of mustard seed ; though it be but as a spark in the ocean ; though it be but as the drop of the dew, in comparison of the river ; yet, blessed, precious Jesus! still this is faith, and it is thy gift. And is it not a token of thy favour? Is it not an earnest of the Holy Spirit, and a pledge of the promised inheritance? Babes in faith, as well as the strong in the Lord, are equally thine : for it is said, that as many as were ordained to eternal life believed ; (Acts xiii. 48.) and to as many as believed, thou gavest power to become the sons of God : so it is by thyself, blessed Redeemer! and not by the strength or weakness of the faith of thy people, their justification before God the Father is secured. Precious is that Scripture which tells us, that by thee all that believe, whether great faith or little faith—*all that believe*, are justified from all things. Acts xiii. 32. But, my soul, while the consciousness of thy possessing the smallest evidences of faith in thy beloved, gives thee a joy unspeakable and full of glory, dost thou not blush to think what ungrateful returns thou art making to thy Redeemer in the littleness of thy faith in such a God and Saviour? Whence is it that thine affections are so warm in a thousand lesser things, and so cold towards Jesus? Whence that his holy word thou so often hearest as though thou heardest not? Whence the ordinances of Jesus' house, the promises of his Scriptures, the visits of his grace; whence these pass again and again before thee, and thou remainest so cold and lifeless in thy affections? Whence that the temptations of Satan, the corruptions of thine heart, the allurements of the world, gain any influence upon thee? Whence that thou art so anxious about things that perish; about any thing, about nothing, deserving to be called interesting; whence so seldom at the court of the heavenly King, where thou oughtest to be found daily, hourly, waiting; and whence, under trials, or the want of answers at a mercy-seat, fretful, impatient, and misgiving —whence all these, and numberless other evils, but from the weakness and littleness of thy love *to* Jesus, thy trust *in* Jesus, thy dependence *upon* Jesus, and thy communion *with* Jesus? All, all arise out of this one sad cause, my soul, thine unbelief. Jesus! Master! look upon me, put the cry with earnestness in my heart, that I may unceasingly, with the Apostles' prayer, be sending forth this as the first and greatest petition of my whole soul—"Lord! increase my faith!"

26.—Thy teeth are like a flock of sheep that are even shorn, which come up from the washing; whereof every one bear twins, and none is barren among them.—*Song* iv. 2.

SEE, my soul, how Jesus sets off the beauties of his church, when made comely in his comeliness, which he hath put upon it. Jesus' whole church forms but one flock; for there shall be one fold and one shepherd. And though it is called a little flock, and a flock of slaughter, yet it is a beautiful flock in the Lord's hand. But wherefore are the teeth of the church said to be like a flock shorn? Probably from their never being exercised but upon divine things: shorn to all desires in which unshorn and carnal persons delight. The believer feeds on Jesus: his flesh he finds to be meat indeed, his blood drink indeed. To the roof of his mouth this becomes like the best wine, which goeth down sweetly, causing even the lips of those that sleep to speak. And how do believers, like sheep, come up from the washing; but when from the washing of regeneration, and the renewing of the Holy Ghost shed upon them abundantly, through Jesus Christ, they come up clean and washed in Jesus' blood, and adorned in the robe of Jesus' righteousness, and are presented before God and the Father, and accepted in the Beloved? And oh! how fruitful are they, like sheep which bear twins! None are barren or unfruitful among them, because they show forth the praises of him who hath called them out of darkness into his marvellous light. The twin graces, if they may so be called, of faith and love, of prayer and praise, mark whose they are, and to whom they belong. The old fleece of nature being taken from them, they are shorn to the world. And the former filthiness and uncleanliness of mind they are washed from to themselves; and hence they come up to mention the loving kindness of the Lord, and to prove that they are neither barren nor unfruitful in the knowledge of the Lord, and in the power of his might. My soul! is this thy state? Are thy teeth like this flock? and thy knowledge and enjoyment of Jesus a real heart-felt enjoyment of him? Canst thou truly relish nothing of food but what hath Jesus in it? Is nothing pleasant to thy taste but this bread of God, which came down from heaven? Comfort thyself then, my soul, that by and by the teeth of death will separate, like the sheep that is shorn, the body of corruption under which thou still groanest, being burdened; and thou shalt come up from the washing in the fountain of Jesus' blood, clothed in his garment of salvation, and made a meet partaker of an inheritance with the saints in light!

27.—Behold how he loved him!—*John* xi. 36.

THE tears of Jesus at the tomb of Lazarus produced that astonishment in the mind of the Jews, that they thus exclaimed! But had they known, or did the whole world know, what I know of thy love to me, thou dear Redeemer of my soul, every one that heard it might with greater wonder cry out, Behold how he loveth him! I would for the present pass by, in my contemplation of thy love, all the numberless instances of it, which I possess in common with thy church and people; for though these in every and in all cases carry with them the tokens of a love that passeth knowledge, yet, for the meditation of the morning, I would pause over the view of Jesus' love to me a poor sinner, not as it is displayed in *general* mercies, even the glorious mercies of redemption, but as those mercies come home, in their *personal* direction to my own heart, even to mine. Think, my soul, what a huge volume thou wilt have to read over in eternity, of Jesus' love to thee, as distinguished, express, personal, and particular. And, amidst all the several chapters of that love, how wilt thou dwell with rapture on those two sweet verses of it, which, like the hymn in one of the Psalms, thou wilt have to chaunt aloud, after the review of every blessing noted down; for *his mercy endureth for ever:* I mean, *first,* that

Jesus should ever look with pity on thee ; and *next* to this, that after such distinguishing grace, the floods of sin and corruption in thee should not have quenched that love and extinguished it for ever.   The thought of Jesus' love, if looked at only in these two points of view, will be enough to employ thy immortal faculties in contemplation, and love, and praise, to all eternity.   Pause, my soul, and take a short view of each.   Jesus looked on thee, loved thee, called thee, redeemed thee, manifested himself to thee, otherwise than he doth to the world ; and this at a time when thousands and tens of thousands are passed by, of temper, mind, disposition, and understanding, in every point of view vastly thy superiors, and far more promising to glorify him !   Bow down, my soul, while thou ponderest over the rich mercy, and refer all the praise and all the glory unto Him, whose free grace, not thy deserts, became the sole cause.   And when thou hast fully turned this astonishing subject over in thy mind, think again, that after such distinguishing grace, how increasingly astonishing it is, that all thy repeated and aggravated transgressions have not extinguished his love towards thee, but that Jesus still loves, though thou hast been, and still continuest, so ungrateful.   Oh ! love unequalled, past all comprehension ! when shall this base, this shameful heart of mine so love thee, as to live to thy glory ?   Lord, I abhor myself in this view of thy grace and my vileness !

28.—And the Lord said, Arise, anoint him ; for this is he.   Then Samuel took the horn of oil, and anointed him in the midst of his brethren.—1 *Sam*. xvi. 12, 13.

Was David singled out from amidst his brethren, to be the Lord's anointed ; and do I not behold in this the representation of Jesus, that Holy One, concerning whom the Lord spake in vision, and said, I have laid help upon One that is mighty : I have exalted One chosen out of the people ? Yes ! thou Lord our Righteousness ! in this I behold thee.   And let my soul make this sweet subject the meditation of my morning song, for surely it is a lovely song, to hail thee, the chiefest among ten thousand !   I behold thee then, thou dear Emmanuel, by the eye of faith, as coming up from everlasting, when amidst that immense multitude of those thou disdainedst not to call thy brethren, thou stoodest forth, in the eternal view, as the glorious One, to be the Christ, the God-man Mediator, for the salvation of thy church and people.

Here, precious Jesus! didst thou appear, to God our Father's view, pre-eminent above thy fellows! And of the whole body, the church, which God our Father in the great decree determined to form as the receivers of grace and mercy, and of eternal life and salvation, thou wert appointed their glorious Head ; that, *in* thee, and *from* thee, and *through* thee, they might become a glorious church, not having spot or wrinkle, or any such thing, but that thou mightest present it to thyself in love. And surely, dearest, precious Jesus! had every individual of thy redeemed brethren been present, as all the sons of Jesse passed in review before the prophet, to have chosen their glorious head, on none but thee could that choice have fallen. All voices would have echoed to Jehovah's proclamation : " Arise, anoint him ; for this is He." Yes! truly, Lord, thou art He whom thy brethren shall praise, and all thy Father's children, with devout rapture and holy joy, shall bow down before thee. Thou art heir of all things, the chiefest and first-born in the womb of mercy. It is thou that art the most entitled to the most full, honourable, and unchangeable right to all thy Father's inheritance. Men shall be blessed in thee, and all nations shall call thee Blessed. My soul! delight thyself unceasingly in this contemplation of thy Jesus. God thy Father hath chosen him. He hath anointed him with the holy oil for salvation, and the Spirit was given unto him, not by measure. And is not God's chosen thy chosen ; the Father's anointed thine anointed! Is there any in heaven, or upon earth, to whom thou art looking for help, or strength, or comfort, or salvation, but to Jesus? Who but Jesus, my soul, wouldest thou have for a Saviour ? What object so desirable as Jesus to claim thy love ? Witness for me, ye sons of light, ye angels that see his face and do his pleasure, that Jesus is my only Beloved, my Hope, my Portion. Shortly I shall join your assembly, and with you bless and adore Jesus in endless song, the fairest and chiefest among ten thousand.

29.—The Marriage of the Lamb is come, and his wife hath made herself ready. And to her was granted, that she should be arrayed in fine linen, clean and white : for the fine linen is the righteousness of saints.—*Rev.* xix. 7, 8.

BEHOLD, my soul, behold that day, that glorious day, in which redemption is to be consummated, in the kingdom of heaven ; when the Son of God brings home his bride, the

church, the full celebration of God's glory, in the happiness
of the redeemed in Jesus, everlasting joy will burst forth.
See how thy nature is then to be adorned! The whole body,
the church, is then to be arrayed in the robes of Jesus' righteousness, having been washed from all their sins in his
blood. And these nuptial ornaments are to be granted or
given to the church; for she hath no righteousness of her
own, but as all along in this world she had professed, so there
in the upper world she triumphantly sings, "I will greatly
rejoice in the Lord, my soul shall be joyful in my God; for
he hath clothed me with the garments of salvation, he hath
covered me with the robe of righteousness, as a bridegroom
decketh himself with ornaments, and as a bride adorneth herself with her jewels." Isaiah lxi. 10. Pause, my soul, over this
view! Is this to be thy adorning in glory? See to it then,
my soul, that it becomes thy covering now. How suited is
it to all thy circumstances! Thou hast no fine linen, nothing
clean, nothing white. Think how comely Jesus' robe of
righteousness must be to appear in! This is the wedding
garment by faith worn at his supper upon earth, and the
same in fruition in which thou art to sit down at his table
above. And oh! how suitable a covering to hide all thy
deformity, to conceal and take away all thy pollution! And
will not this procure thee favour and acceptance with God?
Is it not thus that Jesus' followers are distinguished from men
of the world? Art thou now clothed with it? Hath God
the Spirit put it on? Doth Jesus now send thee these love
tokens as his betrothed; and, in the ordinances of his grace,
doth he grant thee many sweet espousals? Oh! then, my
soul, see to it, that thy righteousness is that of Jesus' own,
with which his church is arrayed, and that these robes are
always clean and white, which are washed in the blood of
the Lamb, for, ere long, the midnight cry will be heard, Behold, the Bridegroom cometh, go ye out to meet him! Oh!
precious Lord Jesus! give me to hear that voice with joy,
that with holy wings of love, in the last office of faith, to be
then swallowed up in sight, I may arise to enter with thee
into the marriage, to sit down with thee for ever

30.—Nevertheless, I am continually with thee.—*Psalm* lxxiii. 23.

YES! my soul, and well is it for thee that it is so; there
is a *nevertheless* in the precious redemption by Jesus, which
secures thee, amidst all thy languishing seasons, when to thy

view it sometimes appears as though the Lord had forgotten
to be gracious, and had shut up his loving kindness in displeasure. And whence this security but in Jesus, and the
covenant engagements of God thy Father in him? The
everlasting worth and efficacy of the Redeemer's righteousness and death, are the same amidst all the changeable circumstances of his people's warfare. By the expression of
being continually with Jesus, is meant, no doubt, that union
with his person, as the sinner's Surety, which gives security
and firmness to the everlasting state and happiness of his redeemed. And it is this which constitutes, not only the safety
of his people now, but the happiness of his people for ever.
Heaven itself, but for Jesus, and the constant flow of righteousness and glory in him, and from him, would cease to be
heaven. The souls of just men made perfect could be no
longer happy nor righteous, but as those supplies flow in
upon their souls from him. So that the everlasting preciousness of Jesus, as the glorious Head of his people, is thus confirmed, and the felicity of the church must be wholly made
up from this eternal union with him. Hence, how precious
the thought, *I am continually with thee!* And is this thy portion, my soul? Art thou alive to this sweet and soul-reviving
thought? Is Jesus, thy Jesus, continually with thee, and
thou continually with him? See to it, that the nearness of
Jesus to thee hath the same effect upon thee, as with things
in nature, when the earth and the inhabitants testify their
sense of feeling. Doth not the earth, and the plants, and the
birds, and every thing look gay, when the sun renews the
face of the earth, and shines with loveliness, to make all nature smile? And shall thy Sun of righteousness arise unobserved or unenjoyed, who comes with healing in his wings?
Oh! precious Jesus! cause me so to live upon thee that I
may be always eyeing thee, in dark seasons as well as bright
hours; that, from never suffering thy dear image to depart
for a moment from my heart, I may be so prepared to behold
thy face in open glory, when the veil of this flesh is removed,
and I awake up after thy likeness, that, though I change my
place, I shall not change my company. In earth or heaven,
yet if with thee, happiness is begun in the soul; and faith,
in lively exercise, is itself an anticipation of glory, by just so
much as the soul realizeth thy sweet presence, in being ever
with the Lord.

11

MAY.

1.—Thou shalt call his name Jesus.—*Matt.* i. 21.

This is one more of the Redeemer's names, which is as
ointment poured forth. As if the Holy Ghost had been graciously consulting the everlasting comfort and happiness of
his people, and therefore commanded the church to know
their Lord by so many different and endearing appellations.
As if he had said, Are you kept back from approaching
him through fear? Oh! no ;—go to him, for he is Emmanuel. So great, as God, that he is able to save! so tender and
near, as man, that he is more ready to bestow mercy than
you are to ask it! Are you kept back for want of righteousness? Be not so, for he is the Lord our Righteousness, and
what you need he hath for you.—Or are you depressed by
reason of sin? Let not this discourage you, for his name is
purposely Jesus, because he, and he alone, shall save his
people from their sins. My soul! what knowest thou prac-
tically and personally of this most blessed name of thy Saviour? It is one thing to have heard of him as Jesus, and
another to know him to be Jesus. There are multitudes who
rest satisfied with the name. The Jews knew him, saw him,
conversed with him ; but they knew him not as a Saviour.
Nay, more than this ; many have had, and still have an his-
torical knowledge and belief that Jesus is a Saviour, but yet
no apprehension or concern for an interest in him. Thus
Balaam, whose eyes were so far opened, but his heart never
affected, as to have visions concerning Christ. But what
an awful account did this impious creature give of himself!
I shall see him, (said he,) but not now: I shall behold him,
but not nigh. Numb. xxiv. 17. What an awful state! Oh,
my soul! bless thy God, thy Jesus, that thy knowledge is not
of the head only, but of the heart. Thou hast not simply
heard of Jesus, but received him as Jesus, to the salvation of
thy soul. Thou hast seen God in Christ ; the Father's name,
the Father's authority in him. Thou hast come to him in
that name, and by that authority as a poor sinner, and found
Jesus precious. And is not Jesus precious to thee? Is not
the very name of Jesus most precious? As one of old expressed it, so hast thou found it, that in this one name of thy

Lord, the whole of the gospel is folded up; it is the light, the food, the medicine, the very jubilee of the soul. Yes! thou blessed, holy, gracious Lord! Yes! thy name is indeed Jesus, for thou art, thou wilt be Jesus. And they that know thy name will put their trust in thee, for thou shalt save thy people from their sins.

2.—And they called Rebekah, and said unto her, Wilt thou go with this man? and she said, I will go.—*Gen.* xxiv. 58.

SEE, my soul, with what readiness Rebekah determined to accompany the servant of Abraham to Isaac. And wilt thou not arise and go forth at the invitation of the servants of Jesus, who sends them to call thee to his arms? Hath he not by the sweet constraining influences of his Holy Spirit, as well as by the outward ministry of his blessed word, made thee willing in the day of his power? Did the servant of Abraham give an earnest of his master's affection in putting the bracelets upon Rebekah's hands, and the ear-rings, and the gold? But what was this to the love-tokens which Jesus himself hath given thee, when he set thee as a seal upon his heart, and as a seal upon his arm, and when all the waters of divine wrath his holy soul had poured upon him for thy sins, and all the floods of corruption, which like a deluge, had overspread thy whole nature, could not quench his love, nor drown it. And if it be demanded, then, from thine own mouth this day, wilt thou go with this man, this God-man, this Glory-man, this Jesus? Wilt thou not instantly cry out, I will go? Yes! thou altogether lovely Lord, thou chiefest and fairest among ten thousand, I will go with thee. I would forget mine own people, and my father's house. For my father's house is a house of bondage. I was born in sin, and shapen in iniquity. A child of wrath, even as others, and by nature dead in trespasses and sins. It is thou, blessed Jesus, who hast delivered me from the wrath to come. It is thou who hast quickened me by thy Holy Spirit to a new and spiritual life. It is thou who hast sent thy servants to call me to thyself, and hast betrothed me to thyself for ever. And is there any that yet asketh me, Wilt thou go with this man? My whole soul would outrun the question, and, like the Apostle, I would answer, To whom else shall I go? Witness for me ye servants of my Lord, ye angels, and ministers of light, I have none in heaven, neither in earth, but him. Yes! thou dearest Redeemer! I will go with thee, follow thee, live with thee, hang upon thee, die with thee, nor even death itself shall part thee and me. Oh! let those precious words of thine, concerning thy church, be sweetly felt in my soul, " I will say, it is my people:" and my whole soul will make her responses to the gracious sound, and say, " The Lord is my God."

3.—Sitting at the feet of Jesus, clothed, and in his right mind.— *Luke* viii. 35.

LOOK at this man, my soul, and see whether thou canst find any resemblance to thyself. Before that he heard the voice of Jesus, he was under the possession of the evil spirit. It is said of him, that he wore no clothes. He dwelt in no house, but abode among the tombs. He was cutting himself with stones. No man could tame him, neither fetters nor chains bind him. Poor miserable creature! And yet, my soul, was not this a true emblem of thy state, and, indeed, of every man's state, by nature? Had not Satan full possession of thine heart and affections, my soul, before that thou becamest savingly acquainted with the Lord Jesus Christ? Did he not lead thee in the pursuit and gratification of thy lusts and pleasures at his will? Thou mightest truly be said to wear no clothes, for, so far from having on the garment of Jesus' righteousness, in those days of thine unregeneracy, thou wert naked, to thy shame, in the filth of nature. Thou didst not dwell in the house of God, nor even delight to go thither. And, as this poor creature abode among the dead, so didst thou live and abide with characters like thyself, dead in trespasses and sins. And as this miserable man was wounding himself, with stones, so wert thou, for thy daily commission of sin was giving wounds to thy soul, infinitely more alarming than the wounds he gave his body. And could no chains or fetters be found strong enough to bind him? so neither did all the solemn commands and threatening judgments of God's holy law act with the least restraint upon thine ungoverned passions. Pause, my soul, over the representation, and acknowledge how just and striking the similarity. Then ask thyself, Art thou now sitting at the feet of Jesus, clothed, and in thy right mind? Yes! if so be, like this poor man, thou hast heard the voice of Jesus, and felt the power of his grace in thine heart. If one like the Son of God hath set thee free, brought thee to his fold, opened thine ear to discipline, and thine heart to grace, then art thou free indeed. What sayest thou, my soul, to these things? Is there this change, this blessed change, from dead works, to serve the living and true God? Oh! then will not the language of thine heart be like Jesus and his church of old? "I will greatly rejoice in the Lord, my soul shall be joyful in my God: for he hath clothed me with the garments of salvation, he hath covered me with the robe of righteousness, as a bridegroom decketh himself with ornaments, and as a bride adorneth herself with her jewels."

4.—The hind of the morning.—*Psalm* xxii. in the title.

THE dying patriarch Jacob, under the influences of the prophetic spirit, pointed to the seed of *Naphtali* as a hind let loose. But it is the church which points to Jesus as the Hind of the morning; for he is, indeed, the loving Hind, and the pleasant Roe. It is sweet and profitable to observe in what a variety of methods the Holy Ghost hath been pleased to give sketches of Jesus. My soul, look at Jesus for thy present meditation as the Hind of the morning. Was he not, from the very morning of eternity, marked under this lovely character? Did not the church speak of him, and desire his appearance, under this same character, when she begged of him, that, until the shadows of Jewish ordinances were passed away, and the day of gospel light should break in upon her, that her beloved would be like a young hart or a roe, upon the mountains of Bether? And was not Jesus, indeed, when he did appear, truly as the hind, which the dogs that compassed him about, and the assembly of the wicked enclosed? Did he not say, in those unequalled moments of suffering, Save me from the lion's mouth, for thou hast heard me from the horns of the unicorns? Yes, precious Jesus! thou art, indeed, the Hind of the morning! In the morning of our salvation, thou camest over the hills and mountains of our sinful nature, with the swiftness of the hind, and the loveliness and gentleness of the roe, to expose thyself to the serpent, and the whole host of foes, for the deliverance of thy people. And having trod upon the lion and the adder, and the young lion, and the dragon, trampled under thy feet; by thy death thou didst overcome death, and him that had the power of death, that is, the devil; and hast delivered them, who, through fear of death, were all their life-time subject to bondage. And now, precious Lord! thou art as the hind slain, the food of the souls of thy redeemed by faith, until

11*

faith itself is done away in sight, and hope swallowed up in
absolute fruition. Oh! let the language of my heart daily,
hourly, correspond to the church of old ; and, during the
shadows of ordinances, and all the dark clouds of unbelief
and temptations with which I am here exercised, let me still
by faith, behold thee as the Hind of the morning, fleeing
swiftly to my assistance, hearing and answering my prayers,
leaping over all the mountains of distance which sin and unworthiness would throw up between thee and my soul, oppos-
ing all my enemies, and beating them under my feet that
would keep me from thee ; until that day, that glorious everlasting day, which will have no night, shall break in upon
my soul, and thou wilt then appear, to my unceasing, uninterrupted joy, the Hind indeed, of the morning. Make haste,
my Beloved ! and be thou like unto a roe, or to a young hart,
upon the mountains of spices.

5.—Believest thou not that I am in the Father, and the Father in me ?—
John xiv. 10.

My soul, thou wilt never sufficiently contemplate this
blessed oneness between the Father and the Son, in the great
work and glory of redemption. Pause, this morning and observe, for the confirmation of thy faith, that as Jesus is one
with the Father in all the essence and attributes of the Godhead, so God the Father is one with Jesus in all the offices
of redemption. God was in Christ's human nature, for he is
said to have been *God manifest in the flesh.* God was in
every name of Christ, every work of Christ, every word of
Christ, every office of Christ, every attribute of Christ. And
hence, in seeing Christ, we truly see God ; in all his grace,
mercy, love, salvation, and every blessing connected with our
present, future, eternal happiness. And what a sweet thought
is that, my soul, for thee to dwell upon ; that as the Father is
in Jesus, and in him dwelleth all the fulness of the Godhead
bodily, so, in consequence, there is a fulness of grace and a
fulness of glory in Jesus, to give out a supply here of the one,
and hereafter of the other, to satisfy the most capacious desires of the souls of his redeemed to all eternity. For the
human nature being personally united to the Godhead in the
person of the Lord Jesus, there must be this fulness everlastingly dwelling. There may be, and for certain purposes
sometimes there are, great gifts and graces of the Spirit
poured out upon the Lord's servants ; but never could the

Godhead be found in any but Jesus. God was in Christ reconciling the world unto himself. Pause once more, my soul, and ask thyself, Hast thou Christ? then hast thou God the Father in him. Where Christ is, God the Father is: and where Christ is not, there God is not. See then, my soul, that this is the standard to ascertain the reality of thy case as it appears before God. Hast thou Jesus for thy portion? then the Father is in him. Dost thou love Jesus? then must thou love the Father in him. Dost thou seek Jesus? then art thou seeking the Father in him. Oh! for grace to discover our true interest in all the Father's covenant engagements and promises, from this very source; that this everlasting oneness between the Father and Son infallibly secures to his people all the blessings of redemption, for in seeing the Son, we literally and truly see the Father, and glorify the Father in Jesus. Amen.

6.—And he said, I am Joseph, your brother, whom ye sold into Egypt. *Gen.* xlv. 4.

WHAT an interview was this in the first manifestation the governor of Egypt made of himself to his brethren! We are told that he wept aloud. His bowels yearned over them. He had long smothered in his own bosom those tender feelings he possessed, of the greatest love towards them; and when he had dismissed every looker-on, and stranger, he broke out in those kind expressions, I am Joseph, your brother, whom ye sold into Egypt. But what were the feelings of the patriarch, compared to those of the Lord Jesus, when he made himself known to his disciples after he arose from the dead; and as he now manifests himself to every poor sinner, whom, by his grace, he makes partaker in the first resurrection, on whom the second death hath no power? I am Jesus, your Brother, (saith that adored Lord;) but he doth not add, whom ye sold for worse than a slave. There is no upbraiding, nothing of our baseness and our sins. And yet we have all not only sold him, but, by our transgressions, crucified him. What a beautiful feature this is in the Redeemer! and how much even the love of Joseph falls short of Jesus! And what endears it still more, is the peculiar attention the Redeemer manifesteth upon the occasion. If there be one of his brethren more distressed and discouraged by reason of sin than another, to him will Jesus direct his manifestation more immediately. Witness the case of Peter after his fall.

Jesus will have the account of his resurrection not only communicated to all, but Peter is mentioned by name.   Go tell
his disciples, and Peter.   As if knowing the apostle might
fear that, having denied Jesus, he might justly be denied by
him.   No, saith Jesus, let Peter be particularly told the joyful
news, to make his heart glad.   And dost thou, dearest Lord,
speak to my soul? Dost thou say to me, I am your Brother?
Art thou not ashamed to call such sinners brethren?   Oh,
thou unequalled pattern of unexampled love! add one mercy
more to the vast account, and let a portion of it kindle a flame
of love in my soul.   I have, indeed, sold thee for a slave,
nailed thee, by my sins, to the cross, and put thee to an open
shame.   But since thou hast redeemed me by thy blood, and
bought the pardon of my sins so dear, and now, by thy triumph over death, art become the first-born among many brethren, and exalted as a Prince and a Saviour to give blessings infinitely superior to those Joseph was exalted to bestow
on his brethren ; behold, Lord, to thee do I come, manifest
thyself still the forgiving Brother, and supply all my wants.
Yes, blessed Jesus! thou art he whom thy brethren shall
praise ; and all thy Father's children shall fall down before
thee.

7.—They shall revive as the corn.—*Hosea* xiv. 7

Sweet promise to comfort a soul like mine, under so many
and such frequent languishing graces!   How often hath it
appeared to my view as if the gracious seed had perished?
It was small, indeed, in its first beginning, like the grain of
mustard-seed ; and no sooner had it appeared, than I per-
ceived it almost choked with the tares of corruption, unbelief,
and Satan's rubbish.   I was soon led to suspect God's work
upon my soul.   Surely, I said, this is not grace.   Presently
I could see no more of it.   I was ignorant that by thus dying
to self the Holy Ghost was opening to my view the only living
in Jesus.   In a moment unlooked for it revived as the corn.
Ah! from whence the source?   Not from self, not from
labours, not from exertions: can dead roots live?   The Holy
Ghost taught me this must be Jesus.   Your life, he said, is
hid with Christ in God.   Here are the springs of grace ;
here, from hence, flow the streams of that river which make
glad the city of God.   Here, then, is faith's view of God's
glory in Christ.   Here is the promise.   They shall revive
as the corn.   And thus it is fulfilled.   In me, (saith that

precious Redeemer) is thy fruit found. Mark this down, my soul. Both root and fruit are in one and the same, even Jesus. Spiritual attainments are in Jesus, not in the greenest buddings or fairest blossoms of our own labours. Live then, my soul, wholly upon Jesus, and then thou wilt revive as the corn. Suppose it trodden down, suppose the tares of the wicked rise to oppose it, yet if Jesus be the root, and the springs of grace in him flow, as they cannot but flow, to keep alive all the branches in him, there shall be, there must be, at last, a glorious harvest. Oh! what a volume doth the soul sometimes read at once in that short promise, " *Because I live, ye shall live also.*" Hail! hail thou glorious root out of a dry ground! Thou wilt send forth the golden ears for thine own garner. Thou wilt weed out every thing that annoys. Thou wilt water, and by the sweet influences of thy blood, thy word, and spirit, thou wilt shine upon the standing corn. And when, by all thy gracious husbandry, (for the whole work and glory is thine,) thou hast caused the plentiful crop to hang down their heads in all the humbleness of self-abasement, as the token of ripeness, thou wilt command thine angel to put in the sickle of death, and take home every stalk and every grain of the precious seed to thy garner in heaven.

8.—Jesus said unto her, I am the resurrection and the life: he that believeth in me, though he were dead, yet shall he live. And whosoever liveth, and believeth in me, shall never die. Believest thou this ?—*John* xi. 25, 26.

PAUSE, my soul, over those divine, those glorious, those soul-quickening, soul-reviving words of thy Almighty Redeemer! What man, what prophet, what servant of the Lord, what angel, but He that is the Angel of the Covenant, One with the Father over all, God blessed for ever, could assume such a language, and prove that assumption, as Jesus did, both by his own resurrection, and that of Lazarus? And mark, my soul, the many precious things contained in this sweet scripture. Observe the blessing itself, even resurrection and life. Observe the source, the author, the fountain of it, Jesus, thy Jesus. Observe *for* whom this stupendous mercy is designed, and *to* whom conveyed, namely, the dead in trespasses and sins, and for the dying, languishing frames of believers. And lastly, observe how absolute the thing itself is; they *shall* live. Oh, precious words of a most precious Saviour. And may I not say to thee, my soul, as Jesus did to Mary, after proclaiming himself under this glorious distinction of character, "Believest thou this?" Canst thou answer as she did, "Yea, Lord, I believe that thou art the Christ, the Son of God, which should come into the world?" This is a blessed confession to witness before God. For if I believe that Jesus be indeed the Christ of God, every other difficulty is removed to the firm belief that, as the Father hath life in himself, even so hath the Son life in himself, and whom he will he quickeneth. Witness then for me, every looker on, angels and men, that my soul heartily, cordially, fully subscribes to the same precious truth, and in the same language as Mary. *Yea, Lord,* I would say to every word of thine concerning thy sovereignty, grace, and love: as thou hast said it, so I accept it: in the very words of thine I take it, and cry out, Yea, Lord, even so be it unto me according to thy word. And now, my soul, under all remaining seasons of deadness, coldness, backslidings, wanderings, and the like, never henceforth forget from whom all revivals can only come. Never look within for them; for there is no power of resurrection in thyself. Can these dry bones live? Yes, if Jesus quickens! And is Jesus less to quicken thee than thy connexion with Adam to have killed thee? Oh! how plain is it that the very wants of the soul correspond to the very fulness of Jesus to answer them. And therefore, when the Lord Jesus saith, I am the Resurrection and the Life, he comes to seek employment in this glorious character, to quicken the dead and revive the living. Oh, Lord! give me to hear thy blessed voice this day, and my soul shall live, and live to praise thee.

9.—A certain Samaritan —*Luke* x. 33.

Look, my soul, beyond the letter of the parable, and see if thou canst not instantly discover who it is that is here meant. Mark how he is described: "A *certain* Samaritan." Not any indifferent undetermined one among the whole mass of men called Samaritans; but an identical certain one: and who but Jesus answers to this character? Said we not well, (said the Jews,) that thou art a Samaritan? Yes, truly, thus far ye said right; for our Jesus is the true Samaritan that came a blissful stranger, from his blessed abode, to deliver us from our lost estate; for his mercy endureth for ever. And, my soul, observe how exactly corresponding to all that is said of this certain Samaritan in the parable thy Jesus proves to have been. Our nature, universally speaking, was going down from Jerusalem to Jericho, when it fell among thieves, and when it was left more than half dead by the great enemy of souls; for we had all miserably departed from the Lord, when Jesus came from heaven to the Jericho of this world, to seek and save that which was lost. And what could the Priest or Levite do by law or sacrifice to help our ruined nature? But when Jesus came and bound up the wounds which sin and Satan had made, by pouring in the balsam of his own precious blood, then he proved himself to be this certain Samaritan; for none but Jesus could have done this, since there is salvation in no other, neither is there any other name under heaven given among men whereby we must be saved. And what is it now, but the same gracious mercy carrying on the same blessed purpose in completing the perfect recovery of our nature? It is Jesus, Samaritan-like, which hath brought us to the inn of his church, hath appointed his servants and angels, who are ministering spirits. to minister in all divine things to the heirs of salvation. He hath commissioned the whole train of ordinances, and providences, and promises, to minister to our good. His holy word, his holy Spirit, are unceasingly engaged to the same blessed end. And what crowns all, and makes our state and circumstances most safe and blessed indeed, is, that Jesus hath commanded all the remaining costs and expenses of our cure to be put down to his account. He saith himself to me, a poor worthless sinner as I am, and to every individual of his redeemed, Whatsoever thou spendest more, when I come again, I will repay. And is it so, my soul? Is not the blessing too great to be bestowed, and thou too worthless to receive it? Oh, no! For it is Jesus who promiseth. That's enough. Hail then, thou certain Samaritan, thou Almighty Traveller through our miserable world! Since the first day that thou didst pass by, and didst behold me in my blood cast out to perish, and didst bid me live, how hath my soul hailed thee, and now and unceasingly will hail thee, as my life, my hope, my joy, my portion for ever!

10.—By the highway side, begging.—*Mark* x. 46.

My soul, learn a lesson from the beggar this morning. And oh, thou blessed Friend of beggars! do thou sweetly make the view gracious to my soul. What was it led this poor man to the highway side to seek alms? Surely his poverty, wretchedness, and a sense of want. And art thou

come forth, my soul, from the same cause and on the same
errand? I presume this creature came forth empty; for had
he been full he would never have come. And art thou so,
my soul? for otherwise it is certain they that are full in
themselves never seek Jesus. But amidst his want and poverty, had this poor beggar hopes that the passers-by would
commisserate his case and relieve him? Yes, no doubt!
though some might overlook and disregard him, all would
not. But, my soul, thy case far exceeds his. Though all
disregard, Jesus will not: and thou art sure he will pass by,
and not only behold thy misery, but give thee needed relief.
Jesus, Master, have mercy upon me! Behold, I am come out
this morning as poor, as wretched, as empty, and as needy,
as though I never before had heard of thy dear name, or
been living upon thy fulness. But thou knowest that I cannot live upon the alms of yesterday, no more than my body
can keep in health from the food received in the many days
that are past, without a new supply. Lord, I know that I am
thine, and that thou art mine. I therefore come to thee for a
suited supply, and surely, thou wilt not send me empty away.
Indeed, Lord, I rejoice that I feel my poverty; for I am
thereby, as an empty vessel, better suited for receiving of thy
fulness. Give in, blessed Jesus, to my poor hungry soul, and
then I shall find cause to rejoice that my emptiness and beg-
gary constrained me to seek thee; and that my need afforded
an opportunity for the display of thy grace. Yes, yes,
blessed Lord! I am not only content to be poor and to be
needy, but to be nothing, to be worse than nothing, so that
thereby my blessed Jesus gets glory in the manifestation of
his love and giving out of his riches. I will glory even in
my infirmities, that the power of Christ may rest upon me.
A beggar still I wish to be, and to lay at thy gate, if but to
glimpse at thy face, and to receive one token from thy fair
hand. Indeed, indeed, then am I most full, when most empty,
to be filled with Jesus.

11.—Let him alone, and let him curse; for the Lord hath bidden him.
It may be that the Lord will look on mine affliction, and that the
Lord will requite me good for his cursing this day.—2 *Sam.* xvi. 11, 12.

My soul, see here a believer in his best frame. To be
sure, it is not always thus with a child of God; but it were
to be devoutly desired always thus to be. But while we admire the faith, let us yet more admire and adore Him, and

his grace and mercy, who gives it. Oh! what a blessed state it is to eye the hand of the Lord in every thing. When Shimei thus cursed David, he passeth by the instrument, and recognizeth the hand of the Lord in the appointment. Let him alone, for the Lord hath bidden him. Sin is at the bottom. The Lord doth not correct for nought. How unjust soever on the part of man, it is both just and right on the part of God. And observe, moreover, the comfort he takes to himself out of it. If my God bid my enemy distress me, is it not that my Almighty Friend may more sweetly comfort me? There is not only a *may be*, but a certainty there *shall be*, in God's requiting evil with good to his people. My soul, never overlook this in any, and in all of thine exercises. Behold his hand in it, be it what it may, and then thou wilt never faint under any burden. Jesus not only looks on, but he it is that permits and appoints. Oh! he is tender even in rebukes. By those means he makes his children more like himself; and, moreover, it is his gracious plan to extract pleasure from pain, and by impoverishing the soul in self, and in creature-love, to turn curses into blessings, and convert loss into gain. Doth the enemy curse you? Doth he come out against you? Oh! then, depend upon it, Jesus is going to confer some special blessing upon you. Thou art to be advanced to great honour, to be made more conformable to his blessed image. Jesus is hereby giving you not only to believe in him, but to suffer for his sake. Precious Lord! grant me then this grace which thy servant David was enabled to exercise; and when the *Shimeis* of the day come forth to curse, let them curse, so thou do but bless. And oh for sweet influences from thee, dearest Lord! that I may know thee and the power of thy resurrection, and the fellowship of thy sufferings, being made conformable unto thy death.

12.—Then said he to Thomas, Reach hither thy finger, and behold my hands; and reach hither thy hand, and thrust it into my side; and be not faithless, but believing.—*John* xx. 27.

WAS Jesus willing to have his wounds searched, rather than his unbelieving disciple should go unconvinced? Look, then, my soul, at Jesus, and he will grant thee a suitable testimony, to hush all thy remaining doubts, if so be, after such manifestations of grace as he hath shown thee, there be a single doubt left behind. Doth not Jesus, in effect, say, in every renewed ordinance, Reach hither thy finger, thrust in

12

thine hand, and the precious blood thou needest shall flow;
for the fountain for sin, for uncleanness, for unbelief, and, in
short, for every necessity of my people, is still open. Is not
this the language of all? Doth unbelief doubt the reality of
the thing itself, like Thomas? Doth unbelief tempt the soul
to doubt the particular efficacy of it to special cases, such as
a man's own? Doth unbelief suggest the circumstances
hopeless from delay, from past neglect, from present unworthiness? In answer to all Jesus speaks, "Reach hither thy
finger; and if a touch will not satisfy thee, thrust thy hand
deeply into my side;" here is enough to silence all fears:
why are those wounds still open? "Wherefore did I appear
to my servant John as a lamb that had been slain, but to
convince, by so palpable a testimony, that I am the same
yesterday, to day, and for ever." Oh for grace to return
the grateful answer to Jesus, My Lord, and my God! My
soul, now thou art commanded, this do. Put forth thine
hand, and leave every other consequence with Jesus. While
Jesus thus gives himself to thee, my soul, do thou make a
complete surrender of thyself to him; for this is the very
exercise of faith that Jesus is come after, and therefore let
him not go away until he hath taken thine whole affections
with him, as thy Lord and thy God.

13.—And one man among them was clothed with linen, and a writer's
inkhorn by his side.—*Ezek.* ix. 2.

PAUSE, my soul, over this scripture. Who could this one
man be, but Jesus, thy Mediator! Did not his garment of
linen mark his righteousness, and the inkhorn to write down
his people, his pierced side? Hath he not written in the
book of life the names of all his redeemed, that none of them
may be lost when he cometh to make up his jewels? And
was it not with an eye to this the soldier pierced his side,
when by his death he had obtained eternal redemption for
them, that he might with his precious blood mark his people,
as a shepherd doth his sheep? Yes, thou dear Redeemer!
surely I behold thee sweetly set forth in this Scripture.
Surely the Holy Ghost, who all along delighted to set thee
forth under various similitudes before the old church, hath
graciously represented thee here. Methinks I behold thee
now coming forth in the white garment of thy spotless
righteousness, with thy pierced side, to mark all thine, before
the destroying angels go forth to the everlasting destruction

of unawakened, unregenerated sinners! Methinks I hear
thy blessed, gracious, compassionate voice, in the same tender
tone of words as thou once didst utter to thy servant John:
*Him that overcometh will I make a pillar in the temple of my
God, and he shall go no more out. And I will write upon him
the name of my God, and the name of the city of my God:
and I will write upon him my new name.* Oh, Lamb of God!
fulfil these blessed promises in my soul! Mark me as thine,
unto the day of redemption. Seal me as a signet in thine
image, and give me that new name which no man knoweth
saving he that receiveth it. Then, amidst burning worlds,
my soul will stand secure, being justified in thy righteousness, and sprinkled with thy blood ; and I shall hear, with
holy joy, that glorious, but awful voice, *Come not near any
man upon whom is the mark.*

14.—If we live in the Spirit, let us also walk in the Spirit.—*Gal.* v. 25.

My soul, take this sweet scripture for thy motto, not only
this day, but every day ; for every day's walk should be the
same, with Jesus by the Spirit. And surely, my soul, if Jesus really, truly dwells in thee, he will manifest that he is
at home, by ruling in thee. It is blessed, and gracious, and
edifying, when out of the abundance of the heart the
mouth speaketh, and like the spouse, the lips drop as the
honey-comb, sweetly of Jesus. But the life of Jesus in the
soul consisteth not in talking only of Jesus, but walking *in*
him, and walking *with* him. But, my soul, how wilt thou
accomplish these things, carrying about with thee, as thou
dost daily, a body of sin and death? There is but one plan,
and that a simple plan, mortifying, indeed, to the pride of
human nature, but giving glory to Jesus! Art thou truly
content to be mortified, so that Jesus be glorified? If so, this
is the only way the apostle hath marked. They, and they
only, that live in the Spirit, will walk in the Spirit. The
same grace which teacheth thee *of* Jesus, must give to thee
power *in* Jesus. As long as Jesus is in view, looked to, and
lived upon, all the blessed effects of the grace from Jesus
will follow, as sure as the rays of light diffuse their brightness when the sun is risen. If, my soul, thou goest forth in
a firm dependance upon Jesus' strength, that strength will
be assuredly perfected in thy weakness ; but if Jesus be lost
sight of, and a fancied strength in thyself supply the place,
this defect in faith will bring forth a defect in practice. My

soul, learn to exercise an holy jealousy over thyself; for after Jesus is once truly known, all thy danger begins at this place: so that the great secret is, to live out of self, upon his fulness; to do nothing but in his strength; to propose nothing but for his glory; and in every step you take, in the whole walk of life, to make Jesus every thing, and depend upon him in every thing; and this is the way to find both security and comfort. Dear Lord! do thou enable a poor worm thus to live, by living in thee; and then, sure I am, I shall be happy, by walking in thee.

15.—Thou shalt also be a crown of glory in the hand of the Lord, and a royal diadem in the hand of thy God.—*Isaiah* lxii. 3.

It is very easy to conceive how the Lord of hosts in the day of salvation becomes for a crown of glory and for a diadem of beauty unto his people, as the prophet hath said, Isaiah xxviii. 5. But that the church, and every individual redeemed of the church shall be the Lord's crown and diadem; oh the wonders of grace! Pause, my soul, over this sweet scripture, and take to thyself the blessedness of it. What a variety of images and similitudes thy God hath made use of, to manifest how highly he prizeth his redeemed! " Yea, he loved the people, (said one of old,) and his saints are in thy hand." He calleth them jewels, precious stones, his treasure, his chosen, his inheritance, his portion, his crown, his diadem! And what a thought it is for thee, my soul, to meditate upon, that though in thyself thou art nothing, yet, considered in Jesus, thou art all this and more; polished, made comely, and glorious, from the comeliness put upon thee, and the glory of Jesus. See then, my soul, the vast mercy in Jesus! A worthless worm made dear to God! How infinitely precious and dear should God in Christ be to thee! Let this encourage thee, then, at all times to come to him. Thou art giving glory to thy God, when thou comest to him, to give out of his fulness to thee. Jesus wanteth needy creatures to be glorified upon, by giving out of his abundance to their necessities; and the more he gives, the more he is glorified. Mark that also, for thy greater encouragement to come to him. The more thou art blessed in his fulness, the more blessed he is in imparting it; so that while thou art his crown of glory, he is glorified in thy redemption. And while thou crownest Jesus' head, in ascribing all the glory of thy salvation unto him, he condescends to make thee a crown of glory in his hand, as a token that thou art his, both by purchase of his blood, the gift of his Father, and the conquest of his grace. Hallelujah!

16.—And he that had been possessed with the devil, prayed him that he might be with him. Howbeit, Jesus suffered him not, but saith unto him, Go home to thy friends, and tell them how great things the Lord hath done for thee.—*Mark* v. 18, 19.

MARK this, my soul, and especially when at any time thy Jesus is so graciously revealing himself to thee, in a way of love that thou art longing to be absent from the body, that thou mayest be present with the Lord; think, then, of what Jesus said to this poor man. The thought of being made instrumental in the hand of the Lord in calling sinners to Jesus, made holy Paul willing to wait in a sinful world, and put off his own happiness. Precious frame of mind! Paul knew also, that if the Lord housed his children from the lions' dens and from the mountains of leopards, as soon as he had brought them to the knowledge of himself, then, in this case, Jesus would have no church in the wilderness. The holy seed would not be found amidst the tares of the earth. Blessed Lord! give grace to every exercised child of thine to think of this; that when, under the various trials with which thy wisdom and love seeth fit to try their graces, they long to be home with thee, and are sending forth the cry of the soul for dismission, they may hear thy voice speaking as to this poor man, "Go home to thy friends, and tell them how great things the Lord hath done for thee." But pause, my soul! Is this thy case? Hath Jesus done great things for thee, and art thou proclaiming it abroad to call others to partake? Suppose one from the throng was to ask thee, What is thy Beloved more than another beloved? What would be thy answer? Wouldest thou say, how he hath blest thee in health, or wealth, or worldly success, or prosperity; in friends, and relations, and the like? And are these all the things or the chief of them that thou couldest speak of? If so, what are these more than carnal men can, and do speak of? The infidel, the Turk, the Pagan, can boast as much! But if thou canst say, "Oh, come hither and harken, all ye that fear God, and I will tell you what he hath done for my soul! I was once darkness, and am now light in the Lord! I was once in Satan's chains, and Jesus hath set me free! I was once like this poor man,

12*

under the possession of sin and Satan; but now I sit down at the feet of Jesus, to hear the gracious words which proceed out of his mouth!" Here, my soul, this is indeed to tell thy friends how great things the Lord hath done for thee. Oh for grace thus to proclaim his adorable name while on earth, until Jesus comes to take me home to himself, there to sound his praise before the whole redeemed church of God for ever!

17.—I am poor and needy, yet the Lord thinketh upon me.—*Psalm* xl. 17

PRECIOUS consideration, my soul, under all thine exercises, the Lord, thy Lord, thy Jesus, thinketh upon thee. Wherefore should I faint, then, under any burden? Surely I may say, as Hagar did at the well, Thou, God, seest me! Surely I may give my God, my Saviour, this name as she did; for she said, "Have I also here looked after him that seeth me?" Yes, however unconscious my poor heart is of the blessed truth, yet a very blessed truth it is; while I am looking after Jesus, he is before-hand, thinking and looking upon me. Precious Lamb of God! I will remember my poverty no more: that is, I will remember it no more, but as it is made the means in thy hand to make me sensible of my need and thy fulness. Art thou thinking upon me? Do I hear thy gracious voice saying to me, " I know the thoughts that I think towards you, saith the Lord, thoughts of peace, and not of evil, to give you an expected end! Oh! then, herein I will rejoice. Poor and needy as I am, let me be more poor, more needy, so but I see my fulness in Jesus. He is thinking of me, providing for me, blessing me. I would not be full for the world, or fancy myself so; for what room should I then have for Jesus? What it will be in heaven, I know not; in the fulness of happiness that is there, though that fulness can only be in and from Jesus. But here below, a full state, or a supposed full state, would be an empty wretched state. No, let me be poor and needy, empty and in want, wretched and helpless, in myself; for then I am sure my Jesus will be most precious. Mark it down then, my soul, this day, and wear it about thine heart as a pleasing consideration—When thou feelest thy need and poverty most, the Lord thy Jesus thinketh upon thee.

18.—The flower of the field.—*Psalm* ciii. 15.

Do I not behold Jesus here pre-eminently set forth above his fellows? Yes, dear Lord! thy people, planted by thy hand, do indeed flourish as a flower of the field; but never any like thee. Indeed, all their loveliness, fragrancy, value, all are only so as derived from thee. Never did God our Father plant so lovely a flower, so sweet, so fragrant a flower, in the field of his garden, in the heavenly Paradise, or the earthly Eden, as when he planted thee. Sweet Plant of Renown! aid my meditations this morning to contemplate thee under this interesting view, as the Flower of the field. And first, let me behold thee as truly the Flower of the field, because thou art altogether of God's right hand planting, and not of man's. The flower of the field hath no father but God, and no mother but the virgin earth. Precious Jesus! thou wert conceived in thy human nature wholly by the over-shadowing of God the Spirit, when thou condescendest, for our salvation, to be born of the virgin's womb. And let me look at thee, oh Lord, under another beautiful illustration of thy nature, as the Flower of the field, when I consider the humbleness and lowliness in which thou didst appear. Was there ever a sweet flower of the field more hid, more obscured, and, when brought forward to view, less regarded, than Jesus, of whom it was truly said, " He was despised and rejected of men ; without form or comeliness, and having no beauty that we should desire him ?" And is there not another thought which ariseth to the mind in the contemplation of Jesus as the Flower of the field? Yes! methinks I behold, in the exposure of the flower of the field to the merciless treading of the foot of the passenger, and to the plucking up or destroying by wild beasts, a striking representation of Jesus, who, in the days of his flesh, was encompassed by beasts of prey, and trodden down of men. Alas! how many even now in the present hour despise thy person, live regardless of thy righteousness, have trodden under foot the Son of God, and count the blood of the covenant an unholy thing! But, precious Jesus! give me to behold thee as the sweet Flower of the field, open to the view of every traveller, and shedding the richness of thy fragrancy, under all the influences of thy Spirit, both in the north wind, and the south wind of thy power. Ye travellers to Zion, come, see this lovely Flower in the open field of his word, his church, his ordinances! Behold the freeness of his bloom, his beauty,

and odour. He sheds his influences, not in a garden in-
closed that ye cannot approach, but in the open field. Here
he stands, as the Plant of Renown, which God hath raised
up. Oh! come to him as the Balm of Gilead, and the Physician there, that the hurt of the daughter of his people may
be healed.

19.—Is this thy kindness to thy friend?—2 *Sam.* xvi. 17.

My soul, borrow the words of Absalom to Hushai, and
make application of them this morning to thyself, as if Jesus,
the best of all friends, were thus reasoning with thee. In
how many ways hath Jesus manifested his love to thee?
Think of this unparalled love in the various ways by which
he hath shown it. He engaged as thy Surety before that
thou knewest any need of one. He took thy nature to fulfil
all those engagements. He loved thee so as to die for thee.
He loved thee so as to shed his blood for thee. He loved
thee so as to wash thee from thy sins in his blood. He
loveth thee now, so as to appear in the presence of God for
thee. He loveth thee so as to be continually supplying thee
with all grace, to visit thee, to smile upon thee, to sanctify to
thee all his appointments for thy good; and will never give
over until he hath brought thee where he is, to behold his
glory, and to partake of it. And hast thou not recompensed
this love, this mercy, in a thousand, and ten thousand instances, with ingratitude, with indifference, with forgetfulness, with disobedience? Is this thy kindness to thy friend?
Precious Jesus! I do remember my faults this day. Oh,
gracious Lord, grant me from henceforth to live wholly to
thee; to be continually eyeing thee, walking with thee, cleaving to thee, hanging upon thee, and to remember thee and
thy love more than wine! Yes, thou dearest Redeemer! I
would pray for grace to set thee always before me, to record
in my heart thy mercies, and to set up in my heart thy person,
to follow thee whithersoever thou goest, to watch the steps of
Jesus, to pursue thee in all the haunts of thy paths, at thy
table, at thine ordinances, in thy word, in thine house of
prayer, in thy providences, in thy promises: every where,
and in all things, where Jesus is, there may my soul be;
that, having nothing to give my Lord to recompense his
bounty, I may at least by his grace follow him, to bless him,
and to manifest that all I am, and all I have, is his. My
soul, see to it, that this is at least thy kindness to thy friend!

20.—Length of days is in her right hand, and in her left hand riches
and honour.—*Prov.* iii. 16.

WHAT is sweetly said of Jesus in one scripture, as the
Glory-wisdom, is as sweetly sung in another scripture, as
the Husband of his church and people. Yes, Lord! thy
right-hand blessings may well be called length of days, for
they are life itself, even life everlasting in thee: and thy left-
hand mercies, which include all temporal good, may well
merit the name of riches and honour, for thou givest to all
that love thee to inherit substance, and thou fillest all their
treasures. There is no substance in any, nothing satisfying,
nothing substantial, where thou art not. Why then, blessed
Jesus, if these things be so, I would say to thee, as the church
of old did, "Put thy left hand under my head, and let thy
right hand embrace me." This will make every thing sweet,
and every thing precious. Even thy left hand blessings, in
the sanctified use of afflictions, sorrow, bereaving providences,
sickness, and the like, even these, being Jesus' appointments,
will bring with them Jesus' blessing; and while thine hand
is under my head, how shall these, or aught else, separate
me from thee? And concerning thy righthand blessings,
in the pardon of my sins, washing me in thy blood, clothing
me with thy righteousness, justifying me with thy salvation,
feeding me, sustaining me, leading me, comforting me, bringing me on, and bringing me through, and by and by bringing
me home, to glory: that where thou art, there I shall be also:
oh, precious Jesus! grant me in this sweet sense to know
thee, and to enjoy thee, in every thing; for sure I am, that
riches and honour are with thee, yea, durable riches and
righteousness.

21.—He found him in a desert land, and in the waste howling wilderness.
Deut. xxxii. 10.

MY soul! behold in this view of Israel thy case and circumstances. Where did Jesus find thee, when he passed by
and bade thee live, but cast out, loathsome in thy person, and
perishing in nature? Remember, then, it was Jesus found
thee, and not thou him. And where wast thou born, and
new-born, and nursed, and educated, and trained? Was it
not in a desert land, and in the waste howling wilderness?
Can any thing be better suited to represent thy state by nature? Is not the heart of man like the heath upon the desert,

that knoweth not when good cometh ?   Is it not like the
ground, dry, parched, and barren ?   And as a wilderness is
a land not inhabited, full of perplexed paths and intricate
ways, without food, without sustenance, and no springs of
water ; can any thing more strikingly resemble the whole
of thy spiritual circumstances, when Jesus called thee from
darkness to light, and from the power of sin and Satan to
himself the living God ?   And as the wilderness is a barren
state, so is it dangerous also, by reason of the prowling beasts
of prey which inhabit it.   And hath Jesus called thee out of
it, brought thee to a city of habitation, and made himself
known unto thee as thy Redeemer ?   Oh ! how sweet is it to
trace all our spiritual circumstances, in the mercy, grace, and
favour, Jesus manifested to Israel, thus beautifully illustrated
and explained, and to see, and know, and truly rejoice in our
unspeakable mercies in Jesus.   My soul ! never forget then
that it was in the wilderness of nature Jesus found thee ! and
hath he indeed brought thee out of it ?   See then that thou
art now coming up from it leaning upon thy Beloved ; hanging wholly upon him, cleaving wholly to him, and determining for thyself, in every remaining period of time, and to all
eternity, to make Jesus thy all, thy life, thy portion, thy shield,
and thine exceeding great reward !

22.—Thy daughter is dead ; trouble not the Master.—*Luke* viii. 49.

MARK, my soul, in the exercises of the father of this child,
and in the happy issue of his application to Jesus, how very
precious it is, to wait the Lord's time for deliverance, and always to keep in view that delays are not denials.   The poor
man's child was nearly dead when he first came to Christ.
And had the greatest dispatch been used, there would have
been still much occasion for the exercise of faith and patience.   But as if this was not enough, another poor sufferer comes in the way to stop the progress of Jesus in the
cure of his daughter, and during this loss of time his child
dies.   My soul ! here is a sweet subject for thee.   Do thy
fears, and unbelief, and doubts, and misgivings, aided by the
suggestions of the enemy, too often prompt thee to think thy
case hopeless ; and every thing joins the cry, Thy daughter
is dead, trouble not the Master ?   Oh ! think what a precious
opportunity all these afford thee to follow up the patriarch's
faith, and against hope to believe in hope.   What cannot
Jesus accomplish ?   Though the daughter be dead ; though

Lazarus be four days in the grave; yet Jesus, who is the resurrection and the life, need only speak the word, and both live. In like manner, when exercises arise to the greatest height, until unbelief suggests all is over, dead frames, a dead heart, deadness to all, then is the very time to believe, in order to see the glory of God. Strictly and properly speaking, Jesus cannot be glorified until the stream of all other resources is dried up. Mark it then, my soul, thy time to trust Jesus is, when nothing in nature, but wholly grace, must trust him. And depend upon it, the greater the difficulty for the keeping faith alive, the greater glory will you give to Jesus in the exercise of it, and the greater glory that blessed Saviour will receive from you in supplying that faith during the dead hour, until the deliverance comes. Hear Jesus' voice in thy instance, be it what it may, as in the case of this distressed father, for the issue will be the same: fear not; believe only, and thou shalt live.

23.—Such an one as Paul the aged.—*Philemon* 9.

AND what was Paul in the moment here represented? Verily an aged servant of his Master, but not retired from the scene of action. Paul, though grown old in the Lord's service, was still as hotly engaged as ever, in the Lord's battle. Art thou such an one, my soul, as Paul was? Then learn from hence, that however many, or however heavy, former campaigns have been, there is no rest for thee this side Jordan, no more than for Paul; no winter quarters for the true soldiers of Jesus Christ. Until thy Captain undress thee for the grave, the holy armour in which he hath clad thee is not to be taken off. Art thou such an one as Paul the aged? Then, like Paul, see that thou art strong in the Lord, and in the power of his might. And how sweet the thought! Thy Jesus, who hath borne thee from the womb, and carried thee from the belly, knows well the burthen of thy increasing years, and all the infirmities belonging to them, and will carry both thee and them. Yes, my soul, those very infirmities which the tenderest-hearted friend sometimes feels impatient at, and even thyself, thou knowest not how to bear, Jesus feels, Jesus commisserates, Jesus will soften! He that hath carried all thy sins, carrieth also all thy sorrows. Doth he not say so? Even to your old age I am he; and even to hoar hairs I will carry you. I have made, and I will bear; even I will carry, and will deliver you, Isaiah xlvi. 3, 4.

Precious Lamb of God! henceforth I cast all my burdens
upon thee. Thou hast never called thyself, I AM, for nothing. Thou hast indeed made me, and new-made me. Thou
hast borne all my sins in thine own body on the tree. Art
thou not both the Alpha and the Omega, both the Author and
Finisher, of my salvation? Oh, yes: thou hast been every
thing to me, and for me, from the womb of creation; borne
me on eagle's wings; made me, and new-made me; redeemed me, in a thousand redemptions, and been better to
me than all my fears! What, indeed, hast thou not done for
me? And now then, being such an one as Paul the aged,
shall I now doubt, or now fear, when every pain, and every
cross, and every new assault from sin, and Satan, bid me go
to Jesus. Oh! for grace, ever to keep in view what thou
hast said and done, and what thou hast promised. Yes, yes:
it is enough; Jesus hath said, "even to your old age I am
he." The same I have been, the same I will ever be. I
will never leave thee, nor forsake thee. Shout, my soul, and
cry out Hallelujah! He that hath been my first, will be my
last; my strength, my song, my salvation for ever!

24.—Then ceased the work of the house of God.—*Ezra* iv. 24.

Ah! how distressed was Zion, when this decree took
place. And yet the history of the church plainly proves
that the hand of the Lord was in it! My soul, are thine
exercises sometimes similar? Doth it seem to thee as if the
work of God in thee was at a stand? nay, as if it was totally over? Pause! recollect there is a set time to favour
Zion. Thy Jesus is of one mind, and who can turn him?
He is everlastingly pursuing the designs of his love. And
as Zion was graven upon the palms of his hands, and her
walls were continually before him, when she appeared in her
most desolate circumstances; so the work of his grace, in
the heart of his people, doth not remit, though, to thy view,
all thy promising beginnings seem to be blighted, and as it
seems in thy apprehension, thou findest growing imperfection. And is not Jesus, by this very means, emptying thee
of self, and all the pride of self-attainments? Is he not pre-
paring thee for his own glory, by removing in thee the rubbish of all creature-confidences? Remember what is said;
When the Lord shall build up Zion, he shall appear in his
glory. Mark here, that it is the Lord that is to build Zion:
and it is the Lord's glory, and not thine, that is to result from

it. The work of the house of God in thee would indeed
cease, if the work was thine, or thou hadst any hand in the
performance of it! But the same almighty hand which laid
the foundation of this house, those hands shall also finish it.
And by this process, the glorious Builder is teaching thee to
cease from thine own works, as Jesus when redemption-work
was finished, did from his. Precious Lord! is this the cause,
and are these the lessons, thou art teaching me, in the deadness, emptiness, and the numberless complaints under which
I daily groan? Oh! then, for grace to cease from self, to
cease from all fancied attainments, and to have my whole
heart and soul centred in thee, in whom alone is all righteousness, grace, work, and fulness. Yes, Lord! the work
is thine, the salvation is thine, the glory is thine, all is thine;
and all that remains for me, is to be for ever giving thee the
just praise that is due to thy most holy name, content to be
nothing, yea, less than nothing, that the power of Jesus may
rest upon me; for when most weak in myself, then am I most
strong in the Lord, and in the power of his might.

25.—And the inhabitant shall not say, I am sick ; the people that dwell
therein shall be forgiven their iniquity.—*Isaiah* xxxiii. 24.

WHAT is this? What happy climate is there where any
of its inhabitants are exempt from sickness? Where is that
salubrious air, that is not impregnated with disease? Surely,
no where but in heaven. But if the cause of sickness be
removed, if the envenomed dart of sin be taken out, and hath
lost its poison, the inhabitant no longer complains, for both
the evil and the pain is gone. My soul, hast thou found this
happy spot? Hath Jesus manifested such views of his pardoning grace, in the all-sufficiency of his blood and righteousness, that thou not only art fully convinced and satisfied
that his blood cleanseth from all sin, but that thou as fully
believest and restest in it for thy salvation, and art of the
happy number of those who believe to the salvation of the
soul? Hath Jesus said to thee, as to the poor man in the
gospel, "Son, be of good cheer, thy sins are forgiven thee?"
Surely, then, thou art the inhabitant the prophet pointed at,
and art no longer sick, but dwelling in the faith, and forgiven thine iniquity. Blessed Physician! I am no longer
sick of that dreadful sickness which is unto death, in an unrenewed, unpardoned, unregenerated state; but I am sick
indeed, and fainting, for the fresh manifestations of thy grace.

13

I am languishing, thou dearest Lord, for the renewed visits of thy love, the enjoyment of thy person, the larger, fuller, more constant discoveries of thyself and thy glory. When wilt thou come unto me? When will the day of everlasting light break in upon my soul? When shall I behold thee among the inhabitants of the upper, brighter world? Oh! ye spirits of just men made perfect, ye who now dwell for ever under the perpetual smiles of Jesus' face; ye who once knew what it was to live in the unceasing desire of his renewed visits, and how precious all his love tokens are—tell him what longings my soul now hath, and what faintings I feel, for his manifestation. Tell him, I charge you, Oh ye daughters of the New Jerusalem, ye that everlastingly behold my Beloved, tell him that I am sick of love!

26.—Thou hast ascended on high ; thou hast led captivity captive : thou hast received gifts for men ; yea, for the rebellious also, that the Lord God might dwell among them.—*Psalm* lxviii. 18

SWEET view of a risen, ascended, and triumphant Saviour. My soul, ponder over these words, and while meditating upon them, see that thou art ascending after thy exalted Head, and partaking in his glories. Jesus is he who hath indeed ascended, far above all heavens, that he might fill all things. He hath led captivity captive; and that not only in conquering all the powers of hell, but taking his people that were in captivity out of the prison-house, and causing them to partake in the felicity of his triumphs. And mark, my soul, what follows: He hath received gifts for men ; or, as the Apostle to the church of Ephesus expresseth the same blessed truth, he gave gifts to men. Eph. iv. 8. And sweetly Jesus hath done both ; for he received that he might give. He needed not for himself, but it was all for his people. He said himself, when speaking to the Father, "that I should give eternal life to as many as thou hast given me." And, my soul, mark another sweet expression in these words; he hath received gifts for men ; or, as the margin of our old Bibles hath it, (and our old Bibles are like old gold, precious things,) he hath received gifts *in the man;* that is, in his human nature, as Mediator, to give out to his people. See then, my soul, all thy blessings are treasured up in Him that is, in one and the same moment, thy God and thy Brother. Oh, glorious thought! oh, soul-comforting truth! Neither is this all: for this sweet scripture points out also for whom he hath received gifts. It is for men. Not for angels, but for men. Not for holy men neither, but for sinners. Not for Jews only, but for Gentiles. "Yea," saith the Holy Ghost, as if the Lord the Spirit would lay an emphasis upon it, that it might be particularly noticed, "for the rebellious also, that the Lord God might dwell among them." Oh, matchless grace! Oh, world of wonders! Fallen angels passed by, and rebels of men taken into favour. Great Father of mercies! what manner of love is this which thou hast bestowed upon our fallen nature? Oh, thou risen and exalted Jesus! send down, Lord, thine ascension gifts. Nay, blessed Lord! come down thyself and dwell among us. Set up thy church in the earth, in the hearts and souls of thy people, and reign and rule there, the Lord of life and glory.

27.—Thine ears shall hear a word behind thee, saying, This is the way, walk ye in it, when ye turn to the right hand, and when ye turn to the left.—*Isaiah* xxx. 21.

My soul, who is this Almighty Teacher, out of sight, but the Holy Ghost? And to what way doth he point, but to Jesus, who is both the way, and the truth, and the life? Art thou ever at a stand? listen to this voice. Art thou about to turn to the right, or left? see how seasonably he is promised to come to direct thee. Condescend, thou gracious, matchless Instructor, to guide me! I shall not fail then to know the wholesomeness of thy teaching, when thou hast opened mine eyes to see the wondrous things of thy law. I shall indeed know that thou art my Director, because thou hast said, "I the Lord teacheth thee to profit." And when thy word comes not in word only, but in power, and in thee the Holy Ghost, surely I shall know it, in that it not only reaches my ear, but will influence my heart; not only will instruct and teach me in the way wherein I should go, but will incline my feet to walk in it. Yes, thou infallible Teacher! I shall know thee to be the Spirit of truth, by guiding me into all truth. I shall know the voice of the Spirit of Jesus, because it will prompt me to follow Jesus. Did I hear a voice, telling me of a way of salvation in a righteousness of my own: did I sit under a teaching which sent me to my tears, and repentance, and alms deeds, by way of recommending me to God; did I listen to the siren song, which told me of safety in myself, and my own best endeavours, and that Christ would do the rest; or did any teach me that I must not come to Jesus until that, by some previous acts of soul-cleansing in prayers and fastings, I had made myself fit: in all these cases, and the like, I should know that they could not be the voice behind me, promised to direct; because it is thy one glorious office, thou holy and eternal Spirit, to testify of Jesus, and to glorify him. When, therefore, I hear the voice behind me, saying, This is the way, walk ye in it; and when it directs me wholly to Jesus; when every thing in this divine teaching enlightens my mind in the knowledge of the person, relation, work, power, grace, righteousness, and love of the Lord Jesus Christ; and when that blessed voice bids me to come unto him, just as I am, a poor, vile, needy, perishing sinner, to venture upon him for life and salvation, and how to receive and improve the Lord Jesus, in his infinite suitableness to all my necessities: oh, how fully verified to my experience is this sweet promise of my God to my soul! Holy Father! cause me to hear this blessed voice, in the daily, hourly path of my pilgrimage; and grant me the spirit of wisdom and revelation, in the knowledge of thy dear Son.

28.—They shall grow as the vine.—*Hosea* xiv. 7.

AND how doth the vine grow? Why, in those soils that are favourable to it, vines are not erect like trees, neither are they fixed, as we do our vines, against walls; but the vine creeps along upon the ground, and rests its tender stalk and branches upon the nearest prop that will stay it. And, my soul, is it not so with the believer that wholly leans upon Jesus, and throws the arms of faith wholly upon Him, as the staff, and stay, and support of all confidence? And there is another property of the vine which carries with it a striking resemblance to the believer, namely, the tenderness of its nature, and danger to which it is exposed. How very weak, and poor, and frail, and helpless is the child of God! What can a believer perform in himself? And what an host of foes is he exposed to! Corruption within, and the enemy on every side, make his case truly like the vine, exposed to the wild beast, and nipping winds, and storms, which every moment threaten to destroy it. And there is a third particularity by which both are known. While flourishing, to what an extensive length will the vine throw out her branches, and what an abundance of fruit will it bear! And doth not the believer, in this sense, grow as the vine, when, from being ingrafted in Jesus, and nourished by him, and from him, his fruit being found, sends forth the graces and fruits of the Spirit, and brings forth some thirty, some sixty, and some an hundred fold? And, to mention no more, what a likeness is there between the dry, unpromising stick of the vine, and the lifeless and unpromising appearance of the believer! As Jesus himself, when upon earth, was like a root out of a dry ground, so all his followers now are men every where wondered at. Precious Jesus! thou glorious Vine of thy church! cause me to be so united to thee, as a branch in thee, the one heavenly Plant thy Father hath planted, that in thee my fruit may be found; that I may be perpetually receiving fresh communications from thee, and living upon thee, and to thee, and rejoicing in thee, the Source and Fountain of all that is gracious here, and the everlasting Spring of glory, happiness, and joy, that shall be hereafter.

29.—As by the offence of one, judgment came upon all men to condemnation; even so by the righteousness of one, the free gift came upon all men unto justification of life.—*Romans* v. 18.

CONCERNING the ruin in which thou art involved in Adam, surely, my soul, thou knowest and feelest it from day to day. No one can persuade thee out of this. Thou art as much concerned in the sin, and consequently implicated in the punishment, of the first man's transgression, as if thou hadst been (and which indeed as thy root and head thou really wert) in the garden with him when he did it. And thou feelest the same disposition to sin, the same rebellion in thy very nature. So that most fully and freely dost thou subscribe to the rights of God's judgment, that condemnation cometh upon all men, because all have sinned. Now then see, my soul, whether, through the same Almighty Teacher who convinced thee of sin, thou art convinced also of the righteousness of Jesus, and art as fully and as truly interested in all that belongs unto him. Now as Adam and his seed are one in sin and its just consequences, so equally Christ and his seed, in the eye of God's law and justice, are one in Christ's righteousness. Remember, my soul, (and it is a great point to remember,) Jesus is never spoken of in Scripture as a single person and as the Christ of God, but as the Covenant Head. He is as much the head, the root, the common stock, of all his spiritual seed, as Adam was the head, and root, and stock, of all his natural seed. So then, as Adam's sin is the sin of all his children, because they are his children; even so the righ-

13*

teousness of Christ, the second Adam, so called, is the righteousness of all his children, because they are his children. This is so plain a truth, that it can need no further argument. The next point now is, in order to enjoy all the comfort and blessedness which ariseth out of this precious doctrine, that thou shouldest be able, my soul, to prove that thou art of Christ's seed. Very fully thou provest from day to day, by the remains of indwelling corruption that ariseth within, that thou art of the stock of the first Adam: how wilt thou prove thy relationship to the second? For as upon the presumption I had not sprung from the stock of Adam, and none of his blood was running in my veins, I should not have partaken of his sin, or been subject to his punishment; so equally evident it is, that if I am not born again and belong to the seed of Christ, I am not interested in him or his righteousness. Blessed be God! the relationship with Jesus, as the glorious Head and Mediator of his people, is as easily to be proved as the relationship with Adam. God promised to pour out of his spirit upon Christ's seed, Isaiah xliv. 3, 4, 5. Hast thou then, my soul, the spirit of Christ, as thou hast the nature of Adam? Is Jesus precious, more precious than gold —his salvation dear—his righteousness thy only confidence? Canst thou, and dost thou, say with one of old, this is all my salvation, and all my desire. Is He whom the Father delighteth in, thy delight—he that is the desire of all nations, thy desire? If these and the like testimonies are in thy experience, my soul, what greater evidences dost thou need, to manifest thy relationship to thy Jesus, as thy corruptions prove thee allied to the old nature. See then, my soul, that thou foldest up this soul-reviving truth for thy bosom, and carriest it about with thee daily wherever thou goest; so will Jesus be thy hope and thy portion for ever.

30.—Renewing of the Holy Ghost, which he shed on us abundantly, through Jesus Christ our Saviour.—*Titus* iii. 5, 6.

PRECIOUS office of the Spirit! Condescend, great God, to grant it to me this morning. Oh, renew my soul with all thy sweet revivals, after a night of sleep, as thou renewest the face of the earth. Oh, send forth, I beseech thee, Lord, all thy graces, as suited to my necessities and the Redeemer's glory, and let it be most abundantly shed abroad through all the faculties of my soul, through Jesus Christ my Saviour Pause, my soul, over the blessed prospect, and, having now pleaded in Jesus' name for the mercy, act forth upon thy God in his promises. Is not every morning a renewing of the Holy Ghost? Is it not said concerning the productions of the earth, that God " sendeth forth his Spirit, and they are created, and thou renewest the face of the earth." See what an evidence the earth gives in this lovely season, in the fruits, and plants, and verdure all around. And are the saints of Jesus of a less sweet smelling savour, when perfumed as they are with the everlasting odour of Jesus' never-failing righteousness ? Do the fields, when renewed by the sun of the morning, look gay, and lovely, and after the dew or the refreshing shower, give out their odour, perfuming the air with their fragrancy ; and shall not the saints of God, when the Sun of righteousness ariseth upon them with healing in his wings, send forth all the blessed effects of that presence which revives the grace Jesus hath planted, and calls forth into exercise the faith he hath given? Shall not the showers of his love, when he comes down in them as rain upon the mown grass, and the dews of the Holy Ghost's renewings, revive all the languishing frames of the soul, and cause even the desert to blossom abundantly, and to rejoice with joy and singing? Yes, yes, thou blessed Lord! methinks I feel thy sweet and gracious renewings : my very heart is refreshed in the thought. Under thy influence I will look up and wait the coming of Jesus. He is near. He comes. I hear him say, " Rise up, my beloved, and come away: for lo, the winter is past, the rain is over and gone, the flowers appear on the earth, the time of the singing of birds is come, and the voice of the turtle is heard in our land."

31.—And Jesus came and spake unto them, saying, All power is given unto me in heaven and in earth.—*Matt.* xxviii. 18.

HAIL then, thou Sovereign Lord of all! I have lately been following thee in sweet and solemn meditation through the seasons of thy humiliation ; now let me behold thee on thy throne. And here I am called upon to contemplate my Lord and my God as possessing universal dominion. Ponder, my soul, the vast extent. Thy Jesus, as God, as one with the Father, possesseth in common with him all power from everlasting. This is his, as God, essentially so ; not given to him, for by nature it is his, being " one with the Father, over all God blessed for ever. Amen," said Paul, so let it be, so shall it be. And so say I, and so saith all! the church: Amen, Amen. But what thy Jesus saith here, in these blessed words, is of a power *given* to him: and that is a power as the Head of his church and people. And although had he not been God, one with the Father, he never could have been suited for the exercise of this power; (for unless he had been the mighty God, how should he have been the mighty Redeemer?) yet being God, and both God · and man, it is precious to consider the power that is given to the Lord Jesus as Jesus, the Head over all things to the church, which is his body, the fulness of Him that filleth all in all. Here then, my soul, let thy thoughts take wing this morning. Behold thy Jesus the Head over all principality and power. See him, by virtue of his Almighty Godhead, exercising and giving energy to the fulness of his power as Mediator; and in this view conceive if it be possible, to what an extent thy Jesus is unceasingly exercising his power for the everlasting benefit of his church and people. All power in heaven: not only among the highest order of created being, angels and archangels, but a power with God the Father to prevail for the eternal salvation of all his redeemed. He left it as a record how he exercised this power when he said before his departure, Father, I will that they whom thou hast given me, be with me where I am, to behold my glory." And he hath power to send the Holy Ghost to all his people. He said himself, before he went away, "If I go not away, the Comforter will not come; but if I depart, I will send him unto you." Here then, my soul, here let thy thoughts be directed, to meditate upon the fulness and extensiveness of that power which thy Jesus possesseth in heaven. Well may it be said that he hath the keys of heaven, when he hath all power with the Father and with the Spirit. And well may it be said that he hath the keys of hell also, when all things in heaven and earth, and under the earth, are subject to his command. And hath he not power then, my soul, suited to answer every want of thine, and of all his church and people? Hath he not power over all flesh, to give eternal life to as many as the Father hath given him? Wilt thou complain, shall the church complain, of any want, while Jesus is upon the throne? Art thou poor, is the church poor, weak, helpless, needy, guilty, polluted, oppressed, exercised? What of all these, and ten thousand other situations, while Jesus lives, and hath all power? Nay, is it not so much the better that the people of Jesus are what they are, that they may be the better suited for his glory, and that their wants may give occasion for the supplies of his grace? Hail! thou Almighty Sovereign, now methinks I would be always poor, always needy, always feeling my nothingness, that all these may constrain me to come to thee: so that every day's necessities may afford a fresh occasion to crown thee Lord of all in a day of grace until I come to crown thee, with the whole church, the everlasting Lord of all in heaven, to the glory of God the Father.   Amen.

JUNE.

1.—The Lord said unto my Lord.—*Psalm* cx. 1.

Some have called this Psalm *David's Creed*. Certain it is that there is scarce an article of a true believer's faith, but what is in it. My soul, look through it this morning, if thou hast time, and see whether it is *thy* creed. If not, look at this precious portion of it, and ask of the Holy Ghost to teach thee the blessed things contained in it. The Lord said unto my Lord: that is, Jehovah said unto my Adonai.   Observe, my soul, that here, as in many other parts of the Bible, one of these words " Lord" is in capital letters, the other in small characters. This no doubt was done by the translators, by way of telling the English reader that the two words in the original Hebrew are not the same. They had no better method of explaining the difference. But by using different sized letters, they meant to say that there is a difference, and the difference seems to be this : the word Lord, whenever used in the Bible in capital letters, signifies Jehovah ; Father, Son, and Holy Ghost: not as a name of office in the work of redemption, but as intimating his own glorious incommunicable essence. The word Lord in small letters, Adonai, is very frequently (as in this Psalm) applied to Christ in his gracious office as the Christ of God and of his people. And a most sweet and precious name it is. It signifies in a double meaning, *first*, his own personal authority and power ; and, *secondly*, that power as exerted and called forth into action for his redeemed. Look at thy Jesus, my soul, as thy Adonai this day, and every day ; and a thousand sweet and precious blessings such a view of Him, as a *ruler*, and a *support*, and a *sustainer*, will open to thy meditation. Yes, all-lovely, all-powerful, all-gracious Adonai ! thou art my Adonai ! In this thy name, which is as ointment poured forth, would I contemplate thee. In this thy name would I rejoice all the day, and in thy righteousness would I be exalted.

2.—Living waters shall go out from Jerusalem ; half of them toward the former sea, and half of them toward the hinder sea : in summer and in winter shall it be.—*Zech.* xiv. 8.

My soul! was not this fulfilled in part when the gospel went forth from Jerusalem ? And is it not now fulfilling, while the same blessed gospel is going forth from sea to sea, and from the river even unto the ends of the earth ? Surely neither the summer's drought, nor the winter's frost, shall dry up or congeal those living waters. But, my soul, hast thou asked of Jesus, as the woman of Samaria did in the moment of Jesus' promise, for those living waters ? Oh ! if thou knowest my soul, this gift of God, and wilt daily, hourly, ask of him, both in summer and in winter, he will give thee these living waters. Oh, contemplate their property, and then, my soul, ask and receive, that thy joy may be full. Jesus himself is this well of living waters ; and wherever he comes, like the waters in Ezekiel's vision, he gives life, and quickens sinners dead in trespasses and sins. Also, Jesus in those streams maintains the life he hath first given. Moreover, Jesus not only maintains, but revives, and renews them, again and again, when the grace of his people languish. Again, these living waters of thy Jesus are always running : here is nothing stagnate, but always flowing. Lastly, into whatever heart Jesus gives them, they shall be, as he hath promised, a well of water springing up to everlasting life. Are these things so ? And have the saints in all ages, and under all dispensations of the church, both in the Old Testament and in the New, been thus supplied ? Is it indeed He, my beloved, who is the same yesterday, and to-day, and for ever, that thus hath supplied, and is supplying, and ever will supply all ? Is it thou, oh thou precious Lamb of God ! that art in the midst of the throne, leading the church above to fountains of living waters, and becoming the same to the church below ? Wilt thou not give of thy fulness to satisfy my thirsty soul in this dry and barren land, where no water is? Yes, yes, my soul, exult with the church of old, for thy Jesus is the same: a fountain of gardens, a well of living waters, and streams from Lebanon, is my beloved!

3.—In his favour is life.—*Psalm* xxx. 5.

OH, for grace to keep this always in view! for then, thou dear Lord, I should never consider my dead frames, or dead feelings, since I well know that thou ever bearest favour and good will towards thy people. For if thy providences frown, or seem to frown, do I not know that behind that aspect thy countenance is the same, always gracious, always favourable, and that thou art invariably pursuing the everlasting happiness of thy people? Let it please thee, my Lord, to grant me this morning such views of thy favour, that I may henceforth trace it in every thing. Was it not this favour that first opened a source of salvation? Was it not this favour that brought me into a participation of it? Was it not this favour that begat me to the knowledge of it—that quickened me to an enjoyment of it—that opened the communication of it, by which thy grace became imparted to my soul? And was it not the same favour that kept alive the incorruptible spark, and maintained it through all attempts of sin, and the world, and the powers of darkness, to extinguish it? Nay, blessed Jesus! what is it now but thy favour that secures me in thy love, and gives me all the inexpressible felicity of mercy, pardon, and peace now, and everlasting glory hereafter? And is not thy favour, then, better than life? Is it not more precious than rubies? Can there be aught desirable like it? Truly, Lord, in thee and thy favour I have life, for thou art both my light and my life: my heart trusteth in thee, and I am helped. Remember me then, oh Lord, with the favour that thou bearest unto thy people; oh visit me with thy salvation!

4.—Awake, O north wind, and come, thou south, blow upon my garden.—*Song* iv. 16.

ARE these the words of my Lord? Yes, surely, they can be no other; for none but Jesus can send the Holy Ghost to his church and people. And, beside, none can call the church *my garden*, but he that is the rightful owner of it. Surely, Lord, it is thine, both by thy Father's gift, and by thy choice,

and by thy purchase, and by the conquests of thy grace, and
by the voluntary surrender of thy people, when thou hast
made them willing in the day of thy power.   And dost thou
call, then, both the north wind and the south, thou dearest
Lord, to blow upon my soul?   Dost thou command all suited
influences of thy grace to visit me, that one may search, and
another warm, my affections, and call thine own gifts and
graces forth in exercise upon thy glorious Person, and thy
glorious work?   Oh, come then, thou Holy Spirit, with all
thy sweet and precious offices!   Come, Lord, to convince
and comfort me, to humble and direct me, to chill my affections to the world, and to warm them towards the Lord Jesus!   Come, thou holy, gracious, Almighty Quickener, Re-
viver, Restorer, and Glorifier of my God and Saviour!   Oh,
if thou wilt make my soul like the chariots of Amminadib,
and cause those graces thou hast planted there to go forth in
a way of love, and desire, and faith, and expectation, and
hope, upon the Person and glory of Him whom my soul
loveth, then shall I cry out, with the church, and say, " Let
my beloved come into his garden, and eat of his pleasant
fruits !"

5.—Have ye received the Holy Ghost?—*Acts* xix. 2.

My soul, ponder over the solemn question again and again,
and then see what answer thou canst give to a point so infinitely interesting and important.   The Holy Spirit is clearly
known by the exercise of his blessed offices in every heart
where he abides, and where he is the glorious inhabitant.
He comes in Jesus' name as an *Ambassador*, to propose to the
sinner a rich and precious Saviour.   He comes as an Almighty *Teacher;* and this condescending office he graciously
exerciseth, in convincing of sin, and convincing of the righteousness of Jesus.   He comes as an *Advocate;* and by his
pleading the cause of a poor sinner's own necessities, and
the cause of a rich Saviour's willingness and ability to supply all these necessities, he manifests himself a most powerful advocate, when, by his constraining grace, he makes the
poor sinner willing in the day of his power.   He comes as an
Enlightener of the dark and untutored mind of the sinner,
and this he doth most effectually, when, by shining in the
heart, he gives the light of the knowledge of the glory of
God in the face of Jesus Christ.   Most gloriously he shines
upon the soul, when, by the ministry of his blessed word,

and by the influences of his divine grace, he leads the mind forth to the contemplation and love of the person, blood, and righteousness of the Lord Jesus Christ. He comes as a *Witness*, also, to testify of Jesus. And this sweet office is manifested in the conscience, when at any time he shows sin to be exceedingly sinful; and that nothing but the blood of Jesus can cleanse from it. And his witness in the soul is proved to the fullest demonstration, when he powerfully brings the guilty conscience under so deep a sense of sin, and so alarmingly concerned for the consequence of it, that nothing will satisfy until Jesus is revealed and brought home to the heart, in all the beauties of his Person, and the fulness and suitableness of his salvation, and formed there the hope of glory. He comes also as a *Comforter*; and oh how sweetly and fully doth he manifest both the power of his Godhead, and the sovereignty and grace of his character, when, by his consolations, as he opens and explains them, and makes application of them as they are in Jesus, he revives the drooping spirit, relieves the distressed spirit, animateth, refresheth, sanctifieth the whole heart, and soul, and mind, and gives a joy and peace in believing, abounding in hope by the power of the Holy Ghost. My soul, what sayest thou now to the question? Hast thou received the Holy Ghost? Surely I do know thee, thou gracious God the Spirit, by these sweet tokens of thy covenant office and character. Lord, I pray thee, be ever with me, and, agreeably to Jesus' gracious promise, abide with me for ever. Oh, may I never grieve thee, by whom my soul is sealed in Jesus to the day of eternal redemption.

6.—Blessed be the Lord, who daily loadeth us with benefits.—*Psalm* lxviii. 19.

BEHOLD, my soul, what a sweet portion for my morning meditation is here. See what thou canst gather out of it, to furnish new songs of praise to the bountiful Lord whose mercies it records. Blessed Spirit! I beseech thee open these precious words of thine to my view. Blessed be the Lord, it saith. Yea, so say I! Blessed be Jehovah. Blessed be the Father, Son, and Holy Ghost, for they are the united source of all my blessings. And blessed be the majesty and glory of God for ever, who daily loadeth his people with benefits. Count over, my soul, each of these blessed expressions, for every word is weighty and ponderous. God not

14

only gives blessings, but daily. His mercies are constant as the morning, unceasing, continual; strength suited to the day, and mercies adapted to every moment. Faith needs no hoards, no banking-houses: nay, it is faith's precious property, and her blessedness, to be always empty, in order that the sweetness of being filled by Jesus may be the better known. But this is not all. God not only daily gives out blessings, but *loadeth* his people with benefits. He openeth the windows of heaven, and poureth out of his grace in such fulness, that there is not room to receive. He makes their souls like the heart of Elihu, as it is said of him, for want of vent, like new bottles, he was ready to burst. So Jesus poureth out his love into the souls of his redeemed, that they are overpowered with his goodness. Knowest thou not, my soul, somewhat of this? Oh yes! I trust I do. Why then, blessed be God, who daily loadeth me with his benefits. And what endears all this in a ten thousand times greater degree, is the assurance that the whole is in a way of salvation. So saith this sweet scripture. He that loadeth us with benefits is the God of our salvation. He that is our God, even he is the God of our salvation. Oh, precious, blessed consideration! then are these blessings everlastingly secured: for He that now daily loadeth us with benefits, will unweariedly do the same to all eternity. He is not only the portion of his people now, but will be so for ever. He not only gives strength to the day, but will be himself our strength to all eternity. And mark it down, my soul, as the most blessed part of those daily benefits, he that thus loadeth the soul with all the benefits of covenant blessings, in the grace, mercy, favour, love. blood, righteousness, and all the sweet tokens of redemption in Jesus, signs and seals every one of them in his dear name: and as he said to Abraham, so he saith to all Abraham's seed, "Fear not, I am thy shield, and thine exceeding great reward." Shout then, my soul, and henceforth let this be thy morning song: "Blessed be the Lord, who daily loadeth thee with benefits."

7.—If there be a messenger with him, an Interpreter, one among a thousand, to shew unto man his uprightness; then he is gracious unto him, and saith, Deliver him from going down to the pit, I have found a ramsom.—*Job* xxxiii. 23, 24.

My soul, how precious are those views in looking back upon where the first discoveries of grace were made. Moses never forgot the first visions of God at the bush; neither did Jacob outlive the remembrance of the first Bethel visit of a God in Christ to his soul; and why should I? Hast thou not known this Messenger, this Interpreter, one among a thousand to show unto thee God's uprightness? Oh, yes! Jesus, by his Spirit, hath shown to me that my God is righteous in all his ways, and holy in his works. When by the blessed discoveries which have been made to me in his word, by his ordinances, providences, judgments, mercies, like the poor creature described in this sweet scripture, when reduced to a mere skeleton, by reason of soul-sickness, driven out of all resources in myself, and utterly despairing of ever seeing the face of God in glory, by any creature attempts, and by all creature righteousness: oh, then it was, thou blessed, glorious Messenger of thine own covenant, thou faithful Interpreter of the mind and will of Jehovah, then it was I was led to see the freeness, fulness, suitableness, and all-sufficiency of a Redeemer's righteousness, and to cast my poor, defenceless, naked, trembling soul, upon the rich, powerful, and altogether-sufficient salvation of thee, my God and Saviour! Oh! how hast thou sweetly and mercifully explained to me the secrets of covenant mercies, the glories of thy person, and the greatness of thy finished work. And now at every step I take, at every portion of thy blessed word I read, when my mind feels the remains of indwelling corruption, and all the lurkings of the enemy's suggestions within; then, then it is I hear the Father's gracious voice: "Deliver him from going down to the pit, I have found a ransom." Yes, precious Jesus, thou art my ransom, and my righteousness for ever!

8.—A red heifer without spot, wherein is no blemish, and upon which never came yoke. And ye shall give her unto Eleazar the priest, that he may bring her forth without the camp, and one shall slay her before his face.—*Numbers* xix. 2, 3.

I REMEMBER well it is said of our Lord Jesus, that, in order to sanctify the people with his own blood, he suffered without the gate. But though I clearly apprehend that the law, with all its sacrifices, was but a shadow of good things to come, and the body was Christ, yet, had not the Holy Ghost been graciously pleased to illustrate and explain by other Scriptures, somewhat either direct, or by allusion, in reference to Jesus, I should have overlooked how, in many striking points, Jesus is here set forth in this type. Surely, Lord, thy spotless purity was beautifully represented in the spotless heifer, here appointed for sacrifice. And the very rare colour of a red heifer, plainly testified the singularity of thy sacrifice. Adam himself was so called, as a token of the red earth from whence he was taken. And when Jesus, as the Son of man, came, to do away all the effects of Adam's sin and transgression, he manifested, by the redness of his apparel, and the blood sprinkled upon his garments, the gracious purposes which all implied. But I do not recollect, in any other type of my Redeemer, a particularity which pointed to the freeness of thy voluntary sacrifice, oh, thou Lamb of God! as the one here represented, in that this heifer was to be one upon which had never come yoke. Nothing, Lord, but thine own free sovereign love, and at the call of God thy Father, prompted thine infinite mind to be the willing sacrifice for poor sinners. There was no yoke, no obligation, nothing to compel thee. Lo, I come, was thy gracious voice, when neither sacrifice nor offering could ransom thy people. Oh, Lord! let the sense of thy freeness in salvation comfort my soul under all heart-straitenings in myself, and the conciousness that there was no yoke upon thee, Lord, but thine own everlasting love, be the sweet constraining yoke on my soul, to bind me to thy love, and to thy service for ever.

9.—I would cause thee to drink of spiced wine of the juice of my pomegranate.—*Song* viii. 2.

WHAT, my soul, hast thou aught to offer to thy Jesus? Will he accept a present at thine hand? Yes, Jesus will accept those goings forth of his own grace, his own gift, in the exercises of faith, and love, and joy, and praise; when, by his own sweet and reviving communications, he hath called to the north wind, and to the south wind, to blow a gracious gale upon my soul, and causeth the very graces he himself hath planted in my heart to send forth all their powers in the enjoyment of his Person and righteousness. And do not forget, my soul, for thine encouragement to this lovely and becoming frame, these will be more grateful to thy God and Saviour than all whole burnt offerings and sacrifices. These will be indeed like spiced wine, and the juice of the pomegranate, when those tears of faith, and love, and repentance, drop at the mercy-seat, in the contemplation of that love of Jesus, which is better than wine. **Help me** then, thou dear Lord, thus to come to thee. Help me, as the poor woman at thy feet did, to shed my tears, and to offer thee this spiced wine: and no longer by sin, and unbelief, and rebellion, to give thee wine mingled with myrrh, as the Jews did at thy crucifixion. Oh God, my Saviour! let it never be said of my soul, from neglect and indifferency to thee and thy sufferings, as thou complainedst of them, "They gave me also gall for my meat, and in my thirst they gave me vinegar to drink." No, precious Lord! if thou wilt shed abroad the influences of thy Spirit in my heart, so as to lead out my whole soul in love to thee, in living upon thee, in contemplating thy glory, thy suitableness, thine all-sufficiency, then will my soul praise thee with joyful lips: and then will my beloved say, as to his church of old, " Thy lips, O my spouse, drop as the honey-comb ; honey and milk are under thy tongue."

10.—My voice shalt thou hear in the morning, O Lord ; in the morning will I direct my prayer unto thee, and will look up.—*Psalm* v. 3.

SWEET thought, my soul, to encourage thee this morning, that thy God in Christ is a prayer-quickening, a prayer-hearing, and a prayer-answering God. Art thou dull, dead, lifeless? one look from Jesus, one influence of the Spirit, will kindle desire, and lead thee to the mercy-seat, and to the throne of grace. Jesus will do more in one moment, to call off thy wandering thoughts, to open to thy views his glory, to reveal to thee what thy wants are, and to give thee a spirit of prayer suited to thy wants and his praise, than all thy laboured attempts, without an eye to Jesus, can do for thee for ever. Whence is it, my soul, that prayer is ever a burden, but because we have lost a sight of Jesus? Why is it that thou art at times so little affected with the remains of indwelling corruption, and canst neither rightly value God's mercies, or be humbled under thy own infirmities? Is it not because thou dost not look up, and behold Jesus in his priestly vesture, waiting to be gracious? Oh, didst thou but eye thy God and Saviour under this blessed character, how wouldst thou feel the preciousness of his great salvation, and haste to unload thyself upon the Lord Christ, and cast all thy burden of coldness, deadness, and sin, upon Him who is mighty to save! Come, Lord, then, I pray thee, with all thy sweet influences, fill my mouth with arguments, and my heart do thou warm with love. I know, Lord, I shall surely speed

14*

this day, this morning, at the mercy-seat, the moment thou
hast loosed my tongue, and enlarged my heart with thy
grace. Yes, yes, blessed Jesus, my voice shalt thou hear,
my voice wilt thou hear in the morning; at the dawn of day,
before cock-crowing, I will direct my prayers to thee, I will
send them up to heaven; and through the day, and all the
day, and seven times a day, will I praise thee, oh thou God
of my salvation, when thou hast caused me to praise thee
with joyful lips.

11.—And my people shall be satisfied with my goodness, saith the Lord.
Jeremiah xxxi. 14.

EXAMINE thine heart, my soul, this morning, and see
whether this blessed promise is really and truly fulfilled in
thy experience. Art thou satisfied with Jehovah's goodness?
Yes, if so be thou hast received that goodness as manifested
and treasured up in the person and work of Christ, and art
so believing as to be living wholly upon it. This is the
grand thing to do: and when it comes to be strictly inquired
into, few, very few, are living so wholly upon it, and so completely satisfied with it, as to be seeking for no additional
satisfaction elsewhere. Now, my soul, as there are but few
that are so fully satisfied with the Lord's goodness in every
thing that concerns salvation, both in providence and grace,
let thy morning thoughts be directed to see whether thou art
one of that happy few. I will, for the sake of shortening the
inquiry, take up the subject from this ground; that thou art
satisfied thou hast an interest in Jesus. Thou hast a long
time since been driven by thy necessities to Christ as a complete Saviour: and thou art resting all thy hopes, joys, and
expectations, upon his blood and righteousness. I will consider this point as fairly and fully determined. Why then,
perhaps, my soul, thou wilt say, Is not this to be satisfied
with Jehovah's goodness? Alas! here is the great defect of
God's people! Though resting on this foundation, how often
may they find their hearts exercised with endless perplexities
how this grace is to be improved, or how that gift is to be
employed. And according as it appears to their view they
have improved the one, or employed the other, their peace
and comfort is proportioned. My soul! do you not see that
this is self-satisfaction, and not being satisfied with God's
goodness? This is setting up the comforts of Jesus' grace
and Jesus' gifts above the glorious Author of those gifts and

graces. To be really satisfied with God's goodness, implies living upon that goodness, and that is Christ himself. Living upon Jesus, acting faith upon Jesus, perceiving all our fresh springs to be in Jesus, and therefore drawing all from him. And, my soul, if thou art thus satisfied with God's goodness, thou wilt find it is injurious to the comfort and blessedness of this life of faith to be ever looking off Jesus to any thing his grace and goodness worketh in thee, lest in the view of the work itself, be it what it may, the source of that work is overlooked, and self-satisfaction, instead of Christ exalting, should creep into thy soul. In every act, my soul, see to it then that all thy satisfaction is in Jesus, as the goodness of Jehovah. Lord, fulfil this sweet promise, and make me satisfied with thy goodness!

12.—And confessed that they were strangers and pilgrims on the earth.— *Heb.* xi. 13.

My soul! hast thou also witnessed this confession before many witnesses? See whether thou hast the same evidences they had. In the first place, they were led to see that here they had no continuing city. Sin, sorrow, sickness, death, inhabited this region. Every thing said to them in that sweet voice of God, Arise ye, and depart, for this is not your rest, because it is polluted. What sayest thou, my soul, to this first view of the subject? Look at it under another. Hast thou learnt, and so learnt as to prize it, the blessedness of that promise, There is a rest that remaineth for the people of God? What sayest thou to this also, my soul? Dost thou see that Jesus is that rest; and he is the object of thy desire in rest? For the prophet saith, He is the rest wherewith he will cause the weary to rest, and he is their refreshing. Isa. xxviii. 12. Hast thou heard, and welcomed his invitation, "Come unto me all ye that labour and are heavy laden, and I will give you rest?" Go one step further in the inquiry. Under these convictions of soul, art thou travelling the heavenly road, asking the way to Zion with thy face thitherward, as a stranger and pilgrim upon earth? Go further yet. Art thou guided as Israel was in the way, by the pillar of cloud by day, and guarded by the pillar of fire by night? Art thou coming up out of the wilderness of this world, leaning upon Jesus? Advance yet further in the inquiry. While the Holy Ghost as the pillar of cloud is going before thee, and thou art resting upon Jesus as thy staff and stay, knowest

thou God for thy father, his word thy guide, his promises thy
treasure, his ordinances thine inns, not to dwell in, but like
the way-faring man to tarry but for the night? And dost
thou draw water with joy out of those wells of salvation?
Pause, my soul, as thou seekest answers to these questions.
Knowest thou the difficulties of a wilderness dispensation;
and the sweets of those streams from that river which make
glad the city of God? Art thou like other travellers, sometimes enjoying fine weather, when Jesus' face, his love, his
mercy, are all in view; and sometimes walking in darkness,
when storms of sin and Satan throw clouds over the gracious
prospect? More especially, art thou the scorn and derision
of the carnal? Do they make thee their subject of laughter,
and art thou the drunkard's song? And lastly, to mention
no more, knowest thou, my soul, what it is sometimes to be
discouraged by reason of the way, while Satan would prompt
thee to go back; but sweetly constrained by Jesus's love, thou
art still the patient follower of them, who through faith and
patience inherit the promises? Hast thou, my soul, these
precious marks of the stranger and pilgrim upon earth?
Oh! then, remember what is said of them to whom the Holy
Ghost bears testimony, and by thy covenant interest in Jesus
behold thy vast privilege in the same blessed promise, God
is not ashamed to be called their God, for he hath prepared
for them a city.

13.—The Master is come, and calleth for thee.—*John* xi. 28.

My soul, mark how gracious the Lord is to his people in
the special and distinguishing tokens of his grace. Jesus
doth not barely send his gospel to the church, or house, or
family, but he speaketh by the soft, but powerful, whispers
of his love, to the individual soul. To thee is the word of
this salvation sent. Hence the soul who feels the sovereignty of his words in the constraining influence with
which it is accompanied, cries out, I shall never forget thy
word, for by it thou hast quickened me. But beside the calls of
his grace in his house of prayer, in how many ways, and by
what a variety of methods, is the Lord Jesus calling upon his
people. My soul! I hope that thou art always upon the
look out, and art getting to thy watch tower, to hear what the
Lord thy God hath to say to thee, by his word, by his providences, in chastisement, in love, and in all the gracious manifestations of his favour. Behold, he saith, I stand at the door

and knock. So Jesus calleth, and so let my soul hear. Now Lord! thou art calling me by thy word and providence in a way of grace; by and by I shall hear thy voice in the hour of death and judgment. And who shall say how very powerful, sweet, and gracious, that call is, when Jesus cometh to take his people home to himself, that where he is, there they may be also. " I hear my Master's voice," said an highly favoured servant of God in the moment of his departure. Perhaps a loud voice, a glorious distinguishable voice to him that is called, when no stander-by is at all conscious of the sound. Hence another said, when he was dying, " I shall change my place, but not my company." Jesus! Master! in that hour be it my happiness to say, Let me hear thy voice, let me see thy countenance ; for sweet is thy voice, and thy countenance is comely.

14.—Who is this that cometh up from the wilderness, leaning upon her beloved ?—*Song* viii. 5.

WHO is it that asketh this question, my soul ? Is it the holy angels, astonished, as well they may, at the gracious condescension of thy Jesus in the grace and favour he hath bestowed upon thee ? Or is it the world at large, looking on with amazement at the love of Jesus to his chosen ? Is it the Jewish church, amazed that Gentiles should be fellow-heirs, and of the same body, and partakers of God's promise in Christ ? Or above all, is it Jesus himself, not because he knoweth not the grace he hath bestowed, but because he admireth the grace he hath given ; and as he did the Centurion's faith, which he himself was the author of, he looketh upon it with pleasure? And art thou, my soul, come up from the wilderness of nature, a dry, barren land, where no water of Life is ; from the wilderness of the world, and from all the unsatisfying and empty pursuits of it ? Art thou leaning upon thy Jesus, cleaving to him, hanging upon him, strengthening thyself upon him, determining, like another Ruth concerning Naomi, where Jesus goeth thou wilt go, and where he lodgeth thou wilt lodge? Is this thy conduct ; and dost thou rest the whole stress of thy present and everlasting happiness upon his glorious person and righteousness ? if so, angels may well look on, and cry out, Who is this to whom the Father of all mercies hath been so gracious ; to whom Jesus hath manifested his love otherwise than he doth to the world ; and on whom the Spirit hath shed his blessed influence to make thee willing in the day of his power? Yes! precious Jesus! I would come up from every thing near and dear in this wilderness state, forget mine own people, and my father's house; I would lean wholly upon thy glorious Person, for my acceptance before God; lean wholly upon thy righteousness, as all-sufficient for my justification; I would lean upon thy fulness, day by day, for the supply of all grace here; and I would lean solely upon the divine efficacy and blessedness of thy blood, to cleanse my soul for everlasting fitness for happiness hereafter. Witness for me, ye angels of light, that this is my beloved, on whom I lean and in whom I trust, and desire to be found, for time and for eternity. Amen.

15.—Now we, brethren, as Isaac was, are the children of promise.—*Gal.* iv. 28.

MARK, my soul, the distinguishing characters of those who are the children of promise, and see whether thou art of this blessed family. For as the law and the gospel are strikingly distinguished from each other, so are the children of nature from those of grace. And how is this to be known? Look at the case Paul hath referred to: Isaac was the son of Abraham. And the Apostle saith that they which are of faith, the same are children of Abraham. And if ye be Christ's, then are ye Abraham's seed, and heirs according to the promise. And as Isaac was a child of Abraham by promise, not by natural power, so believers in Jesus are born, not of blood, nor of the will of the flesh, nor of the will of man, but of God. Hence Paul saith, to Abraham and his seed were the promises made. He saith not to seeds, as of many, but as of one; and to thy seed, which is Christ. Precious truth! The children of promise are of Jesus; for he himself is the one great promise of the Bible. So that from everlasting they are the seed of Christ: their being, their well-being their everlasting being, are all folded up in Jesus, as the oak in all its foliage is contained and folded up in the first and original acorn. Hence they are spiritually begotten, born, nourished, fed, sustained, led, strengthened and carried on, through all the gradations of grace, until grace is consummated in the ripeness of their full stature in glory. My soul! art thou as Isaac was, a child of promise? Oh! live by faith on Jesus, and in Jesus, and see to it, in all thy daily, hourly exercises and experiences, that all the promises of God in Christ Jesus are Yea, and Amen, unto the glory of God the Father.

16.—He shall gather the lambs with his arm, and carry them in his bosom.—*Isaiah* xl. 11.

My soul! mark in this sweet scripture, how Jesus is described, in not only attending to all the various wants of his fold, but to the very method of imparting to their several wants in a way corresponding to his own character and their state. In the fold of Jesus, like the sheep-folds among men, some are sheep and some are lambs; some of advanced age and some of younger standing. Well! where will Jesus put the lambs and the weaklings of his fold? Certainly, if there be one place in the heart of Jesus softer and more tender than another, there the lambs shall lie. And as Jesus himself lay in the bosom of his Father, so the lambs of his flock shall lie in his bosom. Sweet thought to encourage thee, my soul, and all the followers of Christ! Jesus will not thrust out the lambs into the dangers of the wilderness, where the prowling beasts of prey are, nor expose them to over-driving, or the speed with which the more mature sheep can travel. But he will proportion their burden to their back, and their day to their strength. And besides this, he will keep them nearer to himself: his arms shall clasp them; the warmth of his bosom shall nourish them; if they cannot walk, they shall be carried; and when they cannot find their way, they shall be led. Oh! thou great shepherd of thy sheep! is it thus thou sweetly dealest with thy little ones? Hence I see then explained, why it is that young believers, in the first season of their knowledge of thee, find so many blessed refreshings, which they afterwards do not so sensibly enjoy. Yes. Lord, it is thus thou gatherest the lambs and carriest them in thy bosom. And sweetly and seasonably dost thou do all this, and in a way which fully proves thy love and compassion to the necessities of thy flock.

17.—He restoreth my soul.—*Psalm* xxiii. 3.

Yes, Lord! it is indeed thou that bringest back the strayed sheep; for as no man ever quickened, so none can keep alive, his own soul. It was indeed thy promise, and most graciously doest thou fulfil it,—" As a shepherd seeketh out his

flock in the day that he is among his sheep, so will I seek
out my sheep, and bring again that which was driven away."
Ezek. xxxiv. 11, 16.   My soul! mark this trait of character
in thy Jesus for thy morning meditation.   It is well for thee
that restoring work, reclaiming work, reviving work, all is
with Jesus; begins in him, and is carried on and completed
by him, and through his grace in thee.   And it is well for
thee, my soul, that though thou so often failest in all things
towards thy Jesus, yet he never faileth in his love to thee in
any thing.   Sweet consideration! his love, and not thy deserts, becomes the standard for all his tenderness to his people.   And mark it down, my soul, in strong characters, that
Jesus' grace is much shown thy way: he doth not wait our
return, for then we should never return at all; neither doth
he wait our cry for help, but he puts that cry into his soul.
Alas! how often have we wandered and gone away, even
before that we were sensible of our departure.   How blessed
is it then to see and know that Jesus' eye is upon us, and
that before we return to him, he is coming forth to us.   His
love, his pity, his compassion, are the security of his people's
recovery.   Yes, Lord! it is thou that restorest my soul.
Praise to thy name, for thou doest it all in such a way as
proves it to be for thy great name's sake, that thy grace comes
freely and without upbraiding.   "He restoreth my soul, and
leadeth me in the paths of righteousness for his name's sake."

18.—To Him whom man despiseth; to Him whom the nation abhor-
reth.—*Isaiah* xlix. 7.

My soul! let thy longing eyes be directed to Him this day
whom man despiseth, and whom God honoureth, and to
whom he hath given a name above every name.   Pause! in
the contemplation of the wonderful mystery.   Was Jesus
indeed despised, and by the very creature he came to redeem?
Did angels hail his wonderful incarnation, and man despise,
hate, and abhor him!   Be astonished, Oh ye heavens! and
wonder, Oh earth!   But, my soul, go further in the contemplation of this mysterious subject.   What man, what individual man, was it, that could thus requite the unparalleled love
of Jesus?   Alas! not an individual only, but a whole nation;
nay, the whole nature, both Jew and Gentile, abhorred him;
for while in a state of unrenewed nature, to the one he is a
stumbling-block, and to the other his cross is foolishness.   Ah!
is it so, my soul?   Why then it follows that thou, even thou,

my soul, wert once in the same state of hatred, and wert by
nature, as well as others, a child of wrath, despising this wisdom of God in Christ for the salvation of sinners. And art
thou then, my soul, recovered by almighty sovereign grace
from this deadly hatred of nature, and dost thou look this day
with love, with joy, with rapture, and unspeakable delight, to
Him whom man despiseth, to Him whom the nation abhor-
reth ? Is Jesus indeed lovely, the altogether lovely, to thy
view ? Is he precious, nay, infinitely more precious than the
golden wedge of Ophir ? Yes, thou holy One of God, thou
art the all in all to my soul. Witness for me, Oh ye saints!
that are now around his throne, that I have none in heaven
or in earth that I desire beside him. My whole soul desires
to know him, to follow hard after him, to trust in him, to
cleave to him, to hang upon him, and to accept and receive
him ; and to make use of him as the wisdom of God, and the
power of God, for salvation to my soul, as he is to every one
that believeth. Oh! ye sons of men, who are still in the unrenewed hatred of your heart, in your hatred against the
precious Christ of God, what will ye do when He whom ye
now despise shall come to your everlasting shame! Well
might the apostle echo the words of the prophet, for from age
to age the astonishing truth remaineth : " Behold, ye despisers,
and wonder, and perish ; for I work a work in your days, a
work which ye shall in no wise believe, though a man declare it unto you !"

19.—Go thy way, eat thy bread with joy, and drink thy wine with a
merry heart ; for God now accepteth thy works.—*Eccles.* ix. 7.

My soul! here is a sweet subject for thy morning thoughts.
Art thou accepted in the Beloved? Hast thou accepted Jesus,
and God accepted thee in Jesus? Well mayest thou then eat
of the bread of common providences, and drink of the sweet
of all sanctified mercies, for every thing is blessed in Jesus,
and Jesus is blessing thee in every thing. Surely an accepted soul is a blessed soul, for he is blessed in his basket
and in his store: blessed in his lying down, and blessed in
his rising up ; blessed in his going out, and blessed in his
coming home ; yea, blessed in time, and blessed to all eternity. Yes, thou blessed source of all my blessedness! thou
precious Jesus! I will go my way, for thou art my way ; I
will eat my bread with joy, for thou art my bread of life ; I
will drink the wine which thou hast mingled for me, for thy

love is better than wine. And as God my Father accepted me in thee, this forms an everlasting cause of everlasting joy; joy in what I have; joy in what I expect; joy in even what I want, for those very wants will lead me the closer and the nearer to thee; joy in what I fear, for my fear will keep me depending upon thee; joy in what I suffer, for my sufferings are sweetly blessed when they afford a renewed occasion for my Jesus to sooth me under them, and in his time to deliver me out of them; and joy in all I lose, for lose what I may, I cannot lose thee, I cannot lose God's Christ; I cannot lose his love, his favour, his grace, his Spirit, the efficacy of his blood, and the merits of his righteousness. Oh! precious security! precious salvation in the Lord our Righteousness! Shall I not then live up to this heritage, and live under its influence, in the thankful, joyful, use of it from day to day? Go thy way, my soul, go in Jesus as thy way; every day, and all the day, eat thy bread with joy; eye Jesus as the spiritual food, and always present at thy table; drink hourly of his cup of salvation, with a cheerful heart, for thou art accepted in the Beloved.

20.—Grace be with all them that love our Lord Jesus Christ in sincerity. Amen.—*Eph.* vi. 24.

AND dost thou, my soul, with the same affection and love as the apostle, bend thy knee this morning before His throne of whom the whole family in heaven and earth are named! Dost thou look up, and pray that all grace may abound? Oh! what a delightful thought is it, my soul, to warm thy affections, that in the moment thou art waiting at the mercy-seat, thousands are waiting also for the morning blessing. Go then, my soul, and tell thy Redeemer this; tell him that he hath all-suited grace, and that the eyes of his redeemed, as the eyes of one man, are all directed towards him. Yes, thou glorious, rich, and gracious Saviour! we do behold thee still as the Lamb in the midst of the throne, leading thy church which is above in glory to fountains of living waters. And, Lord, we know that thou art equally attentive to thy church in the dry and barren wilderness here below, where no waters are. Vouchsafe, blessed Lord, to supply each soul. Thou hast every grace, suited to all wants; grace to pardon, grace to save, grace to renew, grace to strengthen, grace to bless. Oh, Lord! awaken, convince, humble, comfort, and pour out of thy fulness as our several necessities may be, in

calling, cleansing, justifying, adopting, sanctifying, and build-
ing up thine household, that all grace may abound according
to God's riches in glory by Christ Jesus. Oh! ye attendants
at the heavenly gate! see that ye come not empty away. Remember Jesus is on the throne: eye him there. Behold, the
very grace you need is in his hand; read the love that is in
his heart, and remember that he hath not only the very grace
you need, but every grace, and every mercy for all that wait
upon him. Tell every poor sinner this, and bid him ask in
faith, nothing doubting: tell all you know, and all you meet,
and all you see, that He who is on the throne hath abundant
grace, and wants vessels—the empty vessels of his people, to
give out into. Tell them that his grace exceeds all sense of
grace, all thoughts, all prayers, all praises, all desires; nay,
that he hath exceeding abundantly above all that they can
ask or think. Behold, then, Oh Lord! thy children, thy redeemed, thy family, and let all grace be with all them, and
upon all them that love thee in sincerity. Amen.

21.—Men wondered at.—*Zech.* iii. 8.

MEN wondered at indeed! And every redeemed soul may
truly say, I am a wonder unto many, a wonder to myself.
Oh: thou whose name is Wonderful! both thou, and the
children the Lord hath given thee, are for signs and wonders.
Behold! my soul, how it was fulfilled in Him whose name
is Wonderful, and then thine astonishment will be the less
that it should be fulfilled in his followers. I would contemplate thy Person, blessed Jesus, and behold thee, not barely
wondered at, but despised and rejected of men. The world
gazed at thee, but saw no beauty nor form of comeliness in
thee to desire thee. In thine offices also, how did the multitude despise thee as a Prophet; when blind-folding thee, and
smiting thee on thy sacred head, they tauntingly cried out,
"Prophecy, thou Christ, who is he that smote thee." As a
Priest, what blasphemy did they utter, when they saw enough
to be convinced, and to confess, that thou didst save others,
but thyself thou couldest not save. As a King, when having
nailed thee to the tree, they demanded a proof of thy power
in coming down from the cross. And wert thou not, blessed
Jesus, wondered at in thy words, when they acknowledged
never man spake like this man; yet charged thy doctrines
with blasphemy, and derided thee in them? Wert thou not
the wonder and the hatred of the world, when thy miracles

astonished them, but were ascribed to the agency of Beelzebub? Wert thou not, oh, thou spotless Lamb of God!
wert thou not charged with immorality, and called a wine-
bibber, a sabbath-breaker, the friend of publicans and sinners?
Did the world thus treat Jesus, and call the Master of the
house Beelzebub? Oh! then, my soul, well may they so
treat them of his household! And must it not be so? Yes.
The world knoweth them not, because it knew him not.
They are made a spectacle, a gazing-stock, a reproach, a
bye-word. How unknown in their new birth from God!
how little understood in their union with Jesus! How perfectly hidden from the world their life in the Spirit! What
an everlasting opposition to carnal men are their pursuits,
their pleasures, their happiness, their conversation, their desires! How wondered at their life of faith on the Son of
God! They have meat to eat the world knoweth nothing of,
for they feed upon the person, body, blood, grace, and righteousness, of the Lord Jesus Christ. My soul! hast thou this
rarity of character? Hast thou this blessed singularity?
Art thou wondered at because thou runnest not to the same
excess of riot, but art blameless and harmless, among the sons
of God, in the midst of a crooked and perverse generation?
Oh! blessed, for ever blessed, be His name, who hath called
thee to this high, this glorious, this distinguishing honour,
of being wondered at, and reproached for Jesus' sake! Yes,
Lord! I will not regard the reproach of men, neither be
afraid of their revilings, for "the moth shall eat them up
like a garment, and the worm shall eat them like wool; but
thy righteousness shall be for ever, and thy salvation from
generation to generation."

22.—And they came unto the brook of Eshcol, and cut down from thence
a branch with one cluster of grapes.—*Numbers* xiii. 23.

WAS not this single cluster God's earnest to the people of
the sure possession of the land where those delicious fruits
grew? And was not the size and weight of this one branch
a sample how full and extensive all the blessings, both of the
covenant and of the promised land, should be to the after
possessions of God's people? My soul! dost thou not see in
it then a precious representation of Jesus, that one Branch,
and of all that cluster of blessings which are in him. Well
might the church cry out concerning the Redeemer, "My
beloved is unto me as a cluster of camphire in the vineyards

of Engedi." For whether this camphire, this copher, denotes the vine of Cyprus, or the fruit of the palm-tree, in either, or in both, the soul-strengthening, soul-exhilaiating, soul-healing virtues of his unnumbered excellencies, may well be set forth under the beautiful similitude of the cluster of grapes from the brook of Eshcol. Yes! thou dear Lord! thou hast condescended to compare thyself to the vine; and to thy people thou art indeed a cluster of all that is lovely, sweet, gracious, and endearing. In thee dwelleth, like the berries of the richest cluster, all the fulness of the Godhead bodily. In thee is found all the purity, holiness, harmlessness, and perfection of the human nature, as God manifest in flesh. In thee, as God-man Mediator, we behold the cluster of all spiritual graces; all spiritual, temporal, eternal, blessings, all divine promises; all, all are in thee, to give out to thy people. Neither is there a mercy thy people can want, of grace here, or glory hereafter, but what is treasured up in thee, in a fulness perfectly inexhaustible. Precious Jesus! revive my spirits this day with this view of thee. Give me to see when my soul desireth the first ripe fruit, that thou thyself art all my soul can need. Bring me to the brook of Eshcol, and there let my eyes, my heart, my whole soul, and body, and spirit, feast itself in the contemplation and enjoyment of thy Person, thy graces, gifts, and fulness, until under the full satisfaction my soul findeth, in being eternally filled with thy goodness, I cry out with the church, My beloved is unto me as the richest of all the clusters of copher in the vineyards of Engedi.

23.—And he will destroy in this mountain the face of the covering cast over all people, and the vail that is spread over all nations.— *Isaiah* xxv. 7.

WHAT a precious promise was this, with which the Lord comforted the church under the Old Testament dispensation, that the faithful might look forward to the New Testament dispensation, when Jesus in the holy mountain, where he finished transgression by his triumphant death, would effectually remove the covering which had blackened all faces, and had separated between God and guilty sinners. And, that the gracious promise might be had in everlasting remembrance by the people, the evangelists were commissioned to tell the church, that in the moment Christ died, the vail of the temple was rent in twain, by an invisible hand, from the top

15*

to the bottom. My soul! see how Jesus, thy Jesus, hath most effectually fulfilled this precious promise. There was a vail of covering spread to separate thee for ever from God, had not Jesus taken it away, even the covenant of perfect obedience. God's injured perfections formed also a total separation. And as if these were not sufficient, the vail of sin would have for ever kept up this distance: " Your iniquities have separated between God and you," saith the prophet. But now by his precious undertaking in fulfilling the whole covenant of works, restoring the honour to God the Father's injured perfections, and opening a new and living way by his blood, which he hath consecrated through the vail of his flesh, he hath opened the kingdom of heaven to all believers. Precious Jesus! how endeared to my heart is this view of thee and of thy great salvation! Yes, thou Lamb of God! I have seen by thy Spirit's teaching this deadly face of covering, which by sin hath been cast over all people; and I have seen, by the same Almighty grace, that vail removed by thee. Now, Lord, in thee, and through thee, and by thee, I am led to behold the glory of God in the face of Jesus Christ. And having fled for refuge to the hope that is before me, this hope I have in thee, as an anchor of the soul, both sure and steadfast, and have cast it within the vail, whither thou our Forerunner hast for us entered, even our glorious High Priest for ever, after the order of Melchizedic.

24.—And another angel came and stood at the altar, having a golden censer; and there was given unto him much incense, that he should offer it with the prayers of all saints, upon the golden altar which was before the throne.—*Rev.* viii. 3.

My soul! behold this mighty Angel, even thy Jesus, in his priestly office. Look at him with an earnest eye of faith, before thou goest this morning to the mercy-seat. See his golden censer, with his much incense, and contemplate both the fulness of merit in his own glorious Person, and the fulness of efficacy in his work and righteousness, for the sure acceptance of all his redeemed. Go near, my soul, having boldness to enter now into the holiest by the blood of Jesus. Hear thy great High Priest bidding thee to take shelter under his golden censer, and behold him presenting thy person and thy poor offerings upon the golden altar, even his divine nature, before the throne. Yes, Lord! I would draw nigh in thee, and by thee, convinced that it is wholly from thee, and for thy sake, either my person or my prayers can find acceptance. For thee, and for thy sake, my sins are pardoned, my offerings are accepted, grace is bestowed, communion and fellowship is obtained ; peace in this life, and glory in that which is to come, are the portion of thy people. Hail! thou glorious, gracious, all-sufficient, High Priest ! To thee be glory, in the church, throughout all ages ! Amen.

25.—The eyes of the Lord are upon the righteous, and his ears are open unto their cry.—*Psalm* xxxiv. 15.

My soul! never more allow thyself to suppose that thou art overlooked or forgotten amidst the immensity of God's works. Is it not the province of a father to attend to the wants of his children ? And will not God regard his own, that cry night and day unto him, though he bear long with them ? This was the very argument of our Redeemer. Do you, saith Jesus, that are evil, know how to give good gifts unto your children, and shall not your heavenly Father give his Holy Spirit to them that ask him ? But, my soul, while thou art taking comfort from this view of divine love, take with thee another sweet thought from this precious verse of scripture. Whose eyes are thus upon thee, and whose ears are thus open to thy cries, but those of the Lord Jesus ? Oh, how sweet the thought ! that by reason of the Son of God, as Christ, being in our nature, and he having taken upon him our nature, he hath eyes to see, and ears to hear, such as we have. What a blessed light the Holy Ghost hath thrown over all those precious passages in which God is spoken of as having eyes, and ears, and an arm, and the like, describing himself by human powers ; that it is indeed the divine nature of the Man Christ Jesus. It is Jesus the Mediator, the Redeemer, the exalted and triumphant Saviour, who hath all power in heaven and in earth ; who, having loved his own which are in the world, hath loved them unto the end. My soul ! learn then to behold in all these sweet proportions, that it is Jesus, thy Husband and Brother, as well as thy God and Saviour, (and both forming one glorious Christ,) whose eyes are always upon thee, and whose ears are always attentive to thy cries, and to the cries of all his redeemed.

26.—The Lord possessed me in the beginning of his way ; before his works of old ; I was set up from everlasting.—*Prov.* viii. 22, 23.

PAUSE, my soul, over those most blessed words, and see what glories are contained in them. May God the Spirit glo-

rify Christ to thy view, while pondering these words. Who
is it that speaks them? Is it not Wisdom? Even Christ,
the wisdom of God, as the apostle elsewhere calls him? But
how was he possessed by the Lord, and how set up from
everlasting? Not openly in the human form that he was in
the fulness of time to take upon him for the purposes of redemption; but, as it should seem, secretly, as subsisting in
covenant engagements from everlasting. As Mediator, was
it not? Not as yet made flesh, but (if we may from another
scripture draw the conclusion) as the image of the invisible
God, the first-born of every creature. Coloss. i. 15. What
a glory, beheld in this view, doth this precious scripture,
with all that follows it in the chapter, hold forth! The Son
of God, in covenant engagements from everlasting, was in
time to take into himself manhood, and from the union of
both God and man become one Christ. Hence, from everlasting, Wisdom, one of those natures, is set up and speaks
as a person not separate or distinct from the other nature of
the Godhead, but as in union, and from both, forming (in
covenant settlements) the one glorious Mediator. So that it is
not Wisdom, as a person, speaking, without subsisting in the
Son of God, neither is it the Son of God, without Wisdom
subsisting as such in him, but both forming one identical person, and that person the Mediator, whose name was then secret, but afterwards was to be called Wonderful, when by the
open appearance of the Son of God, tabernacling in a body
of flesh, redemption-work, from everlasting covenanted for
and agreed upon by the several persons of the Godhead, was
to be completed. What a blessed contemplation is here
opened, my soul, to thy diligent and humble inquiry. Here
direct all thy researches; here let prayer ascend for divine
teachings to guide thee; and here behold Him, who, in the
after-ages of his love, made an open display of himself as the
God-man, when he manifested forth his glory, and his disciples believed on him; thus, as the Wisdom-man, declaring
himself as possessed by Jehovah in the beginning of his
way, and set up before all worlds as Jehovah's delight, while
his delights were with the sons of men. Oh! the wisdom of
God in a mystery, even the hidden wisdom which God ordained before the world began!

27.—I am Alpha and Omega, the first and the last.—*Rev.* i. 11.

My soul! if the precious meditation of yesterday be not
wholly gone off from thy poor forgetful mind this day, here

is another blessed view to revive the thought afresh, in looking at the Mediator, as the Alpha and Omega, the first and the
last, in the same covenant engagements. Jesus is indeed, as
the 8th verse of this same chapter expresses it, the Alpha and
Omega, as one with the Father, over all God blessed for ever.
But he is also here the Alpha and Omega, as the Mediator,
both God and man. For he is the first and the last of all
God's thoughts, and in his covenant engagements, of all Jehovah's works, for every thing in creation begins and concludes in him. From everlasting he was set up. So that
though Adam was the first man openly, yet not the first man
secretly, and as subsisting in covenant engagements. Here
again, as was remarked before, and from an authority not to
be disputed, he is the image of the invisible God, the first-
born of every creature, that in all things he might have the
pre-eminence. Precious Jesus! be thou to me the Alpha and
Omega. And as it is plain that Jehovah possessed thee as
the glorious covenant Head of thy people in the beginning of
his way, and before his works of old, so cause me to possess
thee as the all in all, the first and the last, the Author and
Finisher of my salvation.

28.—Carry down the man a present.—*Gen.* xliii. 11

Ah, poor Jacob! how unconscious wert thou that this man,
the governor of Egypt, was so near and dear to thee, and
that his bowels yearned to tell thee how much he loved thee.
And oh, ye sons of Israel! who would have had power to
convince you, while you were bowing down before Joseph
under the dreadful apprehensions which agitated your minds,
and he was assuming a voice of displeasure, that this very
man was your brother? My soul! and what was all this,
heightened to the greatest possible degree in the real love and
affection of Joseph towards his family, compared to that love
of Jesus which passeth knowledge? Jesus is thy Brother,
and he is the Governor, not of Egypt only, but of heaven
and earth. The famine, it is true, is sore in the land, and to
him thou must go for sustenance, or thou wilt perish for ever.
But wilt thou carry down the man a present? My soul,
what hast thou to carry? Not thy duties, nor thy prayers,
thine alms, thy righteousness: these are all filthy rags. Besides, he to whom thou goest needeth not the gifts and offerings of his creatures. His terms are, without money and
without price. Go then, my soul, poor and wretched as thou

art, go to him with a broken and a contrite heart, for that he
will not despise.   And oh! what a volume of mercies, blessings, and graces, is contained in that one word of his, when
he shall say, I am Jesus your Brother!   Precious Jesus! I
would say, thou art indeed a Brother born for adversity. Thou
art he whom thy brethren shall praise, and all thy Father's
children shall bow down before thee.

29.—And they sought him among their kinsfolks and acquaintance, and
found him not.—*Luke* ii. 44, 45.

MAY we not gather a lesson of sweet instruction from the
anxious and fruitless search the parents made for Jesus in
the days of his flesh?   What kinsfolks and acquaintances
shall we now search among for the Saviour? My soul! how
little of Jesus is to be found in this Christless generation!
What parlor conversation makes mention of his name?   Is
it not plain and evident, from the general, nay, almost universal, silence observed in all companies concerning his
name, and offices, and characters, and relations, that Christ is
not there?   Shall we seek him among the professors of the
gospel?   Who are they that honour Jesus?   Not they who
deny his Godhead; not they who deny the influences of his
Holy Spirit; not they who set up their own righteousness as
part, or the whole, of their justification before God. Jesus is
not in that house, in that family, in that heart, among that
people who live in sensuality, profaneness, and impiety.
Where shall we seek Jesus?   Blessed Lord! mine eyes are
unto thee to be taught.   I would say unto thee, in the language of the church, " Tell me, O thou whom my soul loveth,
where thou feedest, where thou makest thy flock to rest at
noon.   O, when I shall find thee without, I would lead thee,
and bring thee into my mother's house, who would instruct
me ; and I would cause thee to drink of spiced wine of the
juice of my pomegranate."

30.—In thee the fatherless findeth mercy.—*Hosea* xiv. 3.

SWEET thought! In Jesus, and the relationship which he
hath condescended to place himself in, all his poor followers
may find a supply to fill up every vacancy. My soul! contemplate Jesus in this blessed feature of character. What
relation do we need? The fatherless are commanded to
look to him whose name is the everlasting Father.   The mo-

therless also, for he hath said, "As one whom his mother comforteth, so will I comfort thee." Doth death make a breach between the husband and the wife? then the scripture saith, "Thy Maker is thine husband, the Lord of Hosts is his name." Are we friendless? "Jesus is the friend that loveth at all times, that sticketh closer than a brother." In short, there is no situation among the affinities of life, the kinder charities of nature, but what Jesus fills, and infinitely transcends all. Pause, my soul; over this view of Jesus, and behold how he graciously proposeth himself to supply all wants, and to fill all vacancies. Jesus is both the Father, the Friend, the Brother, the Husband, the whole in one of all relationships and of all connexions. And amidst all the changes the fluctuating circumstances of human affairs, the frailties and infirmities of our own hearts, and the hearts of others, which sometimes separate chief friends, what a blessed thought it is, " Nothing can separate from the love of Christ!" Precious Lord! give me to cry out with the church, under the full assurance of thine unalterable love, " This is my beloved, and this is my friend, O daughter of Jerusalem."

JULY.

1.—Because of the savour of thy good ointments, thy name is as ointment poured forth.—*Song* i. 3.

WHY, my Lord, is thy name so truly blessed, but because thou hast so endeared it to thy redeemed, by every tie which can gain the affections! Didst thou, even before I had a being, enter into suretyship-engagements for me, that thou wouldest redeem me when fallen, that thou wouldest take my nature, live for me, die for me, become a sacrifice for me, shed thy blood for me, wash me in thy blood, clothe me in thy righteousness, justify me before God and thy Father, become my Advocate, High-Priest, Intercessor, betroth me to thyself here in grace, and everlastingly unite me to thyself in glory hereafter! Didst thou do all this, and art thou still

doing it, making my cause thine own, and following me
with love, and grace, and mercy, every day, and all day, and
wilt thou never leave me nor forsake me! And must not thy
name be as ointment poured forth? Can there be a savour
as sweet, as fragrant, as full of odour, as the name of Jesus?
Precious ointments, it is true, have a smell in them very
grateful; but what savour can be like that, which to the spiritual senses manifests Jesus in his person, love, grace, and
mercy; in whom there is every thing desirable, and nothing
but what is lovely; all beauty, power, wisdom, strength, an
assemblage of graces, more full of odour than all the spices
of the east? Precious Lord Jesus! let thy name be written in my heart, and let every thing but Jesus be for ever ob-
literated there, that nothing may arise from thence but what
speaks of thee; that through life, and in death, the first and
last, and all that drops from my lips, even in the separation of
soul and body, Jesus may form in the close of grace here, and
in the first opening of glory to follow, the one blessed precious
Name, as ointment poured forth.

2.—And thou shalt not be for another man; so will I also be for thee.—
Hosea iii. 3.

My soul, was not God the Holy Ghost representing, by the
similitude of his servant the prophet's marriage with an
adulteress, the astonishing marriage of Jesus with our nature, and his personal union with every individual of his
church and people? Look at this scripture, and see how
sweetly it points to Jesus. The prophet was commanded to
love this woman, beloved of her friend, and yet an adulteress.
He was to buy her also to himself: and he was to charge
her to abide with him, and not to play the harlot any more,
saying unto her, "And thou shalt not be for another man, so
will I also be for thee." Precious Jesus, do I not behold
thee in all this? Can any thing more strikingly shadow
forth thy grace, thy mercy, thy love, to thy people? Was
not our whole nature estranged from thee, when thou camest
down from heaven, to seek and save that which was lost?
Were not all in a state of daring adultery, when thou hadst
from everlasting betrothed thyself to us, in standing up our
glorious Husband and Surety? And how striking the expression; "Then said the Lord unto me, go yet, love a
woman beloved of her friend;" surely at the command of
God thy Father, and not uncalled, unsent, unauthorized,

didst thou come. Our nature was indeed yet beloved of
thee, our best and dearest Friend, though in a state of
spiritual adultery, and wholly gone away from thee. Yes,
blessed Jesus! in defiance of all our multiplied transgressions, it might be truly said, we were yet beloved of thee
our Friend and Brother, born for adversity; for thou wert
then, as now, unchangeable in thy love, the same Jesus yesterday, to-day, and for ever. And surely, Lord, in another
feature the prophet shadowed thee forth: for as he purchased
the harlot, so thou, Lord, before we became thine, didst purchase us by thy blood. And dost thou now say to me this day,
" Abide with me, and thou shalt not be for another man, so
will I also be for thee ?" Oh, condescending God! oh, precious, lovely, all-loving Saviour! Lord make me thine, yea,
altogether thine! Let my whole soul, and body, and spirit,
be all thine, both by the conquests of thy grace, as they are
justly thine, and by the purchase of thy blood, that never,
never more, I may depart from thee, but with the same full
consent as the church of old, I may exult in this blessed assurance: *My beloved is mine, and I am his.*

3.—Now the end of the commandment is charity, out of a pure heart,
and of a good conscience, and of faith unfeigned.—1 *Timothy* i. 3.

SEE, my soul, what Jesus hath secured for thee, by his
gracious undertaking and accomplishment; and which his
servant was commissioned to tell the church, was the very
end of the commandment, namely, charity and love. And
this law of love is given thee, that thou mightest manifest
whose thou art, and to whom thou dost belong; not as a rule
of acceptance, for then that would be to make thy love a covenant of works, but as a sweet testimony of thy affection in
the hand of Jesus. It is a law of love indeed, because the
cords of love, by which thou art drawn, prove it to be so.
Thy obedience is not from slavish fear, for then this would
be bondage, but the love of Christ constrains thee. Thy
love to him makes thee long to be like him. Thy love to
him makes his commandments not grievous but gracious.
Thy love to him makes ordinances precious, because Jesus is
the whole of them. And thy love to him makes all that
belongs to him dear, and in which Jesus requires thy proofs
of affection; not in thy strength, as the poor Israelites were
demanded to make brick without straw, but living in thee,
and working in thee, both to will and to do of his good plea-

sure.   Here, my soul, thou truly findest strength and grace
equal to thy day.   The end of every commandment, as well
as the beginning, is love, for it begins in Jesus, is carried on
in Jesus, and ends in Jesus, and he is all love.   And in him,
and by him, the conscience, the heart, faith, all, are kept pure,
undefiled, and unfeigned, because love in Jesus is at the bottom ; like the chariot of Solomon, paved with love.   Oh,
thou glorious pattern of all holiness ! make me like thyself !

4.—I am among you as he that serveth.—*Luke* xxii. 27.

SURELY there is a blessedness in these words that affords
substance to feed upon.   My soul, read them again and again ;
pause over them, pray over them, and look up to Him, that
thus so humbly, graciously, and lovingly, expressed himself!
Art thou, blessed Jesus, among thy people as he that serveth ?
I know, Lord, that thou didst condescend to become the servant of Jehovah, though thou wert Lord of all, when, for the
salvation of poor sinners, thou didst undertake to veil thy
Godhead, and in our nature to become our Surety.   And I
know, Lord, also, that thou didst, in a very memorable moment, and at a time when (as the Evangelist had it to relate
to the church) thou knewest that the Father had given all
things into thine hands, thou didst condescend to wash thy
disciples' feet.   But art thou still among thy people as one
that serveth ?   Be astonished, Oh heavens ! and wonder, Oh
earth !   All power is thine in heaven and in earth !   And
is Jesus among his people, among his redeemed ones, his exercised ones, as he that serveth?   Pause again, my soul.
Meditate upon the blessed gracious words.   Was there not a
circumstance of trial, when Christ was upon earth, but what
he felt in his human nature, when fulfilling all righteousness ?
Then will it follow, that there cannot be a circumstance of
trial which his members now feel but what he knows ; nay,
what he appoints.   And if he appoints it, is he not looking
on ; nay, measuring out suited strength, suited grace, as the
circumstances shall require ?   And if all this be in Jesus now,
and every minute event, both his ordering, supporting under,
carrying through, crowning ; in all is he not, though Lord
of all, servant of all ; and doth he not now say to every poor
disciple in the present moment, as fully as he did to them in
the garden with him, "I am among you as he that serveth ?"
My Lord and my God, would I cry out, under the same con-

scious shame of my dreadful unbelief, as Thomas did under his. Yes, Lord, thou art still ministering, still serving! And though I lose sight of thee in a thousand and ten thousand instances, where nothing but thy imparted strength could carry me through; yet plain and most evident it is, that in all the blessings of thy finished redemption, thou thyself art giving out, and serving up, grace to thy people. Thou didst first purchase all blessings with thy blood. And now thou ever livest to see them administered by thy spirit. Precious Jesus! thou art ever with me. By and by I shall be with thee, I shall see thee as thou art, and shall be satisfied when I awake with thy likeness.

5.—Thou shalt not wear a garment of divers sorts, as of linen and wool-len together.—*Deut.* xxii. 11.

THOUGH the true believer, who, like the king's daughter, is all glorious within, cannot but know, that as meat commendeth us not to God, so neither doth the necessary dress, which, since the fall, is become suited to cover our sinful bodies, make a part of our holy faith: yet it is highly proper, that persons professing godliness should use great plainness of apparel. The ornament of a meek and quiet spirit, we are told, is of great price in the sight of God. But who should have thought that such a precept as this of Moses had a gospel signification. And yet as Christ was preached under types and figures through the whole law, we may reasonably suppose that not a single command was then given, but what had an eye to him and his great salvation. But if we find the Lord so strict respecting the outward dress of the body, what may we conclude the Lord would enjoin respecting the inward clothing of the soul? If woollen and linen were offensive to be worn together, surely we cannot appear before God in the motley dress of Jesus' righteousness and our own. The fine linen, scripture saith, is the righteousness of saints. With this, which Jesus puts on his people, nothing of our own woollen garments must be worn. The righteousness of a creature, had we any, (which in fact we have none,) cannot be suited to mix with the righteousness of the Creator. And no man that is wise for salvation, would put the old piece of our corrupt and worn out nature upon the new garment of the renewed nature in Christ Jesus. When therefore the Lord saith, Thou shalt not wear a garment of divers sorts, my heart replies, No, Lord! let me be clothed with the

robe of thy righteousness, and the garment of thy salvation;
then shall I be found suited for the marriage supper, when
the King comes in to see the guests at his table.

6.—Nay, in all these things we are more than conquerors through him
that loved us.—*Romans* viii. 37.

MORE than conquerors! mark that, my soul. Conquerors
all the soldiers of Jesus must be, for in his strength they fight,
and he hath himself subdued all our foes, even death the last
enemy, and Satan, whom the God of peace will bruise under
our feet shortly. So that victory is sure. For we overcome
by the blood of the Lamb, by the sword of the Spirit, and by
the shield of faith, whereby we subdue all the fiery darts of
the wicked. But though conquerors, how are we *more* than
conquerors? Yes, through Him that loved us, believers ab-
solutely conquer Him that is himself unconquerable. For,
by union with Jesus, we may be said to have the power with
God, and to prevail. " I will not let thee go," said the praying Jacob, "except thou bless me." A blessing he came for,
and a blessing he would have. So all the praying seed of
Jacob have power through the blood and righteousness of
Jesus, in like manner. Hence Jesus saith to his church,
" Turn away thine eyes from me, for they have overcome
me." Sweet and precious thought! my soul, never lose
sight of it. Through Him that loved thee, and gave himself
for thee, thou art more than conqueror: nay, thy present victories are more than the victories of the church in heaven.
For they have now no more conflicts with tribulation, or distress, or persecution, or famine, or nakedness, or peril, or
sword; but, by Him that loved us, we arise above the midst
of them now, and while troubled on every side, we are not
distressed; while perplexed, are not in despair: the love of
Jesus is seen in these very exercises, and that in very love,
and very faithfulness, the Lord causeth us to be afflicted.
Hence, through him, we conquer them; nay, we are more
than conquerors. We love him that sends the affliction, because we discover his love in it; and as, without that afflic
tion, the love of our Jesus in sending it would in that instance
not have been known, therefore here we have a blessed victory the church above cannot know. Precious Jesus! to thy
love, however, and thy grace, be all the praise and all the
glory; for under thy banner of love alone it is that we are
more than conquerors.

7.—Hope deferred maketh the heart sick: but when the desire cometh it is a tree of life.—*Prov.* xiii. 12.

SURELY, my Lord and Saviour is the sum and substance of this sweet verse! For art thou not the hope of Israel, and the Saviour thereof? And if thou deferrest giving to my soul renewed views of thy pardoning love, or withholdest the renewed visits and manifestations of thy grace, will not my soul languish, and my whole heart be sick? Can I, dear Lord, continue for a moment in health of soul without thee? And art thou not my desire, when thou art the desire of all nations? And when thou comest to my soul in all thy freeness, fulness, suitableness, and all-sufficiency, art thou not the very Tree of Life in the paradise of God? Precious, precious Jesus! give me to sit down under thy shadow with great delight, for surely thy fruit is sweet to my taste. Do not defer thy blessed visit to my soul this morning, for thou knowest, Lord, that though, through thy grace, that sickness of sin which is unto death, thou hast already cured by the application of thy blood and righteousness; yet there is a sickness not unto death, and which my soul will pine and languish under, unless thou renewest me from day to day. Oh, blessed Jesus, I want every moment fresh manifestations, renewed discoveries, of thy presence, grace, and favour! I want to know thee more, to love thee more, to live to thee more; and the deferring these precious mercies maketh my heart sick. Come then, thou blessed Lord, with all thy fulness: my desires are to thee, and to the remembrance of thy name. With my soul have I desired thee in the night: and now, with the first dawn of day, would I seek thee early. And surely, when thou comest, as I know thou wilt come, thou wilt be indeed, and in truth, the Tree of Life. Methinks my soul is now opened by thee for thy reception; and therefore, Lord, do thou now make such rich discoveries of thy person, glory, grace, and love, as may fill every portion of my heart. Nay, Lord, I pray to feel such goings forth of my poor soul, in waiting for thy coming, that, like the queen of Sheba, overpowered in the view of the riches and wisdom of Solomon, my views of thy condescending grace, and a sense of my unworthiness to be so blessed of my God, may melt my whole soul before thee, and, like her, there may be no more spirit in me from such ravishing enjoyments of thy presence.

16*

8.—Ye are my witnesses, saith the Lord, and my servant whom I have chosen.—*Isa.* xliii. 10.

Doth God indeed appeal to the souls of his people for the truth of his covenant love? Oh! the gracious condescension! It is sweet, it is blessed, and a testimony enough to make the heart of every child of God that possesseth it to leap for joy, when the Spirit witnesseth to our spirits that we are the children of God. But it is still carrying on that blessedness with increasing delight, when the people of God themselves become witnesses of covenant love and faithfulness; and, from numberless experiences in themselves, can and do set to their seals that God is true. See then, my soul, this morning, whether thou art one of thy God's witnesses, and thy Redeemer, as the servant of Jehovah, witnesseth *for* thee, and by his sweet influences *in* thee, all that thine heart can wish concerning the word of his grace, and thy fellowship and communion with him. Run over a few leading points in which thou canst, and dost, bear witness for thy God. Did he not remember thee in thy low estate, when he passed by, and bid thee live? Did he not convince thee of sin, and put a cry in thine heart for salvation? Did not God the Holy Ghost convincingly prove to thee, both the infinite glories and perfections of Jesus, and by his gracious leadings constrain thee to a love towards him, dependence upon him, and a perfect approbation of having him for thy Saviour? Did not Jesus so graciously visit thee, show thee his love, his tenderness, his power, his suitableness, his all-sufficiency, as to warm all thy frozen affections into a warmth for him, and attachment to him? And did not thy God and Father, again and again, manifest to thee his covenant love, in accepting thee in Jesus, blessing thee with all spiritual blessings in him, hearing and answering prayer, and proving by all these tokens that he is thy God, and that thou art one of his people. And art thou, my soul, day by day looking up for salvation only in Jesus, and renouncing all other Saviours? Dost thou know all these precious things, my soul, and a thousand more of the like nature, in which thou art bearing daily testimony to the word of his grace? Then surely thou art one of those to whom Jehovah appeals in the blessed scripture of the morning. Think then, my soul, what an honour thou art called to! What a privilege is thine! See to it, my soul, that thou witness for Jesus, whom God hath given for a witness to the people. And while Jesus takes up thy cause before the throne in heaven, do thou plead his cause, and be valiant for his truth, here upon earth. And do ye angels of light, and ye spirits of just men made perfect, witness for me that this Lord is my God!

9.—But he answered her not a word.—*Matt.* xv. 23.

MARK, my soul, this feature in thy Redeemer's conduct towards the poor woman that so long and so earnestly entreated him—Jesus answered her not a word. And yet, from the close of the subject, nothing can be more evident than that the Lord had determined, not only to grant her petition, but to throw the reigns of government, concerning herself, into her hands so completely, that it should be as she would. Learn then from hence how to interpret silence at the throne upon every occasion of thine. In every dark providence, under every dispensation of grace, never forget that Jesus' love is the same. What though he answereth not a word, yet his whole heart is towards his redeemed. Whatever frowns there may be in outward things, there can be none in what concerns the real happiness of his people. Jesus may try, as in the instance of this poor woman, the graces he gives. Faith may be hard put to it, and silence at the throne may make temptations and exercises of every kind more sharp and painful. But Jesus is the same,—his love the same, the merits and efficacy of his blood and righteousness the same. These speak *for* thee, my soul, though they may not speak *to* thee. That's a precious thought; never forget it. And remember, moreover, covenant mercies are not suspended upon our deserts. The free grace of God in Christ depends not upon the will or the worth of man ; according to the beautiful account by the prophet, of the rain, or dew of heaven, which waiteth not for man, neither tarrieth for the sons of men. Henceforth, therefore, my soul, do thou learn to wait at the mercy-seat as cheerful, and with as lively actings of faith, when Jesus answereth not a word, as when thy petitions are all complied with. Men ought always to pray, and not to faint, saith one that could not be mistaken. Oh, for grace and faith to take God at his word, and like Job to say, Though he slay me, yet will I trust in him.

10.—And he is before all things, and by him all things consist.—
Coloss. i. 17.

How doth the apostle mean that Jesus is before all things?
Not as God only, for then the observation would have been
needless; and not as man only, for then how could all things
consist by him? What is it then, my soul? Is it not as
Mediator, both God and man? And was not Christ thus set
up from everlasting? Not openly revealed indeed, neither
openly manifested in a body of flesh, until the fulness of time;
but secretly, and in the divine counsels. What a blessed
thought for the redeemed to exercise their rapturous meditations upon! And is it not this which the apostle hath said,
He is the image of the invisible God? The image! Yes!
that representation of what is in itself invisible; that identical
image concerning which Jehovah, when calling Adam into
existence, said, Let us make man in our image, after our likeness. So then Adam was the first man indeed *openly*, but
not so *secretly*, for it is plain that Adam was made after this
likeness, which was set up from everlasting. Hence this
union of natures, subsisting in one Person, formed the one
glorious Mediator, who is and was before all things, and by
whom all things consist. Here is the foundation then of the
church, and that from everlasting: without this, the church,
and indeed all things beside, had wanted foundation. For
there is nothing created that can stand out of God; and there
was nothing created that could stand in God by a personal
union, but him. What a glorious thought! Cherish it, my
soul! Never lose sight of it! In Christ the Mediator, all
things consist. The church is preserved, redeemed, sanctified, glorified! And how are all his redeemed ones personally and individually secured, but by the same? By him
all things consist. Hence their consisting is in him; they
are living in him, feeding on him, made righteous in his
righteousness, and hereafter will be glorified in his glory. My
soul! think what a world of mysteries thou art in! think
what an unspeakable life is a life of grace here! think what
a world of glory in Jesus hereafter! Now see if thou canst
better enter into an apprehension of those divine words of Jesus, Because I live, ye shall live also. And again, At that
day ye shall know that I am in my Father, and you in me,
and I in you.

11.—If thou knewest the gift of God, and who it is that saith to thee, Give me to drink ; thou wouldest have asked of him, and he would have given thee living water.—*John* iv. 10.

Amidst a thousand precious things concerning Jesus, there are two views of him which are peculiarly so, and which those words of his to the woman of Samaria bring home to the heart in the plainest and most blessed manner. The one is, who and what Christ is in himself; and the other is, the Father's authority in him, so as to give faith in him a divine warrant to act by, when a poor sinner comes to make use of Christ. It is our ignorance in those two grand points concerning salvation which is the sad cause of all our miseries, and the little enjoyment even gracious souls, for the most part, have in Jesus. Now, my soul, do thou meditate upon both these things, this morning, and from these sweet words of thy Saviour see if thou dost not prove what he so graciously saith to be true. First, consider who and what Jesus is as he is in himself. Let thy faith have for its object of meditation the Person and the work of God thy Saviour. In all he wrought, in all he did, in all he accomplished, it was as the surety of his people. And in all the fulness by virtue of it, which is treasured up in him, it is not for himself, for he cannot need it, but it is for his people. So that a poor sinner is as much suited to Jesus for him to give out of his fulness, as Jesus is suited for a poor sinner to supply his emptiness. And therefore, if we did but thus know him, and thus come to him, we should find that he is as earnest to receive every poor sinner, and to give out of his fulness, as that poor sinner can be to come and take. Now, my soul, when thou hast duly pondered over this, look at Jesus in the other point of view also, as the gift of God. Here thou hast a warrant, an authority, nay, a command, to come to Jesus, and to make use of him for every want which poverty, ignorance, and sin, have occasioned in the circumstances of our fallen nature. Christ is the one blessed ordinance of heaven ; Christ is the one, and the only one, appointed way for a poor sinner's acceptance with God. And therefore, did a poor sinner always keep in view that Christ is the gift of God, and that God is honoured when that poor sinner honoureth his dear Son, by believing the record God hath given of him, would not this make every poor sinner happy, in thus glorifying God ? And therefore, my soul, look to it that this is thy daily exercise ; for then thy thirst for Jesus will not be supplied, as from a pool which depends upon dry or wet seasons, but Jesus himself will give thee living water; nay, Jesus will himself be that everlasting living spring in thee, which springeth up unto everlasting life!

12.—And they began to pray him to depart out of their coasts.—
Mark v. 17.

AND was this Jesus whom they desired to depart? Yes! And what had the Redeemer done to merit this treatment? He had dispossessed the evil spirit from the mind of a poor creature, and caused the whole country to be freed from the fury of one whom no chains could bind! Was this the cause? Yes! And is it possible that so divine an act could have had such an effect upon the minds of a whole body of people? What, would these Gadarenes rather have the devil raging among them, in the person of this poor creature, than the Son of God in the kindness of our nature? Pause, my soul. Is it not the same now? Do not men still prefer the raging uncontrolled lusts of their own hearts, the dominion of Satan, and the customs, pursuits, and follies, of the world, to the grace, mercy, and sweet dominion, of Jesus? Do they not in deed, if not in words, say, Depart from us, we desire not the knowledge of thy ways? Pause again, my soul! Was there not a time when the same was thy case? Indeed there was; and is not every one so by nature? And what but an act of grace, like the miracle Jesus wrought on this poor man, can bring any one out of it? Art thou, my soul, brought out of it? Yes, if so be, like him, thou art now sitting at the feet of Jesus, clothed, and in thy right mind. Surely, Lord, thou hast wrought this blessed change upon me. Could I desire thee to depart out of our coasts? Nay; is it not the daily, hourly desire of my heart, that thou wouldst be with me, dwell in me, reign and rule in me, and be my portion, my God, my Saviour, and make me thine for ever? Sweet testimony, in the midst of all my wanderings, coldness, undeservings. Cherish it, my soul. Jesus will not depart from thee. That love which brought him down from heaven to save a world, led him over the lake of Genesaret to save one poor sinner. And he who came in love unsent for, departed not until he was sent away. Oh, ye poor, blind, deluded, Gadarenes! Oh, my poor, equally blind and deluded, countrymen and fellow-sinners, who know not, nor desire to know, Christ Jesus! Who are ye that thus reject the Lord of life and glory, and desire him to depart out of your coasts?

3.—This year thou shalt die.—*Jer.* xxviii. 16.

I HAVE often thought this passage, pronounced on the lying prophet, a most suitable sermon for a birth-day portion, to be sounded in the ears of the sinner: and if qualified with the possibility and probability which arise out of our dying circumstances, it might, when commissioned by the Lord, have a blessed effect. My soul, take it for the meditation of thy birth-day. It *may be* fulfilled this year, it *must be* fulfilled some year, it *cannot be* a very distant year, and there is a birth-day when it *shall be* passed upon thee in the year. And why not the present? Pause! my soul, and meditate upon it, as if this were the very year. And what though carnal men celebrate the anniversary of their birth-day, as best suited to their carnal minds, let thine be wholly spiritual. If indeed a man came into the world laughing, there might be a suitable correspondence in commemorating the annual return of such a birth with laughing; but cries first indicate the birth of a poor helpless creature born to want, and the subject of sin and misery. Can rioting and folly be the proper celebration of such an event? And is there no joy suitable on the return of a man's birth-day? Oh, yes, there is, and ought to be, real, heart-felt joy with every child of God. When a man begins to count birth-days in grace, every return calls for joy in the Holy Ghost. Not for that he was born an intelligent immortal creature only, but for that he was made a new creature in Christ Jesus; not for that he came into the world in a state of nature only, but for that he was brought also into a state of grace; not for that he was of the stock and lineage of Adam only, but of the seed of Christ. Here is an alliance royal, holy, heavenly, divine! My soul! how many moons or years in the new life canst thou mark down? Let this be the arithmetic of thy calculation. And if, like the herald of the morning, the voice should say, This year thou shalt die, oh! how sweet to answer, Lord, my times are in thine hands. Can they be in a wiser, or more tender, or more loving, hand, than Jesus'? Precious Lord! wean me from everything here below, that I may be living nearer with thee, and in thee, and to thee; that as the last year of my pilgrimage lessens to the month, and the month to the week, and the week to the day, nay, to the very hour and moment of my departure from a body of sin and death, the last expiring words on my trembling lips may be of Jesus, and thine, Oh Lord, come home with power and sweetness to my soul, like thine to him on the cross, To-day shalt thou be with me in paradise.

14.—And I only am escaped alone to tell thee.—*Job* i. 19.

My soul, is there nothing in this account which the messenger to Job gave concerning himself which suits thy case and circumstances ? Nay, mayest thou not in a great variety of ways, both in providence and grace, adopt similar language, in which thou art escaped alone to tell ? Pause. Look back to thy boyish days. Nay, look further back, even to the birth and to the womb; for had not the Lord carried thee from thence, surely from the womb wouldest thou have died and given up the ghost. And what was thy childhood, but years of peril and danger, in which multitudes dropped all around thee, so that thou mightest say, while contemplating them, " And I only am escaped alone to tell thee." And where are numbers with whom the stages of thy youth, and years at school were spent ? Where are they ? May it not here again be said, "And I only am escaped alone to tell thee ?" Go on, and trace the wonderful history of the eventful path of riper years ; through what sickness, pains, and death hast thou passed, and mayest thou not, my soul, here again cry out " And I only am escaped alone to tell ?" Oh, the wonders of distinguishing love, even in common providences, towards his people, before that the highly-favoured objects have any consciousness how that love is watching over them, and whereby they are preserved to the day of their calling ! Who shall count the sum of distinguishing mercy, in preserving and upholding providences, during the whole of an unconverted state ! My soul, hadst thou died in any one of these perilous seasons, (and how very near sometimes hath death seemed,) the language of Job's messenger would not then have been thine as it is now, " And I only am escaped alone to tell thee." Pause once more. Art thou now, my soul, indeed escaped to tell of converting grace ? Canst thou now look round, and amidst the dying and the dead in trespasses and sins, unawakened, unconcerned, unregenerated, canst thou indeed, say, " And I only am escaped alone to tell thee ?'' Oh then, my soul, proclaim with earnestness the glorious truth, invite all as far as thy sphere of information can reach, as if thou, and thou alone, wert escaped to tell of the wonders of redeeming love; and let thy daily language be, " O come hither, and hearken all ye that fear God, and I will tell you what he hath done for my soul."

15.—Rivers of waters run down mine eyes, because they keep not thy law.—*Psalm* cxix. 136.

WHO is there of whom this may be said? Jesus, and Jesus only. He wept indeed over his beloved Jerusalem, for he was a man of sorrows, and acquainted with grief. And the love he had to his redeemed, induced a bloody sweat through all the pores of his sacred body. But of every other may it not be said, All seek their own, not the things which are Jesus Christ's. Did we truly love Zion, would not rivers of tears run down at the present languishing state of Zion? Did we feel the full sense of distinguishing grace, would not every heart mourn over the ruins of our common nature? Think, my soul, what a mass of sin ascends as a cloud before the view of the Lord every day from a single heart of the desperately wicked transgressor! Think what an accumulation in a town, a province, an empire, the world. Might not rivers of water run down at the contemplation? And worse, if possible. Think of that higher source of sorrow, in that the only possible remedy for this evil is slighted, and Christ, which is God's one gracious ordinance for the recovery of our ruined nature, is so little esteemed among men. Oh how might the people of God be supposed to have their very souls melted in the contemplation. This, this is indeed the condemnation : this is the soul-destroying sin, that light is come into the world, and men love darkness rather than light, because their deeds are evil. Oh for grace to mourn over a Christ-despising generation. Oh for the Deliverer to arise out of Zion, and turn away ungodliness from Jacob.

16.—I say unto you, there is joy in the presence of the angels of God over one sinner that repenteth.—*Luke* xv. 10.

WHAT a precious information is this, which the Son of God hath given of heaven's joy over every individual instance of the recovery of our poor fallen nature. Surely if angels of light thus participate in the triumphs of our Jesus, well may

sinners rejoice over sinners, whenever a single one is awakened from darkness to light, and converted from the power
of sin and Satan unto God. Think, ye ministers of my God,
what motives arise out of this thought, to stir up your most
earnest exertions in labouring in the word and doctrine.
Ought it not to be the first and most importunate petition at
the mercy-seat, whenever entering upon your labours, that,
by the LORD's blessing upon you, new causes might arise to
call forth this joy in heaven? Nay, ought it not to be the
fervent prayer and hope of faith, at the close of those labours,
and especially every Lord's day, that some souls may have
been awakened, and angels may have rejoiced through your
instrumentality? Can there be a prayer more interesting
upon earth, than when the servant of Jesus saith, "Lord,
crown my labours this day with success?" And can there be a
subject to call forth more animated praise than when at the
close of a sabbath, you look up and say, "Lord, have angels
rejoiced this day over the conversion of any poor sinner in
this congregation?" And no less, ye parents and guardians
of the rising generation, should the same hope prompt ye to
wrestle in prayer with God for the sanctification of your
household? Go on and hope that answers are coming down
to your earnest requests. Perhaps the next joy in heaven
may be over one for whom you have now prayed! Precious
Jesus! it is enough. I bless thee, Lord, for this, among a
thousand other proofs of thy care over us, that the salvation
of poor sinners adds new joy to the felicity of heaven, and
that there is joy in the presence of the angels of God over
one sinner that repenteth.

17.—I go to prepare a place for you. And if I go and prepare a place
for you, I will come again and receive you unto myself, that where
I am, there ye may be also.—*John* xiv. 2, 3.

How shall I ever sufficiently enter into an apprehension
of the love of Jesus? Much less, how shall I ever sufficiently love thee, and adore thee, thou unequalled pattern of excelling love, blessed, precious Jesus? Was it not enough to
have given such palpable evidences of thy love in dying for
poor sinners, but must thou tell them also, before thy departure, the cause for which thou art gone away, and to give
them an assurance, at the same time, that thou wouldest come
again and take them home with thee to glory? Oh help me,
Lord, to love thee, to live to thee, to be always on the look

out for thee, and to rejoice with a joy unspeakable in the promise of thy coming. And, my soul, while thou art taking all the sweetness of those precious words of thy Jesus to thyself, in the prospect of his shortly coming to take thee to himself, let them also have their full comfort under any bereaving providences of thy friends. Wouldest thou regret if an earthly king had conceived such a love to any friend of thine, that he had sent for him to advance him to some high dignity, to make him his favourite, and to load him with honours? Considered as to earthly accommodations, would this advancement of some near and dear friend of thine be distressing to thee, because thou wert to see him no more? Nay, would not the generosity of the prince be highly extolled by thee, and more especially if the messengers which came to fetch thy friend brought with them a promise, that, ere long, a royal guard would be sent to take thee also, to live with thy friend for ever, in the king's palace, and under the king's eye, both enjoying the royal favour? But what would all this fading, dying, perishing, and uncertain grandeur be, to that which Jesus promiseth in these blessed words of the morning? And hath Jesus taken any of thine home to his glory? Are they now at the fountain-head of blessedness, and art thou weeping over their breathless remains? Raise up, my soul, thy thoughts from earth to heaven. Hear the voice that speaks, " Blessed are the dead which die in the Lord." Keep up the constant expectation of thine own call. Walk as on the borders of the invisible world. And above all, so watch the daily hourly visits of Jesus, by his grace, and enjoy the sweet communion and fellowship in spirit, by which he now speaks to his people, and they to him, that when Jesus draws back the curtain of thy bed at death, and appears to thy ravished view in all his glory, thou mayest leave the trembling body, and run to his embraces, crying out, " My Lord, and my God !"

18.—Take us the foxes, the little foxes that spoil the vines, for our vines have tender grapes.—*Song* ii. 15.

My soul, mark the sweetness and tenderness of this precept! Foxes no doubt resemble, in this scripture, the subtle, less open, less discovered, sins and corruptions which lurk in us, like these cunning creatures, under a covering, and perhaps sometimes under a fair covering. Moreover, they may mean also false but fair teachers. " O Israel," said the

Lord, "thy prophets are like the foxes in the deserts," crafty, designing, malignant, and filthy. And in proportion as they put on a more fair and specious appearance, the more are they to be dreaded. Satan never more artfully, nor perhaps more effectually, deceives, than when he is transformed into an angel of light. Moreover, the precept is enforced by that important consideration, that vines (by which, no doubt, are meant believers) have tender grapes. What more tender than a weak conscience? And what more liable to be wounded than the tender principles of young beginners in a life of grace? My soul, look up to Jesus, the Lord of the vineyard, for grace to be on the look out against these destructive enemies to thy welfare. And, conscious that all thy vigilance, without his watchful eye over thee, would never protect thee from foes so shrewd and artful, beg of Jesus himself to take these foxes for thee, and destroy them before thine eyes. "Lord," I would say, "keep me from every enemy which doeth evil in thy sanctuary, and preserve alive in flourishing circumstances all those tender graces of thy Spirit bestowed upon me, that I may bring forth fruit to the praise of thy holy name, and may flourish and spread abroad as the cedar of Lebanon.

19.—Without me, ye can do nothing.—*John* xv. 5.

DEAREST Jesus! I know this in theory, from thy gracious teachings, as well as I know that I am by nature a sinner; but I am for ever failing in this knowledge, when I come to put it into practice. Teach me, Lord, how to preserve the constant remembrance of it upon my mind, that I may never go forth to the holy warfare to subdue a single foe but in thy strength, and never make mention of any thing but thy righteousness, and thine only! Be convinced, my soul, every day, more and more, of this most precious truth, and behold it proved from all the circumstances around thee. See and remark the total inability either of God's judgments or God's mercies to induce the least alteration upon the heart of man, without his grace. Behold the prosperous sinner, bathing in a full river of blessings: himself in health, his circumstances flourishing, his children like olive branches round his table, wealth pouring in upon him from every quarter; and yet he lives without God, and without Christ in the world; and as he lives, so he dies, in the vanity of his mind. See him amidst distinguishing preservations, in battles by sea or land, still preserved, while floating carcases, or opened graves, are all around him: do these things bring his heart to God? Not in the least. The sum total of his character may be comprised in a few words: *Neither is God in all his thoughts.* Look at him in the opposite side of the representation: let such an one be visited with chastisements; in his own person, sickness; in his family, misery; in his substance, want; in short, in all that concerns him, a life of sorrow, care, anxiety, disappointment, ruin: perhaps to all these, a body long the dwelling-place of some loathsome disease, under which he groans, and at length dies, and dies the same unawakened sinner as he had lived. And suppose these accumulated evils had been distinguished also with some more peculiar maladies, in perils in the sea, in perils in the war, in perils among men. Nay, let him be maimed in his limbs, let him be rotting in a prison, let him be worn out with misery from evil upon evil, like waves of the sea following each other; yet still he continues the same hardened unsubdued sinner, under all, and as unconscious of God's rods as the prosperous sinner before described is of God's blessings. Are these things so, my soul, and hast thou seen them? Yes, in numberless instances: Oh then learn, that without Jesus thou canst do nothing! Outward circumstances, unaccompanied with inward grace, leave men just where they found them; and plain it is, that grace alone can change the heart. Lord Jesus, let these loud and crying truths day by day lead my soul to thee! Be thou all in all, my hope, my guide, my strength, my portion; for without thee I can do nothing.

20.—Arise, and go down to the potter's house, and there I will cause thee to hear my words.—*Jeremiah* xviii. 2.

YES, Lord, with the first of the morning will I arise, and go down at thy command, where, by the secret and silent whispers of thy divine teaching, I may gather suitable instruction for interpreting all thy dispensations, both in providence and grace, towards me! Mark, my soul, the vessel marred in the hand of the potter. Alas! how hath our nature been marred since it came out of the hand of our Almighty Potter! Will the potter cast his vessel away? No, he will new make it. Oh, thou glorious Lord! methinks I hear thy words in this, for thou hast not thrown us away, but hast new made us, and more blessedly made us, in Christ Jesus. My soul, art thou indeed thus new made, a vessel unto honour, sancti-

17*

fied and meet for the Master's use? Attend then to thy proper character, and never lose sight of it. Refer every act of
mercy and favour in thy original creation, in thy new creation, when marred by sin, and in all the appointments and
dispensations, both in nature, providence, and grace, in which
thou art placed, to the sovereign will and pleasure of Jehovah,
thine Almighty Potter. All the different forms, and the different ends, for which the whole is appointed, result from his
sovereignty, in which the richest display of wisdom and of
love is shown. Shall the thing formed say unto him that
formed it, Why hast thou *made* me thus? Much less in any
of the dispensations, either in providence or grace, shall any
say, Why dost thou *use* me thus? Precious Jesus! It is
enough to be new made in thee, to be new formed in thy
blessed likeness, to be taken into thy service, and to be made
a meet vessel for the Master's use in thy family. Thy church
is as a great and well-furnished house, where there are not
only vessels of gold and of silver, but also of wood and of
earth. And if my Lord condescend to look on me, to use
me, nay, to bring me into his house and family, that I may
be always under his own gracious eye, how humble soever
the place, or lowly the station, to belong to Jesus is the supreme honour of all his saints. My soul, make frequent
visits to the Potter's house, and never fail to go down there
whenever any temptation from the enemy, or thine own heart,
causeth thee to forget thy creatureship, and the wonders of a
marred creature being new made in Christ Jesus!

21.—The righteous shall flourish like the palm tree.—*Psalm* xcii. 12.

It forms a beautiful illustration, which the Holy Ghost
condescends to give of a true believer's state, as it stands before God, in the allusion not unfrequently made in scripture
to that of the palm tree. The direct tendency of the palm
tree is upwards: it lifts its head, in defiance of all impediments, towards the clouds. Now a true believer in Jesus is
always looking upwards, and directing all his pursuits after
Jesus. His person, blood, and righteousness, are the objects
of his desire. And as the palm tree is said to flourish the
more when trodden upon, and attempted to be crushed, so the
believer most oppressed for Jesus' sake, will flourish in the
graces of the Spirit more abundantly. How fruitful also is
the palm tree! And how much the people of God bring
forth fruit in their old age, when, after long experience, they

have found, that in Jesus alone their fruit is found! How much the palm tree likes sunny places! How precious the Sun of Righteousness is to his people! And as the branches of palm trees are worn in tokens of victory, so the church above are beheld with palms in their hands: and the church below carry the palm of rejoicing, when, from the atoning blood and righteousness of Jesus, they are made more than conquerors through Him that loved them. My soul, art thou flourishing like the palm tree? Yes, if so be thou art planted in Jesus, and watered from the streams of that river which maketh glad the city of God. Yes, if directing all thy views, all thy hopes, all thy desires, to Jesus, thou art living in him, acting faith upon him, making him the Alpha and Omega of hope here, and happiness hereafter. Blessed Sun of Righteousness! shine with such warm, life-giving, fruit imparting, beams of thy rich grace upon my soul, that I may flourish indeed under thy divine influence; and show that *the Lord, who is my rock, is upright, and that there is no unrighteousness in him.*

22.—These shall make war with the Lamb, and the Lamb shall overcome them: for he is Lord of lords, and King of kings; and they that are with him are called, and chosen, and faithful.—*Rev.* xvii. 14.

WHAT an awful thing must sin in its own nature be, which hath introduced such evil into the whole creation of God, in its consequences. One might have hoped, however, that the meek and gentle Lamb of God would have been exempt from the daring rebellion, and that sin would not have bid defiance and waged war against the peaceable, and holy, and harmless, Jesus. But so far is this from being the case, that, in all probability, war first broke out in heaven against the person of God's dear Son, as man's glorious Head, and Mediator, even before the deadly malignity manifested itself against God and his Christ upon earth, in tempting the first man and his wife in the garden of Eden, to rebel against God. Pause, my soul, over this scripture. Who are they here described that make war with the Lamb? Nay, rather, who are they not? All the powers of darkness, all the varieties of the earth, all the inhabitants of hell, all that are under the influence of that evil spirit, which now worketh in the children of disobedience. Under this dreadful banner of open rebellion against heaven, every man by nature is enlisted; and until an act of sovereign grace and power is past, and he that is Lord of lords, and King of kings, overcomes, and brings them under his blessed dominion, all ranks and orders of men are found. My soul, are the weapons of sin fallen out of thine hands? Art thou brought under the conquests of Christ's grace? Hast thou bent the knee of willing homage to the Lamb, who hath bought thee with his blood, and made thee his by his grace? Read thy character, if so, in these sweet words, "And they that are with the Lamb are called, and chosen, and faithful." Art thou *called* with an holy calling? Art thou *chosen*, and fully convinced of this, that had not Jesus first chosen thee, thou wouldst never have chosen him? Art thou *faithful*, in seeking and desiring no other salvation, convinced that there is salvation in no other? Take with thee then, my soul, these precious marks of thy high-calling and fellowship, and see that thou follow the Lamb withersoever he goeth.

23.—One like unto the Son of man, clothed with a garment down to the foot, and girt about the paps with a golden girdle.—*Rev.* i. 13.

MY soul, thou art going this morning to the throne of grace, art thou not? Pause then, and behold Jesus, as John saw him, for the church's joy, in his priestly vestments; for, remember, he is still a Priest upon his throne, and by the oath of Jehovah abideth a Priest for ever. Nay, my soul, be not afraid; draw nigh; hark, surely he calls. Methinks he speaks to thee—"Behold me! behold me. See, I am thine intercessor. For this cause I wear these priestly garments, and, as the high-priest of old represented me, I appear in them down to the foot, and the golden girdle round and beneath the breast. What is thy cause? What blessings and praises hast thou to offer for past grace? And what supplications for present and future favours? Behold my vesture dipped in blood. Think of the everlasting efficacy of my righteousness: and for whom should I make intercession, but for transgressors?" Fall down, my soul, with holy reverence and goldly fear. Jesus will do by thee as he did by John. He will lay his right hand upon thee, and say, Fear not. Oh, precious, precious Lord! thou art indeed he that was dead, and now livest for evermore. And thou livest to see the fruits of thy great salvation faithfully and fully applied to every one of thy redeemed. Thy priesthood is for ever. Thy intercession unceasing. I do behold thee, Lord, by faith, even now standing with the blood of the covenant in thine hand, and presenting me, even me,—poor, wretched, worthless me,—as one of the purchase of this blood! Do I not hear thy voice in those soul-reviving words, "Father, keep through thine own name those whom thou hast given me? Father, I will that they also whom thou hast given me, be with me where I am?" Oh, glorious, gracious, almighty High-priest! thou art indeed a Priest for ever, after the order of Melchisedec. Oh, ye trembling souls! ye who have any cause this day to bring before the court of heaven, look unto Jesus, look within the vail, see Jesus there; look steadily, though humbly, and behold his hands, his side; Zion is still engraven on his palms. Nay, do we not see, may we not read, our very names, as the high-priest bore the names of Israel on his breast, while his hands were lifted up to bless! Yes, Jesus takes up our cause, bears our persons, and all our concerns. And how shall either fail, while he is able to save to the uttermost all that come to God by him, seeing he ever liveth to make intercession.

24.—The stranger did not lodge in the street; but I opened my doors to the traveller.—*Job* xxxi. 32.

THOUGH Job was thus hospitable, yet we know that angels would have lodged in the street, if Lot had not taken them in. Nay, the Lord of angels, when he came a stranger upon earth, had not where to lay his head. He came indeed unto his own, but his own received him not. My soul, pause! hast thou done better by thy Lord? Nay, thou hast not. And though thou knowest the precept the apostle had it in commission to tell the church, not to be forgetful to entertain strangers, for thereby, as in the instance of the patriarch and others, some have entertained angels unawares; yet, my soul, how long did the Lord of life and glory stand without knocking at the door of thine heart, by the ministry of his word and ordinances, saying, "Open to me;" yea, and would have stood to this hour, had he not, by his own sovereign grace, put in his hand, by the hole of the door, and opened to himself. Oh, thou blissful stranger! didst thou, indeed, come from a far country, on this gracious, blessed errand, to seek and save that which was lost; and didst thou find every heart resolutely shut against thee? Didst thou, blessed Jesus, when travelling in the greatness of thy strength, open to thyself an entrance into the souls of thy people, by the sweet and constraining influences of thy holy Spirit? Do thou, then, almighty Lord,

throw open the street-doors of my heart, for thy constant reception! Make them like the gates of that blessed city,
which are never shut, day nor night. And cause my soul,
like the prophet on the watch-tower, or Abraham in the tent
door, to be always on the look out for my Lord's approach, that
I may invite thee, yea, constrain thee, to come in, and abide
with me, and to make thyself known unto me, by the heart-
burning discourses of thy word, and in breaking of bread,
and of prayer. Yes, yes, thou glorious Traveller! who art
perpetually on the visits of thy love, I do know thee; I do sometimes catch a sweet glimpse of thee, and trace the footsteps of
thy grace, in thy word, in thy ordinances, and in the various
ways by which thy presence is discoverable. Indeed, indeed,
thou heavenly Stranger, thou shalt not lodge in the street; but
I will take thee home to my house, to my heart and soul; and
thou shalt sup with me, and I with thee, according to thine own
most gracious promise, and I will cause thee to drink of spiced
wine, of the juice of my pomegranate.

25.—Thou art my hiding-place.—*Psalm* xxii. 7.

Yea, dearest Jesus! thou art indeed my hiding-place. In
every point of view I desire grace so to behold thee. Surely,
from everlasting, in thee, and thy person and righteousness,
were all thy redeemed hid in the counsels of peace and
salvation. And is not every individual hid in thee also, oh!
thou glorious Head of thy church! while in a state of renewed
nature, to be secured from death and the grave, and from the
unpardonable sin; and as one of the apostles terms it, *preserved in Christ Jesus and called?* And when called, and
quickened by grace, what but from having our lives hid with
Christ in God, could keep alive the incorruptible seed, or preserve unextinguished the immortal spark? Whence is it,
my soul, that the smoking flax, which Satan and thine own
remaining indwelling lusts strive to blow out, is not quenched;
or the bruised reed, which appears so continually falling, is
not broken—but because Jesus is thy security, through
whom, and in whom, thy languishing graces revive as the
corn, and grow as the vine? Oh! what springs of grace
must there be for ever flowing from Jesus, though hidden
from mortal view! Surely, Lord, thou art my hiding-place,
and therefore, with thy leave, I will consider thee as a strong
Tower, into which the righteous runneth and is safe. Yes,

both my person and life, both my safety and happiness, both my present peace and everlasting joy, all, all are in thee. Doth any then ask thee, my soul, Where dwellest thou? Tell them, in Jesus, in the clefts of the rock, in the secret places of the stairs, even in Christ himself and his justifying righteousness; secret and hidden indeed from mere men of the world, but revealed from faith to faith to all his redeemed; and into which, tell them, thou hast found shelter from the broken law of God, from the dreadful effects of sin, from death, from hell, and all the powers of darkness. And all these, and numberless other unknown blessings, because Christ is my hiding-place, who hath both preserved me from trouble, and hath compassed me about with songs of deliverance.

26.—And there wrestled a man with him until the breaking of the day.— *Genesis* xxxii. 24.

My soul! here is a lovely portion for the morning. For the morning did I say? Yea, both for night and morning, and, indeed, until the everlasting morning break in upon thee, and all the shadows of the night flee away. For are not all the seed of Jacob, like their father, wrestlers in the actings of faith and the favour of prayer, until they come off, like him, prevailing Israels? And who was this man which wrestled with the patriarch? Let scripture explain scripture, and give the answer. " By his strength," said the prophet Hosea, (chap. xii. 3, &c.) " he had power with God; yea, he had power over the angel, and prevailed; he wept, and made supplication unto him; he found him in Bethel, and there he spake with us; even the Lord God of hosts, the Lord is his memorial." Here then light is thrown upon the subject. He that is called a *man* in one scripture, is called an *angel* in this other. And that we might not overlook nor forget the identity of his Person, as the very man whose name was then secret, (Judges xiii. 18,) but hereafter to be made known, and himself appear openly, the prophet was commissioned to tell the church that he that spake with us, in the person of Jacob our father, was the same that found Jacob in Bethel, even the Lord God of hosts; for that was his memorial. Gen. xxviii. 10, 19. And was it then He, whose name is Wonderful, which wrestled with Jacob? And when the poor patriarch was hard put to it, full of fears, doubts, and distresses, on account of his brother Esau, and was stirring up himself to take hold of God's strength, by way of strengthening himself against Esau, did he that came to strengthen him, first take hold of him, and seem to contend with him, until the breaking of the day? Oh, then, my soul, here learn a sweet and precious lesson against the hour of the many contentions with the *Esaus* of thy warfare; for thou wrestlest not only against flesh and blood, but against principalities and powers, against the rulers of the darkness of this world, against spiritual wickedness in high places. See, my soul, where thy strength is—even in Jesus. See what a blessed example of prevailing in prayer the Holy Ghost hath here set before thee. Look to this God-man, with whom Jacob wrestled and came off successful, and say with Job, Will he plead against me with his great strength? No, but he will put strength in me. Job xxiii. 2, 7. Fill thy mouth with arguments, as Job did. Tell Jesus of thy wants: tell him of his riches, tell him of thy guilt, tell him of his precious blood and righteousness ; and tell him, that thy misery, and weakness, and unworthiness, renders thee a suitable sinner for so gracious a Saviour to get glory by in saving. Go to him, my soul, with these strong, these unanswerable pleas. Jesus will love to hear and to receive them. And while he wrestles with thee, do thou wrestle with him, all the night, in which thou art contending with thy sins within and temptations without, with the errors of the infidel, and the crying sins of the profane. And do as Jacob did, wrestle, plead, supplicate, cry, and take hold of his strength, his blood, his righteousness, and God the Father's covenant-promises in him ; and never give over, nor let him go, until the day break and he blesseth thee.

27.—That thy trust may be in the Lord, I have made known to thee this day, even to thee.—*Prov.* xxii. 19.

My soul, mark for thy morning meditation what is here said. Observe, in the first place, the *general* knowledge the Lord hath given of his saving truth and mercies in Christ Jesus, and which becomes a sufficient warrant and authority for all the world to believe in Christ, and to accept of Christ, to the salvation of the soul. Christ in the word is the Father's authority for every sinner to believe the record God hath given of his Son ; and the rejection of this command will be the condemning sin to every one who despises this plan of salvation, because he hath heard, and then turned his back upon this love of God in Christ Jesus the Lord. My soul, ponder over this view of the subject, and then turn to another sweet and distinguishing property of God's revelation, which he makes by his blessed Spirit, in the *particular* apprehension of it. And this is done in every heart that is made willing in the day of God's power, when the same grace which reveals Christ in the word, reveals Christ also in the heart, the hope of glory. Here the verse of the morning is confirmed, in what God saith, that in order to every child of God putting his trust in the Lord, he hath made known to thee, even to thee, this day. Observe, my soul, the personal application of the divine truth. God, by his Spirit, makes it known to *thee*. It comes like a present sent down from heaven. Who is it for? Read the direction. It is for thee, my soul. Thus faith takes home the contents to the heart, and finding how exactly every thing in Jesus and his salvation suits his own case and circumstances, he lives upon it, feeds upon it, takes it for his portion, trusts in God for the truth of it, and rejoiceth evermore. My soul, hast thou marked these distinct things? And dost thou know how to distinguish rightly between *general* proclamations of mercy, and *special* personal enjoyments of it? Oh, then, live up to the full enjoyment of God's rich mercy in Christ; accept Christ, and use Christ, daily, hourly, to the glory of Father, Son, and Spirit, as the redemption by Christ was intended; and bless God more and more for his unspeakable gift.

28.—As an eagle stirreth up her nest, fluttereth over her young, spreadeth abroad her wings, taketh them, beareth them on her wings ; so the Lord alone did lead him.—*Deut.* xxxii. 11, 12.

HERE learn a lesson, to form some faint idea how the Lord is unceasingly engaged in taking care of his people. If thy God condescends to represent it by such a similitude, is it not both thy privilege and thy duty to mark the several particulars of such grace and tenderness? The eagle not only possesseth, in common with other creatures, the greatest affection for her young, but manifests a vast superiority over every other of the winged tribe, in her management of her brood. She provides for them and protects them, as other birds of the air do ; but in educating them, and the method by which she shelters them from danger, here is displayed such superior wisdom and power as far exceeds whatever we meet with in other creatures. She *stirreth up her nest :* by

18

which we may understand, she suffers not the young eagles
to lay sleeping, but calls them forth to life and exercise. She
fluttereth over them, as if to show them how they are to use
their wings, and fly.   And when she taketh them from the
nest, this is not done like other birds who carry their young
in their talons, and in their haste or flight may drop them—
or, when pursued or fired at by an enemy, may have them
killed and herself not hurt; but the eagle beareth her young
on her wings, so that no arrow from beneath can touch the
young, until it hath first pierced through the heart of the old
bird.   What a sweet thought do these views afford; and
what a blessed instruction do they bring!   My soul, do they
not teach thee, since the similitude is the Lord's own, that
He that hath stirred up the nest of thine old nature, in which
thou wast born, because he would not suffer thee to sleep
there for ever in the unawakened state of sin, and hath
brought thee out, and brought thee abroad, and taught thee
how to fly up, in devout aspirations after him, is the Lord?
Is it not he that fed thee and sustained thee from thy youth,
even until now; taught thee, and hovered over thee, and
caused thee to mount up as upon the wings of eagles;
to run, and not to weary; to walk, and not faint?   Yes,
yes, blessed Jesus! it is thou that hast indeed borne me,
as thou hast said, upon eagles' wings, and brought me
to thyself: so that I see, by this delightful comparison, that
thou wilt not suffer any of thy little ones to perish; for he
that toucheth them, toucheth the apple of thine eye—nay,
while on thy wings, he that destroyeth them, must first destroy thee!   Oh! Lord, give me grace rightly to enjoy and
use such marvellous blessings.   And since, to the wisdom
and strength of the eagle, thou hast now added the tenderness and solicitude of the hen, do thou, Lord, gather me under thy wings, and nourish me with thy love and favour,
that I may be thine for ever, and live here by faith, as hereafter I hope to live with thee in glory!

29.—We, being many, are one body in Christ.—*Rom.* xii. 5.

ONE of the most delightful of all thoughts, and which
when fully enjoyed under the influence of the Holy Ghost,
gives an unspeakable felicity in the heart, is that union and
fellowship of Christ with his church.   Ponder it, my soul,
this morning.   All the members of Christ's body are but one
body, the apostle saith, in Christ; and he is the Head over

all things to the Church, which is his body, the fulness of Him that filleth all in all. I would never, if possible, lose sight of this, because in the perfect conviction and assurance of it must be found all our security and joy. And the way by which this blessed truth, under divine teaching, will be kept alive in the soul, is this: I would behold myself what I am by nature and practice in Adam, and connect by this view what I am by grace and faith in Christ. Now as Adam was the common head of all his seed in nature, equally so is Christ the common head of all his seed in grace. Do I consider that, when Adam sinned in the garden, I as one of his children, and then (as scripture saith of Levi, in respect to his connexion with Abraham) was in his loins, part of himself, and consequently implicated and involved in all the good or bad belonging to him? then it will follow, that in Adam's sin I sinned, and in Adam's condemnation I was included. So then, as Adam did not transgress only for himself, but for all his seed by nature that should come from him; equally so when Christ fulfilled all righteousness, and when Christ expiated all sin by the sacrifice of himself, his seed were considered righteous in him; and his expiatory sacrifice, as the Head of his people, must be, to all intents and purposes, the same as if they had been sacrificed with him. Cherish this thought, my soul! and never allow thyself to behold Christ as the Christ of God, in the capacity of a private or single person, but as the Covenant-Head, the Father's Chosen, the Sent, the Sealed, the Anointed of God, in whom all his members are one body in Christ. See that thou hast the Spirit of Christ, by which thou art proved to be one of his! And for the full enjoyment of all the blessings contained in this union and communion with thy glorious Head, daily and hourly remind God thy Father of all his covenant promises made to Christ as the Head of his church and people, in which the Lord hath said, "I will pour my Spirit upon thy seed, and my blessing upon thine offspring."

30.—My grace is sufficient for thee.—2 *Cor.* xxii. 9.

My soul! gather a rich cluster this morning of those precious fruits, which hang upon the Tree of Life—even upon Jesus. Thou wilt find their taste more sweet and pleasant than all the branches of the vine. Consider the *fulness* in thy Lord. Such a fulness indeed, by virtue of the covenant engagements in Jehovah, is treasured up in Christ, that all

the grace every individual of his seed could possibly want in
time, and all the glory hereafter—all, all is lodged in him.
What a thought is here! Consider also the *freeness* of this
grace. Never, surely, did God give any gift more free than
when he gave his Son.   And, as the apostle from hence
justly reasons, "He that spared not his own son, but delivered him up for us all, how shall he not with him freely
give us all things? When, my soul, thou hast feasted thyself upon the *fulness* and *freeness* of the fruits of Jesus' rich
salvation, gather another rich portion for thyself, with the
hand of faith, in the *suitableness* and *sufficiency* there is in him
for *thee*. Take the sweet words spoken here to Paul, but
not limited to Paul, as if personally addressed to thyself. It
is Jesus now speaks and saith this day, "My grace is sufficient for thee." Which is as if he had said, all the grace I
have is for my people; and I have not only enough for all,
but for every one; and I have it for thee; I have the very
portion which I knew each would want every day, and all
the day, through the whole of their pilgrimage state: from
everlasting I knew their need; and from everlasting I have
laid every individual child's portion by, and do keep it for
him to the moment required; and each shall find a suited
sufficiency, exactly answering to all their wants, and corresponding to all their necessities. Precious thought! Henceforth, my soul, cast all thy care upon Jesus; for thou now
seest how he careth for thee. Morning by morning hear his
voice, speaking personally to thyself, "My grace is sufficient
for thee."

31.—Watchman, what of the night? Watchman, what of the night.—
Isaiah xxi. 11.

WHILE this solemn inquiry may be supposed to have peculiar reference, as addressed to the servants of the Lord, whom
he hath set as watchmen upon the walls of Zion, may it not
be made *personally* to every man's bosom also, as it refers to
himself? And the repeating of it twice should seem to im-
ply the importance and earnestness with which it should be
followed up. My soul! What is the night with thee? Art
thou watching in it more than they that watch for the morning; yea, I say, more than they which watch for the morning? How art thou exercising this watchfulness? Is all safe
respecting thine everlasting welfare? Art thou watching the

approaches of the enemy? Art thou watchful in prayer; watchful for the gracious moments of the Spirit's helping thee in prayer; watchful in guiding thee in the exercise of it; watchful of the Lord's gracious answers to prayer: and, like the prophet on the watch-tower, having given in thy petition to the heavenly court, into the hands of the High-priest and Intercessor, art thou waiting to see what the Lord will say unto thee? Lord, make me eminently watchful in these things. Go on, my soul, in this heart-searching inquiry. Art thou waiting and watching thy Lord's return? What of the night is it now? May not Jesus come at even, or at midnight, or at cock-crowing, or in the morning? Pause, my soul! Suppose his chariot-wheels were at the door, wouldest thou arise with holy joy, crying out, "It is the voice of my Beloved," saying "Behold, I come quickly?" And wouldest thou answer, "Even so, come, Lord Jesus?" Oh! for grace to be of that happy number, of whom the Lord himself saith, "Blessed are those servants whom, at his coming, he shall find so doing."

AUGUST.

1.—In thy name shall they rejoice all the day; and in thy righteousness shall they be exalted.—*Psalm* lxxxix. 16.

SEE, my soul, what a blessed cause is again before thee to begin the month, and to carry it on through every day, and all the day, and in every part of the day, for joy in the name and righteousness of Jesus. And mark it with peculiar emphasis, that it is Jesus, as Jesus the Christ of God; and his righteousness as the righteousness of God, in which all thy rejoicing is, and not in the finest frames or spiritual exercises of thine own. A daily sense of a need of Christ, and as constant a sense of acting faith upon Christ; these form the foundation of every true believer's joy, and make the savour of Christ's name like ointment poured forth. And whence is it, my soul, that all the redeemed are said to rejoice in the name of the Lord all the day, but because the Lord hath saved them and redeemed them for his name's sake? And whence is it said, that in his righteousness they shall be exalted, but because from their union with Christ, as their spiritual Head, they are accepted in his righteousness, and are made the righteousness of God in him! Here's an exaltation indeed, enough to make the heart of the most sorrowful glad, let outward circumstances be what they may, when inward joy and peace in believing give such a blessedness to the believer's view of the name of Jesus. See to it then, my soul, that all thy fresh springs of joy are in him. Be very jealous over thyself, in the happiest moments of thy comfort, that Christ's name, and his righteousness and salvation, lie at the bottom of thy joy. Where is Jesus? I would ask my heart, when I am most at ease and happy? Is He in this happiness? And is this happiness enjoyed, and enjoyed purely, because Christ is in it? Trace this, my soul, through all the parts of salvation, and through all thy paths in grace, and see whether thou art bottoming every hope and every mercy, both for time and eternity, in the name and righteousness of Jesus only : for, depend upon it, as Jehovah hath said, in pardoning and blotting out the transgressions of his people, " I, even I, am he that blotteth out thy transgressions for my name's sake ;" so it is to the everlasting praise of his name, that all the glory of salvation is, and must be, ascribed. Nevertheless, he saved them for his name's sake, that he might make his mighty power to be known!

2.—My Father is the husbandman.—*John* xv. 1.

BLESSED truth, and blessed assurance, to the true followers of Jesus! Yes, Almighty Father! I would pray for thy continual teaching, to behold thee as the Husbandman of thy vineyard the church, in which thou hast raised up the Plant of Renown, the Man whose name is the Branch, the true Vine, in whom, and upon whom, and through whom, all thy redeemed, taken from the olive-tree that is wild by nature, are grafted, and bring forth fruit unto God. Yes, Almighty Father! I would desire grace to behold thee, and while I behold, to love, to praise, to adore thee, that from everlasting thou hast graciously been the Husbandman of thy church. It was in thee, and from thee, as the contriver and appointer of all that concerned redemption, we trace the fountain and source of all that grace, mercy, peace, and favour here, with all the unknown treasures of glory hereafter, which thou hast placed in His most blessed hands, who is the Lord our Righteousness. In every renewed view of Jesus, as the true Vine which thou hast planted ; and in every renewed communication, from his fulness, nourishment, and life-imparting influences ; may it be my happy portion, Oh Lord, to eye thee as the Husbandman, while I feel and know my union in Jesus as the Vine.. And do thou, most gracious God and Father, condescend to act the part of the kind Husbandman still. Let thine eyes be upon me for good, as the Husbandman visits his vineyard. Water, Lord, with the heavenly dew of thy word and Spirit, the dry and languishing plantation. Oh, that the Lord may give showers of blessings, and that he may be to me as the latter and as the former rain, upon the barrenness of my heart. Preserve me, Lord, from the wild boar of the wood, even Satan, that he may never tread me down. Weed out, Lord, the briars and thorns, even the corruptions of my own heart, which would twine themselves with the tender branches. And lop off, Oh Lord, all the superfluous shoots, even the world's enticements, which might prevent fruitfulness in Jesus. In all things, blessed God and Father ! be thou the kind, the tender, the wise Husbandman, in doing for me what thou seest to be needful, however painful to flesh and blood thy pruning dispensations and wintry providences may be found. Do thou purge, as Jesus hath said, every branch that beareth fruit, that it may bring forth more fruit: and by thy gracious Spirit so cause me to abide in Christ, and that Christ may abide in me, that thou, my God and Father, mayest be glorified in my bearing much fruit, to the praise of thy grace, wherein thou hast made me accepted in the Beloved.

3.—Now I know that thou fearest God, seeing thou hast not withheld thy son, thine only son, from me.—*Gen.* xxii. 12.

My soul, ponder these words. By whom were they spoken ? It is said by the angel of the Lord ! Probably the Messenger of the covenant: He who, in the fulness of time, was to make known, face to face, to all Abraham's seed, the whole revelation of Jehovah concerning redemption ! It was a critical moment in Abraham's life, and a trying moment to his faith. It is said, "Now I know." Did not the Lord know before? Oh! yes; but He that gave Abraham the faith, *now* afforded an opportunity for the exercise of it. My soul, how blessed is it to remark, that the largest gifts of grace are dispensed when there is the largest occasion for them. As thy days, so shall thy strength be. And, my soul! do not forget to remark also, that our Isaacs, our children, our earthly comforts, are most likely to be continued to us, when the Lord gives grace and faith to be most ready at his holy will to part with them. When I can say, Lord, all that thou hast given me is thine; and if thou art pleased to take all, or any part, back again, still it is thine own—not mine, but lent. Oh! for grace, like Abraham, to bless a taking God as well as a giving God, and to withhold nothing from him. Pause, my soul, one moment longer over this precious portion! Is there nothing more to be gathered from it? Look again. Read it over once more. Pass beyond Abraham, and contemplate the God of Abraham, and see if thou canst not discover the infinite, unequalled, astonishing love of God the Father typified in this solemn transaction: and while we behold Abraham, at the call of God, giving up his son, his only son, may we not behold God, uncalled, unsought, and without any one cause but his own free, everlasting love, giving up his only begotten Son, as a sacrifice for the redemption of his people? The patriarch gave up his son but in intention; but God, in reality. And, my soul, what oughtest thou now to say to God in the view of this transaction? Methinks I find authority, from these sweet words, to make a paraphrase upon them, and to make application of them, for all and every circumstance with which I may be exercised; and, looking up to God my Father in Christ Jesus, I would say, "Now, O Lord and Father, I know thou dost love a poor, sinful, unworthy worm as I am, seeing thou hast not withheld thy Son, thine only Son, from me!"

4.—And he led them forth by a right way, that they might go to a city of habitation.—*Psalm* cvii. 7.

My soul! what are thy daily exercises concerning the way the Lord thy God is leading thee through a wilderness dispensation? Art thou convinced that it is the *right* way? What if it be a thorny way, a tempted way, frequently a dark way; yet art thou satisfied that it is the *right* way, because it is thorny, tempted, dark, and with numberless other exercises? This is the plan to judge by. And though, my soul, I trust thou hast grace enough given thee to see and know, in thy cool hours of thought, that whatever thy God appoints must be right, and his holy will must be done; yet there is an exercise of grace which goes much beyond these views of the subject, and which a believer is enabled to bring into practice, when he not only submits to a painful dispensation, but rejoiceth in it, because it is the right way. When he saith, I am afflicted; but afflictions are useful. I am in dark and trying circumstances; but these also are useful. I am buffeted by Satan; but this also I find to be right, because Christ is the more endeared thereby, and his strength is perfected in my weakness! My God is bringing me by a right way, to a city of habitation. Of this I am sure. And every step leading to the final attainment, is already marked by infinite wisdom, and provided for by infinite love; and Jesus himself is with me through all the pilgrimage! Hence then, I conclude, that if at any time I am at a loss to see my way, to find comfort in my way, or if I am obstructed in my way; still it is the *right* way, because Jesus himself is the way, and his unerring wisdom is in the appointment! Oh, for grace in lively exercise, to be as satisfied now, of all thy dispensations concerning thy church and people, as when of old in the wilderness; the Lord is leading forth by a right way, to bring to a city of habitation, whose builder and maker is God.

5.—Therefore thus saith the Lord, I am returned to Jerusalem with mercies.—*Zech.* i. 16.

My soul, think what a sad state that land, that church, that family, that heart, is in, where God withdraws but for a moment! This will be one way of rightly appreciating his presence. What a mercy, what an unspeakable mercy, is it when God returns! For until he returns in grace, there will be no return to him in a way of seeking mercy. Pause, my soul, over the thought. Though a child of God loseth not the interest and favour of God in his covenant, because what unworthiness soever, as in ourselves, we must appear in before God, yet in Christ there is an everlasting worthiness, in which his people are accepted and beloved; yet if the Lord suspends his gracious influences to the soul; if Jesus speaks neither by Urim nor Thummim; if the Holy Ghost, though at home *in* the heart, manifests not himself *to* the heart; what shall the soul do? Ordinances are nothing, if the God of ordinances be not in them. To look inward, the soul finds no peace. To look upward, there can be no

comfort. For if the Lord commands the clouds to pour no
rain upon his inheritance, their heaven is as brass, and their
earth as iron. Hast thou, my soul, experienced trying seasons; and though convinced of an interest in Jesus, hast thou
languished after the sweet and blessed visits of his grace?
Listen, then, to this precious scripture; " I am returned, saith
the Lord, unto Jerusalem with mercies." Welcome, Lord,
to my soul, to my heart! Thy presence is better than life
itself. And the mercies thou hast brought with thee, in pardoning, quickening, renewing, reviving, comforting, and
strengthening me, will put more joy in my heart than thousands of gold and silver. There will be no barren ordinances, no barren hearts, no barren land, where our God
comes. Thou hast said, "I will be as the dew unto Israel."
Oh! what a revival in my poor heart; what a revival will
thy presence make in my family! what a revival in thy
churches; what a revival in this dear land of our nativity!
Oh! come, Lord Jesus, come in our midst; and let us hear
thee say, " I am returned to Jerusalem with mercies. Thou
shalt no more be termed forsaken; neither shall thy land any
more be termed desolate: but thou shalt be called *Hephzibah*,
and thy land *Beulah;* for the Lord delighteth in thee, and
thy land shall be married."

6.—Set me as a seal upon thine heart, as a seal upon thine arm : for
  love is strong as death ; jealousy is cruel as the grave: the coals
  thereof are coals of fire, which hath a most vehement flame.—*Song*
  viii. 6.

My soul, is this the language of thine heart to Jesus? Yes,
it is. Can any desire to be nearer Christ than thee? Can
any long more to be worn as a signet upon his arm, and to
lay nearer his heart, than thee? And can any desire more
than thou dost, to be sealed with his Holy Spirit unto the day
of redemption? Surely, my soul, thou longest earnestly for
these precious things, that that arm of Jesus, on which thou
wouldest be set as a seal, may be ever clasping thee; and
that heart of thy Redeemer's upon which thou art engraven,
as the high-priest bore the names of the people of Israel,
may be always folding thee, and bearing both thy person and
thy wants before the throne, and thus unceasing fellowship
may abound with the Father and with his Son Jesus Christ.
And canst thou not say, as the church did to Jesus, " For
love is strong as death; jealousy is cruel as the grave?" For

as death conquers all, and the grave admits of no rival, so thy love to Jesus, which he hath planted in thine heart, hath conquered thee; and no rival, no partner, can divide the throne of thine heart with Jesus. Every thing in thee, concerning Jesus, is as though on fire; and all the flames of thine affection burn with this language: "Whom have I in heaven but thee? and there is none upon earth I desire beside thee. My flesh and my heart faileth: but thou art the strength of my heart, and thou art my portion for ever!" But pause, my soul! Is there not somewhat in those precious words of the morning, in which Jesus may be supposed to say the same to thee? Surely, my soul, if thou lovest him, it is because he first loved thee! And if the real cry of thine heart is to be set as a seal upon his heart, and upon his arm, depend upon it, it is because he hath been beforehand with thee in both. Precious Redeemer! and dost thou indeed bid me set thee in my heart, and on my arm? Lord Jesus! I would wear thee in my heart; I would never, never suffer thee to depart from my arms; I would feel thee *inward*, manifest thee by every *outward* testimony, and as seals upon the arm and upon the breast are in sight, so would I set thee always before me, and tell the whole earth whose I am, and whom I love; that whither thou goest I would go, and where thou dwellest I would dwell: for I am no longer my own, but am bought with a price; therefore I would glorify God in my body, and in my spirit, which are his.

7.—A friend that sticketh closer than a brother.—*Prov.* xviii. 24.

AND who is this, my soul; indeed, who can it be, but Jesus? None among the fallen race of Adam could ever redeem his brother, or, if he could, would have done it at the expense of his own soul. But Jesus did all this, and more, when our cause was desperate, and gave himself a ransom for his redeemed. Oh! for grace to mark the features of his love. It began in eternity; it runs through all time, and continues everlasting. As Jesus is himself, so is he in his love; the same yesterday, and to-day, and for ever. And how hath he shown it? First, by engaging as our Surety; then, paying all our debts; fulfilling the whole law; purchasing our persons; undertaking for our duty; nay, even to the conquering the stubbornness of our nature, and making us willing to be saved in the day of his power? And what is it now? Having accomplished redemption for us by his blood, he is

gone to take possession of a kingdom in our name. There
he still manifests the friend that sticketh closer than a brother; for he takes up all our causes, pleads our suits, and
makes every case his own. And by and by he will come to
take us to himself, that where he is, there we may be also. In
the mean time he supplies all our wants, and this with a freeness, fulness, suitableness, and all-sufficiency, that knows no
bounds, to manifest the unalterable friendship which he bears
us. He visits us continually, sympathizeth with us in all our
afflictions, and increaseth with his tender love the enjoyment
of all our comforts; and all this, and a thousand other
nameless, numberless tokens, Jesus is continually showing, as
proves that his whole heart and soul is ours. So that he is a
faithful, loving, constant, powerful, kind, everlasting, unchanging Friend, that sticketh closer than a brother. My
soul, what wilt thou say to such a Friend? How wilt thou
love him? Oh! precious Lord! I am astonished when I
think of thy love and my ingratitude. But, Lord, it is thine
to love, thine to pity, thine to pardon. Lord, give me grace
to appropriate thee to myself; and while thou art still saying
to me, and to thy church, " I have called you friends"—may
I say, " This is my Friend, and this is my Beloved, O daughters of Jerusalem !"

8.—Henceforth there is laid up for me a crown of righteousness, which
    the Lord the righteous Judge shall give me at that day: and not to
    me only, but unto all them that love his appearing.—2 *Timothy* iv. 8.

PAUSE, my soul, over this blessed verse, and mark the very
weighty things contained in it. Many a soul is for deferring
the thoughts of this great day of God, and concludes, that
the justification of the sinner cannot be known until the day
of judgment. But, my soul, see to it that thou art for bringing the firm and unshaken belief of it into immediate possession and enjoyment now; for surely Jesus hath effectually
and fully provided for it. Whom he called, them he also
justified; and whom he justified, them he also glorified.
See to it then, my soul, that thou dost not suffer thyself to live a day, no, not an hour, in a state of uncer-
tainty, upon a point of such infinite consequence, in which
the pardon of thy sins, and the justification of thy person before God, is so highly concerned. If Jesus be thy Surety,
his righteousness and blood must be thy full justification before God, and his salvation as much now as it will ever be.

Pause then, and ask thine heart, Dost thou love his appearing?
Suppose the trump of God was this moment to sound, wouldest thou love his appearing? No doubt the moment would
be solemn; but would it not be glorious? Is Jesus thine?
his righteousness thine? his blood thy ransom? Wouldest
thou love his appearing if these things were sure? And
what makes them not sure? Art thou looking to any other
righteousness? Hast thou not disclaimed all other saviours?
Ask thyself again: dost thou love his appearing in the season of ordinances, providences, retirements; in his word, in
the visits of his grace; at his table, his house of prayer,
among his churches, his people? Dost thou love his appearing in the conversion of every poor sinner; and doth the
same make thee to rejoice over the recovery of such, as angels do, when one repents? My soul! let these things be
among thy daily meditations concerning Jesus; for then will
thy meditation of him be sweet. And by thus making the
justification of thy person in the blood and righteousness of
Jesus thy daily comfort, thou wilt be prepared to love his appearing, in death, and finally at judgment; that when the
Master comes, and calleth for thee, thou mayest arise with
holy joy, and mount up to meet the Lord in the air, and receive that crown of Jesus' righteousness which fadeth not
away.

9.—And the fire upon the altar shall be burning in it: it shall not be *put*
out. The fire shall ever be burning upon the altar; it shall never
go out.—*Levit.* vi. 12, 13.

PAUSE, my soul! Behold the precept in one verse, and
the promise in the other. The Israelite was not to *put* out
this altar-fire; and Jehovah promised that it should never *go*
out. Neither did it, through all the Jewish church, until
Christ came. And if it be true that it actually did expire (as
it is said it did) the very year Christ died, what is this but a
confirmation of the grand truths of God concerning the putting away sin by the blood of Christ? For is not fire an
emblem, through all the scriptures, of Jehovah's displeasure
against sin? Is not God said to be a consuming fire?
And by its burning, and that miraculously preserved
under all the Jewish dispensation, is it not meant to manifest Jehovah's perpetual wrath, burning like fire against
sin? And as the fire was never extinguished upon the altar,
notwithstanding the numerous sacrifices offered, can any

thing more decidedly prove the inefficacy of sacrifices under the law, how expensive soever they were, to take away sin? And is the fire now gone out; Hath God himself indeed put it out? Then hath he accepted that one offering of the body of Jesus Christ once for all, who came to put away sin, and hath for ever put it away by the sacrifice of himself. Hail! thou great, thou glorious, thou everlasting Redeemer! Thou art indeed both the High-priest and the Altar, both the Sacrifice and the Sacrificer, whose one offering hath both put out the fire of divine wrath, and caused the holy flame of love and peace to burn in its stead, which hath kindled in every heart of thy people. Yes, yes, thou Lamb of God! it is thou which hast delivered us from the wrath to come! Thou hast made our peace in the blood of thy cross. Thou hast quenched, by thy blood, the just fire of divine indignation against sin. Thou hast quenched no less all the fiery darts of Satan. Thou hast subdued the flaming enmity of our hearts, with all their fiery lusts and burning affections. What shall I say *to* thee, what shall I say *of* thee, what shall I proclaim *concerning* thee, Oh thou, the Lord our Righteousness? Lord, help me to begin the song, and never suffer sin or Satan— nay, death itself, for a moment, to make an interruption in the heavenly note: but let thy name fill my whole soul, and vibrate on my dying lips, that I may open my eyes in eternity, while the words still hang there: *To him who hath loved us, and washed us from our sins in his own blood, and made us kings and priests unto God and the Father; to him be glory and dominion for ever and ever.* Amen.

10.—Who hath saved us, and called us with an holy calling, not according to our works, but according to his own purpose and grace which was given us in Christ Jesus, before the world began.—2 *Timothy* i. 9.

MARK, my soul, all the precious things, if thou hast power or time to do so, which are contained in this blessed scripture. Eternity itself will not be sufficient to allow space to enumerate them; neither will thy ripened faculties, even when full-blown and full-fruited, be found sufficient to enter into the complete apprehension of them all. Who is it that is here said to have saved us, and called us with an holy calling, but the holy, glorious, undivided Jehovah, existing in a threefold character of persons—Father, Son, and Holy Ghost? For all have concurred in that blessed work; and all, in the essence of the One Jehovah, must have the joint praise and the joint glory to all eternity. Well, then, put thy salvation down to this glorious account: it is God who hath saved and called thee. Next, mark the order here set forth. Thou art said to be *saved* before thou art said to be *called*. Mark that! salvation precedes our knowledge of it. The covenant engagements of the almighty Covenanters took place from everlasting. For so saith the apostle concerning the hopes of happiness founded on salvation: "In hope," saith he, "of eternal life, which God, that cannot lie, promised before the world began." Next, my soul, take notice of the call itself. It is an holy call; for we are called to the fellowship and communion of Jesus Christ. And as He who hath called us is holy, so are we called to be holy, in all manner of conversation and godliness. See to it, my soul, that thy fellowship and communion is in the holiness and sin-atoning blood of Jesus. Lastly, never my soul, lose sight of the cause of these unspeakable mercies—no, not for a moment. We are saved, and called, not according to our works, but according to his purpose. Hence, what is God's gift, cannot be man's merit: and what resulted from infinite love, from all eternity, cannot flow from creature-love in time. Blessed purpose, and blessed grace! and thrice blessed, being given to us in God's dear Son, even Christ Jesus, before the world began!

11.—By faith Abel offered unto God a more excellent sacrifice than Cain.—*Heb.* xi. 4.

THE Holy Ghost hath here marked down, by his servant the apostle, in the very first offerings which we read of in the Bible, the vast importance of faith; by which it most decidedly proves, that it is faith which gives efficacy to all the offerings of his creatures. Faith in what? Nay—there can be but one view of faith throughout the word of God, namely, faith in the promised Seed, to bruise the serpent's head. This was the first promise which came in upon the fall. Every offering therefore offered unto God, unless it had an eye to this, became offensive. Cain did not offer the first fruit of the ground with an eye of faith in Christ—hence, he was the first Deist the world ever knew. Abel, by faith, offered the firstlings of his flock with an eye to Jesus—and hence the testimony that God respected his offering. What a striking evidence is here, my soul, of the vast and infinite importance of faith. Cain made an offering to God, and, by doing so, he did, as the Deists now do, acknowledge God to be his

Creator; but not looking to him as a Redeemer, and thereby intimating that he needed none, both his person and his offering were rejected. Meditate on this, my soul; and learn, by grace, to mix faith in all that concerns thy soul. Oh! keep an eye on Jesus, convinced that there is no other name under heaven, given among men, whereby we must be saved. And if, through the gracious teachings of the Spirit, in taking of the things of Jesus, and showing unto thee, thou art able daily to apprehend by faith, and bring him, as the bee doth from the flower, his person, his work, his character, his relations, his grace, and righteousness, as the Sent and Sealed, and Anointed of the Father, full of grace and truth; by thus living *upon* him, and living *to* him, and making him what he is to all his people, the Alpha and Omega of thy salvation, faith in him will give a sweet leaven to all thy poor prayers, and praises, and offerings, and thou wilt find favour with God, to the praise of the glory of his grace, who maketh thee accepted in the Beloved!

12.—To the chief singer on my stringed instruments.—*Habakkuk* iii. 19.

My soul, take down thine harp from the willow, and now the night is past, let the first of the morn find thee going forth, in the matin of praise, to the Chief Singer on all the instruments of his grace, which he hath strung thine heart to use to his glory. And who is this Chief Singer, but Jesus? Doth not the prophet say, " The Lord God is my strength, and he will make my feet like hinds' feet, and he will make me to walk in mine high places?" Surely he that is the Lord God of my salvation is the Chief Singer and Chief Musician of my song. And he that will be my portion, my everlasting portion, in the upper world, will be my strength and song in this. Surely David would not have directed, as he hath in such numberless places, his psalms to a singer among men, in the temple service, when the whole scope of the psalm itself treats of the Lord, and of his Christ. The root of the word singer or musician itself means *the end;* and Christ is the end of the law, for righteousness to every one that believeth. Come then, my soul, strike up this morning thy hymn of praise. God the Holy Ghost is exciting thee. It is he which points to Jesus. He shows thee the King in his beauty, and bids thee behold his suitableness, transcendent excellencies, grace, love, favour, glory. Carry, then, all thy concerns to this Chief Musician. Put forth all thy strength to praise him, that while Jesus is attentive to the hallelujahs of heaven, he may hear thy feeble notes amidst all the songs which are offered to him, giving glory to his great name, from the uttermost part of the earth. Follow the prophet's example; and let the goings forth of thy warmest desires be to the Chief Singer on thy stringed instruments:—" The Lord is my strength and my shield; my heart trusteth in him, and I am helped: therefore my heart greatly rejoiceth, and in my song will I praise him."

13.—And every oblation of thy meat-offering shalt thou season with salt; neither shalt thou suffer the salt of the covenant of thy God to be lacking from thy meat-offering: with all thine offerings thou shalt offer salt.—*Leviticus* ii. 13.

PONDER over these words, my soul; and looking up for grace, and the divine teachings, see whether Jesus is not sweetly typified here. Was not Jesus the whole sum and substance of every offering under the law? The Holy Ghost taught the church this, when he said the law was a shadow of good things to come, but the body is of Christ. And did not the church, by faith, behold him as the Salt which seasoned and made savoury the whole? Moreover, as all the sacrifices were wholly directed to typify Him who knew no sin, but became sin for his people, the seasoning the sacrifice with salt, which was also a type of Christ's purity and sinlessness, became a sweet representation to denote that the sinner, when he came with his offering, came by faith; to intimate that he looked for acceptance in the Lord as his sacrifice, and for preservation in the salt of his grace, in Christ Jesus. And who then, among believers now, would ever approach without an eye to Jesus, and the seasoning with this salt all his poor offerings. Lord, grant that the Salt of the covenant of my God may never be lacking; for where Jesus is not, there can be no acceptance. Lord, let me have this Salt in myself, and may every renewed presentation of myself be there salted. Then shall I be as the salt of the earth, amidst not only the putrefactions of the world, but the corruptions of my own heart. Lord, say to us, and impart the blessing of thyself in saying it, Have salt in yourselves; and then shall we have peace with thee. and with one another.

14.—And shall not God avenge his own elect, which cry day and night
unto him, though he bear long with them ?   I tell you that he will
avenge them speedily.—*Luke* xviii. 7, 8.

My soul, mark, for thy encouragement, in all thine approaches to a throne of grace, what Jesus here speaks, and
never lose sight of it.   Remember how well acquainted He
who came out of the bosom of the Father, must be with the
Father's mind and will towards his people, over and above
the gracious exercise of his priestly office in their behalf.
Now, my soul, do mark down distinctly what blessed things
are here promised.   *First,*—God's people are said in it to be
his elect, his chosen, his jewels.   This people, saith God, I
have formed for myself; they shall show forth my praise.
Secondly,—God's people are a praying people: they cry day
and night to him; they are unceasing in their applications;
and they wrestle, like their father Jacob, in prayer.   Lord, I
will not let thee go except thou bless me.   Give me Jesus,
and in him I shall have all things.   He will subdue this corruption ; he will soften this affliction; he will conquer Satan,
and with him all his temptations.   *Thirdly,*—God's people
will and must be exercised.   There will be sometimes long
silence at the throne.   The enemy will endeavour to improve
this to strengthen his temptation : he will suggest, God hath
forgotten thee; he will return no more; he hath cast thee
off.   *Lastly,*—mark what Jesus saith :—" Shall not God
avenge his own elect, who cry day and nigh unto him, though
he bear long with them ?"   Yes, yes ! he will: " I tell you,"
saith One who could not be mistaken, " he will avenge them,
and that speedily."   When the hour of deliverance comes, it
shall come so sudden, so sweet, so unexpected, that all their
long waiting shall be forgotten ; and it shall seem as if that
promise of answering before they called was in it.   And he
will not only bless them, but avenge them of their foes.   And
whence all this, my soul, but because he is the Father of
mercies, and God of all consolation.   His people are his
chosen, the gift of his love, the purchase of Jesus' blood,
the conquests of his Holy Spirit.   Lord, cause me ever to
keep those precious things in remembrance, and to hang on,
and hold out, and never, never to give over pleading in Jesus,
until I hear that precious voice, " Be it unto thee, even as
thou wilt."

15.—The good will of him that dwelt in the bush.—*Deut.* xxxiii. 16.

AND who is this, my soul; who indeed can it be, but Jesus? Surely He is the glorious person. It was good will in the highest possible instance of it, that prompted his infinite mind, from everlasting, to love his people, to engage for them in suretyship engagements, and to stand up and come forth, at the call of God the Father, as the Head of his body the church. It was a continuation of the same good will which prompted him, in the fulness of time, to assume our nature for the purposes of fulfilling those engagements. Then it was, indeed. he dwelt in the bush; for what is our nature, at the best, but a poor dry bramble bush, fit for burn-ing? But yet, by Christ in it, so sustained, and so preserved, that though the bush burns with fire, even the fiery lusts of our corruptions, and the fiery darts of the wicked, and all the fiery opposition of the world, it shall not be consumed. Precious Jesus! what good will hast thou shown, dost thou show, and everlastingly wilt show, to our poor nature, since thou hast been in it; and art now, indeed the dweller in it! And did Moses, when dying, thus connect the first views of thy love, when from the burning bush thou didst make thy-self known to him as God tabernacling in our flesh for the purpose of salvation, with his last views as he was closing his eyes to this world, and looking up to thee as God-man Me-diator, and thus pray for thy good will to the church? Oh, then, let my every day meditation do the same. Lord Jesus! I would seek thee and thy good will beyond all the riches of the earth, and all the enjoyments of the world. Lord! 1 would never forget that it was thy good will which brought thee down from heaven; thy good will which prompted thee to die, to rise again, for poor sinners; thy good will which makes thee wash them from all their sins in thy blood; all the visits of thy grace here, all the glories of redemption hereafter; all are the purchase and the result of thy good will. Precious Lord! do thou, day by day, grant me re-newed tokens of thy good will; and let those visits be so gracious, so sweet, and so continual, that I may think of no-thing else, speak of nothing else, but the good will of my Dweller in the bush. I would pray for grace to spend all the moments of my life here, in receiving from thee grace and love, and bringing to thee love and praise, until thou shalt take me home to live at the fountain of thy good will, and the whole happiness of eternity consist in the praises of

God and the Lamb, and in enjoying the good will of Him
that dwelt in the bush.

16.—I am black, but comely.—*Song* i. 5.

SEE, my soul, whether thine experience corresponds to
that of the church. Hast thou learnt from God the Spirit
what thou art in thyself? Art thou truly sensible of the
many sins and corruptions which lurk under fair appearances, and that, from carrying about with thee a body of sin
and death, as the apostle said he did, in thee, that is, in thy
flesh, dwelleth no good thing? Dost thou appear not only
black in thine own view, but art thou despised for Christ's
sake, and counted the offscouring of all things in the view
of the world? Pause my soul! Now look at the bright
side. Art thou comely in Christ's righteousness, which he
hath put upon thee? Comely in the sweet sanctifying grace
of the Holy Ghost dwelling in thee? Comely in the eyes
of God the Father, from being accepted in Jesus the Beloved?
Comely in Church communion and fellowship, walking in
the fear of God, and under the comforts of the Holy Ghost?
What sayest thou, my soul, to these sweet but soul-searching
testimonies? If thou canst now take up the language of the
church, "I am black, but comely;" lowly in thine own
eyes, self-loathing, self-despising, self-abhorring; but in Jesus
rejoicing, and in his salvation triumphing, all the day; think,
my soul, what will it be when the King, in whose comeliness thou art comely, shall take thee home as a bride adorned
for her husband, and thou shalt then be found, not having
spot, or wrinkle, or any such thing; but shall be everlastingly
holy, and without blame before him in love.

17.—The dead shall hear the voice of the Son of God ; and they that hear shall live.—*John* v. 25.

WHAT a promise is here! and what an encouragement for
every dead sinner to hope, and for every living saint, who is
interested for dead sinners, not to despair. Observe, my soul,
the extensiveness of the mercy: it is the dead. Why all are
dead in trespasses and sins. Is there not hope then for all?
And they that hear shall live. Why then every sinner
should ask his heart, Do I hear? But my soul, mark how
this is done. It is by the voice of the Son of God. Yes,
there is salvation in no other. He saith himself, "I am the

resurrection and the life : he that believeth in me, though he were dead, yet shall he live ; and whosoever liveth, and believeth in me, shall never die." But, my soul, while taking comfort from this blessed passage, as it concerns poor dead sinners, ask thine own heart whether thou hast been the happy partaker of it thyself. Hast thou heard the voice of the Son of God ? Yes, if so be thou livest *in* him, and *upon* him, and walkest *with* him. Jesus' voice is a quickening voice, a life-giving voice, a soul-feeding voice, soul-strengthening, heart-warming, heart-breaking, heart-melting voice ! What sayest thou, my soul, to these examinations ? Oh ! if Jesus' voice hath been ever heard by thee, thou wilt be desiring the renewal of it from day to day ; and thou wilt be saying, in the earnest language of the church, " Let me hear thy voice, let me see thy countenance ; for sweet is thy voice, and thy countenance is comely."

18.—Give strong drink unto him that is ready to perish, and wine to those that be of heavy hearts. Let him drink and forget his poverty, and remember his misery no more.—*Prov.* xxxi. 6, 7.

WHAT is the strong drink of the gospel but the covenant love, faithfulness, and grace, of Jehovah ? And what is the wine of the gospel but the love of Jesus, which the church saith is better than wine ? Tell a poor sinner that is ready to perish, of God the Father's everlasting love towards his people, who were all by nature sinners ready to perish, when God passed by and bid them live. Tell them, that such was God's love that he gave his only begotten Son, to the end that all that believe in him should not perish, but have everlasting life. Tell them of Jesus, his Godhead, his Manhood—both natures united in one Person, forming one Christ. Tell them that faith in his blood will save the soul; that God the Father hath respect only to the person and worth of his dear Son ; and that for his sake, and his sake alone, the greatest saint, and the greatest sinner, if believers, are alike saved. This is strong drink ; and a poor perishing sinner needs the cordial. Neither will the heavy in heart be any more sad, that thus is made to drink of the wine of the gospel. My soul ! hast thou tasted of this strong drink ? Oh ! then, take the cup of salvation, and call upon the name of the Lord. Drink of this cup which Jesus puts into thine hand, and, in his riches, forget thy poverty ; and in his free, and full, and finished redemption, remember thine own misery no more.

Live only to Jesus, and let him be thy strong drink, thy wine, and thy cordial for ever.

19.—My beloved is white and ruddy.—*Song* v. 10.

Pause, my soul, and contemplate thy Redeemer this morning, under this engaging description of his person. It opens a delightful subject for meditation in several points of view. Jesus is white and ruddy, if considered in his *human nature* only. He might be said to be white, in reference to the immaculate holiness of his body, underived as it was from a sinful stock like ours. He was born of the Virgin Mary, by the miraculous conception of the Holy Ghost, and therefore emphatically called, that Holy Thing: agreeably to all which, his whole life was without sin, or shadow of imperfection. "Such an High-priest became us, who is holy, harmless, undefiled, separate from sinners, and made higher than the heavens." Hence Jesus was truly *white* as the Lamb of God, without blemish, and without spot. And was he not *ruddy* also, in his bloody sufferings, when his head was crowned with thorns, and his side pierced on the cross? Was he not ruddy in the garden, when his agony was so great as to force blood through all the pores of his sacred body, which fell in great drops on the ground? Behold, my soul, thy Beloved in both these views, and say, Is he not white and ruddy? But do not stop here. Look at him again, and contemplate the Lord Jesus as the Christ of God, in his *two natures*, divine and human, and say, in the union of both, Is he not white and ruddy? What can set forth the glories of the Godhead, to our apprehension, more lovely than the purity of whiteness, which, as in the mount of transfiguration, became a brightness too dazzling for mortal sight to behold? And what can represent the human nature more strikingly than the ruddiness of the countenance? Adam, the first man, takes his very name from hence; for Adam, or Adamah, signifies, *red earth*. And such, then, was Jesus. And is he then, my soul, white and ruddy to thy view? And is he also thy beloved? Oh, then, let him be thy morning, noon-day, evening, midnight meditation; and let him be sweet to thee, as he is to his church and people—the Beloved who is white and ruddy.

20.—Within the vail, whither the forerunner is for us entered, even Jesus.—*Heb.* vi. 19, 20.

PAUSE over these words, my soul, this morning. Is the vail removed? Was the vail rent in twain, from the top to the bottom, in the hour that Christ died? And did Jesus, as thy High-priest, with all his blood, then enter into the place not made with hands, having obtained eternal redemption for us? Did he enter too as thy Forerunner? Pause over this thought—it is a sweet one. Is Jesus still there? Nay, my soul, look in and see. He calls thee to look unto him—nay, to follow him, having boldness to enter into the holiest by his blood, in the new and living way which he hath consecrated for us through the vail, that is to say, his flesh. And what canst thou see there? Within the vail of the Jewish temple there was the golden censer, and the ark of the covenant, and the golden pot that had manna, and Aaron's rod that budded, and the tables of the covenant; and over it the cherubims of glory, shadowing the mercy-seat. But within that vail, whither our Forerunner is entered, look up my soul, and see Jesus with the golden censer of his own merits and blood; and not the symbols of the covenant only, but he himself the whole of the Covenant, God the Father hath given him for the people; not merely manna, but himself, the living bread, the bread of God, of which whosoever eateth shall live for ever; not the rod of Aaron, but the rod of his power, to make poor sinners willing in the day of his power; not the cherubims of glory, but himself, the mercy-seat, the propitiatory, the sacrifice, High-priest, and all in all. Look up—look in—go in, my soul, after him, by faith, and contemplate him as thy Forerunner; and while all thy faculties, in grace and faith, are going forth in the most lively exercise, hear him say, and let his words sink deeper and deeper in thine unceasing remembrance, " I only go to prepare for you a place. I will come again, and receive you to myself, that where I am, there you may be also." Hail, thou glorious Forerunner, who art made an High-priest for ever, after the order of Melchisedec!

21.—Fear not; for they that be with us, are more than th y that be with them.—2 *Kings* vi. 16.

MY soul! never lose sight of this, which was shown to the prophet's servant in his fright. Though thou seest not, with bodily eyes, the mountain full of horses and chariots of fire in thy defence; yet, with thy spiritual eyes, thou mayest see, infinitely beyond all this, as surrounding thee at all times and in all places, God thy Father, with all his divine attributes and perfections, all engaged, all made over, all pledged in covenant engagements, in Jesus, for thy defence, protection, comfort, security, and guiding thee in all things. There is more in that one assurance than in a thousand worlds, *I will be thy God*—and all in Jesus; yea and amen. Then, moreover, thou hast God thy Redeemer with thee, with all his fulness, all his grace, all his love—his whole heart, his whole soul thine. And thou hast God the Holy Ghost, with all his influences, gift, teachings, .quickenings, consolations, strengthenings. All these are with thee; to say nothing of angels, which are ministering spirits, sent forth to minister unto them which are heirs of salvation. Surely God's attributes, Jesus' graces, the Holy Ghost's comforts, being all thine own, and always with thee; let what armies of men, or legions of evil spirits, assault thee—unbelief, or fear, or doubt, or misgiving; let nothing drive out the recollection, nor remove thy confidence: fear not; for they that be with thee, are more than all that can be against thee. Hallelujah! Amen.

22.—Seeking for Jesus.—*John* vi. 24.

This, my soul, should be thy constant employment. Wherever thou art, however engaged; in going in, or out; at rising up, or lying down: whether in public, or private, in the church, or market-place; the closet, the family, the garden, the field, the house; the question ever arising in the heart should be, Where is Jesus? Blessed Spirit! thou glorifier of my Lord! wilt thou constantly excite this seeking for Jesus in my heart? Wilt thou, Lord, give me every moment a sense of need, then a view of his fulness, suitableness, readiness to impart, then bring Him, whom my soul loveth, and me together; and then open a communication, in leading me forth in desire, and giving me faith to receive, from the infinite fulness of my Lord, and grace for grace? Lord Jesus! I would desire grace to seek thee, as for hidden treasure. I would seek thee, and thee only, oh! my God. I would separate myself from all other things. It is Jesus my soul chooseth, my soul needs. I would trust in nothing beside No duties, no works; neither prayers nor repentance; no nor faith itself, considered as an act of my soul, shall be my

comfort, but Jesus alone I would make my centre ; and every
thought, and every affection, and every desire, like so many
streams meeting in one, should all pour themselves, as rivers,
into the ocean of thy bosom ! And the nearer, as a stream
that draws near the sea is propelled to fall into it, so the more
forcible and vehement let my soul be in desires after thee, as
my soul draweth nearer the hour of seeing thee. Oh! Lamb
of God! give me to be seeking after thee through life, pressing after thee from one ordinance to another ; and when ordinances cease, and all outward comforts fail, then, Lord, may
I gather up (as the dying patriarch did his feet in the bed)
all my strength, and pour my whole soul into thine arms,
crying out, *I have waited for thy salvation, O Lord.*

23.—The beloved physician.—*Coloss.* iv. 14.

My soul! catch a thought of what the apostle here speaks
of the servant, to think of the Master! If Luke the physician was beloved, how much more so ought Jesus to be by
thee in this sweet character. The Son of God came, as the
great Physician of the soul, to heal all that were diseased, to
bind up the broken heart, to give sight to the blind, to set at
liberty them that are bound, and to proclaim the acceptable
year of the Lord! My soul, dost thou know Jesus in this
tender and affectionate office? Hath he examined thy case,
made thee sensible of thy disease; and art thou, through his
mercy, restored to health? Though, through shame and
fear at the first, you would never have made known your
case to him, had he not first, of his own free accord, called
upon you, yet hath he done so? Have you heard him asking the tender question, *Wilt thou be made whole?* And
have you rejoiced to come under his care? Do you know
what it is to have his blood applied to heal the wounds of sin,
his righteousness to cover them, his grace to refresh under
them, and his name, as ointment poured forth, to make a fragrancy for all uncleanness? Moreover, hath Jesus shown to
thee the freeness of his remedies, without payment, without
money, and without price? And doth he do all this, and a
thousand affectionate offices beside, which belong to the Physician, calling himself by that endearing name, Jehovah
Rhophi, I am the Lord that healeth thee? No longer let it
be said, then, Is there no balm in Gilead—no physician
there? but tell to every poor sin-sick soul, Jesus is the beloved Physician, who visits the poor and the needy, and heals

all manner of sickness, and all manner of diseases among the people.   He hath healed me!

24.—God, according to his promise, hath raised unto Israel a Saviour, Jesus.—*Acts* xiii. 23.

MARK, my soul, the blessedness of these words.   Jesus is not only Israel's Saviour, and hath fully answered, in every point, to that glorious character, but here we are led to discover his credentials.   This is faith's warrant—I believe in Jesus.   Why?   He brings with him the name, the authority, the commission of God the Father.   Jesus is the appointment, the ordinance, the method Jehovah hath set forth for salvation.   Sweet thought!   So that, added to all that I behold in the Lord Jesus adapted to my case and circumstances, I here see that Jesus is the Father's Gift, the Father's Sent, the Father's Anointed, full of grace and truth!   Jesus is therefore the great Promise of the Bible; for in him are folded up and contained all the promises.   And I see, also, that God our Father was, and is, the great Promiser!   And I see that God not only gave this rich Saviour to poor sinners, but, according to his promise, raised him up also from the dead, when he had made his soul an offering for sin, to bless them: for it is said, that he was delivered for our offences, and raised again for our justification.   My soul! pause over this blessed account, and look for thine own interest in it.   If God hath raised up to Israel this Saviour, what knowest thou of him?   Hast thou felt thy need of a Saviour?   Dost thou accept the Father's Saviour?   Is Jesus thy Saviour?   Art thou come to him for salvation?   Now God the Father hath raised him up, doth he appear to thee in all his beauties, fulness, suitableness, and complete salvation?

25.—And his servants shall serve him.   And they shall see his face; and his name shall be in their foreheads.—*Rev.* xxii. 3, 4.

MARK these characters, my soul! Jesus hath servants; and they are distinguished from the world.   They serve him. What is it to serve Christ?   The prophet hath described. Free grace hath made them servants, in bringing them from the bondage of corruption into the glorious liberty of the sons of God; and therefore he saith, in the Lord's name, " My servants shall eat, but ye shall be hungry; my servants shall drink, but ye shall be thirsty; my servants shall rejoice, but ye shall be ashamed; my servants shall sing for joy of heart, but ye shall cry for sorrow of heart." How distinguishing these characters! God's servants have the table of Jesus to sit down to; the bread of life, the bread of God, the living bread, which is Jesus himself, to feed upon. They shall drink also; for He that is their living bread, is their living water also—even the water of life, of which whosoever drinketh shall thirst no more; but it shall be in him a well of water springing up into everlasting life. The servants of the Lord shall rejoice, and sing for joy of heart also! Yes! the kingdom of God is not meat and drink, but righteousness, and peace, and joy, in the Holy Ghost. Neither is this all. The servants of the Lord shall see his face. They do now, by faith, in his word, in his ordinances, in his manifestations, visits, grace, and providences! And, by and by, when this vail of covering cast over all people, is totally taken down and removed at death, they shall have a glorious view of the King in his beauty by sight. Moreover, his name is said to be in their foreheads. Yes! It is so: the image of Christ is impressed upon them, as "Holiness to the Lord" was engraven on the mitre of Aaron. Beholding, as in a glass, the glory of the Lord, they are changed into the same image, from glory to glory, even as by the Spirit of the Lord. My soul! what sayest thou to these evidences? Are they thine? Canst thou take the comfort of them to thyself?

26.—The God of our fathers hath glorified his Son Jesus.—*Acts* iii. 13.

SEE, my soul, how every part and portion of scripture is directed to this one subject—to glorify the Lord Jesus! What is the very design of redemption, but to glorify the Lord Jesus? What hath God constituted a church for, but to glorify the Lord Jesus? To what do all the precepts, promises, ordinances, sacrifices under the law, and institutions under the gospel, minister, but to this one end—to glorify the Lord Jesus? Talk they of promises? Why, all the promises of God are, in Christ Jesus, yea and amen, to the glory of God the Father by us. Talk they of the law? Christ is the end of the law for righteousness to every one that believeth. Talk they of commandments? This is the commandment—that ye believe on the name of the only begotten Son of God; and that believing, ye might have life through his name. And how hath the God of our fathers glorified his Son Jesus, in giving him as a Covenant to the people? Hath he not

constituted him the glorious Head, the Mediator, the Husband, the Lord, the Prophet, the Priest, the King of his
people? How hath he glorified him in his person, offices,
characters, relations? How hath he carried him through all
the parts of redemption, in his incarnation, ministry, miracles,
obedience, life, death, resurrection, ascension ; and in all his
triumphs over sin and Satan, death, hell, and the grave?
And having constituted him the universal and eternal Lord
of all, commands that every knee should bow before him, and
every tongue confess that Jesus Christ is Lord, to the glory
of God the Father ! And is there any thing left, by which
the God of our fathers might manifest that he hath glorified
his Son Jesus? Yes! there is one thing more, my soul, by
which the wonderful grace is shown ; and that is, when the
God of our fathers hath glorified his Son Jesus in the heart
of every poor sinner, who gives the glory of his salvation
fully, heartily, completely, to him, and puts the crown of redemption upon the head of Jesus. My soul! hast thou done
this ? Hast thou glorified Jesus in this way, the only way in
which thou canst glorify him, and the Father in him? Then,
if so, what a sweet thought is it, that the God of our fathers,
and thou, a poor sinner, are both agreed in this one blessed
work, to glorify Jesus. And here both meet, in the only possible meeting-place for an holy God and unholy men to
meet ; and both are engaged in one and the same deed—to
glorify Jesus ! Oh! thou Lamb of God! be thou eternally
glorified in my salvation!

27 —I have exalted one chosen out of the people.—*Psalm* lxxxix. 19.

My soul! wert thou refreshed, on the past day, with the
precious meditation of the God of our fathers glorifying his
Son Jesus. Suffer not, then, the blessed subject to pass away
from thy thoughts this day, or any day ; but look at the same
delightful meditation proposed in the words, which God spake
to his Holy One in vision—" I have exalted One chosen out
of the people." Yes! the Lord Jesus, as Man and Mediator,
was chosen, in the infinite mind of Jehovah, Father, Son, and
Holy Ghost, from everlasting. And before that God went
forth in the immediate acts of creation, when that vast mass
of beings the Lord determined to call into existence arose in
his own infinite mind at his command ; this blessed One, this
glorious, this distinguished, this precious individual, which
was to become One with the uncreated Word, in order to

constitute the Wisdom-man Mediator, was from everlasting chosen. This was the glorious act—this was the great appointment. Then Christ Jesus, our glorious Head, our Surety, Redeemer, Saviour, was then set up from everlasting. And, my soul, hadst thou been present, had there been a possibility of such a thing, had the whole church been there, would not every heart, every soul, of his redeemed, have shouted aloud in the contemplation of such a Saviour, and cried out, " He is the altogether lovely, the chiefest among ten thousand." Precious Jesus! thou art indeed lovely in thyself, lovely in thy cross, lovely in thy crown, lovely in all thy gracious acts, victories, triumphs, grace, and mercy. Every thing in thee is lovely; and thou communicatest loveliness to all thy people. Thou hast chosen our inheritance for us—reign and rule over us, and in us; for thou art The Lord our Righteousness.

28.—The creditor is come to take unto him my two sons to be bondmen.—
2 *Kings* iv. 1.

My soul! how doth this affect thee? Art thou in debt? By nature and by practice thou wast miserably so, unless the debt be cancelled. As a creature, and as a sinful creature, thou art in thyself for ever insolvent. Thou hast nothing to pay, and art shut up in a total impossibility ever to pay. And how much owest thou unto my Lord? Alas! my soul, thou owest millions of debts to thy Almighty Creditor. The law thou hast broken: justice demands retribution, conscience condemns, Satan accuses; and the Creditor is come to take, not thy two sons only, but both thy two parts, soul and body, to the prison of death and hell, unless some Almighty Surety hath stept in and paid the dreadful debt, that thou mayest be free. At death, and at judgment that follows, the everlasting release, or the everlasting imprisonment, will take place. And who knows whether the decision may not be to-morrow; nay, whether the same sentence as went forth to the rich man in the gospel is not already gone forth concerning thee— " This night thy soul shall be required of thee?" Pause, my soul! Is it not high time to flee to the Prophet, even to the Prince of the prophets, the Lord Jesus, to tell him thy case, and to seek his deliverance? Hark! doth he say, as the prophet did to the poor woman, " What shall I do for thee? Tell me what thou hast in the house?" Is not Jesus with thee? Is not his fulness suited to thy emptiness? Hast thou

20*

him with thee in the house? Shut then the door: bring,
bring, my soul, all thy empty vessels—Jesus will fill them
all. Nor will his bounty stay until that all thy vessels be
filled; nay, every vessel will fail before that his grace fails.
And when thou art full of Jesus, live on Jesus, and see that
Jesus hath paid thy Almighty Creditor, and left enough for
thee to live on for ever. Oh! the rapture and the joy when
the Almighty Creditor comes, at midnight, or at cock-crowing,
or in the morning, to know the dreadful debt is paid, and to
hear him say, " Deliver him from going down to the pit;
I have found a ransom !"

29.—Have I been so long time with you, and yet hast thou not known
me ?—*John* iv. 9.

PAUSE, my soul, over this question of the Lord Jesus, which
he put to Philip—figure to thyself that the Lord saith the
same to thee; and now see what answer thou wilt give him.
It is a great question: and if thou art able to answer it with
a—" Yea, Lord;" and, from the blessed Spirit's teaching,
thou truly knowest Jesus to be what the scripture saith he is,
and canst as truly, from the receiving that testimony which
God hath given of his dear and ever-blessed Son, set to thy
seal that God is true; then art thou truly happy, and mayest
humbly take to thyself a portion in that blessedness, which
the Lord Jesus pronounced upon Peter from the same grace
manifested : " Flesh and blood hath not revealed it unto thee,
but my Father which is in heaven." Pause then and inquire,
Dost thou know who Christ is ? Art thou perfectly satisfied,
my soul, of the Oneness, in nature, in essence, in glory, in
will, in worship, in work, in design, in attributes, perfections,
power, sovereignty; in short, in all and every thing which
constitutes the Godhead between the Father, and the Son, and
Spirit ? Oh, yes, my soul cries out, I do, through the teaching of my God, most firmly, heartily, and cordially believe
that Jesus is One with the Father over all, God blessed for
ever. Amen. Pause again, my soul, and say, Dost thou as
firmly and heartily believe that thy Jesus, who, in the divine
nature is One with the Father, is no less in the human nature,
which he united to the Godhead for the purposes of salvation,
one with thee, bone of thy bone, and flesh of thy flesh?
Doth this make an equal article in thy creed? Oh, yes; I
am, through the same divine teaching, as fully and perfectly
convinced that He who is, and was, and ever will be, the

uncreated Word, was made flesh, and thereby became the true Emmanuel, God with us, God in our nature. Pause once more, my soul, and say, Dost thou believe that, by this union of God and man, Jesus became the true, the only, the blessed Mediator, the Christ of God, the Sent of God, the Sealed of God, the Anointed of God, the Lamb of God, the Word of God, the Wisdom of God, and the Power of God, for salvation to every one that believeth? Bow down, my soul, with unceasing thanksgivings and praise, to the Author and Giver of faith, for the stupendous discoveries he hath made to thee of himself, while thou cryest out in transports of rejoicing—Lord! all this I believe; and am perfectly satisfied that thou art One with the Father, and art in the Father, and the Father in thee. And while thou thus givest in thy testimony of the Lord Jesus, wilt thou not, my soul, at the same time, under a conscious sense of the distinguishing mercy, cry out also with the astonished disciple—"Lord, how is it that thou hast thus manifested thyself unto me. and not unto the world?"

30.—And thou shalt remember that thou wast a bondman in the land of Egypt, and the Lord thy God redeemed thee.—*Deut.* xv. 15.

Say, my soul, canst thou ever forget the wormwood and the gall of that state of nature, from which the Lord thy God brought thee? Figure to thyself the most horrid state of captivity which the world ever knew; and what could the whole be, bounded, as it must be, by the short period of human life, compared to the everlasting vassalage of sin and Satan, in which thou didst lay when Jesus passed by and brought thee out? No galley-slave, chained to the oar, could equal thy misery, bound with the chain of sin. No duration of misery, bounded by time, equals that endless state of woe to which thou wast exposed. Thou wert a bondman to the power of sin, to the love of sin, to the desire of sin, to the punishment of sin; a bondman to the law of God, to the justice of God, to the displeasure of God, to the threatenings of God; a bondman to thine own guilty conscience; a bondman to thine own corrupt lusts—not one lust, but many—serving, as the apostle saith, divers lusts and pleasures, hateful, and hating one another; a bondman to Satan—a willing drudge—wearing his livery, delighted in his service, though full of sorrow, vexation, and disappointment, and his wages sure death; a bondman to the fear of many creatures among

the inferior creation, many of whom had continual power to
vex and distress thee; a bondman to the fear of death, hell,
and a judgment to come. Was this thy state, my soul, by
nature and by practice? And hath One like the Son of Man
brought thee out? Precious Jesus! what shall I say *to* thee
—what shall I say *for* thee? What shall I render to the
Lord for all the mercies he hath done to me, and for me?
And dost thou say, Lord, that I may remember that bondage
and thy redemption. Oh, may my tongue cleave to the roof
of my mouth, if I forget thee, thou Author of all my joy, and
all my happiness:—nay, if I do not remember thee, and prefer
thy love more than wine. In life, in death, and to all eternity, may my soul hang upon thee, as the bee upon the flower;
and let the fragrancy of thy name be as ointment poured forth.

31.—One thing I know, that, whereas I was blind, now I see.—*Jno.* ix. 25.

THIS is a great thing to say, my soul: on what foundation
dost thou rest this knowledge? If the Lord Jesus hath
opened thine eyes, then indeed thou canst not but discover thy
former blindness; for, during that state of nature, thou literally could discern nothing. And if thy former blindness be discovered, then thy present sight hath brought thee acquainted
with new objects. Pause over the review of both this morning. The blindness of nature to spiritual things is marked
in scripture in strong characters. A poor blind sinner sees
nothing of the light of life. The Sun of Righteousness is not
risen upon him. He discerns nothing of the love of God in
Christ. If he reads the scripture, the veil is upon his heart.
If he hears of Jesus, he sees no beauty in him. Nothing is
nearer to him than the Lord, and nothing further from his
thoughts. To tell him of the sweetness of the word of God,
is strange to him; for he tastes nothing of sweetness in it.
To tell him of the loveliness of ordinances and the sabbaths;
these are strange things in his esteem. My soul, if indeed
thine eyes be opened, thou wilt know that thou wert once indeed blind, in the fullest sense of the word, to all these delightful views of sacred things which now are thy supreme
pleasure and thy joy. Say, then, what hast thou seen to justify
this saying, "One thing I know, that, whereas I was blind,
now I see?" Hast thou seen the King in his beauty?
Hast thou seen with the eye of faith the glories of Jesus?
Yes! if so be all other objects are obscured. The sight of Jesus, as the Christ of God, hath darkened the glory and excel-

lency of all beside. Jesus, as he is in himself, as he is in his offices, characters, relations—as he is to thee and thy happiness—is the one, the only one thing needful; and thou must count all things but dung and dross to win Christ. These, my soul, are blessed tokens that Jesus hath opened thine eyes, and brought thee out of darkness into his marvellous light. By-and-by thou shalt see him as he is, and dwell with him for ever!

SEPTEMBER.

1.—And his name, through faith in his name, hath made this man strong.—*Acts* iii. 16.

MY soul, begin this month, as the Lord in mercy hath enabled thee to begin some that are past, in taking the name of Jesus for thy theme. Let his name be as ointment poured forth, whose fragrancy shall make thee strong, as it made the poor man whole. And as the Lord hath opened a new mouth to thee in grace, do thou take up his name, through faith in his name, in praise and prayer. And see to it, my soul, that through the month, and indeed the whole of life, thou improve his name in every case, in every want, in every need. Depend upon it, his name will answer all. Whatever thy necessities are, in Jesus' name there is a supply for all. Art thou poor? he is rich: sick? he is thy health: weak? he is strong: sinful? he is The Lord thy Righteousness. Every thing, and in every way, upon all accounts, and upon all occasions—his name, through faith in his name, is the universal charm, the everlasting remedy, supply, comfort, strength, of all. Jesus hath every thing, and all things; and he hath them all for his people. Oh! then, my soul, look to Him and his name for the suited grace in every time of need. He will, as the psalmist sweetly reasons, —he will, nevertheless, (notwithstanding all thy undeservings, this *nevertheless* is still in the covenant,) he will save for his name's sake, that he might make his mighty power to be known.

2.—The Lord, the God of hosts, shall be with you, as ye have spoken.—
Amos v. 14.

My soul, pause over this precious scripture, and ask thyself, Is it indeed confirmed to thy experience? And do remark how the promise of the *Old* Testament scripture is confirmed in the *New*. Jesus assured the same, when he said,
"If a man love me, he will keep my words: and my
Father will love him, and we will come and make our
abode with him." Pause, my soul, again, and see whether
both Testaments concurring in the same, and the Holy Ghost
ever abiding with the Lord's people, to confirm his word in the
heart ; are not these promises thine, and art thou not everlastingly enjoying them? Precious Jesus! morning by morning would I besiege thy mercy-seat to put thee in mind of
this promise, which, in its blessedness comprehends every
other. If the Lord the God of hosts be with me ; if the Father graciously come ; if the Son himself come, both to make
their abode, not as a way-faring man that turneth in to tarry
for a night, but to make their abode; and if the Holy Ghost
abide with me for ever—oh, the blessedness of such a state,
the glory of such company! Lord, I pray, be it unto me according to thy word.

3.—Let not the wise man glory in his wisdom, neither let the mighty
man glory in his might, let not the rich man glory in his riches ; but
let him that glorieth, glory in this, that he understandeth and knoweth me, that I am the Lord.—*Jeremiah* ix. 23, 24.

And didst thou, my poor, proud, vain, sinful heart, after so
much as hath been said to thee of Jesus, and so much as thou
hast been feelingly taught thy want of Jesus—didst thou need
this precept? Oh, yes, my soul, every day it had need be
sounded in thy ears, and wrote over again by the Holy Ghost
upon thine heart. Now it is, Lord Jesus, I learn from hence
why thou art so suited to a poor convinced sinner. Thou,
and thou only, art the Lord our Righteousness ; and therefore
let those that know not their own worthlessness, nor thy
glory, boast in what they may ; let others talk of what they
will ; I see plain enough there is nothing out of thee for a
poor soul to rejoice in. The wise man hath no wisdom, but in
thee ; nor the mighty man strength, nor the rich man riches ;
but if thou art my portion, thou art made of God to me, both
wisdom, righteousness, sanctification, and redemption ; and
then indeed I shall glory in the Lord.

4.—A just God, and a Saviour.—*Isaiah* xlv. 21.

My soul, hast thou learnt, from the teaching of God the Holy Ghost, to contemplate him with whom thou hast to do, under these blessed united characters? If thou hast, thou hast found it a blessed and an approved way of opening communion with God, and maintaining that communion alive in the soul. Thou knowest, then, that God, as a just God, can admit of no pardon to sin, but upon the footing of a complete satisfaction; for, without this, his truth and justice would still be violated by unatoned sin. But if thou beholdest God in Christ, reconciling the world to himself, and hast been taught by the Spirit that Christ hath redeemed thee from the curse of the law, being made a curse for thee; that as thy Surety and thy Representative, he hath paid thy debt, and restored that which he took not away; here thou beholdest indeed "a just God, and a Saviour," and hast learnt that precious, blessed truth, how God can be just, and the justifier of every poor sinner that believeth in Jesus. See to it, then, my soul, that thou keepest this precious thought always in view. Always blend together, in all thy approaches to a mercy-seat, that thou art approaching "a just God, and a Saviour." Never lose sight of the high demands of God's righteous law; neither the perfect worth and efficacy of Jesus in his blood and righteousness: and connect always with the blessed view thine own personal interest in that obedience by thy union with him. Then wilt thou as much delight in God's justice as his mercy; and his holiness will be as dear to thee as his love. Then wilt thou understand that blessed truth, and join issue with it in every part.— Surely shall one say, "In the Lord have I righteousness and strength; even to him shall men come; and all that believe in him shall not be ashamed nor confounded, world without end."

5.—The praise of all his saints.—*Psalm* cxlviii. 14.

And who is this, my soul, but Jesus? Is he not indeed both the praise and the glory, the delight and the joy, the portion and the happiness, of all his people? His saints, doth it say? Yes! saints made so by his righteousness and salvation, when taken from among sinners; and when themselves sinners. He hath washed them in his blood, clothed them with his garment of salvation, and granted them an in-

heritance among the saints in light! And is he not their
praise? Indeed, is there any other the object of their praise,
to whom they look up, in whom they delight, but Him, in
whom God their Father hath made them accepted in Him,
the Beloved? Say then, my soul, is he not thy praise, this
day; and will he not be thine everlasting, unceasing praise,
every day, and all the day, and through the endless day of
eternity? Who shall be thy praise but Jesus; his beauty,
his glory, his excellency, in whom all divine perfections
centre? Who shall be thy praise but Jesus, the Mediator,
the Christ of God, whose glory it is to redeem poor sinners,
and make them saints; to give out of his fulness, and grace
for grace? Who shall be thy praise but he that hath made
thy peace in the blood of his cross, and ever liveth to make
intercession for thee? Oh! thou fair and lovely One, the
chiefest among ten thousand; thou art my praise, my glory,
my song, my rejoicing! Every day will I praise thee:
morning by morning will I hail thy name, and night by
night testify thy faithfulness. Here, while upon earth, will
I unceasingly speak of thy praise; and, ere long, I shall
join the happy multitude above, in that song—*To Him that
hath loved us, and washed us from our sins in his own blood!*
Oh! thou that art the praise of all thy saints!

6.—And the Lord turned, and looked upon Peter.—*Luke* xxii. 61.

My soul! hath that eye, that looked so graciously upon
Peter, looked graciously upon thee? Pause, and determine
the point by the effects. Peter went out and wept bitterly.
Hath such impressions of grace been upon thee, my soul?
Hast thou wept over the recollection of sin and a ruined
nature, which is continually manifesting itself in the same
faithlessness and worthlessness as in the apostle? Moreover,
hast thou ever looked with an eye of faith and love to Jesus?
If so, it must have been wrought by this eye of Christ upon
thee, my soul: for, mark it, we never look to him with an
eye of faith, until Jesus hath first looked on us with an eye
of love. If we love him, it is because he first loved us.
Sweet testimony this, if so be thou hast it in thine experience,
that he that turned and looked upon Peter, hath looked on
thee also. Moreover, any thing short of this glance of
Jesus' eye, is short of all to induce true repentance. Peter
heard, unmoved, again and again, the crowing of the cock;
just as we hear, unmoved, the warnings of God's holy word

in his scriptures; until Jesus accompanied the crowing of the cock, which he had admonished the apostle concerning, with his tender and remonstrating look: then, and not before, the blessed effects were wrought. Oh! precious Master! turn, I beseech thee, and look on me; and let that look enter my very soul, that I may look on thee whom I have pierced, and mourn, as one that mourneth for his only son, and be in bitterness as one that is in bitterness for his first-born. Let all my soul's affection be continually going out after the look of Jesus, until eye-strings and heart-strings break and give way; and when they close in the sleep of death, may I, with the eyes of the soul, behold thy face in righteousness, that I may be satisfied when I awake with thy likeness.

7.—For the Lord God of Israel saith, that he hateth putting away.— *Malachi* ii. 16.

AND well is it for thee, my soul, that he doth: for if the Lord God of Israel had dealt by thee *once*, as thou hast been dealing with him *always*, thou wouldest have been ruined for ever. But what is the cause of thy mercies? Is it not the covenant faithfulness of God thy Father, founded in his own everlasting love, engaged in his promise and his oath, to Jesus, and secured in his blood and righteousness? And is this the cause why the Lord God of Israel hateth putting away? Oh! for grace to see the cause, to adore the mercy; and where the Lord God of Israel rests, there, my soul, do thou rest also! See to it, my soul, that thy life of faith, and thy life of hope, are both founded in Jesus, and not in the sense thou hast of these precious things. The things are the same, how different soever, at different times, thy view of them may be. The everlasting worth, the everlasting efficacy, of Jesus' blood and righteousness, is always the same; and his people's interest in it the same, although, from the different view we have of it, at different times, it seems as if sometimes it were lost, and our own state was worse and worse. My soul! upon such occasions call to mind this sweet scripture: "The Lord God of Israel saith, that he hateth putting away." Observe, the Lord not only doth hate putting away, but he saith it, that his people may know it, and properly esteem his unchanging love. Oh! to cry out under the assurance of this precious truth, and to feel the blessedness of what the Lord saith by his servant the prophet: "The Lord thy God in the midst of thee is mighty:

21

he will save; he will rejoice over thee with joy, he will rest in his love, he will joy over thee with singing."

8.—Ye have dwelt long enough in this mount.—*Deut.* i. 6.

PAUSE, my soul, and remark the gracious words of God to Israel. They were just entering the borders of Canaan at that time. Forty years long had they been in a wilderness state: many ups and downs, battles and restings, conflicts and trials. God graciously said, "It is long enough." There is a rest that remaineth for the people of God. Hark, my soul! doth Jesus speak to thee to the same amount? Hast thou indeed *dwelt* long enough in this mount of exercises, sin, sorrow, and temptation? Hast thou *seen* enough of the emptiness of all creature-comforts to satisfy thee? Hast thou *felt* enough of a body of sin and death, which drags down the soul, to make thee groan under it, being burdened? Is there any thing now worth *living* for? Are not the glories above worth *dying* for? Doth Jesus call thee, invite thee, allure thee, to come up to the Canaan which he hath taken possession of in the name of his redeemed; and wilt thou not mount up upon the wings of faith, love, and longing desire, to be for ever with the Lord? Doth Jesus say, Thou hast dwelt long enough here below? And wilt thou not say the same? Doth Jesus call thee to his arms; and wilt thou say, Not yet, Lord? Ah! my soul, art thou indeed in love with this prison? Dost thou wish to wear thy chains a little longer? And is this thy kindness to thy Friend? Precious Lord! break down every intervening thought or passion that would rob thee of thy glory, and my soul of thy presence; and give me to cry out—Hasten, my Beloved! and be thou as a young hart upon the mountains of Bether.

9.—In those days, and in that time, saith the Lord, the iniquity of Israel shall be sought for, and there shall be none; and the sins of Judah, and they shall not be found: for I will pardon them whom I reserve.— *Jer.* i. 20.

WHAT those days and that time refer to is very plain, namely, the day when the great trumpet shall be blown, and when they shall come which were ready to perish: the glorious days of gospel grace by Jesus. For God the Father, having appointed and accepted a Surety for poor sinners, in the blood and righteousness of his dear Son, beholds no

iniquity in Jacob, nor perverseness in Israel. Blessed thought
to comfort a poor soul! that, seen in Christ, and accepted in
the Beloved, there is no condemnation to them that are in
Christ Jesus, who walk not after the flesh, but after the
Spirit. Pause, my soul, over this precious scripture, and
take to thyself the comforts of it. If thou art in Christ, thou
art beheld righteous in his righteousness; and, as thy Surety,
what he wrought and what he suffered was for thee. So
that, in this sense, thou art, as Christ tells the church, all fair,
and there is no spot in thee. So that, amidst all thy groans
for the remains of indwelling sin, (and groan thou dost
daily,) and as thou sometimes art prompted to think, there is
growing imperfection in thee; yet in Jesus, as thou art found
and beheld in him, sin is pardoned, and thy person accepted;
and thou art in a state of justification before God, in the
righteousness of God thy Saviour. And as this is so essential to be known and enjoyed, see to it, my soul, that thou
livest upon it. Go, in the strength of Christ's righteousness,
every day to the throne, pleading that righteousness, and that
only. And under a perfect conviction, that not a single sin
of thine was left out when Jesus bore the sins of his people
on the tree, beg for grace to exercise faith, and to know that
in Jesus thou art justified before God, and that God hath
cast all thy sins into the depth of the sea. Oh! the depth of
the riches, both of the wisdom and goodness of God. What
shall separate from the love of Christ? Surely not sin: for
Jesus hath put away sin by the sacrifice of himself. The
law of God cannot: for that law Jesus, as the sinner's Surety,
hath satisfied. And justice, so far from condemning, now
approves. God is just to his dear Son, as our Surety, who
hath answered all the demands of sin, and therefore hath
forgiven sin, and cleansed from all unrighteousness. Blessed
thought! in this way sin is pardoned in Christ; and in that
day, when God shall arise to judgment, the sin of Judah,
and the iniquity of Israel, cannot be found.

10.—While the king sitteth at his table, my spikenard sendeth forth the
smell thereof.—*Song* i. 12.

THAT was a precious testimony Mary gave of her love to
Jesus; and Jesus himself hath given his approbation of it,
when she anointed Jesus' feet with the spikenard. God our
Father hath anointed his dear Son; and so ought we. Surely
God's Anointed should be our Anointed: and if Mary poured

forth the best of her offerings, my soul, do thou the same.
Indeed, while the king sitteth at his table, and reigneth in
thine heart, the graces will flow. Yes, thou heavenly King!
when thou spreadest thy table, and callest thy redeemed as
thy guests; while thou suppest with them, and they with
thee: the humble spikenard, in the heart of a sinner, awakened by thy grace, and brought forth into exercise, will send
forth all that shall testify love, and praise, and affection, and
duty, and regard. Do thou then, dearest Lord! sit as a king
frequently at thy table. Let me hear thy gracious invitation:
"Eat, O friends! yea, drink abundantly, O beloved!" And
oh! thou heavenly Master! as all at the table is thine; the
bread of life, the water of life, the wine of thy banquet—and
all is thine own, and of thine own do thy redeemed give thee;
let me hear thy voice, let me see thy countenance. And
while thou givest forth thyself with all thy fulness, oh! let
my poor spikenard send forth faith and grace in lively exercise, that I may eat of thy flesh, and drink of thy blood, and
have eternal life abiding in me.

11.—For thou hast been a strength to the poor, a strength to the needy
in his distress, a refuge from the storm, a shadow from the heat, when
the blast of the terrible ones is as a storm against the wall.—*Isaiah*
xxi. 4.

WHO so poor as Jesus' poor? Who so needy as the needy
of the Redeemer? The world knoweth them not, because it
knew him not. And as the Master was, so are his servants
in this world. But, my soul, observe how sweetly Jesus is
all this. A strength to the poor in his distress, by taking all
the storm himself. He is a shadow from the heat, the heat
of the wrath of a broken law, which Jesus bore himself, when
he died to expiate the breaches of it. His blood and righteousness cool the heat of sin, and quench all the fiery darts
of the wicked: these terrible ones which beat upon a poor
sinner, like a storm against the wall. Moreover, when the
showers of wrath shall fall at the last day on the wicked;
when that horrible tempest of fire and brimstone, the Psalmist
speaks of, shall come down on the ungodly; Jesus will be
an hiding-place from the storm, and a covert from the tempest: not a drop can fall on those that are undr him, and
sheltered by his blood and righteousness. As the church is
now said to sit under his shadow with great delight in this
wilderness state, and his fruit sweet to her taste; so when

she is fairly come up out of it, having all along leaned upon her Beloved, and having entered with him into his glory; there will be both security and delight, everlasting safety and joy. Precious Jesus! thou hast been a strength indeed to my poor soul; and thou wilt be my portion for ever! Oh! give me to see my daily need of thee, to feel my poverty and weakness: the exercises of persecution, both without and within; that from all the terrors of the law, the claims of guilt in the conscience, the remains of indwelling sin in a body of death, which is virtually all sin—the accusations of Satan, the just judgments of God; in thee, thou One glorious Ordinance of heaven, precious Lord Jesus! I may behold myself secure in thee, and continually cry out, in the language of thy servant the prophet: *Surely shall one say, In the Lord have I righteousness and strength; even to thee do I come; and never shall I be ashamed or confounded, world without end.*

12.—And as Moses lifted up the serpent in the wilderness, even so must the Son of man be lifted up; that whosoever believeth in him should not perish, but have eternal life.—*John* iii. 14, 15.

Pause, my soul, over these words, and remember that they are the words of Jesus. Call to mind the wonderful event, to which Christ refers, in the church's history, in the wilderness, as related, Numb. xxi. 5, 9. Israel had sinned: and the Lord sent fiery flying serpents among the people, which bit them, and they died. In their distress they cried unto the Lord; and the Lord appointed this method of cure:—A figure of a serpent was made in brass, to which Israel was commanded to look only, and be healed. They who did so, lived. If any refused, he died. This was the ordinance of God. "Now," saith Jesus, "as Moses, at the command of God, lifted up the serpent, so must I be lifted up; that whosoever believeth in me shall never perish, but have eternal life." Now, my soul, mark what the Saviour saith, and see the blessedness contained in his precious assurance. It was a serpent that stung the Israelites! It was the old serpent, the devil, which poisoned our nature at the fall. All his temptations, assaults, and poisons, are fiery. And when the dreadful effects of sin are felt in the awakened conscience, how do they burn with terrors in the soul? What could the dying Israelite do, to heal those venomous bites?—Nothing. Would medicine cure?—No. Was there no remedy within the power of man?—No; it baffled all art—it resisted all at-

tempts to heal. Such is sin. No prayers, no tears, no endeavours, no repentance, can wash away sin. If the sinner
be restored, it must be by the interposition and mercy of God
alone. Now observe the method God took with Israel. A
figure of brass: and if, as some men tell us, any thing shining like brass, to look upon when the head and brain is diseased, would make the person mad; so far was this serpent
of brass likely to cure, that it was the most unpromising thing
in the world to accomplish it. But yet it was God's command; and that was enough. It infallibly cured. Look
now to Christ. Here also is God's appointment, God's command, God's authority. Christ was made in the likeness of
sinful flesh; and though holy in himself, yet becoming sin
for us, that we might be made the righteousness of God in
him. This single precept is, "Look unto me, and be ye
saved." What, must I do nothing, bring nothing, take nothing?—No, The answer is, "Look unto me." This is the
appointed way. Christ is the One only Ordinance; Christ
is the Altar, Offering, High-priest. "If thou liftest up thy
tool upon it, thou hast polluted it." Christ is the Father's
gift for healing. In Jesus there is a fulness to heal. Faith,
then, hath a double plea—the authority of God the Father,
and the fulness of salvation in God the Son. Lord! I take
this for my warrant. Help me, thou blessed Spirit! so to
look, so to depend; so to fix my whole soul, on this complete
remedy for all my need, that heaven and earth may witness
for me, I seek salvation in no other, being most fully convinced that there is salvation in no other; neither is there
any other name under heaven, given among men, whereby
we must be saved.

13.—And thou shalt write them upon the posts of thine house, and on
thy gates.—*Deut.* vi. 9.

SEE, my soul, what a gracious provision the Lord made
for the glory and honour of his Israel, that every traveller
passing by might say, "Here dwelleth an Israelite indeed!
He hath the name of the Lord of hosts upon his house!"
And did it please the Lord God of Israel so to have his people
known; and shall it not be my desire to have thy name,
Lord, upon the gates of my house? Shall any pass by my
door ignorant that a lover of the Lord Jesus dwelleth there?
Nay, shall I not esteem it my highest honour to have it
known whose I am, and whom I serve, in the gospel of his

dear Son ? Shall I be ashamed of that name before which every knee bows in heaven and in earth ? Oh, Lord, Jesus! not only write thy name upon the gates of my house, but engrave it in the centre of my heart, my affections; my first, and last, and earliest, and latest thoughts! Let it be my rapture and my joy, to speak out of the abundance of my heart concerning thee and thy great salvation! In all I say, in all I do, let it be manifest that I am in pursuit of Him whom my soul loveth. Let every action tend to recommend thy dear name; and whether at home or abroad, in my house or family, when lying down or when rising up, let all creation witness for me, that the love, the service, the interest, the glory, of my God in Christ, is the one only object of my soul's desire; and let every thing speak this language— " Whom have I in heaven but thee ? and there is none upon earth I desire but thee: and though my flesh and heart faileth, yet thou art the strength of my heart, and my portion for ever."

14.—And he must needs go through Samaria.—*John* iv. 4.

AND what was there, blessed Jesus, that constrained thee to this necessity ? Was it because there was a poor adulterous woman there that needed thy grace, and the hour was come for her conversion ? Sweet thought! let me cherish it this morning. Was there not the same *needs be* for the Father setting thee up, from everlasting, for the Head of thy church and people ? Could there have been a church without thee ? And when thy church had fallen by sin, what archangel could have recovered her but thee ? Why then there was a *needs be,* that thou shouldest take the nature of thy people upon thee, and come to seek and save that which was lost ! And as it is said of thee, concerning this poor woman, that he must needs go through Samaria ; so must it be equally said, Jesus must needs go to Jerusalem, to save Jerusalem sinners by his blood. Oh, yes, there was a blessed necessity upon thee, thou Lamb of God ! that thou shouldest do all this. *Ought not Christ to have suffered these things, and to enter into his glory ?* My soul, indulge this precious thought yet further, and see if there be not a *needs be* in thy Jesus for numberless other occasions. Is there not a blessed necessity that Jesus should give out of his fulness to his people ? Is there not a *needs be,* when his blessed gospel is preached, that he should be present to give virtue and efficacy to the word delivered? Might not every poor waiting needy sinner say, There is a blessed necessity Christ should be here? Surely he is constrained by his promise, that where two or three are met in his name, he is in the midst of them; and therefore he will come, he will bless his word, he will give out of his fulness; for he knows my need, and the need of all his people present. Nay, is not the glory of our Jesus depending upon the receiving of his poor, and making them rich by his bounty? Go one step further, my soul, this morning, as it concerns thyself. Doth not Jesus know now thy state, thy want, thy circumstances, and that thou art waiting for thy morning alms, before that thou canst leave his gate? Then is there not a *needs be* that he, who was constrained to pass through Samaria, should come to thee? Precious, precious Jesus! I wait thy coming; I long to hear thy voice. What I need thou knowest. And as thy glory and my salvation are both blended, do for me, Lord, as shall best conduce to this one end, and all will be well. Jesus will be glorified, and my soul made happy. Amen.

15.—As for me, I am poor and needy; yet the Lord thinketh upon me.— *Psalm* xl. 17.

My soul! sit down and reckon up thy true riches. See what are thine *outward* circumstances, and take an inventory of all thine *inward* wealth. Thou art, by nature and by practice, one of the children of a bankrupt father, even Adam, who lived insolvent, and died wretchedly poor in himself, having entailed only an inheritance of sin, misery, and death, with the loss of divine favour, upon the whole race of his children. By nature and by practice thou art poor in the sight of God, despised by angels on account of thy loathsome disease of sin; thine understanding darkened, thy will corrupt, passions impetuous, proud, self-willed—all in opposition to the law of God: exposed to all present evil, everlasting evil, a slave to Satan, a willing captive in his drudgery; hastening daily to death, to the *second* death, and with an insensibility which is enough to make every heart mourn that beholds thee. Such, my soul, was thy state by nature; and such, and far worse, would have been thy state for ever, had not Jesus interposed, and looked upon thee, and loved thee, when thou wast cast out to perish, and no eye to pity thee, nor help thee from thy ruin. My soul! canst thou now say, though poor and needy, the Lord thinketh upon thee? Oh, blessed Jesus, thou dost indeed think upon me and provide for me; and hast given me to see, to feel, my poverty, need, and misery, and to live wholly upon thee and thy alms from day to day. Yes, Jesus, I would be poor, I would be needy; I would feel yet more and more my nothingness, worthlessness, poverty, wretchedness, that Jesus may be increasingly precious, and thy salvation increasingly dear. Oh, for grace, as a poor needy debtor, daily to swell my debt account, that my consciousness of need may make thee and thy fulness increasingly blessed. Let it be my daily motto—" As for me, I am poor and needy; but the Lord thinketh upon me."

16.—I will strengthen them in the Lord, and they shall walk up and down in his name, saith the Lord.—*Zech.* x. 12.

My soul, mark these words, how precious they are; and mark the Speaker and Promiser, and consider how sure they are. Is not this God the Father speaking of the church, and most graciously assuring the church that he will strengthen the church in Jesus, the church's glorious Head? Is not this said with an eye to Christ, who is represented in another part of this blessed prophecy as calling upon the church to attend to him, who is come to build the temple of the Lord, and to bear all the glory; and who expressly saith that the church shall know that He, the Lord of hosts, is sent by the Lord of hosts unto his people? Who but the Lord of hosts could build the temple of the Lord of hosts; or who but him bear all the glory? Zech. vi. 12. So, then, my soul, observe that Christ is the strength, as well as the righteousness, of his redeemed: and do observe further, that when at any time thou art strengthened in Jesus, it is the Father's gracious hand and office which is manifested in this merciful act. If thou art drawn at any time to Jesus, it is the Father's sweet constraining love that thus works upon the soul, John vi. 44. If thou enjoyest at any time some new and delightful revelation of Jesus, which lifts thee up with a joy unspeakable, remember, my soul, from whom the blessing comes; and learn to ascribe the mercy, the distinguishing mercy, as the apostle did, to the Father's grace, when it pleased him to separate thee from thy mother's womb, and called thee by his grace to reveal his Son in thee. Gal. i. 15, 16. Yes, Almighty Father! it is thy special mercy, both to give thy Son, and with him all things, to the highly-favoured objects of thine everlasting love. It was he who, from all eternity, did contrive, order, will, appoint, and prepare, the great salvation of the gospel; and choose Christ as the Head, and the church as the body, of this stupendous work of redemption. It is thou which hast carried on and executed all the great designs; and it is thou who dost strengthen and complete the whole in the final salvation of all the members of it, in grace here, and glory hereafter. Blessed, holy, compassionate Lord God! for Jesus' sake fulfil this promise daily in my soul: bear me up, carry me through, and strengthen me in the Lord my God, that I may indeed walk up and down in his name, until thou bring me in to see his face in thine eternal home, and dwell under the light of his countenance for ever.

17.—Brethren, pray for us.—1 *Thes.* v. 25.

My soul, mark how earnestly the apostle sought an interest in the prayers of the faithful. And if so eminent a servant in the church of Jesus thus entreated to be remembered by the brethren at the mercy-seat, how needful must it be that the brethren should remember one another; not only ministers to pray for the people, but the people for their ministers. "Brethren, pray for us," should be the constant request of every lover of Jesus. Methinks I would ask every one that I knew to be a constant attendant at the heavenly court, to speak for me to the King, when he was most near, and in the enjoyment of his presence. Tell the Lord, I would say, that his poor prisoner needs his alms, longs for his grace, and is waiting the anxious expectations of his visits. Beg for me, that I may live always under the blessed tokens of his love; that I may be ever living near the Lord, and strong in the grace which is in Christ Jesus. And do tell his Sovereign Majesty that the one great object of my soul's desire is, that I may have increasing views of the infinite dignity of his Person, work, merit, offices, relations, characters; and, in short, every thing that relates to One so dear, so lovely, so glorious, and so suited to a poor sinner, as the Lord Jesus Christ is in all things. And do add for me, that my humble suit is, that after he hath given me all his gifts and graces that he sees needful for me in my pilgrimage state, that Jesus will give me yet more than all, by giving me himself, and causing my heart to be dissatisfied with all but himself; for until Jesus himself be my portion, I shall have not what I want. It is not enough to give me life; but He himself must be my life. It is not enough to give me rest, unless He himself is my rest, and I rest in him. Precious Jesus! I would say, in thyself is all I need : all to pardon, all to justify, all to sanctify, all to glorify, all to satisfy, all to make happy, here and for ever. Brethren, let this be your prayer for me, and it shall be mine for you ; that Jesus be the all in all of our souls, and our portion for ever.

18.—The King is held in the galleries.—*Song* vii. 5.

AND who but Jesus is King in Zion? As one with the Father over all, God blessed for ever, he is indeed the King eternal, immortal, invisible ! And as Mediator God-man, he is my God and King, both by his conquest of my heart, and the voluntary surrender of my soul. Yes, blessed Jesus ! I not only hail thee my God and King, but I would have every knee bow before thee, and every tongue confess that thou art Lord and King, to the glory of God the Father. But, my soul, what are those galleries where thy King is held ? Are they the scriptures of truth where Jesus is held and retained, adored and admired ? Or are they the public ordinances of thine house, or the place where thine honour dwelleth ; or the secret chamber, or the closet, of retirement and meditation ; when thou comest to visit thy people, and when thou knockest at the door of their hearts, when thou comest in to sup with them, and they with thee ? Well, my gracious, condescending Lord ! be they what they may, or where they may, methinks, like the patriarch, when thou comest to wrestle with my poor, heedless, and sleepy heart, I will hold thee in the galleries, and say, as he did, " I will not let thee go, except thou bless me." I would say, as another famous patriarch did, " My Lord, if I have found favour in thy sight, pass not away from thy servant. Rest yourself under the tree ; and I will fetch a morsel of thine own bread, and of thine own giving, and comfort ye your hearts : for therefore are ye come to your servant." Gen. xviii. 3, 5. I would entreat thee, Lord, not to be as the wayfaring man, that turneth in to tarry but for the night : but I would hold thee in the galleries of thine own graces, in thine own strength, imparted to my poor soul ; and I would beg of thee, and entreat thee, to tarry until the dawn of day, and make thyself fully known unto me, in breaking of bread, and in prayer. Yes, my adorable King ! my Lord and my God ! I would detain thee in the galleries, I would hold thee fast, I **would not let thee go**, until that I had brought thee into my mother's house, the church—and until thou hadst brought me home to thine eternal habitation which is above; and there to sit down at thy feet to go out no more, but at the fountain-head of joy to drink of the spiced wine of the juice of the pomegranate in everlasting felicity.

19.—I have set before thee an open door, and no man can shut it.— *Rev.* iii. 8.

BLESSED Jesus! thou hast indeed done all this, and more. Thou art thyself the Door into thy fold here below, and to thy courts above; for thou hast said, by thee, whosoever entereth in, shall go in and out, and find pasture: and it is thou that hast opened a new and living way by thy blood. Thou art the only possible way of access to the Father. And because thou hast opened it, no man can shut it; for thou ever livest to keep the way, which thou hast once opened, still open, by thy all-prevailing intercession. Yes, thou heavenly Lord! the gate is never shut, day nor night. In the preaching of thine everlasting gospel, all the ends of the earth shall see this salvation of our God. And, as thou hast graciously said, all that come to God by thee shall never be shut out. The word, the authority, the warrant, of Jehovah, is gone forth to this purpose. Thy blood and righteousness secure it. The Spirit sets his seal to it. Thou wilt receive, thou wilt bless, thou wilt cause all the Father hath given thee to come to thee; and thou wilt keep the door always open for all comers. Oh! heavenly way! oh! precious, endless salvation! My soul! see to it that thou art entered in, and there abidest securely. Oh! ye, my fellow sinners, yet without, rouse up from your carnal security and sloth, before the Master of the house hath arisen and shut to the door; and ye then, too late, cry out—Lord, Lord, open to us. Now is the accepted time; now is the day of salvation!

20.—Behold the man whose name is The Branch.—*Zech.* vi. 12.

MY soul! listen to the call, and behold this wonderful Man, whose name is THE BRANCH! Mark the wonderful features of his person. This is one of the prophetical names of Him, in the faith of whom, as the Redeemer of Israel, all the Old Testament saints died. The Branch of the Lord —the Branch of Righteousness; or, as he is elsewhere called, the Nazarene. But observe how very descriptive of his nature is this title. He grows up out of his place. And where is that?—In the eternal counsel of Jehovah. Who shall declare his generation? He is indeed a rod out of the stem of Jesse, and a branch out of his roots. But all this as the root himself of David: planted in the eternal purpose of God's own sovereign decree, and budding forth as a branch in all the periods of his incarnation, death, resurrection, ascension, glory. And what a Branch of never-failing loveliness, and everlasting verdure and fruitfulness, in all the proclamations of his gospel, converting sinners, and comforting saints! And what an eternal perennial Branch to all his redeemed in grace and glory. Hail, thou glorious, wonderful Man, whose name is The BRANCH! Thou art indeed, as the prophet described thee, beautiful and glorious in the eyes of all thy redeemed. On thee, Lord, would I hang all the glory of thy Father's house, and all the glory of my salvation. May it be my portion to sit under thy shadow with great delight here, until thou bring me home to sit under thee, the Tree of Life, in the Paradise of God, in the fulness of enjoyment of thee for ever.

21.—Ye shall be baptized with the Holy Ghost.—*Acts* xi. 16.

BLESSED promise! realize it, oh thou Holy Spirit! day by day, in and upon my soul. Bring me under the continued baptisms of thy sovereign influence, and cause me to feel all the sweet anointings of the Spirit sent down upon the hearts and minds of thy redeemed, as the fruits and effects of Jesus' exaltation, and the promise of God the Father! Yes! blessed Spirit! cause me to know thee in thy person, work, and power; in all thy offices, characters, and relations. I need thee, day by day, as my Comforter. I need thee, as the Spirit of truth, to guide me into all truth. I need thee, as the Remembrancer of the Lord Jesus, to bring to my forgetful heart all the blessed things he hath revealed to me. I need thee, as the Witness of my Jesus, to testify of my wants, and his fulness to supply. I need thee, as the Glorifier of my Lord, to take of his, and show to me. I need thee, as my Advocate and Helper, in all my infirmities in prayer. I need thee, as the Earnest of the promised inheritance, that I may not faint, nor want faith to hold on and hold out in all dark seasons. I need thee, Lord; nay, I cannot do a moment without thee, nor act faith, nor believe a promise, nor exercise a grace, without thy constant, thine unceasing,

agency upon my poor soul. Come then, Lord, I beseech
thee, and let me be brought under thine unceasing baptisms.
Shed abroad the love of God my Father in my heart, and
direct me into the patient waiting for Jesus Christ!

22.—The justifier of him who believeth in Jesus.—*Romans* iii. 26.

AND who is this, indeed who can it be, but Jehovah? It is
God that justifieth. Who is he that condemneth? But, my
soul, mark how each Person of the Godhead is revealed in
scripture under this character; as if to convince every poor
sinner that is looking for redemption in Israel only in Jesus,
that God can be just, and yet the Justifier of him that believeth in Jesus. God the Father justifieth the poor believing
sinner: for he manifests that he is faithful and just to forgive
us our sins, having found a ransom in the blood of his Son
for sin, whereby he is faithful to all his covenant-promises in
pardoning us, having received at our Lord's hand double for
all our sins. God the Son justifieth also his redeemed: for
it is expressly said by the prophet, "In the Lord shall all the
seed of Israel be justified, and shall glory." And that God
the Holy Ghost justifieth, is as evident also: because it was
through the Eternal Spirit the offering of the body of Jesus
Christ was offered, by which Christ is said to have been justified in the Spirit; and believers are said to be justified by
virtue of it in the name of the Lord Jesus, and by the Spirit
of our God. Hence all the Persons of the Godhead concur
in the act of justifying every believer in Jesus! by whom we
have peace with God, fellowship with the Father, and with
his Son Jesus Christ. Here then is a portion to live upon
through life, in death, and to all eternity.

23.—Is there no balm in Gilead? Is there no physician there? Why
    then is not the health of the daughter of my people recovered?—*Jere-
    miah* viii. 22.

YES! there is both balm in Gilead, and a Physician there!
For the blood and righteousness of Jesus is the truest balm;
and Jesus himself a Sovereign and an Almighty Physician.
But if that blood be not applied, if Jesus be not known nor
consulted, how shall health be obtained? My soul! hast
thou known thy disease, felt thy disorder: art thou convinced
that it is incurable by all human means—no medicine, no
earthly physician, can administer relief? **Hast thou known**

these things? And, convinced of the infinite importance of seeking elsewhere, art thou come to Jesus? What sayest thou, my soul, to the inquiry? Art thou acquainted with Jesus? Hast thou made known thy case to him? And hath he told thee all that is in thine heart? Hath he taken thee under his care? Is he administering to thee the balm of Gilead? Oh! my soul, see to it that nothing satisfieth thy mind, until that thou hast heard his soul-reviving voice, saying, *I am the Lord that healeth thee.* Exod. xv. 26. Seek it for thy life. Say unto the Son of God—*Speak but the word, Lord, and my soul shall be healed.*

24.—How much owest thou unto my Lord?—*Luke* xvi. 5.

My soul! if this question, which the unjust steward put to his lord's debtors, was put to thee, concerning that immense debt which hath made thee insolvent for ever, what wouldest thou answer? Never couldst thou conceive the extent of it, much less think of paying the vast amount. A debtor to free grace for thy very *being ;* a debtor to free grace for thy *well-being ;* ten thousand talents, which the man in the parable owed his master, would not be sufficient to reckon up what thou in reality owest thy Lord, for even the common gifts of nature and of providence. But when the calculation goeth on in grace, what archangel shall write down the sum total? To the broken law of God, a bankrupt: exposed to the justice of God; to the dreadful penalty of everlasting death ; to the fears and alarms of a guilty conscience ; to the worm that dieth not; to the accusations of Satan, unable to answer one in a thousand. My soul, how much owest thou unto thy Lord? Are there yet any other outstanding debts? Oh! yes, infinitely and beyond all these. What thinkest thou, my soul, of Jesus? How much owest thou to the Father's love in giving, to the Redeemer's love in coming, and to the Holy Ghost in making the whole effectual to thy soul's joy; by which Jesus hath paid all thy debts, cancelled all the demands of God's righteous law, silenced Satan, answered justice ; and not only redeemed thee out of the hands of everlasting bondage, misery, and eternal death, but brought thee into his everlasting kingdom of freedom, joy, and glory. Say, say, my soul, how much owest thou unto thy Lord? Oh, precious debt! ever increasing, and yet everlastingly making happy in owing. Lord Jesus, I am thine, and thy servant for ever : thou hast loosed my bonds.

25.—Thou shalt prepare thee a way, and divide the coasts of thy land (which the Lord thy God giveth thee to inherit) into three parts, that every slayer may flee thither.—*Deut.* xix. 3.

SWEET thought to my soul, that He who is the *refuge* is also the *way* to every poor soul-slayer, who hath murdered his own soul by sin. And who, my soul, could prepare thee this way, but God thy Father, who gave both Jesus for the way, and Jesus for the refuge? And how hath God the Spirit pointed to the way, cast up and prepared it, by taking up the stumbling-blocks out of the way, as God saith of his people? Isaiah xlvii. 14. Is it not God the Holy Ghost that sets Jesus up, as Moses did the serpent; points to his person, to his blood, to his righteousness, as the sanctuary and the city of refuge to every poor sinner that is the man-slayer of his own soul? And if what the Jews have said be true, that magistrates once a year made it their duty to have the roads examined, lest any obstruction should arise to block the path of the poor fugitive; and that they were obliged to set up a post at every turning and avenue, with the word *Miklat—Refuge,* upon it, to direct the murderer in his flight; well may ministers every day, and all the day, stand in the gates of the city, and in the high places of concourse, pointing to Jesus, and crying out, "Behold the Lamb of God, which taketh away the sin of the world!" Precious Lord Jesus, lo, I come to thee: thou art my city of refuge—thou art the *Miklat* of my soul! Under thee, and in thee, I shall be safe. Cease, ye avengers of blood, your vain pursuit: Christ hath taken me in. Thou shalt answer for me, oh Lord, my God.

26.—And they shall hang upon him all the glory of his father's house.— *Isaiah* xxii. 24.

AND who is this but Jesus, the true *Eliakim* and Governor of heaven and earth? Jesus sweetly explained it himself, when declaring himself possessing the key of David. Rev. iii. 7. And hath not God the Father literally given all things into his hands? Is there any thing which Jehovah hath kept back? Hath it not pleased the Father, that in him should all fulness dwell? Is not Jesus the Head over all things to the church, which is his body? Is he not the Almighty Lord and Treasurer of all things—grace here, glory hereafter? And is not our Jesus the Administrator of all things in the world, both of providence and grace? My soul, is there aught remaining to hang upon Jesus? Pause. Hast

thou hung upon him all the glory of thy salvation? Pause
again; my soul. Is *all* and every tittle given? Is there
aught kept back? Is there any *Achan* in the camp of thy
heart? Forbid it, Lord. See to it, my soul, (for it is thy
life,) that thou art hanging all the glory of the Father's
house upon Jesus. Make him not only the Alpha, but the
Omega also of thy salvation. And as the Father loveth his
Son, and hath given all things into his hands; so do thou
come to him for all things, receive from him all things, and
ascribe to him all things, in the receipt of grace here, and
glory hereafter—that Christ may be all, and in all, to the
glory of God the Father. Amen.

27.—He hath not despised nor abhorred the affliction of the afflicted:
neither hath he hid his face from him: but when he cried unto him,
he heard.—*Psalm* xxii. 24.

My soul! behold Jesus the Lamb of God in this sweet
scripture. Is it not said of him, that in the days of his flesh
he offered up strong crying and tears, and was heard in that
he feared? Though he were a son, yet learned he obedience
by the things which he suffered. And was Jesus the holy
One, the afflicted One, also? Was he truly so, when he bore
thy sins? And was this the time to which this scripture
refers, when God the Father had respect to the sufferings of
Jesus, and neither despised nor abhorred them? Did the
Father behold him then through the whole as the sinner's
Surety, and graciously accept Jesus, and the church in him?
Oh, then, my soul, think of this in all thy trials and afflictions.
Carry all thy sins and sorrows to the throne. Jesus knows
them all, sees them all—nay, appoints them all. He is always
looking upon them, and presenting thee in himself to the
Father. And depend upon it, as thy afflictions are not only
known to him, but appointed by him, he will measure out no
more to thee than he will sanctify. And so far from abhor-
ring or despising thy affliction, he will with every sorrow
grant support, and with every temptation make a way to
escape. Go then, my soul; cast all thy care upon him; for
he careth for thee.

28.—And there was a rainbow round about the throne.—*Rev.* iv. 3.

Mark this, my soul, and connect with it what God said
after the destruction of the old world by water:—" I do set

my bow in the cloud, and it shall be for a token of a covenant between me and the earth. And I will look upon it, that I may remember the everlasting covenant between God and every living creature of all flesh." And was not this rainbow round the throne which John saw, to tell the church of Jesus, on whom the Father is always looking, to remember his everlasting covenant of grace? And what doth it say but this—there shall be no more a deluge, nor floods of vengeance poured out upon the sinner that believes in Jesus? He looks to Christ, while the Father beholds Christ; he trusts in Jesus, whom the Father hath trusted with his honour: he accepts Jesus as the whole of the covenant, in whom the Father beholds the whole of the covenant fulfilled. Help me, Lord, in the view of every renewed token of the rainbow in the heavens, to connect with it the promise of Jehovah to his poor redeemed upon earth. Yes, blessed Lord! there is a rainbow round about the throne; and Christ is the Bow which Jehovah hath set in the cloud. On him, my soul, gaze and feast thy ravished eyes. On him thy God and Father looks, and is well pleased.

29.—And it came to pass, when the vessels were full, that she said unto her son, Bring me another vessel. And he said unto her, There is not a vessel more. And the oil stayed.—2 *Kings* iv. 6.

Do I not see Jesus and his fulness here? His giving out never ceaseth, until we have no more empty vessels to receive. And surely it is but proper the oil of grace should stay when there are no more souls to be supplied. Pity indeed would it be, that any thing so precious should be spilt on the ground. My soul, art thou not poor as this poor woman? Is the creditor come to take thee for bondage? Cry mightily to Jesus, the Lord God of the prophets. And wilt thou borrow vessels to receive his bounty? Borrow not a few; for every vessel must fail before that Jesus fails. Hast thou filled all? See then that thy Almighty Creditor is paid from Jesus' bounty; for he hath paid all thy debt: and see that thou live henceforth on Jesus' fulness. Oh, bountiful Lord! let me learn from hence sweet lessons of faith. There is no narrowness in thee, but all fulness. All thou hast, moreover, is for sinners. And, precious Lord! art thou not glorified in giving out to sinners? Is it not thy glory, thy delight, so to do? Art thou not pleased when sinners come to thee? Oh, for grace to come to thee, and to know and believe that it is thy glory and thy pleasure to receive them. Indeed, indeed thou keepest open house—an open hand, an open heart. Lord, give me daily, hourly, to come empty to thee to be filled, with grace here, and glory hereafter!

30.—And this day shall be unto you for a memorial.—*Exodus* xii. 14.

It is blessed to end the month, and end every day, as we would wish and desire to end life, blessing and praising God in Christ; rising from the table of divine bounties, and thanking the great Master of the feast. Pause, my soul, and see whether, in the past month, such hath been thine experience of sovereign grace and unmerited mercies, that thou canst now set up thine Ebenezer, and mark this day for a memorial. What visits hath Jesus made to thee, my soul; and how hath thine heart been drawn out after him? Hath the Father, as well as the Son, come and made his abode with thee? Hath the Holy Ghost, the glorious Inhabitant in the souls and bodies of his people, manifested his continued presence to thee? This day is indeed a memorial, if, in summing up the wonderful account of divine manifestations and divine love in providence and grace, during the month now nearly closed, and the years already passed, thou canst mark down the blessed enumeration. And will not my Lord, while the day is not passed, and yet remains to be added to the month, will he not make it memorable by some renewed favour? Oh! for some new visits from Father, Son, and Spirit,—this morning, this day, and all the day! As long as I live I would have my soul going forth in exercises of faith and love upon the person of Emmanuel, that I may carefully mark down the numberless instances of it: here, I would say, Jesus visited me; here it was he met me; here he showed me his loves, and made the place and day ever memorable by his grace.

OCTOBER.

1.—Shiloh.—*Gen.* xlix. 10.

PRECIOUS name of the Lord Jesus! how blessed hath it been in all ages to thy people! Oh! Lord, make it as ointment poured forth this morning to my soul. Both Jews and Christians alike agree in it, that it belongs only to the Messiah. And how then is it that they do not see Christ in it, even our Jesus, who suffered under Pontius Pilate, and died, as Caiaphas predicted the expediency, that one man should die for the people, and that he should fulfil the dying patriarch's prediction, by gathering together in one the children of God which were scattered abroad? That Jesus answered to Jacob's prediction, and none but Jesus ever did, is evident from their own testimony:—"We have a law," said they to Pilate, "and by that law he ought to die." Now, then, they themselves hereby confess that, as Jacob prophesied, the Lawgiver was not departed from Israel when Christ came. And when they added, "We have no king but Cæsar," certain it was, from their own testimony, the sceptre was gone out of the family of Judah, when the heathen emperor was king. Think of these evidences, my soul, and feast thyself upon the precious name of thy Shiloh. Thy Jesus, thy Shiloh, thy Almighty Deliverer, is come. He is both thy Law-giver and thy Law-fulfiller; thy God and thy King, who sprang out of Judah. Oh! thou glorious Shiloh, let my soul be gathered to thee, to live upon thee, and to thee, and do thou, Lord, arise out of Zion; and, when the fulness of the Gentiles be completed, let both Jew and Gentile be gathered into one fold, of which be thou the ever-living, ever-loving, ever-governing Shiloh! to bless them in thyself for ever. Amen.

2.—By night on my bed I sought him whom my soul loveth.—*Song* iii. 1.

PAUSE, my soul, over this account which the church gives of herself, and see whether such be thine exercises. It is night indeed in the soul whenever Christ is absent, or his presence not enjoyed. And though, blessed be God! the believer's interest in Christ varies not, yet his joy in the sense of safety is not always the same. Though it be the bed of affliction, or the bed of sickness, it is not the bed of carnal security, when the soul seeks Jesus. We cannot be said to be in a cold, lifeless, and indifferent state, while Jesus is sought for. It may be night indeed, it may be a dark season; yet, nevertheless, when we can say, With my soul have I sought thee in the night, yea, with my spirit within me will I seek thee early—surely this earnestness implies grace, and love, and desire, in lively exercise. However dull, stupid, and unprofitable, at times, ordinances and means of grace may seem; still grace, like the live coal under the embers, is not gone out, nor extinguished. Him whom my soul loveth frequently breaks out, and plainly shows that Jesus still lives and reigns within. Oh! precious Lord! thou art still the lovely one, the chief one, and the fairest among ten thousand. Be thou my all in all, the hope of glory.

3.—Even the righteousness of God which is by faith of Jesus Christ unto all, and upon all, them that believe; for there is no difference.— *Romans* iii. 22.

HERE, my soul, is a morning portion for thee! Surely here is enough for a morning portion, for poor believing souls to live upon to all eternity. Mark, my soul, what is here said. That righteousness of the Lord Jesus Christ, which he wrought out for his church, is the righteousness of God: for, as he was God as well as man, his righteousness was, to all intents and purposes, the righteousness of God. Now the sin of Adam, and the sins of all Adam's children, put the whole together, form but the sins of *creatures;* consequently, the righteousness of the Lord Jesus Christ is more than an equivalent, a more full payment than their debt can demand, because it is the righteousness of the *Creator.* Sweet thought! for God is more honoured by Christ's obedience, than dishonoured by our disobedience. And observe, my soul, how this righteousness is the church of Christ's, namely, by faith; it is unto all, and upon all, that believe. It is received by faith. The scripture language of this unspeakable mercy is, that as it was imputed to Abraham for righteousness, so it shall be imputed unto us also, if we believe on Him that raised up our Lord Jesus from the dead. This is another delightful portion of this precious verse. Neither is this all—for, as if to encourage the poorest, weakest, and most timid believer, this righteousness of God, which is by faith of Jesus Christ unto all, and upon all, that believe, *hath no difference* in its blessed effect. All partakers of it are alike partakers. By him, (that is, by Christ,) the scripture saith, all that believe are justified from all things. Acts xiii. 39. So that, though the faith of an Abraham or of a Peter might have been vastly greater than the timid Ananias, or the poor man that came to Christ for his son, saying, " Lord, I believe, help thou mine unbelief;" yet the justification by Christ, to all, is one and the same—it is to all, and upon all, that believe; for there is no difference. Oh! precious righteousness of the God-man Christ Jesus!

4.—Behold, I am with thee, and will keep thee in all places whither thou goest: for I will not leave thee, until that I have done that which I have spoken to thee of.—*Genesis* xxviii. 15.

HERE is a promise to Jacob, and not to Jacob only, personally considered, but to Jacob's seed. For the apostle Paul was commissioned, by the Holy Ghost, to tell the church of Jesus, that we, as Isaac was, are the children of promise. Hence this, like all other promises in Christ Jesus, is yea and amen. Pause then, my soul, and ask thyself, What hath the Lord spoken to thee of? Hath he met with thee in Bethel, as he found Jacob? And hath he there spoken unto thee? How wilt thou know? Very plainly. Jesus hath met with thee, hath indeed spoken unto thee; if so be thou hast seen thine own unworthiness and sinfulness by nature and by practice; and if thou hast seen the King in his beauty, even Jesus, in his own glory, suitableness, and all-sufficiency, as a Saviour; and inclined thine heart by his grace to believe in him, to depend upon him, and to live to him and his glory. What sayest thou, my soul, to these things? Is this promise, made to Jacob and his seed, thine? If so, live upon Jesus, and plead the fulfilment of it daily, hourly! Say to him, my soul, Lord! what hast thou spoken to me of, but mercy, pardon, peace, and grace, with all spiritual blessings, in Christ Jesus? And what have I to depend upon, or what indeed can I need more, but thy promise and the great Promiser? Yes, Lord Jesus! I do depend, I do believe. Surely thou wilt never leave whom thou hast once loved; and therefore thou wilt not leave me, until thou hast done that which thou hast spoken of in grace here, and wilt complete in glory hereafter.

5.—He goeth before you into Galilee: there shall ye see him —
Mark xvi. 7.

MARK this, my soul. In all thy goings forth, look out for
thy gracious, glorious Forerunner; and see whether the
same going before thee of thy Lord hath not been from everlasting. Was it not Jesus that was set up as the Head of his
people from everlasting? Did he not then go before them,
when he went forth for the salvation of his people? In the
council of peace, did he not go before them; not only before
we knew our need, but before we had a being? In all his
covenant-engagements, as the Surety of his people, he went
before them. And in all his offices, characters, and relations,
he was preventing us with the blessings of his goodness.
And in the personal salvation of every individual of his redeemed, was not Jesus beforehand in quickening, illu-
minating, redeeming, mercy? *If we love him, is it not because he first loved us?* And what is it now? Do not his
mercies go before our prayers; and before we call, doth not
Jesus answer? And will it not be so during the whole day
of grace, even to the eternal day of glory? Precious Jesus!
surely thou art going before me into Galilee. Oh! for grace
to follow the Lamb whithersoever he goeth. And do thou,
Lord, walk with me, and talk with me, as thou didst to the
disciples in the way; and make thyself known unto me in
continual manifestations, and in breaking of bread, and in
prayer.

6.—Trust in him at all times; ye people, pour out your heart before him.
God is a refuge for us. Selah.—*Psalm* lxii. 8.

MY soul! the Holy Ghost hath marked this verse with
Selah ; therefore pray observe it. You see the argument for
trust, because God—that is the Elohim—is a refuge. Yes!
God the Father is a refuge, in his covenant-engagements,
word, oath, promises. God the Son is a refuge, in his sureti-
ship-engagements, in his perfect righteousness, in his blood-
cleansing, sin-atoning death and salvation; and in all his securities of grace here, and glory hereafter. God the Holy
Ghost is a refuge, in all his blessed offices, characters, and
relations; by which he undertakes and fulfils all the purposes of salvation, in the glorifying the Father and the Son,
to every poor believer's joy and comfort. And wilt thou not,
my soul, then trust to this glorious Elohim? Wilt thou not
pour out thyself before him, and trust in him at *all* times, at

any time, at *every* time? Nay, wilt thou not call upon all the people to this soul-rewarding service, and tell them of his grace and glory? Come hither, I would say, and hearken, all ye that fear God; and I will tell you what he hath done for my soul. Oh! let us magnify his name together; for he is a Rock, and his work is perfect.

7.—Looking for that blessed hope, and the glorious appearing of the great God, and our Saviour Jesus Christ.—*Titus* ii. 13.

PAUSE, my soul, over these sweet and solemn words! Is Jesus my hope? Surely then it is a blessed hope; for all blessings are in him. Art thou looking for his appearing? Pause—for the thought is solemn. How shall I know? Suppose this moment the trumpet of the archangel was to sound, Arise ye dead, and come to judgment—my soul! art thou ready? Pause once more. Do I long for Jesus' appearing now, in the conversion of every poor sinner? Do I rejoice to hear at any time, that a soul is born to God? If so, is not this looking for his appearing? Again—Do I long for Jesus' appearing in the after-manifestations of his grace to the souls of the people? for this is to rejoice with them that do rejoice, and to prove a family interest. Again—Is Jesus precious to me; and do I long for the renewal of his visits, as the earth longeth for the rising sun? When I read his word, sing his praise, call upon his name, mingle in the congregation, go to his table; is his appearing upon all these occasions precious now, and are his love-tokens sweeter to my soul than honey, and the honeycomb? If, my soul, thou canst bear a cheerful testimony to these things, and canst truly call them blessed *now;* surely the hope of Jesus' *second* coming is blessed also, and thou canst well subscribe to the apostle's words; for his appearing being now *gracious,* will then be *glorious,* in the appearing of the great God and our Saviour Jesus Christ.

8.—But him they saw not.—*Luke* xxiv. 24.

MARK, my soul, what is here said. Though Jesus sought out his disciples in the morning of his resurrection, and was found of them that sought him not; yet many sought him not, while he was thus gracious to many that looked not for him. So is it now. Many, like those women, have seen the sepulchre as it were of Jesus, heard his word; nay, many saw his body when on earth, yet saw not God in Christ in him. "The grace of God," saith the apostle, "hath appeared unto all men;" that is, the gospel grace is preached in common before believers and unbelievers; but believers only see Jesus as the wisdom and the power of God for salvation: of others it may be said, as here, *but him they see not.* Oh! precious Jesus! give me to see thee as the Sent and Sealed of the Father, that my soul may have such a saving sight and knowledge of thee as the apostle had, which flesh and blood cannot reveal, but the Father only which is in heaven. Oh! heavenly Father, give me the Spirit of wisdom and revelation in the knowledge of thy dear Son; and do by me as by Paul—reveal thy Son in me.

9.—And all mine are thine, and thine are mine; and I am glorified in them.—*John* xvii. 10.

PRECIOUS testimony of a precious truth. See to it, my soul, that thou suffer not these blessed words of Jesus to drop from thy remembrance; but make them the everlasting meditation, not only of this morning, but every morning, and every day, and all the day; and mark thine interest in them. All Jesus' treasures, in his people and his grace, are still the Father's; for as Jesus and the Father are one in essence and in will, so also in property. And the Father's giving the church to Jesus, with all blessings in him, doth not alienate the Father's right. So in like manner, all that Jesus hath are the Father's, and Christ is glorified in them. It is a blessed order in the work and purpose of redemption, to trace the Father as the original Giver, Fountain, and Source of all. And then to trace them as Jesus', by virtue of his being the glorious Mediator. And hence the Holy Ghost is said to take them as Jesus', and show unto the people. The Holy Ghost doth not take them immediately from the Father, but mediately from Christ; because, without the person and work of Jesus, they never could have been communicated to us. So that Christ is glorified by the Holy Spirit in the hearts of his people, when that blessed Spirit takes them, and gives them, and shows them, not immediately as the Father's, but as the fruit and consequence of Christ's merits and death: and thus showing the common interest both of Father and Son, in all the blessed things of salvation. My soul! dost thou understand these precious things? Oh then live in the enjoyment of them, and see that Jesus is glorified and the Father glorified, in his dear and ever blessed Son.

10.—That ye may know how that the Lord doth put a difference between the Egyptians and Israel.—*Exod.* xi. 7.

WHO shall mark down all the properties of distinguishing grace! What a vast difference doth grace make, in this life, between him that serveth God and him that serveth him not! And what an everlasting difference will be made in the life which is to come! My soul! make this thought the subject of thine unceasing meditation. Thou canst not walk the street, nor go to public worship, nor watch the Lord's dealings in all the vast and numberless dispensations going on in life, in the wide world of providence and grace, but what every thing speaks, in the language of the Morning Portion, of the difference there is still put between the Egyptians and Israel. Every thing proclaims it, every event confirms it. And do not overlook the great point of all. It is the Lord that doth all this. Who maketh thee to differ from another? Oh! for grace to be always on the watch-tower to mark this, and for grace to acknowledge it. Precious Jesus! thou art the Source, the Fountain, the Author, the Finisher, of all. Oh! the depth of the riches, both of the wisdom and knowledge of God! How unsearchable are thy judgments, and thy ways past finding out!

11.—He wakeneth morning by morning; he wakeneth mine ear to hear as the learned.—*Isaiah* l. 4.

WHO is this but Jesus in his human nature, of whom the Prophet speaks? Eminently to him doth it refer, to whom was given the tongue of the learned, that he might know how to speak a word to him that is weary. Precious Lord! it is indeed thy province, and thine only, to speak a word to weary souls, and to be the rest wherewith thou causest the weary to rest, and to be their refreshing. Not only to give them rest, but thyself to be their rest. Not only to give them salvation, but thyself to be their salvation.—But, blessed Lord! may not a poor soul like myself say of thee also, that thou wakenest me morning by morning? for who is it but Jesus, that by the sweet influences of the Spirit wakens his people morning by morning, and openeth the ear to hear, and the eye to see, and the heart to feel, the blessed tokens of his coming? Have I not found thee, Lord, wakening my soul sometimes before the dawn of day, and calling my soul up in gracious meditation, to attend to the soft whispers of thy love? Have I not heard thee saying, as to the church of old, Rise up, my love, my fair one, and come away? And hast thou not made my soul, or ever I was aware, like the chariots of Amminadib? Do thou, Lord, waken me, I beseech thee, morning by morning, and while thou art thus speaking to my soul, let mine answer be, My voice shalt thou hear betimes, oh Lord, in the morning ; early will I direct my prayer unto thee, and will look up. My soul shall wait for thee, more than they that watch for the morning, yea, I say, more than they that watch for the morning.

12.—And this man shall be the peace, when the Assyrian shall come into our land.—*Mic.* v. 5.

WHAT man is this but the Glory-man, the Mediator between God and men, the man Christ Jesus? And what peace, when all enemies oppose the soul, but peace in the blood of his cross? Yes, my soul, Jesus is the wonderful man, who alone could make thy peace. For as it was by one man's disobedience many were made sinners, so by the obedience of one shall many be made righteous. And none but one in our own nature could redeem that nature, for the right of redemption belonged only to him. Leviticus xxv. 25. And none but one in our nature could atone, could bleed, could die, and rise again, that he might be the Judge, both of the dead and living. Oh! precious Jesus, how suited wert thou by the union of thy two natures, as God and man, and God-man, both in one, to be our glorious Mediator, and to be the Lord our righteousness. Yes, precious Lord. God hath said it, and my soul evermore rejoiceth in the blessed truth : this man Christ Jesus shall be my peace, my glory, my salvation, my refuge, when the Assyrian shall come into our land.

13.—Jesus made a surety.—*Heb.* vii. 22.

MY soul, look at Jesus as a Surety, and as *made thy Surety* this morning.—Blessed view, if so be the Holy Ghost will enlighten thine eyes to see him under all these characters. First, a Surety. We are all ruined by a debt, incapable of being ever paid by any, or by all, the fallen sons of Adam.

Jesus steps in, becomes a Surety for our debt, and pays the whole by his obedience and death. But we owe a duty also, as well as a debt. Jesus becomes here again the Surety. He will put his Spirit in us, and we shall live. He becomes also a Surety for promises, that all God hath promised for his sake, shall be fulfilled in him, and in us for him. But he is not only a Surety, but *made* a Surety; for the Father's name, and the Father's authority, is in him. It is God the Father which saith, I have given him for a covenant. Precious thought for faith to act upon. And, my soul, is not Jesus *thy* Surety? Yes, if while the Father thus freely gives, thou as fully receivest, and art looking to no other. Say then, my soul, is it not so with thee? Is not Jesus thy all in all, thy Surety, thy Sponsor, thy Redeemer? And dost thou not say, Thou shalt answer for me, oh Lord my God? Oh! comprehensive word, Jesus made a Surety!

14.—Behold, I give you power to tread on serpents and scorpions, and over all the power of the enemy.—*Luke* x. 19.

ASTONISHING the mercy, and wonderful the privilege, manifested to the followers of the Lamb! Poor, and weak, and helpless, as they are in themselves, yet how strong in the grace that is in Christ Jesus. My soul, never lose sight of these blessed things. In Jesus thou art not only a conqueror, but more than conqueror. As the armies in heaven overcame by the blood of the Lamb, so here below, it is all in him, and by him, the victory is obtained. God will bruise Satan under our feet shortly; but it is God that must bruise him, and it is he that must put him under our feet. Oh for grace to see where our strength is, and as cheerfully to ascribe all to him; that He in whom we are made to tread on serpents and scorpions may have the glory due to his name, and He who gives the strength may have the praise.

15.—Whose names are in the book of life.—*Philippians* iv. 3.

How is this known? It must be a blessed privilege this, and highly desirable to attain, if there be a true scriptural testimony to it. That there is a book of life, in which the record is made of the people of the Lamb, is without all dispute, from many parts of scripture. The church of the first-born are said to have their names written in heaven; such as are chosen of God in Christ before the world began.

But these are secret things, which belong to the Lord our God. Yet it is said, the secret of the Lord is with them that fear him, and he will show them his covenant. Hence, therefore, is not the Bible a copy of this book of life? Are there not scriptural marks and characters given, by which the correspondence is proved? In both, they are distinguished by one and the same name and character. They are called the *people*, the *seed*, the *offspring*, of Jesus. They are his by gift, by purchase, by conquest, by a voluntary surrender. They are known by the character as well as by name. They seek salvation only in Jesus. God is their Father, Jesus their Redeemer, the Holy Ghost their Sanctifier. My soul, see thy name in bible characters answering to this persuasion, and be assured, that the original writing of the book of life in heaven, and the book of God for life upon earth, which is his written word, is in exact correspondence. Blessed Jesus, give me in this way to know whose I am, and to whom I belong, and then assured shall I be, that my name is in the book of life.

16.—We will make thee borders of gold, with studs of silver.—*Song* i. 11.

My soul, ponder over these words. What borders of gold shall be made for the believer, but the robe of Jesus' righteousness? And what silver but the garment of his salvation? If thou art clothed with this, my soul, thou wilt shine indeed, with more lustre than all the embroidery of gold and precious stones, which perish with using. But mark, my soul, who it is that makes them, and who puts them on thee —Surely none but God. And observe how all the persons of the Godhead are engaged in this work. *We* will make thee, is the language. Yes, Jehovah Elohim, who said, *Let us* make man, at the original creation : the same now saith, at the new creation, *We will make* thee borders of gold, with studs of silver. And is not the hand of God the Father in this blessed, gracious act, in the gift of his Son to the poor sinner? Is it not Jesus who hath wrought out a robe of salvation for the poor sinner? And is it not the Holy Ghost, who puts on the blessed adorning upon the poor sinner, in taking of the things of Jesus, and showing unto him? Oh, precious testimony of a precious God in Christ. Be it unto me, Lord, according to thy word. Let me be thus clothed and adorned, and I shall be happy now, and happy to all eternity.

17.—And on the cities of Judah shall the flocks pass again under the hands of him that telleth them, saith the Lord—*Jeremiah* xxxiii. 13.

SEE, my soul, what a blessed scripture is here. Meditate upon it this morning. Whose hands can these be but Jesus'? For whose are the flocks but his? Is he not in all the scripture said to be a Shepherd, and the good Shepherd, that giveth his life for the sheep? And would he give his life for sheep he knew not? Surely, that is impossible. Moreover, did not the Father give them to him? Did he not receive them from the Father? And did he not know them, and count them over, when he received them? I know my sheep, saith Jesus, and am known of mine. And observe, the flocks are said to pass *again* under his hands. A plain proof that they have all passed before. Nay, is it not said that he *telleth* them? Yes! He calleth them all by name, and leadeth them forth, and goeth before them. And he saith himself, Of all thou hast given me, I have lost none. Precious scripture of a most precious Saviour. How then can any be lost? If Jesus knew them when he received them, counted them over, set his seal upon them, and they must all pass again under his almighty hand, how shall one, even one, be found wanting, when he maketh up his jewels? Poor weather-beaten shorn lamb of Jesus' fold, whosoever thou art, think of these things, when wandering, or cold, or in darkness, or on the mountains. Jesus will seek thee out in the dark and cloudy day. He will bring thee home, and thou shalt lie in his bosom, and by and by dwell with him for ever: for he is, he must, he will still be Jesus.

18.—And God heard their groaning, and God remembered his covenant. *Exod.* ii. 24.

THIS is a precious scripture. My soul, put a note upon it. No sigh, no groan, no tear of God's people can pass unobserved. He putteth the tears of his people in his bottle. Surely then he can never overlook what gives vent to those tears, the sorrows of the soul. Our spiritual afflictions Jesus knows, and numbers all. How sweet the thought! The Spirit maketh intercession for the saints, with the groanings which they cannot utter. And do, my soul, observe the cause of deliverance. Not our sighs, nor our groanings, nor our brokenness of heart; not these, for what benefit can these render to an Holy God? But God hath respect in all to his own everlasting covenant. Yes, Jesus is the all in all of the covenant. God the Father hath respect to him. For his sake, for his righteousness, for his atoning blood, the groanings of his people find audience at the mercy-seat, and redress. And God hath respect to his own word, his oath, his promises to his dear Son. Oh! blessed assurance! Oh! precious security! How shall any poor groaning child of God go unheard, unpardoned, unrelieved; who hath double security, in the glory of God the Father's sovereign grace, and covenant word and oath, to depend upon: and the everlasting covenant righteousness and atoning blood of God the Son to be found in? Here, my soul, rest, for ever rest, thy sure claim to grace and glory.

19.—There shall be no more thence an infant of days, nor an old man that hath not filled his days; for the child shall die an hundred years old, but the sinner being an hundred years old, shall be accursed.—*Isaiah* lxv. 20.

My soul! contemplate, this morning, the auspicious and blessed effects brought into the circumstances of mankind by the gospel. Not only shall there be new heavens, and a new earth, but new hearts, new minds, new dispositions to enjoy them. If any man be in Christ, he is a new creature. Old things are passed away, and all things are become new. And among the many blessed changes that shall take place in consequence of Jesus' salvation, all untimely deaths are done away. Indeed, there can be no such thing as an untimely death to those who are in Christ: for a voice from heaven pronounced all blessed that die in the Lord. A child new born, if born also in Christ, an infant of a day, if a gracious day, is as ripe for glory as if an hundred years had passed over him. Indeed, he is an hundred years old in Jesus. Sweet thought! what a blessedness, dearest Jesus, hath thy great salvation introduced into the circumstances of thy people. But what an awful thought! the life of an unawakened, unregenerated sinner, though protracted to an hundred years, is lengthened only to misery. As he came into the world, so he goes through it, and so he goes out of it, an unrenewed sinner! Oh, distinguishing grace! oh, great salvation!

20.—Christ is all, and in all.—*Coloss.* iii. 11.

Hail, thou great, thou glorious, thou universal Lord. To thee, blessed Jesus, every knee shall bow. Thou art all in

all, in creation, redemption, providence, grace, glory. Thou
art all in all in thy church, and in the hearts of thy people:
in all their joys, all their happiness, all their exercises, all
their privileges. Thou art the all in all in thy word, ordinances, means of grace, the sum and substance of the whole
Bible. Speak we of promises? Thou art the first promise
in the sacred word, and the whole of every promise that follows; for all in thee are yea and amen. Speak we of the
law? Thou art the end of the law for righteousness to every
one that believeth. Speak we of sacrifices? By thy one
sacrifice thou hast for ever perfected them that are sanctified.
Speak we of the prophecies? To thee give all the prophets
witness, that whosoever believeth in thee shall receive remission of sins. Yes, blessed, blessed Jesus, thou art the all in
all. Be thou to me, Lord, the all in all I need in time, and
then surely thou wilt be my all in all to all eternity.

21.—All are your's; and ye are Christ's; and Christ is God's.—1 *Cor.*
iii. 22, 23.

Oh! what a rich inventory is here. All things, all blessings, all gifts, all grace, all mercy; all, all, the Christian's.
And observe, my soul, on what it is suspended—if ye are
Christ's. And whose art thou, my soul, but his? Hath not
the Father given thee to him? And hath not the Son of
God bought thee with a price? Hast thou not made a voluntary surrender of thyself to Jesus, and given thyself to him
in an everlasting covenant which cannot be broken? Oh!
yes, yes; all this is certain. Lord, grant me grace, and faith
in lively exercise, that I may now take to myself all the blessedness of it by anticipation, until I come to realize the whole
in absolute enjoyment, in glory. Christ is mine, and with
him, heaven is mine; God the Father is mine; the Holy
Ghost is mine; all covenant blessings are mine; ordinances,
means of grace, the holy book of God, all are mine here, and
will be my portion for evermore. Hallelujah.

22.—The Lord will command his loving kindness in the day time, and
in the night his song shall be with me, and my prayer unto the God
of my life.—*Psalm* xlii. 8.

Both night and day open sources of comfort, when Jesus
is present, and when Jesus sanctifies. How, indeed, my soul,
canst thou be otherwise than comfortable, while Jesus is with

thee, and manifesting himself unto thee? And do observe, my soul, the sweet expression in this verse. Thy Lord, thy Jesus, will both create blessings and command them. His loving kindness, which is better than life itself, will make daylight in the soul, when otherwise it is night. And his love will shine, as the stars in the darkest night sparkle with more lustre, with increasing brightness, when dark providences are around. Nay, Jesus will give songs in the night, when all things else are out of tune. Do thou, Lord, do thou, my Lord, command then thy loving kindness both by day and night; and my prayer and praise shall both go forth to thee, the God of my life, and it shall put more gladness in my heart, than when corn, and wine, and oil, increase.

23.—Now therefore go, and I will be with thy mouth, and teach thee what thou shalt say.—*Exod.* iv. 12.

My soul! pause over this sweet promise which the Lord gave to Moses; for surely the same is in effect said to every minister, every child of God, and every believer. He that made man's mouth, will give every thing suitable to the mouth, and proportion every thing to the necessity of his people. And do, my soul, remark the comprehensiveness of the promise. Will not He who undertakes to be with the mouth, be also with all the renewed faculties of the soul? Jesus gives the tongue of the learned. Jesus gives grace to the lips, understanding to the heart, eyes to the blind, feet to the lame: thy bread shall be given, and thy water shall be sure; and thy defence shall be the munition of rocks. Go then, my soul, go wheresoever the Lord leads: for he saith, Be not afraid, I am with thee, I am thy God. Learn, my soul, then to eye Jesus in all, and depend upon it, Jesus will bless thee in the use of all. Make his glory thy aim, and thy happiness will be his glory.

24.—And the remnant of Jacob shall be in the midst of many people as a dew from the Lord, as the showers upon the grass, that tarrieth not for man, nor waiteth for the sons of men.—*Micah* v. 7.

Observe, my soul, the character given of Jacob's seed, and bless the Lord for being included in the number. For so saith the apostle, If ye be Christ's, then are ye Abraham's seed, and heirs according to the promise. Mark then their characters. They are a *remnant*. But they are God's remnant, being in covenant with God in Christ; and as such, distinguished and separated from the world. They are a people that dwell alone, and not reckoned among the nations. They are in the midst of many people, but belong to none of them. For though living in the world, they are not of the world, but chosen out of the world. They are, moreover, as a dew from the Lord. Beautiful resemblance! For as the dew is from heaven, so believers in Christ are born from above: not of the will of the flesh, nor of the will of man, but of God. Moreover, they are as showers upon the grass; meaning, that as Jesus is promised to come down as showers upon the mown grass to refresh his people, so his people live in a constant dependence upon Jesus, and receive out of his fulness, while all the earth is dry as stubble around them. Moreover, as the rain waiteth not for man, but wholly falls from God's appointment, so grace is not dispensed for man's desert, but the Lord's free bounty. Oh! precious promise, or rather precious cluster of promises,—and all in Jesus.

25.—My beloved is unto me as a cluster of camphire in the vineyards of Engedi.—*Song* i. 14.

How full indeed, how infinitely full, abundant, and soul-satisfying, is Jesus, in all that concerns life, light, grace, glory! A cluster of all is Christ; whether the *copher* of medicine to heal, or of sweetness to satisfy, or of riches to enlarge, or salvation to impart. Every way, and in every thing that is lovely or desirable, Jesus is a cluster indeed to his people. And whether we meet him in the valley or the mount, in the plains of Jericho, or the vineyards of Engedi, neither place nor situation, neither state nor circumstances, make any alteration in our Beloved; he is, he must be, Jesus, and that is always lovely.

26.—He went on frowardly in the way of his heart; I have seen his ways, and will heal him.—*Isa.* lvii. 17, 18.

PAUSE, my soul, over this sweet scripture: and while thou readest it, wilt thou not cry out, with David, in the contemplation of the overwhelming mercy, " And is this the manner of man, O Lord God?" 2. Sam. vii. 19. Think, oh my soul, how it was with thee, when in the days of thy unregeneracy thou wentest on frowardly in the way of thy perverse heart. Who could have stopped thee, had not sovereign grace? And how justly might the Lord have said, I have seen thy ways, and will punish thee ; will give thee over to a reprobate mind, and forsake thee for ever. Oh! the riches of grace, when, from my very unworthiness, the Lord took occasion to magnify his love and mercy. Oh! Lord Jesus! do thou incline the heart that thou hast healed to live to thy praise, and let the life that thou hast saved from destruction, be spent in thy service.

27.—I have chosen thee, and not cast thee away.—*Isaiah* xli. 2.

Is this thy portion, my soul? Hath the Lord thy God indeed chosen thee ? Hath he manifested his love to thee in so distinguishing a way ? Take comfort, then, in all thine exercises, when seasons of darkness and discouragement are around ; think of God's choice, and venture on God's love! Art thou distressed, exercised, afflicted ? Dost thou call on God and find no answer? Doth the enemy tempt thee to doubt ? Doth thine own unbelieving heart misgive thee ? Still recollect, Jesus knows all. He chose thee—and he that chose thee, knows all thine exercises ; nay, he himself hath appointed them. And remember, thou wast not forced upon him. It was his own free choice first made thee his: and his own love will be the security of thy present dependence. Jesus resteth in his love : he hateth putting away. Cast down as thou art, thou are not cast off. Though fallen, he can raise. Though dejected, he can and will comfort. Sweet thought! He will turn again; he will have compassion upon us; and he will cast all our sins into the depths of the sea. Hallelujah!

28.—Casting all your care upon him, for he careth for you.—1 *Pet.* v. 7.

Yes, blessed Jesus, I would cast all upon thee: sins, sorrows, trials, temptations. Thou art the Almighty Burden-bearer of thy people; for the Lord Jehovah hath laid on thee the iniquity of us all. And as thou bearest all our sins, so thou carriest all our sorrows. And dost thou not bear all the persons of thy redeemed ? Dost thou not bear all our troubles, all our exercises, all our temptations, trials, difficulties ? The government is upon thy shoulder; the care of the churches is all with thee. And shall I not cast all my care upon thee? Shall I be careful for many things, while Jesus saith, " Cast thy burden upon the Lord, and he shall sustain

thee ?"   Oh for grace to set loose to all things, and to leave
all things with thee !   Lord, do thou bear me up when I am
falling, support me when weak, uphold me against all mine
enemies, carry me safe through a life of grace here—and,
finally, bring me home to thy glory to behold thee, and dwell
with thee for ever.

29.—He sent his word, and healed them.—*Psalm* cvii. 20

OF all the subjects to comfort our minds in the recollection
of the mercies in Jesus, the authority and name of Jehovah
in the appointment comes home with the greatest comfort to
the heart.   This is faith's warrant—this is faith's confidence.
Who sent Jesus; who sent his word ; who is it that gives
validity and efficacy to salvation ?   Jehovah.   " Beware of
him," saith the Lord, " my name is in him."   And how then
can my soul fail, or any promise in Christ pass unfulfilled,
when Jehovah sends, and Christ completes the work the Father gave him to do.   Blessed Jesus, may I always look to
thee under this precious character: and may I hear thee
speaking under that solemn but blessed title, " I am the Lord
that healeth thee."

30.—Thy shoes shall be iron and brass ; and as the day so shall thy strength be.—*Deut.* xxxiii. 25.

WHAT a thought that is which the word of God furnisheth, in the view of everlasting engagements, that a suitable
strength is laid up for every emergency.   God's love hath
provided adequate supplies to the wants of all his people.
What strength of enemies shall be equal to the everlasting
strength of God ?   What shall drain the resources of everlasting love ?   What shall dry up the streams which flow
from an everlasting fountain ?   Jesus therefore will proportion the back of his people to the burden.   His grace shall
be sufficient for all : it shall be sufficient for you, it shall be
sufficient for me, for every one, for all.   Sweet thought !   Oh
for grace to keep it always in remembrance !

31.—There remaineth therefore a rest to the people of God.—*Heb.* iv. 9.

BLESSED motto for the close of the month, or the day, or
year ; after being fatigued with the thoughts, and cares, and
anxieties, of life.   My soul, delight thyself in the thought of

it—look forward to the speedy enjoyment of it. Like the prophet's vision, it will come: wait for it. No sorrow you have gone through will ever come over again. No persecution already felt shall exactly be again practised. The same trial shall not be again known. Every day, every hour of the day, we are nearer home. Precious consideration! And Jesus is the rest of his people. Lord, in thee alone I find rest: be thou my hope, and be thou my portion for ever.

NOVEMBER.

1.—For thou wilt light my candle.—*Psalm* xviii. 28.

PRECIOUS consideration! It is the Lord that lighteth the candle of his people. And if the Lord light it, what power can put it out? Cherish, my soul, the faith this thought awakens, amidst all the darkness around thee and in thee. Hath the Lord indeed given thee light? Dost thou in his light see light! In the light of God the Father, dost thou behold God the Son; and, by the enlightening of the Holy Ghost, hast thou the light of the knowledge of the glory of God in the face of Jesus Christ? Oh, the blessedness of such a state of light, and life, and knowledge; how is it possible then any more to be in darkness, when the Lord himself is my everlasting light, and my God my glory? Now consider the reverse of this in creature-enlightening. "How oft," saith Job, "is the candle of the wicked put out?" And how exposed is it to be every moment put out; for it is not of God's kindling. A *fleeting* of its own oil will do it. What is called a *thief* in the candle will do it. It may be *blown* out; it may be *snuffed* out; or if none of these causes occur, yet of itself it must shortly *burn* out. For what is our life but a vapour? My soul, ponder these things. Hath the Lord lighted thy candle? Is Jesus thy light, thy joy, thy sunshine, thy morning star, thy all in all? And hath he risen upon thee, never more to go down? Oh, then, though all thou knowest, all thou beholdest now, is but as the faint taper of the night, compared to the glory of that day which shall be revealed, yet take to thyself by faith all the sweet

24

comforts of thy state of grace, and say—It is the Lord that
hath lighted my candle; the Lord my God will enlighten all
remaining darkness: I shall see thy face in glory, and
shortly awake up after thy likeness.

2.—But the Comforter, which is the Holy Ghost, whom the Father will
send in my name, he shall teach you all things, and bring all things
to your remembrance, whatsoever I have said unto you.—*John* xiv.
26.

Oh, blessed Spirit, to whom I owe such unspeakable mercies! Let me, Lord, contemplate thee this day under this
gracious, kind, compassionate office, of the Comforter. Thou
art indeed the Holy Ghost the Comforter. And how mercifully dost thou sympathize with all the followers of Jesus
in their various afflictions, both of soul and body! How
tenderly dost thou show us our sins, and lead to Jesus' blood
to wash them away! How sweetly dost thou visit, encourage,
strengthen, instruct, lead, and guide, into all truth? And
how powerfully at times, by thy restraining grace, dost thou
enable us to mortify the deeds of the body, that we may live!
Hail, thou holy, blessed, almighty Comforter! Oh, let thy
visits be continual! Come, Lord, and abide with me, and be
with me for ever. Manifest that thou art the Sent of the
Father and of the Son, in coming to me in Jesus' name, in
teaching me of all the precious things concerning Jesus, and
acting as the Remembrancer of Jesus; that in thee, and by
thy blessed office-work, I may know, and live in the sweet
enjoyment of fellowship with the Father, and with his Son
Jesus Christ, through the influences of thee, the Holy Ghost
the Comforter!

3.—And in that day there shall be no more the Canaanite in the house
of the Lord of hosts.—*Zech.* xiv. 21.

Oh, precious day of God, when will it arrive? Shall the
house of Jesus be indeed delivered from all false pastors, all
corrupt worship, and the Lord have turned to the people a
pure language, that they may all call upon the name of the
Lord, to serve him with one consent? Shall my soul indeed
be freed, not only from all the sorrows, pains, evils, and
afflictions, of sin around me, but what is infinitely better than
all, from the very being and indwelling of sin within me?
Shall the fountain of corruption, both of original and actual

sin, be dried up, so that I shall never think a vain thought, nor speak an idle sinful word any more? Is there such a day, in which the Canaanite shall be wholly driven out? Oh, blessed thought! precious, precious promise. Oh, dearest Jesus, to what a blessed state hast thou begotten poor sinners of the earth by thy blood and righteousness. Hasten it, Lord. Cut short thy work, thou that art mighty to save, and take thy willing captive home from myself, and all the remaining Canaanites yet in the land, which are the very tyrants of my soul.

4.—For I know that ye seek Jesus which was crucified.—*Matt.* xxviii. 5.

Is it indeed known unto my Lord that I seek him? Doth Jesus know that I desire him more than my necessary food? Ye angels of light, that watched over his sepulchre, do ye witness for me that he is more precious to me than gold, yea, than the golden wedge of Ophir. And can I, do I, humbly appeal to him that readeth the heart and knoweth all things, and say, Thou knowest, Lord, that I love thee? Be comforted then, my soul: He whom thou seekest will be soon found of thee. He is near at hand. He hath never been a wilderness to his people; neither hath he ever said to the praying seed of Jacob, Seek ye my face in vain. While thou art seeking him, he is looking on thee. And the very desires in thine heart of seeking him, it is Jesus hath kindled. And nothing can be more sure than that He who kindled them in thine heart did not kindle them in vain. Sweet thought. I bless thee for it, thou gracious Lord!

5.—The king hath brought me into his chambers.—*Song* i. 4.

YES! he who is King of nations, King of saints, is my God and King also; for he hath an universal empire, being One with the Father over all, blessed for ever! Amen. To him I bow the knee, and humbly and gratefully desire to put the crown of my salvation on his adorable head. And what hath this Sovereign done for thee, my soul? Oh! record his praise; tell it to saints and sinners all around. This great, and glorious, and condescending King, hath not only brought thee out of darkness and the shadow of death, but hath brought thee into his chambers. What chambers? Chambers of sweet communion and fellowship; chambers of love, of grace, of mercy, of redemption, of ordinances, and of all

covenant blessings. He hath taught me of his love and my
privileges in him, and so assured me of my everlasting safety
in him and his finished salvation ; that by-and-by, when,
from those outward chambers of grace, he hath accomplished
all his blessed purposes concerning me, he will bring me
home into his inner chambers of light and glory, from whence
I shall go out no more, but dwell in them, and in the presence
of God and the Lamb, for ever and ever. Hallelujah!

6.—For the Father himself loveth you, because ye have loved me, and
have believed that I came out from God.—*John* xvi. 27.

SEE, my soul, how thy Jesus hath endeared to thee the
Father in the assurance of his love. And wilt thou not feel
thine whole affections going forth in continual love after
him? Was it not thy Father which, from everlasting gave
thee Jesus as thy Saviour, and gave thee to Jesus that he
might redeem thee? Was it not from the same precious
source that Jesus came as a Saviour, and a great one, to redeem thee, and other great sinners? Is it not thy Father,
that hath adopted thee into his family in Jesus, and given
thee the spirit of adoption, whereby thou criest Abba Father?
And doth he not accept thee in Jesus, bless thee in Jesus,
nourish thee with the body and blood of Jesus, clothe thee
with the righteousness of Jesus, and give thee all temporal,
spiritual, and by-and-by will give thee all eternal, blessings in
Christ Jesus? Nay, even his chastisements have nothing in
them of wrathful punishment, but fatherly love and mercy in
Jesus! Oh, my soul, pause, and behold what manner of
love the Father hath bestowed upon thee, that thou shouldest
be called a child of God! And wilt thou not then from henceforth and for ever say unto him, in Jesus, My Father! thou art
the guide of my youth, for thou hast commanded me so to
call thee. Jeremiah iii. 19.

7.—And yet there is room.—*Luke* xiv. 22.

Room! where, and for whom? Room in the gospel of
salvation, and for poor perishing sinners, in the blood and
righteousness of Jesus Christ. Room in the heart of God
the Father ; in the love, grace, mercy, and peace of God the
Son ; and in the teachings, influences, and fellowship of God
the Holy Ghost. Room in the plentiful provisions of grace,
the calls of the gospel, the ministration of the word and or-

dinances in the house of prayer. *Whosoever will*, is the gracious invitation; whosoever feels his heart made willing in the day of God's power, *let him come and take of the water of life freely.* Lord, is there room for me ? Thousands, and tens of thousands, have found room, through thy grace inclining them to come; and yet the scripture sweetly saith again this day, And yet there is room. Oh, give me grace to see that I am one of the invited, one of the happy number that hath found room; and from experiencing the blessed fulness, riches, grace, suitableness, and all-sufficiency in the blood and righteousness of Jesus for poor sinners, I may proclaim every where around, that others may find the same, that yet there is room. And oh, Lord, grant, that while yet there is room, multitudes that are ready to perish may come. And then all thy royal guests whom thou bringest to thy banquet, and who find room in all the mercies of Jehovah for redemption here below, will find room in the house not made with hands, eternal in the heavens.

8.—The people shall dwell alone, and shall not be reckoned among the nations.—*Numb.* xxiii. 9.

Mark, my soul, the character of God's Israel, and remember that they are the same in all ages. Distinguishing mercies are sweet mercies. God's people dwell alone, in the everlasting appointment of the Father, by whom they were set apart, and formed for his glory, and given to his Son. They dwell alone, in being brought into the church of Jesus, as the redeemed and purchased by his blood. They dwell alone under the sweet influences of the Spirit, by whom they are known, distinguished, regenerated, and sealed, unto the day of redemption. Thus set apart, thus formed, thus given, thus redeemed, thus purchased, thus sealed, surely they are not reckoned among the nations, but are supposed to show forth God's praises, who hath called them out of darkness into his marvellous light. My soul, what saith thy experience to these things? Oh, how different the state, the circumstances, the new birth, the fellowship, pursuits, way, life, and work of God's people, from the world. Blessed Jesus! cause me to dwell alone from the nations around : but let me not dwell a moment without thee; but do thou come with thy Father and the Holy Spirit, according to thy sweet promises, and make constant abode with me.

24*

9.—And many of them that sleep in the dust of the earth shall awake, some to everlasting life, and some to shame and everlasting contempt.—*Daniel* xii. 2.

WHAT a morning will this be! how distinguished from every other! Lord, how often do I now awake, with thoughts of earth, and sin, and trifles, and vanity! How have I opened mine eyes this morning? Was it, dearest Jesus, with thoughts of thee? In that solemn morning, there will be no longer dreams as now, even in our waking hours: for all childish imaginations, shadows, doubts, and fears will be done away. Precious, blessed Lord Jesus! cause me, morning by morning, while upon earth, to awaken with sweet thoughts of thee. Let the close of night, and the opening of the day, be with thy dear name in my heart, on my thought, and on my lips: and in that everlasting morning, after having dropped asleep in Jesus, and in thy arms by faith, may I awake up in thy embraces, and after thy likeness, to be everlastingly and eternally satisfied with thee.

10.—For such an High Priest became us, who is holy, harmless, undefiled, separate from sinners, and made higher than the heavens.—*Heb.* vii. 26.

WHAT a sweet thought! Surely, as a poor sinner, I need an High-priest to act for me. I cannot, I dare not, approach in myself, and with my poor polluted offerings, without one. But he that intercedes for me, must be himself holy, free from sin: his sacrifice holy, his obedience holy, and in all points suited to his office, and my necessities. Cherish, then, the thought, my soul. He that is thine High-priest, is all this, and infinitely more. So holy in himself, that not the shadow of sin was in him. So harmless, that in his mouth was found no guile. So undefiled, that though he took all the sins of his people upon him, yet in himself he was free from all sin. So separate from sinners, that though he took the nature of man, yet wholly underived from man ; and so much higher than the heavens, that his own personal holiness infinitely transcended the holiness of angels. For while they are said to be charged with folly, Jesus is the Holy One in whom the Father declared himself well pleased. Meditate, my soul, on these precious features in thy Jesus, at all times, and upon all occasions : and more especially, when thou drawest nigh the throne of grace in and through this glorious Mediator. And moreover, for thy further comfort and encouragement to come

boldly to the mercy-seat, forget not to recollect the still further blessed thought, that this holiness of Jesus is the righteousness of all his people; for he was made sin, when he
knew no sin, that they might be made the righteousness of
God in him. And, as if this was not enough, Christ glorified not himself to be made thy High-priest, but was called
to it, as was Aaron. Go then, my soul, go to the precious,
the holy, the harmless, the undefiled, High-priest, Christ Jesus, in whom, and in whose righteousness and atoning blood,
thou mayest always have boldness to draw nigh, to find
grace, and mercy to help, in all time of need.

11.—And in that day there shall be a root of Jesse, which shall stand
for an ensign of the people ; to it shall the Gentiles seek ; and his
rest shall be glorious.—*Isaiah* xi. 10.

JESUS is both the root and the offspring of David, and the
bright and morning star; and, therefore, is not this the day,
the very day, the joyful day, in which he was set up, as
God the Father's ensign from everlasting, for salvation in the
council of peace? And was he not brought forth, and set
up, and proclaimed, as God's salvation to us poor Gentiles in
the fulness of time, as well as the light of his people Israel?
Surely it can have reference to no other. Precious Jesus! I
do indeed behold thee, as set up from everlasting. Thou
wert so exhibited in the council of peace; and thy goings
forth were from everlasting, when thou wentest forth for the
salvation of thy people. In the Bible, thou art the great
Promise, and the whole of the promises. Thou art the
whole of the law and the prophets. Both the Old Testament
dispensation, and the New Testament grace, all pointed to
thee, and in thee they had their completion. Thou art the
Father's ensign of redemption, the signal of war with sin,
with Satan, and all the powers of Hell and corruption. Lord!
to thee do I seek; under thy banner, and in thy strength,
would I enjoy a rest which indeed must be glorious. And
oh, thou blessed Spirit of all truth! when at any time the
enemy cometh in like a flood, do thou lift up thy ensign, even
Jesus, as a standard against him.

12.—And they shall come which were ready to perish.—*Isaiah* xxvii. 13.

WHAT a blessed promise is this to a poor sinner, that is
conscious of his being in perishing circumstances. My soul,

pause over it this morning. Art thou not, if considered out
of Christ, in perishing circumstances, by reason of the captivity of sin? Art thou not perishing under the sentence of
God's broken law; under the just judgment of God, the
alarms of thine own guilty conscience, the accusations of Satan, the fear of death, and the prospect of judgment and eternity? And doth this sweet scripture hold forth a provision
for such perishing circumstances? Doth it really say, that
such shall come? Nay, that they *shall* come, whatever obstructions, either from within or without, shall block up the
way? Will the Lord enable them, lead them, help them,
nay, constrain them to come, in defiance of all impediments?
Oh! precious, precious Jesus! may the blessing of him that
is ready to perish come upon thee: for thou dost indeed make
the widowed heart, and the sorrowful heart, to sing for joy.
Blessed be thy name, for that thou hast made me willing in
the day of thy power!

13.—Christ hath given himself for us, an offering and a sacrifice to God,
for a sweet smelling savour.—*Eph.* v. 2.

If, when Noah offered by faith his sacrifice at the coming
forth from the ark, the Lord smelled a sweet savour in it, because both the ark and sacrifice was a type of his dear Son;
how fragrant and acceptable must have been the substance,
when Jesus offered himself without spot to God? Behold
him by faith, my soul, in that hour, in the full incense of his
own merit, the censer of his own offering, and the golden
altar of his own nature! And while God, even the everlasting Father, accepts Jesus as thy Surety, in the fragrancy of
his offering, wilt thou not by faith so apprehend the sweet
influence of his person, work, and righteousness, as to rejoice
before God in the sure acceptance of thyself and all thy poor
offerings in the Beloved? Oh, let a throne of grace be a
daily, hourly, testimony for thee, that all thy approaches here
are under the incense and intercession of Jesus; and all thine
hopes and expectations of glory hereafter, are all founded in
him and his finished salvation. Yes! thou Lamb of God!
let all witness for me, that thou, and thou alone, art the Lord
my Righteousness, and that I seek salvation in no other, most
perfectly assured from thine own Spirit's teaching, that there
is no other name under heaven, given among men, whereby
we must be saved. Hallelujah!

14.—And the parched ground shall become a pool, and the thirsty land springs of water.—*Isaiah* xxxv. 7.

OH! how refreshing is this promise to my poor, dry, barren, thirsty soul! Surely every poor sinner like me, that knows his own leanness and poverty, will feel the blessedness of it; for whether he be in the sapless state of unawakened nature, or whether in a scorched or languishing state, from the want of the renewings of grace, nothing can be more refreshing than such a promise. Precious Jesus! do thou revive the languishing frame of thy people; do thou pour water upon him that is thirsty, and floods upon the dry ground. Oh what a fulness, blessed Lord! there is in thyself to supply all. Surely thou art, as the church said, " A fountain of gardens, a well of living waters, and streams from Lebanon." Do thou then, oh Lord, send forth this day, this blessed day, such copious streams from thyself as may cleanse, revive, comfort, satisfy, and strengthen, all thy churches. Lord, cause me to drink of the rivers of thy pleasure; for with thee is the fountain of life.

15.—At our gates are all manner of pleasant fruits, new and old, which I have laid up for thee, O my beloved.—*Song* vii. 13.

YES, blessed Jesus! at the gates of ordinances, and the word of thy gospel, all the pleasant and precious fruits of the Spirit, which come in new and fresh supplies from thee, are indeed laid up. And oh! how sweet and refreshing are they, brought home and laid up in my heart, by thy divine power, when thou enablest me by faith, and in thy leadings and strength, to go forth and bring them home, and to live upon them, and feed upon them, from day to day. And shall I not then blessed Jesus! by the endearing name of my Beloved, call upon thee to command the north wind, and the south wind, to blow upon thy garden in my heart and in my soul, that the spices may flow; and that then my Beloved may come into his garden, and eat of his own pleasant fruits which his grace alone planted, and which his Spirit bringeth forth and ripens.

16.—Thou shalt weep no more: he will be very gracious unto thee at the voice of thy cry; when he shall hear it, he will answer thee.— *Isaiah* xxx. 19.

LISTEN to this, my soul. Ponder over every precious word in it. Are not all tears dried from thine eyes, when behold-

ing that complete salvation in which thou art interested, in
Christ Jesus? Believers are commanded to sorrow no more,
as others without hope. And doth Jesus indeed wait to be
gracious, nay, very gracious? Is it possible to consider, that
He, who hath all power in heaven and in earth, waits upon
a poor worm of the dust, and this in order to be gracious?
Come then, my soul, unto the mercy-seat. Do thou wait for
him who thus waits for thee. And as soon as thy Lord
hath heard, and answered one prayer, do thou follow it up
with another. Remember that he waits to be gracious; and
Jesus is glorified in giving out of his fulness, to supply the
wants of his people. And what petitions, my soul, hast thou
now before the throne? What mercies art thou waiting for?
Lord, help me to know my need, and thy fulness to supply.
Help me to be for ever bartering my poverty for thy riches,
and my sins for thy righteousness: that while thou art coming forth to me in mercy, my soul may be going forth to
meet thee in prayer; and while Jesus is loading me with
benefits, my poor heart may for ever be proclaiming his
praise.

17.—And he was clothed with a vesture dipped in blood.—*Rev.* xix. 13.

Oh, thou bleeding Lamb of God! didst thou thus appear
to thy servant John, to tell him, and the church through him,
that thy priesthood and thy sacrifice are of the same everlasting nature and efficacy as thy person and thy finished
work—the same yesterday, and to-day, and for ever? And
didst thou thus manifest thyself, by way of assuring thy poor
needy follower that thou delightest in thine office, and lovest
to be employed! Was it not, dearest Jesus, to this end, and
as much in effect, as if thou hadst said, See, I wear these
priestly garments: behold my vesture still fresh with the
blood which I offered, in the day of my sacrifice on the cross,
for my redeemed; and for whom I still appear in the bloody
robe, as a proof of its everlasting efficacy. For whom, but
for my people, do I wear this vesture? My soul, art thou
looking now, with an eye of faith, within the veil? Hast thou
a blessing to ask at the court of heaven this day? Fly then
to Jesus. Behold him still as John beheld him, and hear
what he saith. Remember, his blood speaks; for so the
Holy Ghost declares—it speaks better things than that of
Abel; for Abel's blood cried for vengeance: Jesus' pleads for
mercy. And doth it not speak *to* God for pardon; and *from*

God in covenant promises of pardon? Oh, the blessedness to behold Jesus clothed with a vesture dipped in blood, in confirmation that we have redemption through his blood, the forgiveness of sins, according to the riches of his grace.

18.—Good news from a far country.—*Prov.* xxv. 23.

FROM a far country indeed! for it is no less distant than from heaven to earth; and from beings as opposite as holiness and sin could make—even from God to man, from a rich Saviour to poor sinners. And so remote, that had not this good news been sent, heaven must have remained at an eternal distance, as an inaccessible region. And what is the good news itself? The angels who were first sent to proclaim it, called it glad tidings of good things, of great joy to all people. And, indeed, such glad tidings it contains, as language fails to describe. It is pardon, mercy, and peace, to poor rebels. It holds forth joy, happiness, and everlasting felicity, to sinners, enemies, and the fallen race of men. God revealed, sin atoned, Satan conquered, death destroyed, hell vanquished, heaven opened. And these not all. This good news informs also of the stupendous way by which the blessings are given, and everlasting happiness secured. Jesus, the Son of God, the Author, the Finisher, the Source, Cause, Sum, Substance, Beginning, End, and Portion, of all his people. These, among an infinite and endless volume of mercies are contained in the good news from a far country; but we must enter upon that country, to which indeed we are invited by the proclamation of the gospel, before that we shall fully know, or even conceive, the thousandth part of what God hath laid up for them that love him. My soul, hast thou heard this good news? Dost thou know the joyful sound? Art thou truly alive to the blessed things contained in it, and anxious to be interested therein? Oh! then, meditate upon them; give thyself wholly to them. And while men of the world, from the world are seeking their chief good, and asking one another, What news? do thou turn a deaf ear to every other relation of a dying world, from which thou art dying daily, and let thy meditations be all the day, and let thine eyes prevent the night-watches to dwell upon this good news, and this only, which cometh from a far country.

19.—The strength of sin is the law.   But thanks be to God which giveth
   us the victory, through our Lord Jesus Christ.—1 *Cor.* xv. 56, 57.

PAUSE, my soul, over this solemn, but yet sweet verse. The
strength of sin is the law. Does sin derive strength from the
law ? Yes, for the motions of sin, which is in our members,
gathers strength from the precepts in God's holy law, just as
pent up waters, that are increasing from various sources, will
swell and rage the more because they are restrained. And
this is what the Apostle means, when he saith, " Sin, taking
occasion by the commandment, wrought in me all manner of
concupiscence." For the mass of indwelling corruption is
stirred up, and excited into action, by the law. The Lord, in
rich mercy, teaching us by this very process, that so totally
corrupt is our nature, that we do not know the whole workings of sin, until, by the holiness of his commandment, we
are led to see and feel a disposition to break it : like the first
transgressors in the garden of Eden, who lusted to eat of the
forbidden fruit, because it was forbidden. So that the very
precepts of God, by the sin of our nature, become the means
of giving strength to that sin of our nature. The law of
God, in this instance acts upon the heart, as when the gar-
dener's spade uncovers the surface of the earth, and the worms
which before lay concealed, appear. The worms were there
before, but they did not appear before. In like manner, the
law turns up the heart, and then appears the sin which,
though there before, lay undiscovered. Is this thy case, my
soul ? And dost thou still carry about with thee such a body
of sin and death ? Well might Paul call it the mystery of
iniquity. And well might Paul from his deeper knowledge
in the anatomy of the heart, cry out so greatly under the burden of it. Oh ! precious, precious, precious, Lamb of God !
how little understood, and less regarded, even by those that
know somewhat of thee in the riches and greatness of thy
salvation, is it considered, in ten thousand instances which
pass away in the gulph of forgetfulness over our unthinking
minds ? Lord, give me to see and feel, yet more and more,
that in myself I am virtually all sin ! And, Oh Lord, give
me to see and feel, yet more and more, that thou, and thou
alone, art my Righteousness. And let the Apostle's hymn
of praise be henceforth, daily and hourly mine—" Thanks
be to God which giveth us the victory, through our Lord Jesus Christ."

20.—Christ, the Wisdom of God.—1 *Cor.* i. 24.

THINK, my soul, what wisdom is contained in that one word, and that one person, Christ. An whole eternity will not be sufficient to read over the immense volume! Wisdom in planning, wisdom in executing, wisdom in completing, thy great salvation. And what a world of wisdom, in the two natures united in one person—the God-man, the Glory-man, the Wisdom-man, Christ Jesus. And oh! what wisdom in making sin, which strikes at God's sovereignty, the very means of manifesting God's power and love. Such is the wisdom of God in Christ, that sin, which in its nature becomes productive of the greatest dishonour to God, should be rendered subservient to produce the greatest glory. My soul, ponder these things. Then ask thyself, Is there not a wisdom in this vast subject, as far as it concerns thee, yet more wonderful than all? Yes, for surely the greatest of all mysteries in this wonderful volume, to thy view, is, that thou, even thou, shouldest be made the subject for the exercise of such wisdom, as Christ the wisdom of God, and the power of God, for thy salvation. And all this even against thy determined resolution to ruin thyself. Well mayest thou join the apostle in his overwhelming song of praise, and cry out, Oh! the depth of the riches, both of the wisdom and goodness of God!

21.—And righteousness shall be the girdle of his loins, and faithfulness the girdle of his reins.—*Isaiah* xi. 5.

MARK these expressions, my soul, concerning thy Covenant God in Christ. The Lord condescends by them to represent both his righteousness and faithfulness, as they are engaged to make good the purposes of redemption, in the Father and the Son. Jehovah's righteousness, and Jehovah's faithfulness, are blessed securities for this purpose; for so saith the Holy Ghost. God is faithful and just to forgive us our sins. Wherefore? Because Christ is the end of the law for righteousness, to every one that believeth. And do not overlook the striking figure of the girdle which is chosen to represent it by: for as a man binds on the girdle round his loins as a strengthener, so Jehovah takes to himself the righteousness of his dear Son. Let him take hold, saith Jehovah, of my strength, to make peace with me, and he shall make peace with me, Isaiah xxvii. 5. This is the girdle of Jeho-

vah, which compasseth him about, and cleaveth to him all
around. So that his people, whether they are behind or before, may lay hold of the girdle of his perfections, and hang
upon them, and depend upon them: and even when God's
providences seem to frown, or the Lord seemeth to have
turned his back upon them. Oh for grace and faith both in
Jehovah's covenant faithfulness, and Christ's righteousness,
thus to trust, and thus to stay ; for he is faithful that hath promised.

22.—Come, buy wine and milk, without money, and without price.—
Isaiah lv. 1.

SURELY no man can plead poverty as an excuse for not
buying, when the things sold are not only without money,
but without even the proposals for money: not only without
ready money, but without any money. Here is not even a
price given. My soul, remember this. The poorer the
wretch, the more welcome to this market. But what are
the things sold ? Both wine and milk. A blessed variety
in the gospel feast—wine to cheer, and milk to nourish.
Yes, blessed Jesus, thy love is better than wine ; and thy salvation more healing than milk. Besides, it comes free, it
comes pure, it comes in plenty. And it far, very far, exceeds
the strongest wine, and the richest milk. For though wine
may remove a temporary heaviness, yet it was never known
to raise the dead. But thy love, blessed Jesus ! hath raised,
and will keep alive for ever, sinners dead in trespasses and
sins, and preserve the languishing graces of thy saints.
Come then, my soul, obey the gospel-invitation this day, and
every day ; come, buy these precious things without money,
and without price. Come, ye poor, needy, perishing sinners ;
come, every one of you, and buy—there is enough in Jesus
for us all. And depend upon it, not one of you will be sent
empty away, if you come empty to be filled, and hungering
to be satisfied. This is the only mark and evidence of every
real purchaser. If Jesus, with all his blessings, be welcome
to your heart, you are welcome to take of his free salvation.
Lord ! I am come this day, and every day. Now let me
hear thy voice: " Eat, O friends ! drink ; yea, drink abundantly, O beloved."

23.—If the Lord were pleased to kill us, he would not have received a burnt-offering and a meat-offering at our hands; neither would he have shewed us all these things.—*Judges* xiii. 23.

PRECIOUS faith this of the wife of Manoah, and sound and conclusive reasoning. My soul, hath the Father, who gave thee Jesus for a Saviour, accepted thee in Jesus? Hath the Father, who sent his dear Son to be the Saviour of the world, accepted Jesus for thy Saviour? Hath the Holy Ghost showed thee the glorious things of redemption in his blood, the forgiveness of sins according to the riches of his grace? And hath he given thee to believe in the record, that God hath given eternal life, and that this life is in his Son? Oh! then say, with the wife of Manoah, Surely the Lord would never have done all this, neither would he have showed me all these things, had he not intended my salvation! Treasure up, then, these past tokens of favour: consider present evidences of mercy, and say, Is not Jesus still precious? Are not my desires after him? And small as you sometimes think your hope, yet would you, my soul, relinquish it for a thousand worlds? Oh, then, my soul, hang upon Jesus, cleave to Jesus, hold fast on Jesus. Never would the Lord have showed me the beauty, glory, fulness, suitableness, and all-sufficiency of Jesus, nor enabled my soul to hold up Jesus in the arms of my faith for acceptance, if the Lord had been pleased to kill me.

24.—Behold I send an angel before thee, to keep thee in the way, and to bring thee into the place which I have prepared. Beware of him, and obey his voice, for my name is in him.—*Exod.* xxiii. 20, 21.

WHO can this be, my soul, but Jesus? He, and he only, who is the whole of the covenant, is also the Messenger, and the Angel of the covenant. Jehovah hath never put his name in any other; neither given his honour to any other. But in Jesus he is eternally well pleased, and hath given all things into his hand. Pause then, my soul, and contemplate this holy, this blessed, this only begotten of the Father, full of grace and truth. I see in Him all the glory, the sovereignty, the wisdom, grace, and goodness, of the Father. And he is Jehovah's salvation to the ends of the earth. And wilt thou then, my gracious God and Father, send Jesus before me in all my way, to keep me, to guide me, and to bring me in, to behold thy glory in the face of Jesus Christ, and to dwell with thee for ever? Oh! Lord Jesus! I would desire

grace so to beware of thee, so to love thee, so to obey thee, so
to adore thee, so to make thee my all in all, my life, my love,
my joy, my present, my everlasting hope and portion, that in
life, and death, in time, and to all eternity, Jesus may be my
glory and salvation for ever and ever.

25.—Once have I sworn by my holiness, that I will not lie unto David.—
Psalm lxxxix. 35.

WONDERFUL condescension. Was it not enough that Jehovah gave his Son to poor sinners; gave his word, his promise, that all that believe in him should not perish, but have
everlasting life? But as if consulting the weakness of our
faith, confirmed it with an oath: pledged his holiness to Jesus,
and to poor sinners in Jesus, for the sure accomplishment of
all covenant engagements, in the blood and righteousness of
his dear Son. Oh, my soul, never, never more call in question the truth of thy gracious God. Say with Job, " Though
he slay me, yet will I trust in him." What are afflictions,
trials, darkness, poverty? These are in me, and about me,
but no obstructions to the efficacy of Jesus' righteousness, or
the Father's faithfulness. Read under every one of them the
charter of rich sovereign grace; hear what God hath said,
what God hath sworn; and believe the record that God hath
given of his dear Son:—Men shall be blessed in him. Jesus
shall see the travail of his soul, and be satisfied. Here then
rest, my soul! God hath sworn once by his holiness: Jesus
hath once died, the Just for the unjust, to bring sinners unto
God. Return to thy rest; the Lord hath dealt, my soul,
bountifully by thee.

26.—And it shall come to pass, that every thing that liveth, which
moveth whithersoever the rivers shall come, shall live.—*Ezek.* xlvii. 9.

LISTEN to this promise, my soul, and make it the subject
of this morning's meditation, of this day, and every day.
See how rich, how extensive, it is in the life-promising power.
And the river of life in Jesus possesseth all these blessed
effects. To every poor sinner, brought into this rich stream,
it gives life, spiritual life, eternal life. And who shall describe the length, the breadth, the heights, the depths, of it?
Not only extending over all the continent of the earth, but
from the borders of hell to heaven, and from one eternity to
another. And its sovereignty is such, that it bears down all

before it—washing away sin, and guilt, and misery; diffusing streams of life, and grace, and mercy; opening sources of joy, and peace, and happiness, for ever and for ever. Oh, precious, precious Jesus! make glad my soul with the streams of this river: be thou the fountain of all my happiness, and let all my springs be in thee.

27.—For lo, I will command, and I will sift the house of Israel among all nations, like as corn is sifted in a sieve, yet shall not the least grain fall to the earth.—*Amos* ix. 9.

BLESSED promise to my poor soul, sifted and blown about by temptation! Look then to Jesus with it, and plead it under every new sifting time. Corn must be sifted, for it is much covered at times with tares and chaff. And so must the seed of Jesus, that the precious may be known and separated; for what is the chaff to the wheat, saith the Lord? Oh, Lord! if it please thee, for thou knowest the necessity of it, sift me, try me, separate me, not only from the ungodly, with whom I am constrained to dwell, but from myself, from my own trifling, vain conversation, from the corruption of the indwelling sin in my fallen nature, from the vain thoughts which lodge within me. Yes, precious Jesus! sift all and every thing which is unsuitable to thee, and let the whole fall through the sieve, that thou alone mayest remain with me: for sure I know my God hath said, though his Israel be sifted, yet not the least grain of the true wheat shall be lost.

28.—For, when we were yet without strength, in due time Christ died for the ungodly.—*Romans* v. 6.

MY soul! fold up this sweet and precious scripture, and carry it about with thee in thy bosom, and in thine heart, that it may help thee on at any time, and at all times, when thy strength seems gone, and there is no power left. Was it not when the whole nature of man was without strength, that Christ was given of the Father? And was it not equally so, when Christ came to seek and save that which was lost? And was it not in due time, when Christ died for the ungodly? due time in his resurrection, due time in his ascension, when he ascended up on high, led captivity captive, and received gifts for men, yea, even for the rebellious, that the Lord God might dwell among them? Go further yet, my

25*

soul, as it concerns thyself—Was it not due time indeed, when Jesus passed by, and saw thee in thy loathsome state of sin, cast out to perish, and when no eye pitied thee, that then his eye compassioned thee, and bid thee live? Who more ungodly than thee? Who more weak? Who more undeserving? Did Jesus then look upon thee, call thee, strengthen thee when thou wast without strength, and hath helped thee to this hour? Oh, then, trust him now, trust him for ever. His strength is made perfect in thy weakness. And depend upon it, when thou art most weak in thyself, then is the hour to be most strong in the Lord, and in the power of his might. He that in due time died for the ungodly, will be thy strength in the time of need.

29.—Until the day break, and the shadows flee away, I will get me to the mountains of myrrh, and to the hills of frankincense.—*Song* iv. 6.

METHINKS I would have every poor sinner, until the day-dawn of awakening grace breaks in upon his soul, get away to the ordinances of God in the mountain of the Lord's house: there he should live, there wait, until the Lord speaks to his soul. And methinks I would have every poor sinner that is awakened, until the day of glory breaks in with an everlasting light upon him, get away to the gospel mountain, where the odour of Jesus' incense, and the savour of his blood and righteousness, become sweeter than myrrh, and more fragrant than frankincense. Here, Lord, cause me to get away from all surrounding impediments, and to be constantly found waiting, that my soul may drink in the fresh, reviving, renewing streams, until Jesus himself, the Morning Star, breaks in upon my soul, to lead me home to his everlasting glory, in his bosom for ever.

30.—It is high time to awake out of sleep; for now is our salvation nearer than when we believed.—*Romans* xiii. 11.

SOLEMN consideration! What time is it with thee, my soul? Let me ask with the prophet, Watchman, what of the night? The morning cometh, and also the night. Perhaps there may be but a step between me and death. Am I really awakened from the sleep of carnal security? Am I alive from spiritual death? Am I dead to the world, but alive unto God through Jesus Christ our Lord? Oh, Lord Jesus! impress these solemn inquiries upon my soul yet more and more: since everlasting happiness, or everlasting misery, hangs upon the decision. My beating pulse is hastening to fulfil the appointed number. Even while I think of these things the account is increased. Every fleeting breath is one the less to take. Lord, make me wise to remember my latter end.

DECEMBER.

1.—Praise waiteth for thee, O God, in Zion.—*Psalm* lv. 1.

Is this the language of my heart? Am I indeed waiting until that Jesus be ready to receive my poor praise? Hath God the Holy Ghost prepared my heart? Oh, then, hasten to him, my soul, with thy morning offerings, poor as they are; for sure I am, Jesus is waiting to be gracious. God will accept both thee and thy offering in him the Beloved! Go forth to meet him as early and as often as thine heart can wish: depend upon it, thy Redeemer will be beforehand with thee, and is waiting thy coming. Neither thy praise nor thy prayer can outrun his love; for both are the blessed effects of his grace, and of his own quickenings. Precious Jesus! grant me to come as often as I need thee. And, Lord! if thou wilt grant me this blessing, I shall never be from thee, for I need thee every moment.

2.—It is written in the prophets, And they shall be all taught of God. Every one therefore that hath heard, and hath learned of the Father, cometh unto me.—*John* vi. 45.

MARK, my soul, these precious words of thy Jesus. It was one of the Old Testament promises, that all God's children should be taught of him. And as this condescension of God, in teaching, implied the Father, so the blessed consequence and effect of it should be, that every one thus taught proved his being a child, and inclined his heart to come to God in Christ as a Father. My soul, art thou come? Art thou looking to, leaning upon, trusting in, walking with, and seeking for, Jesus? Is he the Lord thy Righteousness, thine only righteousness: thine only hope, thine only confidence? Dost thou, like the Apostle, count all things else but dung and dross to win Christ, and to be found in him? Courage then, my soul! These are blessed tokens of thine adoption-character. None but God the Father, by his Holy Spirit, could have taught thee these things. None but He that revealed his Son in the heart of the Apostle, could have been thy Teacher. Thou hast both heard and learned of the Father; and, in proof thereof, thou art come to Christ for life and salvation. Fold up, then, this precious scripture in thy bosom for thy daily use, and examine thine interest in Christ continually, by a mark so sure and infallible. And remember what the Lord Jesus hath said, as a collateral testimony to the same blessed truth: all that the Father giveth me (saith Jesus) shall come to me: and him that cometh I will in no wise cast out.

3.—Whether our brethren be inquired of, they are the messengers of the churches, and the glory of Christ.—2 *Cor.* viii. 28

WHAT a blessed account is here given of the children of God to all inquiries concerning them. See, my soul! whether thy experience corresponds to it, and mark their character. They are not only brethren to one another, but to Christ also: for we are told that he is not ashamed to call them brethren. Precious condescending Saviour! Moreover, they are the messengers of the churches. What is that? A messenger, in scripture, is called also an Angel. And if the brethren of Jesus do know, and can speak of him as his people should, then are they like angels come down from the court of heaven, to relate what they have seen and know of the king in his beauty, and their hearts glow with a warmth of earnestness to proclaim his glory, and his love to poor sinful creatures here below. Neither is this all. For they are the glory of Christ. Mark this, my soul, and dwell with rapture upon it. A true believer in Jesus is the glory of Jesus. Not only because he gives glory to the Redeemer for his grace, but because Jesus derives glory from his redemption. Not only because the poor sinner hath everlasting happiness from Jesus; but Jesus hath everlasting glory from that poor sinner's salvation. Never lose sight of this, my soul, when thou goest to Jesus. Indeed, indeed, Jesus is glorified in receiving thee, in pardoning thee, in blessing thee, in giving to thee of his fulness. And the

Father is glorified in this great salvation by his Son. Oh! what encouragement is this to faith; what inducement to come to Jesus. Lord! how ought I to blush when I think how little glory I give to thee in not seeing that thy church and thy people are thy glory, in being saved and redeemed by thee!

4.—Come, see the place where the Lord lay.—*Matt.* xxviii. 6.

LORD! I would desire grace to accept the call, for it is always profitable to have faith in lively exercise. I would pray that my meditation might frequently take wing, and view the memorable sepulchre of my Lord. Did Jesus once lay in the grave? Surely death never had such a prisoner before! But did Jesus lay so low for me? Am I shortly to lay there? Sweet consoling thought! The grave is now softened, and the chambers of death are perfumed with the fragrancy contracted from his holy incorruptible body.—But is there not another place where the Lord lay? And doth not the Angel invite his people to see him there are also? Yes! Jesus lay in the bosom of the Father from all eternity. And doth he not lay there now, and will he not through all eternity? But can I see him there? Yes. For if by faith I behold Jesus as the Christ, the sent, the sealed of the Father; in seeing him, I see the Father also. He saith this himself, John xiv. 9. And again, John xiv. 20. At that day ye shall know that I am in my Father, and you in me, and I in you. Blessed assurance. Jesus is one with the Father: and all his people one with him. And as he is in the bosom of the Father, so are they in his, and there shall dwell for ever and ever. Hallelujah. Amen.

5.—It pleased the Father to bruise him: he hath put him to grief.—
Isaiah liii. 10.

THE depths of wisdom were explored to furnish redemption, and to find a Person competent to accomplish it. And when found, the depths of love were broken up, to make it complete. My soul, read over the mysterious volume which the Lord hath in part opened before thee. It cost the Father his thoughts from all eternity, to appoint a plan by which, consistent with his holiness and his justice, thou mightest be saved. It cost the Father his Son, his dear Son, his only Son, before that thou couldest be redeemed. Jesus must die

ere thou canst live. Pause over the subject as it is here expressed. It pleased the Father to bruise him. Jesus, who
was in himself holy, harmless, undefiled, separate from sinners, and made higher than the heavens ; he, who knew no
sin, must be made sin ; he, who never merited wrath, must
be made a curse. Read on ; Jesus must die—And by whom ?
Not by Jews, nor Gentiles only : not simply by high-priests,
and governors among men : but by God the Father. He
must bruise him, and put him to grief. For though Jesus
was taken, and by wicked hands crucified and slain, yet all
this, we are told, was by the determinate counsel and fore-
knowledge of God. And is there yet another chapter of
wonder in this mysterious volume ? Yes ! what can it be ?
Namely, that all this was for sinners, for rebels, for enemies ;
nay, my soul, for *thee !* Wonder, O heavens, and be astonished, O earth ! Had our whole nature been bruised to all
eternity in the mortar of divine wrath, for the sin of our nature, what would all this have been to the sufferings, agonies,
and death, of the Lamb of God ? And didst thou die for
me, oh thou unequalled pattern of love and mercy ; and by
thy stripes is my soul healed ! Precious Jesus !

6.—If ye ask any thing in my name, I will do it.—*John* xiv. 14.

Is it so, blessed Jesus, that if I go to the Father in thy
precious name, my petitions shall be certainly heard, and answered ? Lo, then I come. I feel my faith and confidence
imboldened in this gracious assurance. And as thou knowest, Lord, this day, what is most suited for me, let thy wisdom choose, and let thy love bestow, that very grace and
mercy, be it what it may. And let a throne of grace witness
for me, that I seek it wholly on Christ's account. I consider
it as good as given, from the high love my God and Father
bears towards his dear Son, as my Surety and Saviour. And
although in the moment that I ask with this boldness of faith,
I see and know in myself, that I have nothing to recommend
me to thy favour, as in the least meriting that favour, but
much, very much, to make me an object in meriting thy displeasure : yet looking up in Jesus, depending upon his blood
and righteousness, and wholly asking in his name, and for
his righteousness' sake only, I am encouraged to hope that I
shall not ask in vain. Oh, then, Lord ! hear for Jesus' sake,
and let my petition and prayer be answered, that the Father
may be glorified in his Son.

7.—And we know and have believed the love that God hath to us.—
1 *John* iv. 16.

Who hath known and believed in terms equal to the greatness of the mercy itself, the love of God to the poor sinner?
God's love must be an infinite love, and consequently the display of it must be infinite also. God, we are told, commendeth his love to us, in that while we were yet sinners, Christ
died for us. Had God loved and delighted in saints that
loved him, this would have been love. Had God taken the
holy angels into a nearer acquaintance with him, this would
have been love. But when he raised beggars from the dunghill, and took rebels from the prison to sit upon his throne;
and at a time when his justice would have been magnified in
their destruction, to prefer sinners, haters of God, and despisers of his grace; to bring them into the closet and nearest
connexion with him, in the Person of his dear Son, and all
this by such a wonderful plan of mercy as the incarnation
and death of Jesus—who hath ever calculated the extent of
such grace? Who hath thoroughly known, or considered,
or believed, in any degree proportioned to the unspeakable-
ness of the salvation, the love that God hath to us? Oh!
Lord! add one blessing more. Cause my cold heart to grow
warm in the contemplation of it: and let it be my happiness
to be daily studying the breadth, and length, and depth and
height, and to know the love of God, which passeth knowledge, that I may be filled with all the fulness of God.

8.—Gad, a troop shall overcome him : but he shall overcome at the last.—
Gen. xlix. 19.

Is there nothing, my soul, in this sweet promise, that suits
thy case and circumstances? Was not Gad one of the children of Israel? And are not all the seed of Israel interested
in the promises? Was the tribe of Gad for a time brought
down, and brought under, by a troop of foes? And are not
all the seed of Israel oppressed and brought into subjection?
Was not that glorious Israelite, the great Captain of our salvation, made perfect through sufferings? Think, my soul,
what troops of hell assaulted him! But was the issue of the
battle with him doubtful? Neither is it now. In his blood
and righteousness, all the seed of Israel shall be justified and
overcome by the blood of the Lamb. What then, though
there be troops of lusts within, and legions of foes without:
troops from earth, and troops from Hell, may, and will, as-

sault thee! but look unto Jesus, It is said of his people of old, that they had an eye unto him, and were enlightened, and their faces were not ashamed. So now, Jesus undertakes for thee, and for thy faith. He saith, I will be an enemy to thine enemies, and an adversary to thine adversaries. God the Father is looking on: angels are beholding: all heaven is interested. Nay, hadst thou but eyes to see, thou wouldest behold, like the Prophet's servant, mountains around thee, full of horses and chariots of fire, all engaged for thy defence. Shout, then, for the battle is already obtained by Jesus for all his people. Though a troop may overcome the Gadites of the Lord, yet shall they overcome at the last. Thanks be to God who giveth us the victory through our Lord Jesus Christ.

9.—-For he said, Surely they are my people, children that will not lie: so he was their Saviour.—*Isaiah* lxiii. 8.

OH! what a tenderness of expression is contained in these words! Jesus not only takes his people into relationship with him, but undertakes for their faithfulness. In the birth of God's everlasting purpose, this was done from everlasting: so that in one and the same moment, we are his people, his children, his brethren, his wife, his redeemed, his fair one, made comely in his comeliness, and in his blood cleansed, and in his righteousness justified, before God. And observe, my soul, the grounds of this relationship: Surely, he saith, they are my people. Not only as God's workmanship and property, but as his purchase. Not only in first giving them being, but in giving them new being in Christ Jesus. The Lord hath taken them into covenant with him in Christ, and granted them a charter of grace and salvation in Jesus. Sweet and precious thought! God the Father, whose right they are by creation, hath given them to his Son. And Jesus hath made them his, both by his own purchase, and the conquests of his grace: therefore he hath an interest in them, and in all that concerns them. Surely, saith Jesus, they are my people, my jewels, my treasure, my hidden ones. And observe further, how he speaks *for* them as well as *of* them : They will not lie. How is this? Why, they are children of the covenant. And because he hath undertaken for them, therefore he was their Saviour ! Oh! the preciousness of such a Saviour, to every circumstance, to every state, in every way, and upon every occasion in life, in death, in time, and to all eternity. Jesus! thou art indeed a Saviour! thou art truly called Jesus, for thou hast saved, and thou wilt save, thy people from their sins.

10.—But there the glorious Lord will be unto us a place of broad rivers and streams; wherein shall go no galley with oars, neither shall gallant ship pass thereby.—*Isaiah* xxxiii. 21.

SEE, my soul! how thy God condescends to represent himself ·to thee as thy God, under various similitudes, so as to strengthen thy faith and thy confidence in him. He that is thy gracious Lord, is also thy glorious Lord; for he is both a Sun and a Shield: and he that gives grace, will give glory; one is the earnest of the other. Well, then, this glorious Lord will be there. Where? Why in Jesus, in *thy* Jesus, God in covenant with him: he will be unto thee a place of broad rivers and streams. What is that? Why, us Jerusalem had no navigable rivers or seas, to defend her from the approach of enemies all around, so God's people are unprotected by nature, or by art, and lie open to their foes. But what they want in nature, shall be abundantly made up to them in grace. And as they have no art nor contrivance in themselves, God's wisdom and love will provide true counsel for them. Since they have no sea for their frontier, God in covenant love will himself be their sea, their ocean, their bulwark. And what galley or ship shall pass God to attack his people? Surely none can. And observe, my soul, as God himself will be rivers, and broad rivers too, to defend, so will he be streams to provide, and full streams to provide plentifully all possible blessings. Hallelujah. Shout, my soul, as the church of old, and say, A Fountain of gardens, a Well of living waters, and Streams from Lebanon, is my Beloved!

11.—And he shall sit as a refiner and purifier of silver. And he shall purify the sons of Levi, and purge them as gold and silver, that they may offer unto the Lord an offering in righteousness.—*Malachi* iii. 3.

MY soul, contemplate this gracious office of thy Jesus, and then see, whether he hath as graciously wrought it on thee. Jesus found our whole nature, when he came to save it, wanting refining and purifying indeed. By the operation of his holy word, and by the influences of his blessed Spirit, he brings the souls of his people into the furnace of purification. By the fire of troubles, of afflictions, of persecutions, he melts down their stubborn nature there. By the Spirit of judgment, and by the Spirit of burning, he purgeth their dross, taketh away their tin, and forms all his people into vessels of mercy and sanctification, that he may at length present them unto himself, a glorious church, not having spot or wrinkle, or any such thing; but that they may be without blame before him in love. And what endears him to his people under this blessed character as their Refiner, is this, that all the while the process is going on, Jesus sits by, watches over them, tempers the fire in exact proportion to what it should be, and suffers not the enemy to fan it a jot more than his love and wisdom see it fit to be. Is this the case, my soul, with thee? Are all the fiery trials thou hast gone through regulated, kept under, and blessed, by thy Jesus, to so much good? Oh! my foolish heart! how have I repined in my affliction, because I saw not Jesus' hand in the appointment, nor discerned his love carrying me through it. Blessed Refiner! henceforth give me to see thee. And do thou sit in this most needful office over my soul, that as all true believers are of the royal priesthood, being sons of Levi, and made kings and priests to God and the Father, never may my soul come out of the furnace of thy purification, until that I am enabled, by thy grace, to offer to the Lord an offering in the blood and righteousness of Jesus, whereby alone I can find acceptance with God in grace here, and glory hereafter.

12.—Take this, and divide it amongst it yourselves.—*Luke* xxii. 17.

PRECIOUS Lord! such was thine unbounded love to thy people, that thou gavest all to them! And, dearest Jesus, what didst thou reserve for thyself? And how wise was thy love manifested. To every one grace according to the measure of the gift of Christ; for the purchase of redemption, in the case of all, cost thee the same. If, indeed, a lamb of thine be weak, or diseased, or torn, or scattered, thou wilt take it to thy bosom, while thou wilt gently lead those that are with young. But every one, and all, shall have thy care: all, as their several wants may be. Here, then, Lord, to thy table I would come. Thy death hath confirmed all thy purchased blessings. And in thy holy Supper I would seek grace, that my right may be confirmed in them. Before God, and angels, and men, I would take the seal of thy gift. In thy blood thou hast signed them: in the word of thy gospel thou hast recorded them: in the ordinances of thy church they are published and brought forth: and by thy Spirit thou givest the tokens and the pledges of them to thy redeemed. Witness for me, then, ye angels of light, that I accept of all in Jesus and in his free gift, the purchase of his blood, and the tokens of his love. Sweeter are they to my mouth than honey and the honey-comb. Blessed Jesus! thy love is better than wine!

13.—The Tree of Life.—*Revelation* xxii. 2.

LEAD me, oh Holy Ghost, by the hand of faith, this morning into the paradise of God, and cause me to sit down under the tree of life; and for a while, before the world breaks in upon me, enable me to meditate on its beauties, its loveliness, and its fruit. Is it not Jesus which I behold in this charming similitude? Surely Jesus is to me the Tree of life, for I have no life but in him! And it is not only he which gave me life at the first, but preserves it, maintains it, and will preserve it for ever. He saith himself, Because I live, ye shall live also. And as he is himself the life of my soul, so every thing in him is the promoter of my life. His fruit also is all my sustenance, all I want, all I desire, all I can truly enjoy. He bears twelve manner of fruits. Yes! for there is in him both fulness and variety: pardon, mercy, and peace, in the blood of his cross; favour with God, affection with men; the Spirit's gifts, graces, influences; comfort in this life, happiness and joy in that which is to come. And every month these fruits abound. Yes! He saith himself, My fruit is better than gold, yea, than fine gold: and my revenue than choice silver. I will cause them that love me to inherit substance; yea, I will fill all their treasures. Nay, the very leaves of this tree of life are for the healing of the nations. And how healing indeed is Jesus, in his word, his ordinances, his providences, his promises, his dispensations? Neither is this all: the tree of life grows in the midst of the street, and is open in every gospel-ordinance, both to Jews and Gentiles, both to bond and free. He is also on either side of the river. The church above, though sitting under the full enjoyment of him, doth not keep him wholly to herself. Blessed be his name, he is as much for the glory and happiness of his church here below, on this side of the river of death. And is this Tree of life, this Jesus, mine? Oh! the vast privilege! I bless thee, oh, thou Holy Spirit, for giving me the knowledge of him now by faith: and ere long, I hope to sit down for ever in the paradise of God, in the unceasing enjoyment of him, from whence I shall arise no more, but dwell under his branches for ever.

14.—Nevertheless, he saved them for his name's sake, that he might make his mighty power to be known.—*Psalm* cvi. 8.

PAUSE, my soul, over this verse, and observe how thy gracious God took occasion, from the misery of Israel, and even from their unworthiness, to magnify the riches of his grace. Israel had highly sinned : they had provoked the Lord ; and their provocations were aggravated from the spot where they were committed, for it was at the sea, even at the Red Sea, that memorable sea where the Lord had made a path for their deliverance. And wherefore then did he save them? Wherefore did not the Lord drown them in the depths of the sea, for their unbelief and hardness of heart? This sweet scripture gives the reason. He saved them for his name's sake. His name was engaged in covenant-promises. And his glory was magnified in making good his engagements, notwithstanding all their undeservings. And what saith this doctrine to thee, my soul? There is a *nevertheless* with thee also, from God's covenant engagements *in* Christ, and *to* Christ, thy glorious covenant-head, notwithstanding all thy unworthiness and provocations. Though I fail in all, God's covenant fails in none. Though my unbelief breaks out like Israel's, even at the red sea of Christ's blood ; yet the efficacy of that blood is still the same, and the Father's engagement to his dear Son, by virtue of it, never can fail. His own love is the standard of his grace, and not my deservings. His name's sake, and not my merit, the rule of his favour towards his people ; and all in Jesus. Fold up, then, this blessed scripture, my soul, for thy daily meditation, and learn to bless the freeness of that grace, which hath for its object the glory of God's name, and no motive for thy salvation, but God's glory in Christ Jesus.

15.— Knowing that tribulation worketh patience.—*Romans* v. 3.

HAVE former trials been blessed to thee, my soul? Why then, depend upon it, this, be it what it may, will be also. The covenant love and faithfulness of God in Christ, are both the same now, as they ever were. If the Lord hath hitherto been making all things work together for good, so will he now. Only pause and consider why it must be so. Thy

God is the same God as ever: is he not? And his love to
thee the same, because it is in Jesus. His covenant the same.
His promises the same. The blood and righteousness of the
Lord Jesus in efficacy the same. Well then, as all the perfections of God are engaged for God's people, certain it is,
that no trial to his people can arise which he knew not, nay,
which he appointed not, and for which he hath not made a
suitable provision. Well then, what trouble of thine can be
so great, as to counteract and overcome divine strength?
What burthen so heavy that Jesus cannot bear? What afflictions so painful that Jesus cannot soften? What grief so
scorching, as to dry up the streams of God's love? Hear
then his words: *In your patience possess ye your souls.* My
soul, rest in this. Let past experience bring thee present
confidence. See that all thy fresh springs of patience flow
from Jesus. Wait patiently for the Lord, by believing in
him. And depend upon it, thy present tribulation, of what
sort or kind soever it is, will terminate, like every former, in
bringing glory to God, and comfort to thy soul.

16.—He that is surety for a stranger shall smart for it ; and he that
hateth suretiship is sure.—*Prov.* xi. 15.

BLESSED Jesus! well is it for me, that thou didst not hate
to become a Surety. For hadst thou so done, and refused
the vast undertaking, I must have perished for ever. And
hadst thou consented to have become a Surety only for friends,
and those only that loved thee, still here again I should have
been lost. But when thou condescendest to become a Surety
for me, oh Lord! it was not simply for a stranger, but for a
rebel, a hater and despiser of thee, and of thy great salvation.
Oh the love of God that passeth knowledge! And how,
blessed Jesus, didst thou indeed smart, and wert crushed and
broken, when for my dreadful debt of sin, which surpassed
all the angels of light to pay, it pleased the Father to bruise
thee, and to put thee to grief. Oh matchless love of a most
compassionate Saviour! Methinks I see thee taking my
place under the angry eye of God's broken law. Methinks
I see thee striking my worthless name out of the bond of the
covenant of the law of works, and putting thine own in.
Methinks I still hear thee, like another Judah, who in this
was evidently thy type, saying to God and the Father, I will
be Surety for him: at my hands thou shalt require him. Oh
Lamb of God! I bless thee as my Surety. I acknowledge

thee as my glorious Sponsor. I was a stranger indeed, and thou hast owned me, and brought me home. I was in debt, and insolvent, and thou hast cancelled the whole in the blood of thy cross. I was naked, and thou hast clothed: sick and in prison, and thou hast visited, healed me, and brought me out. I was lost, and thou hast redeemed and saved me. Oh what shall I render unto the Lord, for all the benefits he hath done unto me? Bless the Lord, oh my soul! and all that is within me, bless his holy name.

17.—Fear not; I have the keys of hell and of death.—*Rev.* i. 17, 18.

Is it Jesus, all precious, all lovely, all powerful Jesus, saith this? He who hath redeemed my soul from hell, mine eyes from tears, and my feet from falling? And hath Jesus, my Husband, my Brother, my Redeemer, the keys both of hell and of death? Why then it is impossible for any to open death's door, one moment before that he give the appointment. And doth he command me to fear not? Oh, then, my soul! dismiss all anxiety about thy departure. Thy time is in Jesus' hands. The keys are hanging at thy Redeemer's girdle. Never fear neither, to die as thou hast lived, and art living, in a believing frame in Jesus. This is as much suited to a dying time, as it is to a living time; for with this thou mayest go out of the world, as safe as living in it. To live is Christ, and to die is gain. God's covenant love, and God's covenant promises in Jesus, are the same. They are both in death and life, fixed and sure. When Jesus therefore comes, when the Master calls for thee, wilt thou feel reluctant? What! reluctant to go to Jesus? Is this thy love, thy kindness, to thy friend? Forbid it, dearest Lord. No! my precious, blessed Jesus! open the gate of death to me *when* thou pleasest, *where* thou pleasest, and *how* thou pleasest. Sure I am thou wilt be present, and that's enough for me. And when the ground of all sensible comforts is sinking under me, oh for a vigorous effort of faith, communicated by thee, that I may drop the body, and leap at once into thy arms, with the last cry of faith, Lord Jesus receive my Spirit, for thou hast redeemed me, O Lord, thou God of truth!

18.—For through him we both have access by one Spirit unto the Father.—*Ephes.* ii. 18.

Who would have thought that so short a verse should contain so much sweetness? And who would have conceived

that in it the gracious offices of all the Persons of the Godhead, as they are mercifully exercised towards a poor sinner,
are described? Is not the access to a throne of grace, the
work, the leading of God the Holy Ghost? Surely, he is
the Spirit here spoken of. And through whom can a poor
sinner have access to the mercy-seat, but in Him, and by
Him, and through Him, whom the Father heareth always?
And to whom should the regenerated adopted child of God
have access, but unto his God and Father in Christ Jesus?
Are then all the glorious Persons of the Godhead thus revealed, as engaged in every poor sinner's approach to the
heavenly throne? Oh for grace to give to each, and to all,
the praise, and glory, and love, due to such transcendent
mercy; and in a conscious sense of being interested in
this great salvation, to cry out with the Apostle. Now
thanks be unto God, who always causeth us to triumph in
Christ.

19.—God is faithful, by whom we were called unto the fellowship of his
Son Jesus Christ.—1 *Cor.* i. 9.

THINK, my soul, what a dignity believers in Jesus are
called unto, when brought into a nearness of communion
with their glorious Head, in any exercise of trials or affliction for his sake. God is faithful in the appointment. How?
In that it proves God's fulfilment of his covenant promises,
when Jesus and his members are considered by him as one.
God is faithful in manifesting this oneness and fellowship, in
making the members conformable to their glorious Head, by
trials or sufferings. God is faithful in sending the affliction.
And God manifests his faithfulness in guiding through it,
and supporting under it. The trial itself, be it what it may,
is a discovery of the covenant love and faithfulness of Jehovah. Nay, God would not have manifested his faithfulness
to a believer without it What a sweet consoling thought
this is to the afflicted exercised followers of the Lamb, under
their trials! My soul! do thou look at the subject, and learn
from it to consider all tribulations in this view, and what a
blessedness will pour in upon thee from so doing. Hath the
Lord called thee to exercises? Hath the progress of them
led thee more to Jesus? Hath the issue of them tended to
endear Jesus? Oh, then, proclaim God's faithfulness! I
know, Lord, (said one of old under trials,) that thy judgments are right, and that thou in very faithfulness hast af-

flicted me. Precious Jesus! what a dignified path is tribulation, when we are enabled to see thy footsteps going before,
marked with blood.

20.—The blood of Jesus Christ his Son cleanseth us from all sin.—
1 *John* i. 7.

My Soul, sit down for a while by this crimson fountain,
and duly ponder over this glorious property of thy Redeemer's blood. Oh, the sovereign efficacy of it! For it not
only cleanseth sin, but all sin : not only others' sins, but our
sins : not only the present evil of sin, but the everlasting evil
of it : not only now, but for ever. It cleanseth from all sin.
Pause, my soul! Is there any other laver to wash away sin ?
Can prayers, or tears, or repentance, or ordinances, or com-
munions, or duties, or alms ? Oh no. We must say of
every thing, and of all things, out of Christ, and void of
Christ, as Job did concerning his friends, Miserable comforters
are ye all ; physicians of no value. Here then, my soul,
seek thy cleansing, and here only. And while to this fountain thou art daily brought by the Holy Ghost, look up and
behold the whole assembly of the redeemed above, who are
now standing around the throne, owing their bliss and their
cleansing to the same source. Listen to their songs of joy,
and catch the notes, to sing even now the same song of rejoicing. They have washed their robes, and made them
white in the blood of the Lamb. And *therefore* it is, and for
no other cause, that they are now before the throne, and
serve the Lord in his temple day and night.

21.—Then I restored that which I took not away.—*Psalm* lxix. 4.

Whose words are these ? They can be none but the words
of Jesus ; for none ever made restoration but him ; and none
but him could say, I took nothing away. And what was
taken away ? God's glory was taken away by sin: and,
consequently, man's happiness also. For when Adam sinned,
he robbed God of his glory, and robbed himself and all his
posterity of God's image, and with it all happiness. Nay,
my soul ! thou hast done the same in every renewed act of
disobedience. And in breaking the divine law, thou hast
justly lost the divine favour. And hath Jesus, all-precious
Jesus, restored all these ? Yes, blessings on his name, he
hath ! And what renders it ten-fold more gracious, he hath

so done it, as never to be lost any more. By his finished
work of salvation he hath restored to God his glory. And
by his obedience and death, as our Surety, he hath restored
to man his happiness. The favour of God we lost by sin :
Jesus hath restored it by justifying us, in his righteousness.
The image of God we lost by rebellion : Jesus hath restored
to us this image, in sanctifying us by his holiness. So that
every way, and in all things, Jesus hath made up the breach,
and the poor sinner who is led by grace to believe in Jesus,
stands more complete and secure now than before the fall.
For if Adam had never sinned, nor his children in him, yet,
after all, their righteousness before God would have been but
the righteousness of creatures. Whereas now, in Jesus, the
believer stands accepted and secured in the righteousness of
the Creator. Hail then, thou Almighty Restorer of our
fallen nature ! In thee, Lord, would my poor soul triumphantly say, have I righteousness and strength : even to thee
shall men come ; and all that believe in thee, shall never be
ashamed nor confounded, world without end.

22.—Having made known unto us the mystery of his will, according to
his good pleasure, which he hath purposed in himself.—*Eph.* i. 9.

MY soul! pause over these volumes of divine truth : for
they are not as so many simple words, but contain vast volumes indeed, and such as a whole eternity will not afford
space to read over and finish. The first is a large one indeed—even the mystery of God's will : namely, the mystery
of redemption, originating in the divine mind, before all
worlds. And this is not the smallest part of it, that it should
be made known in any degree or measure to thee, my soul :
a poor creature of a day, and that day, a day of nothing but
sin. The *second* volume in this vast subject is another precious part of the same glorious truth, namely, that this mercy
of God in Christ is the sole result of God's good pleasure.
No foresight, no merit, no pretensions of thine, my soul ; no,
nor the merits of archangels, becoming in the least, the
cause. For though a gracious God hath taken occasion to
make a glorious display of the depths of his grace, from the
depths of men's ruin : yet it was not our state, but his good
pleasure, which laid the foundation of our recovery by Jesus
Christ. And the *third* volume in this stupendous subject is,
that He that planned, executed and finished it. As none but
infinite wisdom could purpose, so none but infinite power

could accomplish. Pause, my soul, and contemplate the vast mercy! It comes from a God in Christ, as the first cause; and reverts back again to God in Christ, as the final end. Hallelujah!

23.—Lo, I come!—*Psalm* lx. 7.

WHAT a longing had Old Testament saints for the Lord Jesus' coming! And what an earnest wish and prayer it is among New Testament believers, for Jesus' coming by the visits of his grace, and the sweet influences of his Holy Spirit, from day to day! My soul! methinks I would realize by faith this day, even this very day, these words of thy Redeemer, as if he were now standing at the door of thine heart, and asking for admission. And shall I not say, under this sweet impression, Come in, thou blessed of the Lord! wherefore standest thou without? Oh, blessed Jesus! when I consider the many precious instances of thy coming, set up from everlasting in thy goings forth for the salvation of thy chosen—thy anticipation, in thy visits before the season of thy tabernacling in our flesh: thy visits to the patriarchs and prophets: thy manifestation openly to the people: thy secret, sweet, and inexpressibly gracious visits now, and thy promised return in the clouds at the final consummation of all things: oh, Lamb of God! dost thou say, Lo, I come? Oh for the earnestness of faith, in all her devout longings, to cry out with the church of old, and say, Make haste, my Beloved, and come; oh, come quickly, Lord Jesus!

24.—God sent forth his Son made of a woman.—*Gal.* iv. 4.

How little did Adam suppose, when he charged God foolishly, (as, by the way, it may be observed all sinners do by this plan,) in attempting to palm off his sin upon God, that the Lord in after ages would put distinguishing honour upon the woman, in which the man should bear no part. The woman, said Adam, whom thou gavest to be with me, she tempted me, and I did eat. Thus endeavouring to throw the whole blame of his transgression upon his gracious Benefactor. It is as if he had said, Hadst thou not given me this woman, I should not have disobeyed thy command. Now observe, my soul, God's benignity and grace upon this occasion. The seed of the woman, said God, shall bruise the serpent's head. Not the seed of the man, but of the woman.

And when the fulness of the time was come for this promise to be accomplished, God sent forth his Son, made of a woman, without the intervention of an human father, but by the miraculous impregnation only of the Holy Ghost. As if to honour the weaker vessel, and to open a source of peculiar comfort in the female breast. As if God had said, in answer to Adam's daring impiety, Though all the redeemed among men shall partake in this great salvation, yet the woman shall have in it an eminent token of divine favour. And as the accursed enemy of God and man did first beguile the woman, from the woman shall arise Him, that shall destroy the Devil. The blessings of redemption shall begin with the woman, to her peculiar honour, and to the serpent's everlasting shame. For He that in after ages shall do away more than all the evil of sin and the fall, by the sacrifice of himself, shall be born of a woman. And thus the Lord manifested forth his grace, in silencing Adam's unbecoming expostulation. Oh! the wonderful way and method of our wonder-working God.

25.—And the Word was made flesh, and dwelt among us.—*John* i. 14.

TURN aside, my soul, this day, from every vain and worldly thought, as Moses did at the bush, and behold by faith the accomplishment of what he then saw in type and figure, of this great sight which the Lord hath made known unto thee. —The Word, the uncreated Word, even the eternal Son of God, taking upon him the nature of man, and uniting both in one Person, that by the union he might be a suitable Saviour for his people. As God, he was mighty to save, and fully competent to the wonderful act. As man, he was a suitable Saviour, for the right of redemption belonged to him. And as both, He, and He alone, could become a proper Mediator, to reconcile and bring together God and man, which by sin were at variance. This was the glorious news angels posted down from heaven to proclaim. This was the song of heaven, for which they sung, Glory to God in the highest, and on earth peace, good will to men. My soul! canst thou join the song? Yes, if so be thou hast received Christ in those glorious characters; if, as for this divine purpose he was born in our streets, he is born in thy heart also, and formed there the hope of glory. Oh! it is a blessed thing to have true scriptural views of the Lord Jesus, and so to receive him, as Jehovah hath set him forth, the Christ of God. Amen.

26.—Jesus Christ of the seed of David.—2 *Timothy* ii. 2.

SWEET thought! Jesus will have regard to both sexes, in his incarnation. He will be of the seed of the woman; he will be also truly and properly man. As both the man and woman had sinned, so redemption shall be for both. But in the holy nature, in which as Redeemer he will come, he will partake of none of their sins. The man shall have no hand in his generation. And the womb of the woman shall be but the deposit of "that holy thing" so called, (Luke i. 35,) by the miraculous conception of the Holy Ghost. So that the body which God the Father prepared him, belonged to both, but was unconnected with either. He must be truly man; for the law had said, Every male that openeth the womb shall be called Holy unto the Lord. He must be a priest; and no woman could minister in that office. He must be a prophet; and no woman could exercise that province, for it is not permitted for a woman to speak in the church. He must be a king; and the kingly office belongeth not to the weaker vessel. But both sexes shall be equally at the same time concerned in the blessed event of his incarnation. The woman is saved in the child-bearing of this Redeemer, and the man brought into favour and reconciliation; for as by man came death, by man came also the resurrection of the dead. So that, as the Apostle strongly and satisfactorily concludes, there is neither Jew nor Greek, there is neither bond nor free, there is neither male nor female, but ye are all one in Christ Jesus.

27.—For the mountains shall depart, and the hills shall be removed: but my kindness shall not depart from thee, neither shall the covenant of my peace be removed, saith the Lord that hath mercy on thee.— *Isaiah* liv. 10.

WHAT a rest is here, for a poor redeemed sinner to stand firm upon, in time and to all eternity! Well may he cry out concerning Jesus, and his great salvation in him, He is a rock, and his work is perfect. Yes! yes, thou Lord God of my salvation: thou art my dwelling-place in all generations. My soul, look all around thee, look within thee, look every where about thee. Search, behold, examine diligently, what else will or can afford thee any security. And think what a dying world it is in which thou art dwelling, or rather travelling through. What friend, what brother, what child, what relation, can give thee help of soul, or even of body, when thou most shalt need it? Think what a day, a week, an hour, may bring forth! Amidst all these changes, is Jesus thine? Doth he tell thee, that though mountains depart, and hills be removed, his salvation and the Father's covenant of peace is the same? Shout, shout, my soul, and begin the song, which in a dying hour will only swell louder: Salvation to God and the Lamb!

28.—The eyes of the Lord thy God are always upon thee, from the beginning of the year, even unto the end of the year.—*Deut.* xi. 12.

OH for grace to live always under an abiding sense of this most blessed truth. My soul, never forget it, if possible, but always possess in recollection an abiding apprehension of Jesus' gracious presence. And do thou, dearest Lord, when thou art coming forth in mercies, give me grace to be going forth to meet thee with praises; and while thou art bartering thy riches for my poverty, let all thy bounties be doubly sweetened in coming from thine own hand, and being sanctified by thy blessing, that I may receive all to my soul's joy, and to the praise of the Father's grace in Christ Jesus. Amen.

29.—Not one thing hath failed, of all the good things which the Lord your God spake concerning you.—*Joshua* xxiii. 14.

SAY, my soul, in looking back the past year, canst thou set thy seal to this truth? Is there a promise which thy God hath not fulfilled? Is there an instance in which God hath forfeited his word? Canst thou point to the time, or place, in any one trial, or under any one affliction, in which thou hast not found God faithful? Give then the Lord the honour due unto his name. If not one thing hath failed, proclaim his glory, set forth his praise, declare his truth, let the father to the children make known that God is faithful. And oh! let thine heart bear testimony to what must be said of all his Israel, in all ages, What hath God wrought!

27

30.—Then Samuel took a stone, and set it between Mizpah and Shen, and called the name of it Eben-ezer, saying, Hitherto the Lord hath helped us.—1 *Sam.* vii. 12.

DID Samuel do this? Was that servant of the Lord, who lived not to see Christ in the flesh, so full of faith in the coming Saviour, and in the experiences of Jehovah's faithfulness in what was past, that he set up his Ebenezer? Surely, my soul, thou wilt blush to be outdone by the prophet, when thou hast not only seen the day of the Son of man completed, but felt his power. Oh, my soul! let thine Ebenezer be Jesus! Let the stone thou settest up, be indeed the Rock of ages. Yes, my soul! set up Jesus indeed, in all places, at all times, upon all occasions. And oh, Lord! do thou by thy blessed Spirit set up thyself in my heart, and enthrone thyself there, and reign and rule there foreever. Surely, my soul! Jesus is thine every day Ebenezer ; for he not only hath hitherto helped, but he doth help, and will help, and be himself thine Help, thy God, thy Portion, thy Jesus, for evermore.

31.—And the Lord spake unto Moses, saying, Speak unto Aaron, and unto his sons, saying, On this wise ye shall bless the children of Israel, saying unto them, The Lord bless thee, and keep thee. The Lord make his face to shine upon thee, and be gracious unto thee. The Lord lift up his countenance upon thee, and give thee peace. And they shall put my name upon the children of Israel, and I will bless them. *Numbers* vi. 22 to 27.

PAUSE, my soul, and in these sweet words behold thine almighty Aaron, even Jesus, in his everlasting priesthood, day by day, thus blessing his people. Observe, the blessing in the name of the Lord Jehovah is thrice pronounced, as if to teach the plurality of persons in the Godhead. And observe also, after this blessing thrice pronounced, Jehovah, as if to intimate the unity of the divine essence, declares, I will bless them. My soul, mark each. The *First* may be considered as the personal blessing of God the Father, whose gracious office it is in the work of redemption to bless and keep his people. The *Second* is the peculiar mercy of Jesus, whose face is always upon his people, and his grace their portion. And the *Third* is the work of God the Holy Ghost, when his blessed influences are shed abroad upon the soul, in the light of his divine countenance. And, my soul, observe further, how personally this blessing from the HOLY THREE IN ONE is to each individual: it is to *thee,* even to *thee.* And, my soul, do not forget nor overlook this vast privilege in the blessing. Aaron the great high-priest of the church, could only *pray* for the people that these mercies *might* be upon them; but thy great High-priest, the Lord Jesus, *confirms* them. His language is, Father *I will*. And God having raised up his Son Jesus, hath sent him to bless us. Here then, blessed, precious Jesus! thou Great High-priest of my soul! close the day, every day, close the year, close my life, whenever thou shalt be pleased to call me home, in thus blessing me. Lord! put thy name upon me, and upon all thy church and people, and we shall be most blessed indeed, in life, in death, and for evermore, Amen: Hallelujah: Amen!

THE END.

www.ingramcontent.com/pod-product-compliance
Lightning Source LLC
Chambersburg PA
CBHW031942080426
42735CB00007B/228